DORIS LESSING
Conversations

Ontario Review Press Critical Series
General Editor, Raymond J. Smith

DORIS LESSING
Conversations

edited by
Earl G. Ingersoll

ONTARIO REVIEW PRESS
Princeton, New Jersey

Many deserve recognition for their contributions to this collection. At Brockport, librarian Robert Gilliam assisted in the gathering of materials, and Jeanne Saraceni, of the College's Document Center, prepared the manuscript. Patricia Featherstone, Heidrun Neth, and Patricia Siegel provided valuable assistance in the editing and translating of interviews. Paul Schlueter, a "dean" of Lessing scholarship, generously shared materials from his archives and offered valuable advice. More than anyone, of course, Doris Lessing quite simply made this collection possible.

Library of Congress Cataloging-in-Publication Data

Lessing, Doris May, 1919–
    Doris Lessing : conversations / edited by Earl G. Ingersoll.
    (Ontario Review Press critical series)
    Includes index.
1. Lessing, Doris May, 1919–   —Interviews.   2. Women authors,
English—20th century—Interviews.   I. Ingersoll, Earl G., 1938–
II. Title.   III. Series.
PR6023.E833Z467   1994   823'.914—dc20   93-43760
ISBN 0-86538-080-5 (pbk. : alk. paper)

Typesetting by Backes Graphic Productions
Printed by Princeton Academic Press

ONTARIO REVIEW PRESS
Distributed by George Braziller, Inc.
60 Madison Ave., New York, NY 10010

Contents

Introduction

FEW WRITERS HAVE VOICED more misgivings about the value of interviews yet submitted to as many of them as Doris Lessing. The two dozen conversations in this collection were selected from over 100 in which she has participated in the past three decades. Those 100 or so interviews run the usual gamut in a writer's interviews. Among those not included here are many of the "celebrity interview" variety in which it is the writer's fame that generates the interview. Such interviewers may know little or nothing of the writer's work and occasionally may even begin with that confession, as though their busy lives as journalists somehow justify their not having completed their "assignments" in preparation for the interview. It is just this preoccupation with the writer's personality that Mrs. Lessing has found particularly frustrating. As she has insisted on several occasions recently, being interviewed, especially following the appearance of one of her publications, is a part of book promotion that she submits to, often without enthusiasm. The interviews in this collection of "conversations" are generally "literary" interviews. The interviewer, frequently an academic or writer, can be expected to ask informed questions.

If Mrs. Lessing has misgivings about the interview as a literary form, they are grounded in her commitment to the writer's craft. As one who is especially sensitive to language, she is dismayed by the narrow confines of the interview format. Seldom does the interviewee have the opportunity to prepare for the questions to be posed, and her views on complex issues or problems must be limited to a spoken response without the opportunity to revise. In such conversations, it is obviously impossible to say to one's questioner: "Give me an hour to think about that question, before I respond," or "Could you ignore what I've been saying for the past two minutes so that I might begin again?" or "May I reorganize the points that I am trying to make?" Clearly, she has felt the pressure toward oversimplification that such a format can easily produce. She herself has written about interviews in an article aptly entitled "Never the Whole Truth?" appearing in a recent issue of *British Journalism Review* (Winter 1990):

> The slightest involvement with the machinery of interviews has to convince you that no one cares about facts. How many have I sat through, uninterested in the questions I am asked, which I have probably answered dozens of times before. I do this, I hope, amiably, with every appearance of interest: before any interview or 'promotion' trip I resolve never to seem impatient or bored, and to answer every question as if for the first time. But more than once, an interviewer,

sensing I am not totally enthralled, has leaned forward at the end to enquire if perhaps there is something not yet mentioned that I would like to discuss. But on saying 'Yes—so and so—' a look at first of incredulity, and then of boredom settles on his or her face, because what I have just said is not exciting enough, does not feed myths about writers. But an interview is 'dead' if the interviewee tells the interviewer what to ask. Why bother to have an interview at all? (The publishers have an instant reply to this.) The point is, the interviewer's questions do interest him, her, and represent in some way the readers. When a German interviewer flounced off, 'If you are not going to talk about your personal life...' she was right. That is what interested her and therefore her readers. (Her fault was not to say in advance that this is what she expected me to talk about.) But it is a remarkable fact that of what must now be hundreds of interviews all over the world—you would be surprised how many interviews a writer doing 'promotion' is expected to agree to—only two or three stay in my mind as good ones— that is, based on real insight. I am not joking when I say that writing about writers has long since lost the idea that truth should be the aim.

What is at stake here is vital to Mrs. Lessing's concerns with contemporary thinking, or perhaps its absence. As one well-versed in the subversion of language by political ideologies, she is acutely aware of the need to escape the entrapment of received notions and the morass of professional jargon. From her point of view, her interviewers frequently pose questions that are nearly impossible to answer, largely because they are not really questions at all. They are assertions disguised as questions, mini-lectures to which she occasionally replies, "Well, you've already said it." Beyond that, however, she is aggravated by the contemporary tendency to insist on putting everything into compartments, a sort of perverse legacy of nineteenth-century scientists who felt an inordinate pleasure in labeling and categorizing phenomena. In speaking with fellow-writer Brian Aldiss, she has a famous laugh at the expense of an unidentified but eminent critic, who kept repeating in a review of *The Fifth Child* on the radio, "But you can't categorize this book; you can't categorize it," as though if we only could, then we would no longer have to think about it.

Mrs. Lessing has participated in a large number of interviews not merely because hers has been such a significant voice in the last thirty years, but because she is a genuinely international writer, as is evident in interviews conducted in places as far from her London home as Singapore and in interviews originally appearing in French, Italian, German, Spanish, Danish, and Norwegian newspapers and magazines. She has been a much-sought-after speaker around the world. That should not be surprising, given her background.

Doris Tayler Lessing was born in 1919 of English parents in Kermanshah, Persia (Iran). Her father had survived the First World War with psychological as well as physical wounds. Like many veterans, he was dismayed by England and took a bank job in Persia, hoping to start over in a different country. In her words, he was something of a dreamer, and when he happened on an agriculture fair he suddenly decided to move his family to Southern Rhodesia, as Zimbabwe was then called. Mrs. Lessing grew up in Southern Africa, where Marxism attracted her, along with many other sensitive young whites, since it seemed the only political ideology addressing itself to racial injustice. In 1949, as a young woman in her late twenties, she left her second husband Gottfried Lessing and accompanied by their son Peter moved to London where she has continued to live. She brought with her the manuscript of *The Grass Is Singing.* It was not her first attempt at the novel, since as she has told her interviewers, she destroyed the manuscripts of two earlier apprentice works. Its critical success and modest royalties launched her as a writer. Years later, she has been amused at her innocence in assuming that she would be able to support herself and her son through writing, but then, as she remarks, writers in mid-century England seldom aspired to the huge sales and royalties to support extravagant life styles that young writers often hope for today.

During the '50s and '60s, *The Grass Is Singing* was followed by the five volumes of her *Children of Violence* series. The first three in the series—*Martha Quest, A Ripple from the Storm,* and *A Proper Marriage*—as she herself admits, drew heavily upon her own experience as a young woman. Her next novel, *The Golden Notebook* (1962), was not part of the *Children of Violence* series. Still probably her best-known work, *The Golden Notebook* began an accelerated movement away from the autobiographical impulse in her fiction. Unfortunately, her readers have often been unwilling to accept her assertion that the women characters are not Doris Lessing in disguise. Those readers have had particular difficulties with *The Golden Notebook,* which some American feminists tried to read as a bible of Women's Liberation. As Mrs. Lessing repeats throughout the later interviews, she had quite different interests in her famous novel and has deeply resented its appropriation as a weapon of sexual politics. Indeed, one distinct theme in these interviews is Mrs. Lessing's attempt to rescue her own fiction from her readers who often want to reduce its complexity to their own narrow points of view.

In many ways, *The Four-Gated City* is among Mrs. Lessing's most important novels. Like *The Golden Notebook,* it is one of those novels written for readers in the future. She has often indicated her sadness that there are no nineteenth-century novels giving readers in this century a better understanding of a movement like Chartism, for example. She goes on to say that she had hoped *The Golden Notebook* would offer future readers a clearer sense of what sensitive, thinking people were concerned with in mid-century England. *The Four-Gated City* fulfills that need for the '60s. However, it also points toward her continuing interests throughout the '70s and '80s, especially toward her interest in the "space fiction" that would precipitate a kind of crisis in her literary reputation.

Central to her later interests is the attempt to move out of the realist mode that brought her critical acclaim and a large readership for her earlier fiction. *Briefing for a Descent into Hell* and *The Memoirs of a Survivor* are the clearest evidence of that movement away from conventional realism toward "inner space." Both are "difficult" novels because they demand more "willing suspension of disbelief" than many of her readers have been prepared for, even though fictional exploration of "insanity" in *The Golden Notebook* and the apocalyptical last section of *The Four-Gated City* point in that direction. And then, almost to demonstrate that she had not said farewell to the realist mode, *The Summer Before the Dark* appeared in 1973, between *Briefing* and *Memoirs*, creating difficulties once again for those bent upon "categorizing" her writing or smoothly plotting the course of her "career."

More than anything, it was toward her problematical "space fiction" that *The Four-Gated City* pointed the direction. In 1979 she launched the *Argos in Canopus* series with the "novel" *Re: Colonised Planet 5, Shikasta*. If its readers were surprised and puzzled, it was in part because they had not paid enough attention to the increasing presence of science fiction on the literary scene in her watershed novel, *The Four-Gated City*. These same readers may also have misread Mrs. Lessing's interest as an attempt to join the virtually universal chorus of scoffers at this "sci-fi," to use the persistent "mainstream" and media term of amused disdain for a fiction damned in part for its popularity. She has preferred the term "space fiction" for the *Canopus* series, not because she wants to dissociate it from "science fiction," but only because she admits to having too little formal training to claim that her writing is "*science* fiction." As she indicates in the interviews that follow, she turned to space fiction because it alone offered her the opportunity to range freely in time and space and to find metaphors to express her concern with contemporary problems and issues.

The response to the *Canopus* series among her readers, both professional and "common," has been astounding. In reviews of the novels, in critical articles, and in letters to Mrs. Lessing herself, many readers have indicated their dismay that she has been wasting her talent writing fantasy. Some who have been particularly dismayed are those readers still waiting for her to write another *Golden Notebook*, or at least a "women's book," like

The Summer Before the Dark. She has persisted, however, past the second *Canopus* novel, *The Marriages of Zones Three, Four, and Five*, which is about as close as she has come in the series to pleasing that readership. The latest three novels in the *Canopus* series are more similar to *Shikasta* than to *Marriages*. One of these, *The Making of the Representative for Planet 8*, has led to yet another new departure for her writing, the libretto for the opera of the same name, written in collaboration with Philip Glass, an artist whose work has also had its share of detractors.

The most recent of the *Canopus* novels deliberately ends without a clear sense of closure. As Mrs. Lessing indicates, she plans a sixth novel and perhaps even more in the series. She has been "sidetracked," she says, by *The Fifth Child* and *The Good Terrorist*, as well as by *African Laughter*, her memoirs of four visits to Zimbabwe, and by the first volume of her autobiography. The two novels that "sidetracked" her might be misread as her bowing to the pressure of those readers bent upon returning her writing to the realist mode. Certainly, they are more realist than the fiction beginning with *Briefing*; they represent, however, in the clearest fashion, Mrs. Lessing's insistence upon her own artistic integrity and the freedom to write in diametrically opposed modes, as they suit her differing interests as a writer.

Although she is perhaps best known as a novelist, we ought not to ignore her accomplishment in other genres. In addition to essays and memoirs, she has published well over a dozen collections of shorter fiction; indeed, her most recent work at this writing is *The Real Thing* (English title *London Observed*) a collection of short stories and sketches. As she comments in the interviews that follow, she has also had a love affair with the theater—*Play with a Tiger* was produced in London in the early '60s—with all the passion and heartbreak implied by that commonplace metaphor.

Mrs. Lessing's awareness of her own reputation and her frustrations with the "business" of being a writer are no more clearly evidenced than by the Jane Somers affair. Ten years ago, she decided to write and publish a novel under a pseudonym. She did so—twice—in what she later published in her own name as *The Diaries of Jane Somers*. In part she wanted to explore her suspicion that the publication of books had become commercialized to such a point that the exigencies of the marketplace and the "bottom line" had clearly obscured traditional interests in literary merit and cultural value. Those who know her writing were not taken in by what she has termed the "hoax" of the Jane Somers novels and, indeed, some became "co-conspirators," if you will. Others were not so fortunate. Publishers' readers and book reviewers who wrote the customarily "patronizing"—her term—encouragements of this hypothetical "first novelist" were obviously not amused, when they had damned with faint praise novels by Doris Lessing. Similarly, publishers who turned down the manuscripts without even sending them out to be professionally evaluated were not happy with what the "hoax" had demonstrated. As she became aware, the marketers of books were most concerned that as an unknown writer "Jane Somers" had no "personality" to help them to sell the book. Besides, would there be an "author" to be interviewed as part of their marketing strategies?

The series of conversations has been arranged chronologically from her interviews in the early '60s to one as recent as 1993. The early interviews appear, despite Mrs. Lessing's apprehension that her views have changed over the past two decades. Most of the interviews have already appeared in print, some in journals as well known as *The Paris Review*, others, however, have appeared in smaller magazines such as *Kunapipi* and *Glimmer Train Stories*, where they are less readily accessible. Some appear here for the first time as transcriptions of taped interviews, notably those with writers Studs Terkel, Brian Aldiss, and Claire Tomalin. The collection includes translations of interviews in French and German. These pose problems because of the obvious infelicities of style inherent in translations of translations; however, they contain valuable interchanges and emphasize the genuinely international nature of her readership.

The conversations appear with the permission of both those who hold rights to them and Mrs. Lessing, who had the opportunity to read and approve the manuscript. The interviews have been edited to enhance consistency in mechanics, notably American spelling, and to reduce the redundant or unimportant material endemic in the transcriptions of spoken versions of the language. Wherever passages have been omitted in reprinted interviews, the notation "//" indicates such omissions, especially when a hiatus in the text might otherwise be distracting. Occasionally, repeated passages have been preserved to serve as bridges from point to point, or, more importantly, to allow Mrs. Lessing to emphasize points. She herself says, "As I have said and it bears repeating . . . " or words to that effect. As she reminds us, interviews are an indication more often of the interviewer's interests than the interviewee's. However, the reader will discover in these conversations a range of responses to issues and concerns in Mrs. Lessing's writing. Taken together, they represent a record of a life in writing.

Earl G. Ingersoll
October 1993

Chronology

1919	Born 22 October, in Kermanshah, Persia (Iran); parents, Alfred Cook Tayler and Emily Maud McVeagh. Her brother, Harry, was born in 1921.
1924	Moved with her family to a farm near the small town of Banket, Southern Rhodesia (Zimbabwe), where her father grew tobacco and corn.
1933	Ended her formal education at a Roman Catholic high school in Salisbury.
1939	Married Frank Wisdom, a civil engineer. Their children John and Jean remained with their father when their parents were divorced in 1943.
1943–49	Worked as a secretary and stenographer in Salisbury. Participated in a small political group with Marxist roots, but the Communist Party was not sanctioned by the colonial government.
1945–49	Married to Gottfried Lessing, a Marxist immigrant. Their son Peter, born in 1947, accompanied his mother to London when his parents' marriage ended in divorce and his father returned to East Germany to assume a government post.
1950	*The Grass Is Singing* (Michael Joseph; New York, Crowell).
1951	*This Was the Old Chief's Country* (Michael Joseph; New York: Crowell, 1952).
1952	*Martha Quest,* the first volume of *Children of Violence* (Michael Joseph; New York: Simon & Schuster, 1964).
1953	*Five: Short Novels* (Michael Joseph; Harmondsworth: Penguin, 1960).

1954   *A Proper Marriage,* the second volume of *Children of Violence* (Michael Joseph; New York: Simon & Schuster, 1964). Received Somerset Maugham Award of the Society of Authors for *Five: Short Novels.*

1956   *Retreat to Innocence* (Michael Joseph; New York: Prometheus, 1959).

1957   *The Habit of Loving* (MacGibbon and Kee; New York: Ballantine, Crowell, Popular Library).

1958   *A Ripple from the Storm,* the third volume of *Children of Violence* (Michael Joseph; New York: Simon & Schuster, 1966).

1962   *The Golden Notebook* (Michael Joseph; New York, Simon & Schuster). *Play with a Tiger: A Play in Three Acts* (Michael Joseph).

1963   *A Man and Two Women* (MacGibbon and Kee; New York: Simon & Schuster, Popular Library).

1964   *African Stories* (Michael Joseph; New York: Simon & Schuster, Popular Library, 1965).

1965   *Landlocked,* the fourth volume of *Children of Violence* (MacGibbon and Kee; New York: Simon & Schuster, 1966).

1966   *The Black Madonna* and *Winter in July* (Panther).

1967   *Particularly Cats* (Michael Joseph; New York, Simon & Schuster).

1969   *The Four-Gated City,* the fifth volume of *Children of Violence* (MacGibbon and Kee; New York, Knopf).

1971   *Briefing for a Descent into Hell* (Jonathan Cape; New York, Knopf).

1972   *The Story of a Non-Marrying Man and Other Stories* (Jonathan Cape); American title *The Temptation of Jack Orkney* (New York, Knopf).

1973   *The Summer Before the Dark* (Jonathan Cape; New York, Knopf).

1974   *The Memoirs of a Survivor* (Octagon; New York: Knopf, 1975).

1976   Received the French Prix Medicis for Foreigners.

1978   *Stories* (New York, Knopf).

1979   *Re: Colonised Planet 5, Shikasta*, the first volume of *Canopus in Argos: Archives* (Jonathan Cape; New York, Knopf).

1980   *The Marriages between Zones Three, Four, and Five*, the second volume of *Canopus in Argos: Archives* (Jonathan Cape; New York, Knopf).

1981   *The Sirian Experiments*, the third volume of *Canopus in Argos: Archives* (Jonathan Cape; New York, Knopf).

1982   *The Making of the Representative for Planet 8*, the fourth volume of *Canopus in Argos: Archives* (Jonathan Cape; New York, Knopf). Received the Shakespeare Prize of the West German *Hamburger Stiftung* and the Austrian State Prize for European Literature.

1983   *Documents Relating to the Sentimental Agents in the Volyen Empire* (Jonathan Cape; New York, Knopf).

1984   *The Diaries of Jane Somers* (New York: Random House), two novels originally published under the pseudonym Jane Somers as *The Diary of A Good Neighbor* and *If the Old Could...* (Michael Joseph, 1983–84; New York, Knopf).

1985   *The Good Terrorist* (Jonathan Cape; New York, Knopf).

1986   Received the W. H. Smith Literary Award.

1987   Received the Palmero Prize and the Premio Internazionale Mondello.

1988   *The Fifth Child* (Jonathan Cape; New York, Knopf).

1992   *African Laughter* (New York, HarperCollins). *London Observed* (HarperCollins); American title *The Real Thing: Stories and Sketches* (HarperCollins).

DORIS LESSING
Conversations

Talking as a Person
Roy Newquist

Newquist: When did you start writing?

Lessing: I think I've always been a writer by temperament. I wrote some bad novels in my teens. I always knew I would be a writer, but not until I was quite old—twenty-six or -seven—did I realize that I'd better stop saying I was *going* to be one and get down to business. I was working in a lawyer's office at the time, and I remember walking in and saying to my boss, "I'm giving up my job because I'm going to write a novel." He very properly laughed, and I indignantly walked home and wrote *The Grass Is Singing.* I'm oversimplifying; I didn't write it as simply as that because I was clumsy at writing and it was much too long, but I did learn by writing it. It focused upon white people in Southern Rhodesia, but it could have been about white people anywhere south of the Zambezi, white people who were not up to what is expected of them in a society where there is very heavy competition from the black people coming up.

Then I wrote short stories set in the district I was brought up in, where very isolated white farmers lived immense distances from each other. You see, in this background, people can spread themselves out. People who might be extremely ordinary in a society like England's, where people are pressed into conformity, can become wild eccentrics in all kinds of ways they wouldn't dare try elsewhere. This is one of the things I miss, of course, by living in England. I don't think my memory deceives me, but I think there were more colorful people back in Southern Rhodesia because of the space they had to move in. I gather, from reading American literature, that this is the kind of space you have in America in the Midwest and West.

I left Rhodesia and my second marriage to come to England, bringing a son with me. I had very little money, but I've made my living as a professional writer ever since, which is really very hard to do. I had rather hard going, to begin with, which is not a complaint; I gather from my

American writer-friends that it is easier to be a writer in England than in America because there is much less pressure put on us. We are not expected to be successful, and it is no sin to be poor.

Newquist: I don't know how we can compare incomes, but in England it seems that writers make more from reviewing and from broadcasts than they can in the United States.

Lessing: I don't know. When I meet American writers, the successful ones, they seem to make more on royalties, but then they also seem to spend much more.

I know a writer isn't supposed to talk about money, but it is very important. It is vital for a writer to know how much he can write to please himself, and how much, or little, he must write to earn money. In England you don't have to "go commercial" if you don't mind being poor. It so happens that I'm not poor anymore, thank goodness, because it's not good for anyone to be. Yet there are disadvantages to living in England. It's not an exciting place to live; it is not one of the hubs of the world, like America, or Russia, or China. England is a backwater, and it doesn't make much difference what happens here, or what decisions are made here. But from the point of view of writing, England is a paradise for me.

You see, I was brought up in a country where there is very heavy pressure put on people. In Southern Rhodesia it is not possible to detach yourself from what is going on. This means that you spend all your time in a torment of conscientiousness. In England—I'm not saying it's a perfect society, far from it—you can get on with your work in peace and quiet when you choose to withdraw. For this I'm very grateful—I imagine there are few countries left in the world where you have this right of privacy.

Newquist: This is what you're supposed to find in Paris.

Lessing: Paris is too exciting. I find it impossible to work there. I proceed to have a wonderful time and don't write a damn thing.

Newquist: To work from *A Man and Two Women* for a bit. The almost surgical job you do in dissecting people, not bodily, but emotionally, has made me wonder if you choose your characters from real life, form composites or projections, or if they are so involved you can't really trace their origins.

Lessing: I don't know. Some people I write about come out of my life. Some, well, I don't know where they come from. They just spring from my own consciousness, perhaps the subconscious, and I'm surprised as they emerge.

This is one of the excitements about writing. Someone says something, drops a phrase, and later you find that phrase turning into a character in a story, or a single, isolated, insignificant incident becomes the germ of a plot.

Newquist: If you were going to give advice to the young writer, what would that advice be?

Lessing: You should write, first of all, to please yourself. You shouldn't care a damn about anybody else at all. But writing can't be a way of life; the important part of writing is living. You have to live in such a way that your writing emerges from it. This is hard to describe.

Newquist: What about reading as a background?

Lessing: I've known very good writers who've never read anything. Of course, this is rare.

Newquist: What about your own reading background?

Lessing: Well, because I had this isolated childhood, I read a great deal. There was no one to talk to, so I read. What did I read? The best—the classics of European and American literature. One of the advantages of not being educated was that I didn't have to waste time on the second-best. Slowly, I read these classics. It was my education, and I think it was a very good one.

I could have been educated—formally, that is—but I felt some neurotic rebellion against my parents who wanted me to be brilliant academically. I simply contracted out of the whole thing and educated myself. Of course, there are huge gaps in my education, but I'm nonetheless grateful that it went as it did. One bit of advice I might give the young writer is to get rid of the fear of being thought of as a perfectionist, or to be regarded as pompous. They should strike out for the best, to be the best. God knows, we all fall short of our potential, but if we aim very high we're likely to be so much better.

Newquist: How do you view today's literature? What about the recent trend toward introspection?

Lessing: Well, I haven't been to America, but I've met a great many Americans and I think they have a tendency to be much more aware of themselves, and conscious of their society, than we are in Britain (though we're moving that way). By a coincidence I was thinking this afternoon about a musical like *West Side Story*, which comes out of a sophisticated society which is very aware of itself. You wouldn't have found in Britain, at the time that was written, a lyric like "Gee, Officer Krupke." You have to be very socially self-conscious to write *West Side Story*.

Newquist: What do you feel about the fiction being turned out today? Does it share the same virtues and failings as theater or can it be considered separately?

Lessing: Quite separately. You want to know what contemporary writers I enjoy reading? The American writers I like, for different reasons, are Malamud and Norman Mailer—even when he's right off center he lights rockets. And Algren. And that man who wrote *Catch-22*. And of course, Carson McCullers. But I only read the books that drift my way; I don't know everything that comes out.

Newquist: How do you feel about critical reactions to your own works?

Lessing: I don't get my reviews anymore. I read reviews if they turn up in the papers I get, but I go through them fast and try to pay little attention to what is said. I think the further I'm removed from this area—reviews, the literary squabble-shop—the better.// You see, the literary society in London is very small and incestuous. Everyone knows everyone. The writer who tosses a scrap of autobiography into an otherwise fictional piece (which writers always have done and always will do), he's not credited with any imagination. Everyone says, "Oh, that character's so and so," and "I know that character." It's all too personal. The standards of criticism are very low. I don't know about American critics, but in this country we have an abysmal standard. Very few writers I know have any respect for the criticism they get. Our attitude is, and has to be, Are the reviews selling books or not? In all other respects, the reviews are humiliating, they are on such a low level, and it's all so spiteful and personal.

Newquist: Do reviews sell books in England?

Lessing: My publishers claim they help build a reputation and that indirectly they do sell books. This is probably true. But in Great Britain everything is much more cumulative and long-term than in America. One simply settles in for what you call the long haul. But "reputation"—what are reputations worth when they are made by reviewers who are novelists? Writers aren't necessarily good critics. Yet the moment you've written a novel, you're invited to write criticism, because the newspapers like to have one's "name" on them. One is a "name" or one is not, you see. Oh, it's very pleasant to be one, I'm not complaining, I enjoy it. But everyone knows that writers tend to be wrong about each other. Look at Thomas Mann and Brecht—they were both towering geniuses, in different ways, and they didn't have any good word for each other.

Ideally we should have critics who are critics and not novelists who need to earn a bit to tide them over, or failed novelists. Is there such an animal, though? Of course, sometimes a fine writer is a good critic, like Lawrence. Look at something that happened last year—I wrote a long article for the *New Statesman* about the mess socialism is in. There was a half-line reference to X. To this day, people say to me, "that article you wrote attacking X." This is how people's minds work now. At the first night of one of Wesker's plays, up comes a certain literary figure and says, his voice literally wet with anxiety, "Oh, Wesker is a much better playwright than Osborne. He is, isn't he?" He felt that someone's grave should be danced on. He was simply tired of voting for Osborne. Tweedledum and Tweedledee. In and out.

You're going to say the literary world has always been like this. But what I said about the theater earlier applies—nothing wrong with the audience who likes *Who's for Tennis?* and the critics who do. It's all theirs. But they should keep out of the serious theater. Similarly, of course, the literary world is always going to seethe with people who say, I'm bored with voting for X. But writers should try to keep away from them. Another bit of advice to a young writer—but unfortunately economics make it almost impossible to follow: Don't review, don't go on television, try to keep out of all that. But, of course, if one's broke, and one's asked to review, one reviews. But better not, if possible. Better not go on television, unless there is something serious to be said (and how often is that?). Better to try to remain what we should be—an individual who communicates with other individuals, through the written word.

Newquist: To return to *A Man and Two Women*. Which stories in this collection would you choose as personal favorites?

Lessing: That's very difficult. I like the first one, titled "One off the Short List" because it's so extremely cold and detached—that one's a toughy. I'm pleased that I was able to bring it off the way I did. Then there were a couple of zany stories I'm attached to. The story about incest I liked very much—the one about the brother and the sister who are in love with each other. Not autobiographical at all, actually; perhaps I wish it were. And I like "To Room 19," the depressing piece about people who have everything, who are intelligent and educated, who have a home and two or three or four beautiful children, and have few worries, and yet ask themselves "What for?" This is all too typical of so many Europeans—and, I gather, so many Americans.

Newquist: Perhaps life without challenge or excitement amounts to boredom.

Lessing: Life certainly shouldn't be without excitement. The Lord knows that everything going on at the moment is exciting.

Newquist: But hasn't boredom become one of our most acute social problems?

Lessing: I don't understand people being bored. I find life so enormously exciting all the time. I enjoy everything enormously if only because life is so short. What have I got—another forty years of this extraordinary life— if I'm lucky? But most people live as if they have a weight put on them. Perhaps I'm lucky, because I'm doing what I want all the time, living the kind of life I want to live. I know a great many people, particularly those who are well-off and have everything they are supposed to want, who aren't happy.

Newquist: Right now a great many criticisms are leveled against bored Americans who have a surfeit of what they want. Is this true of England?

Lessing: I think that England is much more of a class society than America. This street I live on is full of very poor people who are totally different from my literary friends. They, in turn, are different from the family I come from, which is ordinary middle class. It isn't simple to describe life in England. For instance, in any given day I can move in five, six different strata or groups. None of them know how other people live, people different from themselves. All these groups and layers and classes have unwritten rules. There are rigid rules for every layer, but they are quite different from the rules in the other groups.

Newquist: Then perhaps you maintain more individuality.

Lessing: The pressures on us all to conform seem to get stronger. We're supposed to buy things and live in ways we don't necessarily want to live.

I've seen both forms of oppression, the tyrannical and the subtle. Here in England I can do what I like, think what I like, go where I please. I'm a writer, and I have no boss, so I don't have to conform. Other people have to, though. But in Southern Rhodesia—well, there one can't do or say what one likes. In fact, I'm a prohibited immigrant in South Africa and Central Africa, although I lived in Rhodesia twenty-five years. But then, the list of people who are prohibited in these areas is so long now.

I am not as optimistic as I used to be about oppressive societies. When I opened my eyes like a kitten to politics, there were certain soothing clichés about. One was that oppressive societies "collapsed under their own weight." Well, the first oppressive society I knew about was South Africa. I lived close to it, and I was told that a society so ugly and brutal could not last. I was told that Franco and his Fascist Spain could not last.

Here I am, many decades later, and South Africa is worse than it was, Southern Rhodesia is going the same way, and Franco is very much in power. The tyrannical societies are doing very well. I'm afraid that the liberals and certain people on the Left tend to be rather romantic about the nature of power.

I'm not comparing tyranny to conformity. The point is that people who are willing to conform without a struggle, without protest to small things, who will simply forget how to be individuals, can easily be led into tyranny.

Newquist: But isn't there strength in the middle road? In the area that lies between Fascism and Communism?

Lessing: I don't know. I hope so, but history doesn't give us many successful examples of being able to keep to the middle. Look at the difference between British and American attitudes toward Communism right now. Sections of America seem absolutely hypnotized by the kind of propaganda that's fed to them. Now, if it is true that Communism is a violent threat to the world, then Britain—which has a different attitude— has been eating and working and sleeping for twenty years without developing ulcers, but America has ulcers. I would say that we are doing a better job of keeping to the middle of the road. You've got some rather pronounced elements who would like to head for the ditch or force a collision.

Hasn't America been enfeebled by this hysterical fear of Communism? I don't think you sit down to analyze what the word "Communist" means. You end up in the most ridiculous situations, as you did in Cuba. When you see what a great nation like America can do to muddle this Cuban thing you can only shrug your shoulders. Please don't think I'm holding out any brief for my own government, but we're in a lucky position. I mean, England is. We're not very important, but America holds our fortunes in their large and not very subtle hands, and it's frightening. When I went to Russia, in 1952, I came to the not-very-original conclusion that the Americans and Russians were very similar, and that they would like each other "if." Now I see you moving closer and beginning to like each other, so now both of you are terrified of the Chinese, who will turn out (given fifteen years and not, I hope, too much bloodshed and misery) to be just like us, also. All of these violent hostilities are unreal. They've got very little to do with human beings.

Newquist: And very little to do with the arts?

Lessing: The arts, nothing! I was talking as a person, not a writer. I spent a great deal of my time being mixed up in politics in one way or another, and God knows what good it ever did. I went on signing things and protesting against things all the while wars were planned and wars were fought. I still do.

Newquist: To get back to your career, what are you working at now?

Lessing: I'm writing volumes four and five of a series I'm calling *Children of Violence*. I planned this out twelve years ago, and I've finished the first three. The idea is to write about people like myself, people my age who are born out of wars and who have lived through them, the framework of lives in conflict. I think the title explains what I essentially want to say. I want to explain what it is like to be a human being in a century when you open your eyes on war and on human beings disliking other human beings. I was brought up in Central Africa, which means that I was a member of the white minority pitted against a black majority that was abominably treated and still is. I was the daughter of a white farmer who, although he was a very poor man in terms of what he was brought up to expect, could always get loans from the Land Bank which kept him going. (I won't say that my father liked what was going on; he didn't.) But he employed anywhere from fifty to one hundred working blacks. An adult black earned twelve shillings a month, rather less than two dollars, and his food was rationed to corn meal and beans and peanuts and a pound of meat per week. It was all grossly unfair, and it's only part of a larger picture of inequity.

One-third of us—one-third of humanity, that is—is adequately housed and fed. Consciously or unconsciously we keep two-thirds of mankind improperly housed and fed. This is what the series of novels is about—this whole pattern of discrimination and tyranny and violence.

Newquist: You have mentioned becoming involved with mescaline. Could you describe this in more detail?

Lessing: I'm not involved with it. I took one dose out of curiosity, and that's enough to be going on with. It was the most extraordinary experience. Lots of different questions arise, but for our purposes the most interesting one is: Who are we? There were several different people, or "I's" taking part. They must all have been real, genuine, because one has no control over the process once it's under way. I understand that experiences to do with birth are common with people having these drugs. I was both giving birth and being given birth to. Who was the mother, who was the baby? I was both but neither. Several people were talking and in different voices throughout the process—it took three or four hours. Sometimes my mother—odd remarks in my mother's voice, my mother's sort of phrase. Not the kind of thing I say or am conscious of thinking. And the baby was a most philosophic infant, and different from me.

And who stage-managed this thing? Who said there was to be this birth and why? Who, to put it another way, was Mistress of the Ceremony? Looking back, I think that my very healthy psyche decided that my own birth, the one I actually had, was painful and bad (I gather it was, with forceps and much trouble) and so it gave itself a good birth—because the whole of this labor was a progress from misery, pain, unhappiness, toward happiness, acceptance, and the birth "I" invented for myself was not painful. But what do I mean, we mean, when we say "my psyche"—or whatever phrase you might use in its place ?

And then there's the question of this philosophic baby, a creature who argued steadily with God—I am not a religious person, and "I" would say I am an atheist. But this baby who was still in the womb did not want to be born. First, there was the war (I was born in 1919) and the smell of war and suffering was everywhere and the most terrible cold. I've never imagined such cold. It was cold because of the war. The baby did not want to be born to those parents (and remember the baby who was also its own mother) and this is the interesting thing, it was bored. Not the kind of boredom described in my story "To Room 19." But a sort of cosmic boredom. This baby had been born many times before, and the mere idea of "having to go through it all over again" (a phrase the baby kept using) exhausted it in advance. And it did not want, this very ancient and wise creature, the humiliation of being smothered in white flannel and blue baby ribbons and little yellow ducks. (Incidentally I'll never again be able to touch or look at a baby without remembering that experience, how helpless a baby is, caged in an insipid world of comfort and bland taste and white flannel and too much warmth.) This creature said to God, Yes, I know that boredom is one of the seven deadly sins, but You created me, didn't You? Then if You gave me a mind that goes limp with boredom at the experiences You inflict on me, whose fault is it? I'll consent (this baby said) to being born again for the millionth time, if I am given the right to be bored.

But as the birth proceeded, the pain, the boredom, the cold, the misery (and the smell of war) diminished, until I was born with the sun rising in a glow of firelight.

Yes, but who created all this? Who made it up?

It wasn't me, the normal "I" who conducts her life.

And of course, this question of I, who am I, what different levels there are inside of us, is very relevant to writing, to the process of creative writing about which we know nothing whatsoever. Every writer *feels* when he, she, hits a different level. A certain kind of writing or emotion comes from it. But you don't know who it is who lives there. It is very frightening to write a story like "To Room 19," for instance, a story soaked in emotions that you don't recognize as your own.// That is a literary question, a problem to interest writers. But that creature being born wasn't a "writer." It was immensely ancient, for a start, and it was neither male nor female, and it had no race or nationality. I can revive the "feel" or "taste" of that creature fairly easily. It isn't far off that creature or person you are when you wake up from deep sleep, and for a moment you don't recognize your surroundings and you think: Who am I? Where am I? Is this my hand? You're somebody, all right, but who?

The Inadequacy of the Imagination
Jonah Raskin

Jonah Raskin's interview was conducted on the campus of the State University of New York at Stony Brook in spring 1969. It originally appeared in *New American Review* 8 (1970) and was reprinted in *A Small Personal Voice,* ed. Paul Schlueter (Knopf, 1977). Copyright © 1970 by Jonah Raskin. Reprinted with permission.

Raskin: I felt that in your most recent novel, *The Four-Gated City,* you wanted to reach out directly to the new audience which has been shaped by television and the atmosphere of violence.

Lessing: I want to reach the youth. Maybe because I was determined to reach people the form of the book has been shot to hell. The first version was too long, and the second time I wrote it the form changed. I've had *Children of Violence* set up for twenty years. By the time I wrote the last volume I'd put myself into a damned cage, but it's probably better now that I've heaved the rules out.//

Raskin: How do drugs fit into your sense of the changes of the mind?

Lessing: I took mescaline once. I've taken pot a bit. Drugs give us a glimpse of the future; they extricate us from the cage of time. When people take drugs they discover an unknown part of themselves. When you have to open up, when you're blocked, drugs are useful, but I think it's bad for people to make them a way of life because they become an end in themselves. Pot should be used with caution, but not banned. I'm against all this banning. I think people can expand and explore their minds without using drugs. It demands a great deal of discipline. It's like learning a craft; you have to devote a lot of time, but if you can train yourself to concentrate you can travel great distances.

Raskin: In your fiction you explore large tracts through dreams, don't you?

Lessing: Dreams have always been important to me. The hidden domain of our mind communicates with us through dreams. I dream a great deal and I scrutinize my dreams. The more I scrutinize, the more I dream. When I'm stuck in a book I deliberately dream. I knew a mathematician once who supplied his brain with information and worked it like a computer. I operate in a similar way. I fill my brain with the material for a new book, go to sleep, and I usually come up with a dream which resolves the dilemma.

Raskin: The dreams in *The Golden Notebook* are points of intensity and fusion, aren't they? Anna sees fragments—a lump of earth from Africa, metal from a gun used in Indochina, flesh from people killed in the Korean War, a Communist party badge from someone who died in a Soviet prison—all of which represent crises in contemporary life.

Lessing: The unconscious artist who resides in our depths is a very economical individual. With a few symbols a dream can define the whole of one's life, and warn us of the future, too. Anna's dreams contain the essence of her experience in Africa, her fears of war, her relationship to Communism, her dilemma as a writer.

Raskin: Do you think that the Freudian concepts are valid?

Lessing: There are difficulties about the Freudian landscape. The Freudians describe the conscious as a small lit area, all white, and the unconscious as a great dark marsh full of monsters. In their view, the monsters reach up, grab you by the ankles, and try to drag you down. But the unconscious can be what you make of it, good or bad, helpful or unhelpful. Our culture has made an enemy of the unconscious. If you mention the word "unconscious" in a room full of people you see the expressions on their faces change. The word recalls images of dread and threat, but other cultures have accepted the unconscious as a helpful force, and I think we should learn to see it in that way too.

Raskin: How did you create the character of Mrs. Marks, "Mother Sugar," in *The Golden Notebook?*

Lessing: My own psychotherapist was somewhat like Mrs. Marks. She was everything I disliked. I was then aggressively rational, antireligious, and a radical. She was Roman Catholic, Jungian, and conservative. It was very upsetting to me at the time, but I found out it didn't matter a damn. I couldn't stand her terminology, but she was a marvelous person. She was one of those rare individuals who know how to help others. If she had used another set of words, if she had talked Freud talk, or aggressive atheism, it wouldn't have made a difference.//

Raskin: You've also been at the center of many political conflicts. Near the end of *The Golden Notebook* Anna says that "at that moment I sit down to write someone comes into the room, looks over my shoulder and stops me.... It could be a Chinese peasant. Or one of Castro's guerrilla fighters. Or an Algerian fighting in the FLN. They stand here in the room and they say, why aren't you doing something about us, instead of wasting your time scribbling?" I feel a tension between my life as a writer and my political activity. Could you tell me how you have felt about this situation?

Lessing: // I am intensely aware of, and want to write about, politics, but I often find that I am unable to embody my political vision in a novel. I want to write about Chinese peasants, the Algerians in the FLN, but I don't want to present them in false situations. I don't want to leave them out either. I find it difficult to write well about politics. I feel that the writer is obligated to dramatize the political conflicts of his time in his fiction. There is an awful lot of bad socialist literature which presents contemporary history mechanically. I wanted to avoid that pitfall.

In the scene from *The Golden Notebook,* which you've mentioned, I was trying to introduce politics and history into Anna's world.

I'm tormented by the inadequacy of the imagination. I've a sense of the conflict between my life as a writer and the terrors of our time. One sits down to write in a quiet flat in London and one thinks, Yes, there's a war going on in Vietnam. The night before last, when we were having dinner here, the police were raiding the university and arresting students.

Raskin: How do you view the future?

Lessing: I'm very much concerned about the future. I've been reading a lot of science fiction, and I think that science-fiction writers have captured our culture's sense of the future. *The Four-Gated City* is a prophetic novel. I think it's a true prophecy. I think that the "iron heel" is going to come down. I believe the future is going to be cataclysmic.

Raskin: You're pessimistic, aren't you? Don't you think that my generation has been liberated, and is liberating much of the society? Our values aren't commercial.

Lessing: I'm not saying that the youth have commercial values. In the 1960s the youth have had a great deal of freedom. It has been a wonderful moment in history. During the period of "flower power" I met some young Canadian poets who assured me that flowers were mightier than tanks. They talked sentimental rubbish. It's too late for romanticism. Young people in this decade have been allowed freedom; they have been flattered and indulged, because they are a new market. Young people coming to the end of this era are hitting exactly what previous generations before them have hit—that awful moment when they see that their lives are going to be, unless they do something fast, like the lives of their parents. The illusion of freedom is destroyed. A large part of the student protest is indirectly due to the fact that after seven or eight years of lotus eating, young people suddenly realize that their lives may be as narrow, as confined, as commercially oriented, as the lives of their parents. They don't want that life, but they feel trapped. This feeling can be good or bad depending how it's used.//

Raskin: It seems to me that your political experience in Africa would be relevant to the experience of white and black radicals today. Could you say something about it?

Lessing: The Communist Party in South Africa was like a seven-year flower which blooms and vanishes. It came into existence in the '20s but it spread and burgeoned toward the end of the '30s. The Communist Party had an enormous effect on politics because it ignored the color bar. In the Communist Party white and black people worked together on the basis of equality. Unfortunately, there were more whites than blacks in the party. If there was a Communist Party there today it would have to be predominantly black. But I don't see how blacks can organize anything coherent at the moment. What's likely to happen is sporadic outbreaks of violence by heroic anarchists. Another weakness of the South African Communist Party was its attitude toward the Soviet Union. But it organized trade unions and blacks. When it was banned it went underground and collapsed. Only a handful of brave individuals survived.

Raskin: The black South African is much more exploited and oppressed than the Afro-American, I imagine.

Lessing: The Africans are fed lies day and night. Every African township has police spies and government informers. A great section of the African population is corrupt, bought off. The black worker, especially the miner, lives in what amounts to a concentration camp. He's policed, doctored, fed, watched. He hasn't got freedom. He's well fed by African standards, but he's a slave. South Africa is a fascist paradise. It's one of the most brilliant police states in history.

Raskin: Some of the things you've said about radicals and repression remind me of the ending of *The Golden Notebook,* which has puzzled me. Could you explain it?

Lessing: When I wrote *The Golden Notebook* the left was getting one hammer blow after another. Everybody I knew was reeling because the left had collapsed. The scene at the end when Molly goes off and gets married and Anna goes off to do welfare work and joins the Labour Party was intended as a sign of the times. I was being a bit grim about what I observed about me. Women who had been active for years in socialist movements gritted their teeth and said, "Right, the hell with all this politics, we'll go off and be welfare workers." They meant it as a kind of joke, but they carried out their program. They did everything and anything that took them out of politics. Women who had refused to get married because they were dedicated to the cause made marriages which they would have found disgusting five years earlier. They regarded it as a kind of selling out. Brilliant Communist Party organizers went into business and entertainment and became rich men. This didn't happen to everyone, but it happened to many Communists.

Raskin: Many of the New Left students are from Old Left families who are now well off. The sons of famous Establishment professors are in SDS. How do you see the generations?

Lessing: The strain of watching the horrors becomes so great that middle-aged people block them out. My generation doesn't understand that young people have penetrated below the surface and have seen the horrors of our civilization. We've been so damned corrupted. Humanity has got worse and worse, puts up with more and more, gets more and more bourgeois. The youth have realized this.

I have always observed incredible brutality in society. My parents' lives and the lives of millions of people were ruined by the First World War. But the human imagination rejects the implications of our situation. War scars humanity in ways we refuse to recognize. After the Second World War the world sat up, licked its wounds ineffectually, and started to prepare for the Third World War. To look at the scene today, to see what man has done to himself, is an incitement to young people to riot. I'm surprised that the New Left isn't more violent.

I hope you don't regard me as unduly bitter. Humanity is a brave lot of people. Everyone of my lot has had to fight on two fronts. Being a Red is tough. My personal experience isn't bad, but friends of mine have been destroyed. The revolutionary movements they were working in sold them down the river. The ex-Communists of my lot have lost a certain kind of belief.

Raskin: What is it you've lost? Isn't it possible that the political struggles of my generation can revive that belief?

Lessing: The ex-Communists of my lot can't be surprised by anything. There is no horror that one cannot expect from people. We've learned that.

Well, yours is a new, young generation, and with a bit of luck the New Left won't have the kind of hammering my generation did. Maybe it'll be different. Maybe it'll not be the way I think it will be. But you and your generation need a calm to negotiate the rapids.

Learning to Put the Questions Differently
Studs Terkel

Studs Terkel's radio interview was conducted in Chicago
June 10, 1969. Printed by permission of Studs Terkel.

Terkel: The passage which you just read from *The Four-Gated City* seems
one of the keys to the book. Lynda, who is the wife of a friend of your
protagonist Martha Quest, has been considered mad, and Martha finds
out something, doesn't she?

Lessing: Well, you see, I've done my homework on this point without ever
planning to do it, because it so happened that for the last twenty years,
without ever intending to do it, I have been ever involved with psychiatrists or social workers dealing in what we call "madness," or have had very
close friends who have been quote, unquote "mad" in one way or
another. This is not anything that I had planned to do; it has just
happened this way. What one experiences gets into one's work!

When I wrote this book, although I had a fairly clear idea of certain
things I wished to say, other things I discovered as I wrote. Lynda is the
character who fascinates me the most in this book, because she is the
crystallization of a great deal of experience in a form I never expected. I
found out a great many things about what I think through Lynda. Lynda
is like a lot of people I've known who spend their time in and out of
mental hospitals. This is getting more and more common. I have no
doubt at all that a lot of people will either be in mental hospitals
themselves or have friends who are in and out of mental hospitals and live
their lives in a twilight of drugs. I mean by "drugs"...

Terkel: ...sedatives, tranquilizers...

Lessing: ...that cycle of chemical things which people get put full of.
These people, I maintain, are probably not mad at all, or a great many of
them are not or never have been mad. Just before I left England, I met a
doctor who'd been working in America, and he said that there is a
different approach here to schizophrenia. In England people can go to a
doctor and be told that they're schizophrenic, but it's happening less and

less here, I'm told. This "disease"—in quotes again, because I don't think it is one—has been broken down, and almost as it were spirited away by words as if it ceases to exist because doctors say it doesn't exist and because they dish out drugs. I think what's going to happen in the next— all right, for argument's sake, let's say—ten years is a lot of rethinking is going to take place about what schizophrenia is. I think we're going to have a lot of surprising conclusions to what schizophrenia is, and what we are, in fact, doing is to suppress and torment—I can use very strong language about this because I have dear friends who go through this misery and it's hard to be cool about seeing people being tormented. In short, a lot of perfectly normal people, with certain capacities, are being classed as "ill."

Terkel: Let's dwell on this. This seems to be the recurring theme. You deal with certain circles, literary people, people in the midst of cataclysmic events—the time of Suez and after—writers in difficulty. Martha Quest is searching, is she not, throughout? She wants to find out what it's about, really, who *she* is.

Lessing: Yes, that's what we're all doing. I chose that *name* when I started the first book in this series twenty years ago almost blindly, you know. I reread *Martha Quest,* the first volume, recently and I was fascinated to see that all those themes are there which bear right throughout this cycle.

Terkel: But the cycle and these themes have developed because in the meantime things have happened in the world in these twenty years too, right along with it—to you as an individual as well as to the world itself— that make your themes all the more critical and pertinent now.

Lessing: I understood that when I chose the title for the sequence, *Children of Violence. Violence* is now a vogue word; it's a cliché: we're living in a violent time. When I chose it, it was *far* from being that.

Terkel: It's as though in a sense the writer is a prophet; you were prescient in that sense. You as a writer, as a creative spirit, obviously were sensing something in the world in which you were living.

Lessing: I don't think that writers have any more sense than anyone else, actually. We can express things better. Our function as writers, I maintain, is to express what other people feel. If we're any good, it's because we're like other people and can express it.

Terkel: Then it's a question of art and craft, and you must express what is a universal feeling is what you're saying, in a way. Getting back to Lynda and Martha, obviously you are expressing what many, particularly sensitive people are feeling.

Lessing: More and more, you see—I looked at the figures recently, but I've nearly forgotten because my head for figures is appalling—but I know the proportion of our hospital beds now occupied by people who are quote, unquote "mad" is unbelievable, something like half. And it's going up all the time. But the capacity for the human race to take things for granted is what's so terrible. We say that the number of people going mad is going up because of the "greater stress" people are under. But what is this supposed "greater stress" that they're under? What in effect is happening to make people become sensitive in this particular way? Do we ask the right questions about it? Is it enough to say that we're driven mad by motorcars and the tension of society? What else is happening to us?

Terkel: In *The Four-Gated City* too you dwell on various events that overtake the country. You also dwell on personal relationships, as well as the new generation of children who make this tremendous leap forward. Is it because the leaps are so overwhelming today too?

Lessing: We can't talk about this without throwing out a whole lot of generalizations, which I shall now throw out. You see, I don't think that I say anything madly original, but I do think perhaps that I'm better at putting facts together; I think I'm quite good at seeing things in juxtaposition.

If I say that two world wars haven't done humanity any good—it's not a very original observation—but do we remember at all times, do we actually wonder what effect two world wars have had on some young person in university who is driving the authorities mad by his behavior? I'm astounded by the lack of imagination of *some* older people. I don't like this business of "generation gap"—it's a great cliché: there's a gap between some members of the younger generation and some members of the older generation. But a large number of the older generation talk about young people as if the young people have inherited the same world they inherited. And they have not, and the world is so terrible—and marvelous. Its possibilities are so incredible. And these young people are reacting very intensely to a situation which no generation has had to face before, including a very strong possibility of never getting to live to be thirty or forty. They all know this. And if their mothers and fathers don't realize that this is a part of their thinking, then they're very stupid and very insensitive. I think they're a marvelous generation, not that I'm one to dish out the praise because I think they've got great lacks as well.

Terkel: You say "lacks," and your book, through Lynda, is almost a plea for the imagination of possibilities. You speak of a "lack of imagination." The "lack of imagination of possibilities" obviously fascinates you.

Lessing: Yes, I think we're living in a time that's like the middle of an atom blast, with everything bad and good happening together, because we don't know what's going to come out of what we're living through now. Everything's changing so fast that we can't grasp the changes. This is the essential thing. The kids are trying at least to grasp them, and they haven't sunk back in some drunken, suburban haze, which is what some of their elders are doing.

Terkel: The elders live in a martini haze, and yet they condemn the young for what they might describe as the "pot scene." The young see a double standard, don't they?

Lessing: Yes, they do. What I'm troubled about the youth is that they're too complacent. It's an interesting thing to say since they're always being as bold as they are. But none of them has ever experienced fighting in an atmosphere which is against them. I know that the police beat them up and authority hates them and a lot of the older generation hates them with real vindictiveness, this is true—but the fact is that there is a freemasonry among the young: they stand by each other, support each other, approve of each other, even though they may disagree with each other. I think what's likely to happen in this country and other parts of the world—in fact, it's inevitable—is that it's not going to continue to be that a large mass of the youth are more or less of one mind.

A large section of that youth are going to be bought by authority and bribed probably by flattery. You're going to find the fighters down to a minority, because it's always like this. There's never been a time when the fighting's not been done by a minority, and the mass of the citizens are staid, conservative, and frightened. What are these kids then going to do? At the moment I don't see youth thinking about how they're going to react when they haven't got this mass support of their own generation. I don't think they realize what it's like to be out on a limb fighting by themselves.

Our generation knows this very well, because we've seen it, we've lived through it. We know very well that when the heat gets turned on, people run, and when it gets unpleasant a few people remain fighting. And when public opinion—that's the point—turns against something, not many people last. This, these kids haven't had yet, and this is why I think they're very vulnerable, because they don't know yet.

For instance, I'm taking that group of people which I think is the most savagely brutal and stupid lot in the world—white South Africans—who are at the same time, if you meet them, kindly, friendly, nice human beings. I remember, when the Second World War ended, the Fascists in Nazi Germany who we knew were everything that history says they were, and I then met them and they were no different from you or me; they'd been in a different historical set-up—that's all. Until these kids know that there isn't one of us who, put in a different set-up, wouldn't be brutal, savage, exploitive, they know nothing about how history works.

There is no original virtue in being twenty-two on a college campus. To be young is a minimal requirement—after all, everyone's been young; it's a grace, but not a very long-lasting one. Have they, in fact, been doing their homework and looking at how many large groups of people in the world now are living in Fascist countries, to be condemned by the same standards that they use to condemn society in America? Have they asked what's going to happen to them in ten years' time, when the heat goes up? Because if they've not thought this out, then they're as good as defeated.

Terkel: This is a theme without ending—the theme of man and circumstance. In Hannah Arendt's book *Eichmann in Jerusalem,* with its subtitle "The Banality of Evil"—and we face now too the evil of banality—she says that Eichmann was indeed not a beast: he was a man who acted *beastly.* Isn't this what you're saying, that the possibilities are within?

Lessing: Yes, can you imagine in 100 years' time, if anyone is alive then, that anyone's going to look back to the Second World War and say, "Oh, those beastly Germans"? They're going to say that the world allowed a certain type of government to take power in Germany, and a very small group of people in other countries protested what was going on; but we're all going to be implicated in this kind of guilt. And they're going to look back on what we're living through now and say, "These people allowed"—I'm not going to list the horrors, because we all know them—"to happen," even though we're terribly nice, good, kind, charming, delightful people. Right?

Terkel: We come here to this question of the individual. I remember my own experience, and again this is all reflected in *The Four-Gated City,* hearing a group of men in South Africa, all of them charming, genial, singing the Schubert *lied,* "Das Lindenbaum," all Afrikaaners, accepting and bolstering apartheid in its most horrendous forms. But, as you say, personally, because I was white, they were charming, wholly removed from the world around them.

Lessing: Bernard Shaw said somewhere the most terrifying thing: "Is it really necessary for Christ to be killed in every generation to save those who have no imagination?" Well, is it? People are so unprepared for the fact that a man can be a nice person as an individual yet support the most appalling policies. This shouldn't happen after what the human race has experienced.

Terkel: You're talking about roots too, aren't you? You're really talking about a knowledge of the past, knowing what happened and why it happened?

Lessing: Well, you said last night that these kids behave as if history started three years ago, and that's what their hang-up is, because it hasn't.

Terkel: It comes back to that again.

Lessing: I really don't want to go on about the kids, because I admire them and I think they're very brave. I feel differently. There are so many of my generation who are against them and who are vindictive. I'm not prepared to criticize them too much.

Terkel: Before we return to *The Four-Gated City,* you've been traveling for about five weeks now through America, and you said that somewhere in the Midwest you saw some incredible antagonism toward the young by our contemporaries.

Lessing: Yes, I met it absolutely nakedly. I think a great many older people are envious, and critical because they're envious. But I hadn't before ever met the naked hatred of the young that I met in the Midwest: they *hated* young people. It's really ugly to see it. And these are teachers who are supposed to be teaching these kids.

Terkel: And you were saying that one of the reasons you think is envy of a certain joyousness among the young.

Lessing: Yes, there's a great style and joy and a good humor—that's the great thing they've got.

Terkel: Getting back to *The Four-Gated City*, could I ask you how you chose that title?

Lessing: It's a phrase that comes out of mythology, and it's in the Bible, spread all over the folklore of every conceivable part of the world. I chose it because the structure of *Children of Violence* goes in fours—each book is divided into four—and this is four again. It's a very ancient symbol, and also I had a dream in which I saw what I later discovered to be an Egyptian theme: the sacred cow stands on great white legs and the hind legs are the people of the city. It was a beautiful dream, in technicolor—just at the time I was trying to work out what I was going to call this book.

Terkel: There's an old Negro spiritual called "Twelve Gates to the City." I take it this theme is universal, this matter of gates.

You spoke of there not being enough imagination. Earlier we were talking about the horrors of behavioral scientists who follow a certain pattern, manipulative people, and you were saying there's another aspect of life that these men never even dream of, and many of us don't— possibilities of experiencing.

Lessing: Yes, they treat human beings as if they were rats; they do their research on rats and pigeons. They can't ask the right questions. But I think it's a mistake to attack and criticize a phenomenon which is not going to be very important in five years' time, because these people are very *little* people. I gather they're quite important in the scientific struc- ture, but I'll lay a bet, any sum you care to mention, that what they stand for will be dead in a very short time because they're too small, too limited, too narrow-minded to . . . This is the problem in these discussions: there's never enough time to go into these matters.

I think that one of the things that's happening everywhere is that we're breeding new kinds of imagination and ways of thinking and experienc- ing. Actually they're very old and we find them in cultures we tend to describe as primitive; they're backward technologically, but they're not backward in any other way and probably more advanced than ours. What is going to happen, I think, is a discovery that many ways of experiencing and sensing the world which we describe as superstitious are not anything of the kind. If you look at what's going on everywhere—well, your country has a genuine feeling of new possibilities—you find these surprising people who would describe themselves as rationalists and die to defend that old-fashioned label are using ways of perceiving that our culture doesn't admit: one of them is the use of dreams, which actually is rather respectable in our society, so it gets made use of; but also different forms of extrasensory perception are being seriously researched and accepted. And have you really ever thought about how the atmosphere's changed about something like telepathy in ten years? Of all places it was the Soviet Union that suddenly made the announcement that they were experimenting into the use of telepathy for space travel. Now this sounds like space fiction—I'm a great reader of space fiction. Here in space fiction you find some novel so incredible that you think it's a fantasy and it's in the newspaper the next day.

Terkel: Coming back to Lynda and Martha, the protagonist in *The Four-Gated City*, we see that Martha, the sane woman, the secretary, the arranger, suddenly comes to lean toward Lynda's way of thinking, doesn't she?

Lessing: Yes, what happens is that Martha lives in this house with Lynda who has this label slapped on her: Lynda's the nutty one, she's mad. But Martha, by being with Lynda, begins to understand that what Lynda is doing is experiencing things in a different way. I try to explore what certain kinds of madness are. I'm inclined to think that schizophrenia is not madness at all. We've been dogmatic about this. I don't want to say that schizophrenia is just this; I don't like this business of saying something is only *that*.

Terkel: I'm fascinated by this character Lynda.

Lessing: One of the ideas that helped create Lynda was a woman I knew in London who was fifteen before she realized that everybody didn't know who was at the other end of the telephone and didn't hear what other people were thinking. She knew what other people were thinking, and in short she discovered that far from everyone being like this she was very much by herself and she learned to shut out the world. Lynda is a girl who has a very solitary childhood, and through a series of circumstances she comes under pressure, cracks up emotionally as God knows how many people do in adolescence—because everybody's a bit crazy in adolescence—and is classed as a schizophrenic and a variety of other things, has a lot of treatment such as shock treatment, insulin treatment, the whole gamut, and is so damaged that she spends the rest of her life in and out of mental hospitals. At the same time, she has these *powers*, increasingly, the capacity to *hear* what people are thinking and to *see*.

Now I would like to define this, because a lot of people have this capacity. They have labels stuck on them by doctors and psychiatrists, and they don't know in fact what they have. A great many people overhear what other people are thinking. It's a capacity that can be developed if you are patient, are prepared to make mistakes, and you're not bulldozed by the scientific way of thinking, which hasn't learnt to put its questions right. They have to learn how to put the questions differently. The way they are putting the questions now means that they're not able to learn.

The other capacity that a lot of people have is they see pictures inside their eyelids; a great many people see them when they're ill, tired, under great strain, or before they go to sleep. There's a word for that— "hypnagogic." The doctor will say, "Oh yes, that's a hypnagogic thinga- majig—dismissed!" This capacity is what they refer to in the Bible as the seer's visions, something which in our culture is not supposed to happen at all, and therefore it's just ignored. Now this too can be developed, and it's got nothing to do with time.

I'm really well aware that this is going to sound nutty: this particular thing *can* be, not always, out of time. It's on a different time length, wave- length. It can take different forms: it can be in black-and-white, it can be in technicolor, it can be in a series of stills, like shots from a movie, frozen shots, it can be like a movie running—a lot of different things. I saw in *Scientific American,* just before I left, an article on research done on children. I've completely forgotten—is it eidetic children?—that is, chil- dren who, if you project an image, maintain this image. They've done a lot of research on that, you see.

Terkel: It's funny that you mention that because the other night on TV Jacob Bronowski said that William Blake had this particular attribute that you just described.

Lessing: He also had a lot of others, quite clearly.

Terkel: But this matter of image, "Blake could *see,*" this is Bronowski talking, "Blake could *see* clearly, wholly, in absolutely all dimensions" that which you just talked about.

Lessing: It's the "eidetic"—the capacity to hold an image in front of your eyes as if it were a photograph. That's not what I was talking about when I spoke of seeing the pictures moving or the stills; that's something else.

Why I was talking about that was to describe how the scientist dealt with it: the test as to whether the child was telling the truth or not was the amount of detail he could come up with from this picture. You see, now if he was able to remember the exact number of buttons on a coat or the hairs on the pussycat's tail, he was telling the truth, and, if not, he didn't have this capacity. This is a scientific mind working, you see. If I meet you on the street tomorrow morning, we have a chat, and we go away; and if you were in an observant mood and I was, you couldn't say what I'd been wearing and I couldn't say what you'd been wearing. If someone had said, "How's he looking?" I would say, "I don't know; he looked much as usual." But we'd have absolutely no doubt at all that we'd met each other, even if we couldn't remember a single detail. Right? We'd go to the stake that we'd met each other, even though we could say no more than that. The scientists are not yet able to measure what happens when you and I meet on the street, or *what* meets on the street. *What* meets, when we meet on the street?

Terkel: Is it two bodies, two pairs of eyes, two pairs of legs, or is it something in addition to that?

Lessing: Right, something in addition to that, which everybody responds to, but which we can't yet measure. What is it?

Terkel: You're saying the questions are wrong questions. And the questions are asked wrong because there's a cynicism or skepticism involved, talking about the child who sees this in his mind, so they're really not so much curious about what the child saw but questioning the veracity of the child.

Lessing: I think they have an unconscious, or perhaps not so unconscious, bias to prove that these things don't exist. This is their problem. I met a girl in New York who said she read this book *[The Four-Gated City]* and she had a great burden taken off her because she was like Lynda. She suddenly realized she'd never been ill. Now this made me so happy.

Terkel: The passage you read at the very beginning dealt with that specific point that she'd been told she was crazy but she wasn't really.

Lessing: There are hundreds of thousands of people who have been tortured by doctors and psychiatrists in a way which they regard as so barbarous. The whole range of treatments used in mental hospitals are savage and cruel and terrible and destroy people.

Terkel: It's as though we're in Neanderthal times at this moment in treatment.

Lessing: Yes. Why is it that *we* have allowed to come about the state of affairs where a human being sits behind a desk and says, "Such-and-such is wrong with you," and we believe him? Why do we allow this kind of thing to be done to us? Now that's a much more interesting question, because the history of medicine is not one that encourages us to believe that they are likely to be right. Putting it at its mildest, they are extremely conservative and inflexible and unimaginative and continually damning new ideas; but in spite of the fact that psychiatry is a new and very feared thing, we will take their word, we allow them to slap a label on this—*why* do we?

Terkel: Do you know R. D. Laing?

Lessing: Yes, I do, and his work. I think he hasn't gone far enough. I admire him because he has battled with the English medical establishment and changed the plan so as to make it possible to ask questions in a way it simply wasn't possible before.

Terkel: You mention the psychiatrist who is detached, who has this patient on the couch, whereas Laing is saying *he* must also adhere to his own vulnerability. I think he uses the phrase "fellow passengers."

Lessing: I once saw on television Laing and some other doctors of his school who have had a great influence, contrasted with the old-fashioned kind, and what came out was the marvelous compassion of one and the cold violence of the other.

Terkel: So it brings us back again to...

Lessing: Oh, I wanted to say something very interesting. In *The Four-Gated City* I imagined that there were doctors tucked away in health services, psychiatrists working on these capacities; I hadn't finished that section before I started hearing of doctors who, in fact, keeping their mouths shut, are working away in your country and in Britain and in the Soviet Union; using the whole facade of what they have to work with, they are researching extrasensory perception and schizophrenia. So it's happening! These doctors, who at the moment have to keep quiet because they'd lose their jobs, are going to make a very great difference.

Terkel: *The Four-Gated City* has an appendix which I would describe as apocalyptic. An event occurs, the exact nature you don't describe—perhaps a plague—I assume it's many things. You're implying that unless the imagination is used we face disaster. Is that it?

Lessing: Well, I'm a bit gloomy about the future. I don't see a big shooting war because they say they've too much to lose, but some kind of accident is inevitable, because it's happening now, some smaller thing going wrong all the time. I think parts of the world will be damaged so badly that they can't be lived in for a while, and there will be a very great deal of various poisons in the atmosphere, and we don't know the effect this will have on the human organism. We can imagine it. Like everything else, it will have good effects and bad effects. Everything always goes in double harness: there's no such thing as a totally bad thing or a totally good thing; they always go together.

Terkel: Do you see any way in which this could be prevented? I'm not asking you for a panacea now, or a nostrum. You just see it as inevitable?

Lessing: You can't pick up a newspaper without reading warnings from scientists about what we're doing. I can't remember the name of this bloke who said that there is a very fine layer of substance around our earth on which the whole of life depends. We're pumping so much rubbish up there that we're changing that layer. The forecasts are various, because after all nobody knows very much, even scientists. We could destroy all organic life.

Terkel: If this is likely to happen, we come back to lack of imagination again, don't we? Through these characters, Martha and Lynda, you're saying that there's something in the human psyche not yet explored?

Lessing: It couldn't be with human beings as they are now; I think we're evolving into better people perhaps. As a part of this vortex we're in, it's possible that we're changing into people with greater capacities for imagination, and that we are going to be regarded as the "missing link," the transition people, and we'll have much better people.

Terkel: You know that old Chinese curse that the science-fiction writer Arthur C. Clarke uses: may you live in interesting times.

Lessing: Yes, indeed, we are living in interesting times.

Terkel: Let me ask you a question, which I know has become increasingly tiresome, yet being in America you've been asked it so often. To many militant women in America, you are the Simone de Beauvoir of Britain, particularly because of *The Golden Notebook*. I suppose you encounter this very often, because you're laughing. Now this always throws you, doesn't it?

Lessing: No, I've got terribly bored with it—that's the truth—because I don't think *The Golden Notebook* is about what they say it was about. Now I can modestly say that it has a large variety of themes, one of them being the sex war; but I now find myself, because I'm overreacting and impatient, in what sounds like a lack of sympathy for women who I know are often under very heavy pressure. But I think this whole trouble between men and women is a symptom of something very much bigger. We're not going to solve what's wrong between men and women by handing insults to each other. Something else has to be put right.

The climate has changed in Britain very sharply, and you'll find there's very much less tension between the younger generation, men and women, and people in my age group. Why? There are always physical things which change these emotional reactions, which people tend to forget. If you get a balance between the sexes, a lot of tension goes out. You should provide day nurseries and equal wages for women. My personal bias is not to sit around discussing psychology; one should be out battling for better nurseries and equal wages. That's where this battle has to be fought.

Terkel: So you see this quote, unquote Women's Liberation as not unrelated to the human battle itself; that is, not something separate and apart?

Lessing: I think people are scared stiff and they're beating hell out of each other, that's all, in one way or another. I can't find anything helpful to say about this, you see, because I think it's a minor thing—the cause of great unhappiness, but it's not the most important thing.

Terkel: You happen to be a writer who is a woman. These characters, Lynda and Martha, could've as easily been two men, couldn't they?

Lessing: Yes.

Terkel: You deal with many fascinating aspects of the contemporary world, but we come back to this theme that man has not yet discovered his possibilities.

Lessing: No, I think they're just beginning. We're on the threshold. We should be alert all the time for what we're overlooking. You see, I don't think some things are going to happen; they're happening *now*. We should try to be more awake to what's happening in our friends and ourselves because even just slightly more awake we could begin to see things happening. We always talk as if things are going to start happening in fifty years' time. But we overlook what's happening now. Will you name me a society ever that hasn't had great blind spots that afterwards people look backward on and wonder how it's possible that those people were so blind? What are our blind spots?

Terkel: So it's asking the impertinent question, the hitherto unasked question?

Lessing: Yes, it's always a good idea in any set-up where there's that question or that idea which seems most stupid and ridiculous to ask whether it really is so stupid and ridiculous.

One Keeps Going
Joyce Carol Oates

It is a bright, fresh, cold day in London, one of those excellent winter days
that seem to promise spring. But it is already spring here, by the calendar,
the spring of 1972, not winter, and one's expectations are slightly thrown
off—everything has been blooming here for months, and now trees are in
full leaf, the sun is a very powerful presence in the sky, but still it is
strangely cold, as if time were in a permanent suspension. Walking along
Shoot-Up Hill in Kilburn, London, I am aware of people's steamy
breaths—in mid-May!—and as always I am a little disconcerted by the
busyness of main thoroughfares, the continual stream of taxis and shiny
red double-decker buses and private automobiles, and the quiet that
attends this commotion. It seems so unexpected, the absence of horns,
the absence of noise. Americans in London are disoriented by the
paradox of such enormous numbers of people crowded into small areas
without obvious intrusions upon one another, or even obvious visual
displays of their crowdedness. It is usually the case that a one-minute walk
off a busy road will bring one to absolute quiet—the pastoral improbabil-
ity of Green Park, which is exactly like the country and even smells like
the country, a few seconds' stroll from Piccadilly on one side and the Mall
on the other—and Doris Lessing's home, only a few hundred yards from
Kilburn High Road, incredibly quiet and private, as remote a setting as
any home deep in the country.

She lives in the top-floor flat of a handsome, sturdy, three-storied
house on Kingscroft Road, a short, curving street of single and semi-
detached homes, with brick or stone walls that shield their gardens from
the street. There is a fragrant smell of newly-mown grass in the air, and
the profusion of flowers and full-leafed trees seem out of place in the
cold. Upstairs, the large room that serves Mrs. Lessing as both a dining
room and a workroom looks out upon a yard of trees, delicate foliage that
is illuminated by sunshine just as I am shown into the room.

It is a room of spacious proportions: at one end a wide windowsill given over to trays of small plants, at the other end an immense writing desk covered with books and papers. The flat—fairly large by London standards—is well-lived-in and comfortable, filled with Mrs. Lessing's own furniture, rugs, pillows, and many shelves and tables of books.

Doris Lessing is direct, womanly, very charming. She wears her long, graying black hair drawn into a bun at the back of her head; her face is slender and attractive, exactly the face of the photographs, the "Doris Lessing" I had been reading and admiring for so long. Meeting her at last I felt almost faint—certainly unreal—turning transparent myself in the presence of this totally defined, self-confident, gracious woman. I had arrived at Kilburn half an hour early, in order to wander around, to see the neighborhood in which she lived; and now, meeting her at last, I marveled at how easily the space between us had been crossed. Surely everything must seem to me a little enchanted.

When I had left the Kilburn underground station, however, I had paused at a news agent's stand to read in amazement of the attempted assassination of George Wallace. I explained to Mrs. Lessing that I was still stunned by the news—that I hardly knew what to think—that I felt depressed and confused by this latest act of violence. And, like many Americans in foreign countries, I felt a sense of shame.

Mrs. Lessing spoke very sympathetically of the problems of violence in contemporary culture, especially in America. "But everyone had guns when I was a child, on the farm," she said, referring to her childhood in Southern Rhodesia. "They went out and shot snakes; it seemed quite natural, to kill. No one ever seemed to ask: Why? Why kill? It seemed entirely natural." She asked me some very perceptive questions about the political climate in the United States: whether anyone would take Wallace's place (since it seemed, this morning, that Wallace might not recover), whether I thought the long, courageous years of effort of the antiwar protesters had really done much good? She seems more sympathetic, generally, with the United States—or with the liberal consciousness of the United States—than with England; when I remarked upon this, she said that her writing seemed to her better understood in the United States.

"In England, if you publish regularly, you tend to be written off," she said. "In America, one has the impression of critics scrutinizing each performance—as if regarding one's efforts at leaping hurdles, overcoming obstacles, with interest."

I asked about the response in England to a recent novel, the very unusual *Briefing for a Descent into Hell* (1971). "The readers who best understood it were the young," she said.

Briefing for a Descent into Hell is "inner space fiction" (Mrs. Lessing's category), and shows a remarkable sympathy with the "broken-down" psyche. It is the record of the breakdown of a professor of classics, his experience of a visionary, archetypal world of myth and drama, his treatment at the hands of conventional psychiatrists, and his subsequent—and ironic—recovery into the mean, narrow, self-denying world of the "sane." An afterword by the author makes the fascinating observation that the defining of the "extraordinarily perceptive" human being as abnormal—he *must* have "something wrong with him"—is the only response one can expect, at present, from conventional medical practitioners. I asked Mrs. Lessing if she were sympathetic with the work of Ronald Laing, whose ideas resemble her own.

"Yes. We were both exploring the phenomenon of the unclassifiable experience, the psychological 'breaking-through' that the conventional world judges as mad. I think Laing must have been very courageous, to question the basic assumptions of his profession from the inside.... In America, the psychiatrist Thomas Szasz, in *The Manufacture of Madness,* has made similar claims. He has taken a very revolutionary position."

Mrs. Lessing has known people who have experienced apparently "mystical" insights. After the publication of that iconoclastic book, *The Golden Notebook* (1962), she received many letters from people who have been in mental asylums or who have undergone conventional psychiatric treatment but who, in Mrs. Lessing's opinion, were not really insane—not "sick" at all.

I asked whether the terms "mystical" and "visionary" weren't misleading, and whether these experiences were not quite natural—normal.

"I think so, yes," she said. "Except that one is cautioned against speaking of them. People very commonly experience things they are afraid to admit to, being frightened of the label 'insane' or 'sick'—there are no adequate categories for this kind of experience."

Because this is a problem I am encountering in my own writing, I asked Mrs. Lessing whether she felt it was extremely difficult to convey the sense of a "mystical" experience in the framework of fiction, of any kind of work intended to communicate naturalistically to a large audience. She agreed, saying that in England, at least, there is a tendency for reviewers to dismiss viewpoints that are not their own, that seem outside the ordinary response. I mentioned that Colin Wilson, in treating most sympathetically the writings of the American psychologist Abraham Maslow (in his *New Pathways in Psychology: Maslow and the Post-Freudian Revolution*), received at least one review that attempted to dismiss him as "clever," and that I believed this quite symptomatic of English literary reviews in general.

Mrs. Lessing, who has met Colin Wilson, said that reviewers and critics have been intent upon paying him back for his early, immediate success with *The Outsider*, written when he was only twenty-three; but that he is erudite, very energetic, and an important writer. However, critical response to a book like his, or any book which attempts to deal sympathetically with so-called "mystical" experiences, will meet opposition from the status quo.

One of the far-reaching consequences of Doris Lessing's two recent books, *Briefing* and *The Four-Gated City*, will be to relate the "mystical" experience to ordinary life, to show that the apparently sick—the "legally insane"—members of our society may, in fact, be in touch with a deeper, more poetic, more human reality than the apparently healthy. But both novels are difficult ones, and have baffled many intelligent readers. When I first read *The Four-Gated City*, in order to review it for the *Saturday Review*, I was astonished at the author's audacity in taking a naturalistic heroine into a naturalistic setting, subjecting her to extraordinary experiences, and bringing her not only up to the present day but into the future—to her death near the end of the twentieth century. I could not recall ever having read a novel like this. And it is the more iconoclastic in that the novel is the last of a five-part series, *Children of Violence*, begun in 1952, tracing the life of Martha Quest, an obviously autobiographical heroine.

I asked Mrs. Lessing what she was working on at present, if she were continuing this exploration of the soul; but she said that, no, in a way she might be accused of a slight "regression," in that the novel she has just finished concerns a woman whose marriage has disintegrated and whose life is suddenly hollow, without meaning. "The title is *The Summer Before the Dark*, and the woman in it, the woman who loses her husband, goes to pieces in a way I've witnessed women go to pieces." Her own marriages, she mentioned, were not very "permanent," and did not permanently affect her; but this phenomenon of a woman so totally defined by her marriage has long interested her. More immediately, she was planning a collection of short stories: the American edition to be called *The Temptation of Jack Orkney*, and the English edition *The Story of an Unmarrying Man*. She was arranging a visit to the United States for a series of five lectures, to be delivered at The New School, and she was very much looking forward to the trip—she wanted to visit friends, and to travel, if possible, to the Southwest.

Her last trip to the United States was in 1969, when she gave a number of lectures at various universities. At that time she met Kurt Vonnegut, "a bloke I got on with very well," whose writing she admires immensely. This struck me as rather surprising, since to me Doris Lessing's writing is of a much more substantial, "literary" nature than Vonnegut's; but their similar concerns for the madness of society, its self-destructive tendencies, would account for her enthusiasm. She spoke of having heard that Vonnegut did not plan to write anymore—which I hadn't heard, myself—and that this distressed her; she thought he was very good, indeed. She mentioned *Slaughterhouse-Five* as an especially impressive book of his.

Less surprisingly, she felt a kinship with Norman Mailer, and believed that the critical treatment he received for *Barbary Shore* and *The Deer Park* was quite unjustified; "they're good books," she said. I mentioned that the exciting thing about Mailer—sometimes incidental to the aesthetic quality of his work—was his complete identification with the era in which he lives, his desire to affect radically the consciousness of the times, to dramatize himself as a spiritual representative of the times and its contradictions, and that this sense of a mission was evident in her writing as well. "In beginning the Martha Quest series, you could not possibly have known how it would end; and the sympathetic reader following Martha's life cannot help but be transformed, along with Martha," I said. Mrs. Lessing was understandably reticent about her own writing—and perhaps I embarrassed her by my own enthusiasm, though I did not tell her that she was quite mistaken in her feeling that her writing might not have the effect she desired: *The Golden Notebook* alone has radically changed the consciousness of many young women. Was there anyone else with whom she felt a kinship? She mentioned Saul Bellow, and of course D. H. Lawrence, and Nadine Gordimer. (Mrs. Lessing cannot return to the country of her childhood and girlhood, Southern Rhodesia, because she is a "prohibited immigrant"; homesick for the veld, she had her daughter send her several color photographs of African flowers, which are on display in her flat.) At the back of her mind, she said, is a work "about two men in prison," which she is not writing (as Kurt Vonnegut was "not writing" for decades the story of the Dresden fire bombing which is the ostensible subject of *Slaughterhouse-Five*); perhaps this work, which she may someday do, is related to her Southern Rhodesian background.

What most excited her about America was, during her visit, the spirit of liberality and energy in the young. She gave a lecture at the State University of New York at Buffalo in 1969, when that university was in a state of turmoil (a condition that the national press unaccountably overlooked, focusing news stories on Columbia and Berkeley), then flew to Stony Brook, which, though hardly a radical institution at the time, immediately erupted into student riots and rampages, brought on by a long history of police harassment over drugs. After visiting these two universities, Mrs. Lessing was scheduled to fly to—of all places—Berkeley, where she gave another lecture. She was most favorably impressed by the students, and young people in general, with whom she became acquainted. I asked her if she might like to teach full-time, but she said she would hesitate to take on a position of such responsibility (she had been offered a handsome job at City College, which she declined with regret), partly because she considered her own academic background somewhat meager. "I ended my formal education at the age of fourteen, and before that I really learned very little," she said. It struck me as amazing: a woman whose books constitute a staggering accomplishment, who is, herself, undisputably a major figure in English literature of the twentieth century—should hesitate to teach in a university! It is rather as if a resurrected Kafka, shy, unobstrusive, humble, should insist that his works be taught by anyone else, any ordinary academic with ordinary academic qualifications, sensing himself somehow not equal to what he represents. Perhaps there is some truth to it. But I was forced to realize how thoroughly oppressive the world of professional "education" really is; how it locks out either overtly or in effect the natural genius whose background appears not to have been sufficient.

Mrs. Lessing said that connections between English writers and universities were quite rare, but that in the United States it seemed very common. I explained that this was because of the existence of creative writing programs in the United States, which were not narrowly "academic," but which allowed a writer-in-residence to meet with students once or twice a week, giving him much time for his own work. In England, many writers are forced to work in publishing houses or on magazines. The publishing world in London, Mrs. Lessing said, is always changing; editors are always switching publishers, publishing houses disappear and new ones appear.//

I asked her if she was pleased, generally, with her writing and with its public response. Strangely, she replied that she sometimes had to force herself to write—that she often was overcome by the probable "pointlessness" of the whole thing. I asked Mrs. Lessing if she meant that her own writing seemed to her sometimes futile, or was it the role of literature in society.

"I suppose one begins with the idea of transforming society," she said, "through literature and then, when nothing happens, one feels a sense of failure. But then the question is simply *why* did one feel he might change society? Change anything? In any case, one keeps going."

I told Mrs. Lessing that her writing has worked to transform many individuals, and that individuals, though apparently isolated, do, in fact, constitute society. Her own writing, in my opinion, does not exist in a vacuum, but reinforces and is reinforced by the writing of some of her important (and nonliterary) contemporaries—Ronald Laing, Abraham Maslow, Buckminster Fuller, Barry Commoner—and many other critics of the "self-destructing society."

"Yet one does question the very premises of literature, at times," Mrs. Lessing said. "Has anything changed? Will anything change? The vocal opposition to the war in Vietnam, in America—has it forced any real change?"

"I think there have been changes, alterations of consciousness," I said.

Mrs. Lessing received my opinion respectfully, but it seemed clear that she did not share it. She went on to remark that she felt rather out of touch with current writing since she kept to herself, generally, and did not make any attempt to keep up with all that was being written. She asked me about the English writers I admired. When I told her that I very much liked V. S. Naipaul's *In a Free State,* she agreed that Naipaul was an excellent writer. "But somehow I don't feel a rapport with him, the kind of sympathy I feel for someone like Vonnegut, even though he writes about a part of the world, Africa, I know very well."

Of the younger English writers I admired, only Margaret Drabble was a familiar name to Mrs. Lessing. She liked Miss Drabble's writing but had not yet read *The Needle's Eye;* I told her that I thought this novel shared some important themes with her own work—the conscious "creating" of a set of values by which people can live, albeit in a difficult, tragically diminished urban world.

"Well, whether literature accomplishes anything or not," Mrs. Lessing said, "we do keep going."

When I left Mrs. Lessing's flat and walked back down the hill to the underground station, I felt even more strongly that sense of suspension, of unreality. It seemed to me one of the mysterious paradoxes of life, the inability of the truly gifted, the prophetic "geniuses" (an unforgivable but necessary word) to comprehend themselves, their places in history: rare indeed is the self-recognized and self-defined person like Yeats who seems to have come to terms not only with his creative productivity but with his destiny. Doris Lessing, the warm, poised, immensely interesting woman with whom I had just spent two hours, does not yet know that she is *Doris Lessing.*

Yet it is natural, I suppose, for her not to know or to guess how much *The Golden Notebook* (predating and superseding even the most sophisticated of all the Women's Liberation works) meant to young women of my generation; how beautifully the craftsmanship of her many short stories illuminated lives, the most secret and guarded of private lives, in a style that was never self-conscious or contrived. She could not gauge how *The Four-Gated City,* evidently a difficult novel for her to write, would work to transform our consciousness not only of the ecological disaster we are facing, the self-annihilating madness of our society which brands its critics as "mad," but also of the possibilities of the open form of the novel itself. Never superficially experimental, Mrs. Lessing's writing is profoundly experimental—exploratory—in its effort to alter our expectations about life and about the range of our own consciousness.

Her books, especially the Martha Quest series, *The Golden Notebook,* and *Briefing for a Descent into Hell,* have traced an evolutionary progress of the soul, which to some extent transforms the reader as he reads. I think it is true of our greatest writers that their effect on us is delayed, that it may take years for us to understand what they have done to us. Doris Lessing possesses a unique sensitivity, writing out of her own intense experience, her own subjectivity, but at the same time writing out of the spirit of the times. This is a gift that cannot be analyzed; it must only be honored.

The Capacity to Look at a Situation Coolly

Josephine Hendin

Josephine Hendin's interview was conducted in New York on WBAI Radio December 30, 1972. The transcription was prepared and edited by Patricia Featherstone. Printed with the permission of Bill Thomas, Director, Pacifica Radio Archive.

Hendin: In *The Temptation of Jack Orkney and Other Short Stories* one thing that interested me particularly was your story "Report on a Threatened City," where creatures from another planet come down to earth to warn everyone of an imminent disaster, and no one seems to want to pay attention. When they try to warn the young people they're in a state which you describe as "disabling despair." You say while they are more clear-headed than their elders, more able to voice and maintain criticisms of the wrongs and faults of society, they're not able to believe in their own effectiveness or ability to do anything about it. Is this how you see young people?

Lessing: Well, not all of them, of course. But I do think, certainly in England, I don't know about this country, that there are large numbers of young people who might have been political perhaps a few years ago, but who seem to be perhaps numbed. Well, I'm not surprised, if you look at what's going on everywhere. Let's put it this way: I'm very glad that I'm not twenty, because I don't think I would be able to regard what's going to happen with all that equanimity. About what goes on here, as I say, I don't know at all. Quite a common thing to see in England is groups of young people living together on some basis or another, often quite informalized. They don't say, "I'm going to set up a group of young people." It's what seems to happen. A feature of this is that people tend to be unambitious and work out some kind of rather relaxed, informal sort of style of living, which is very interesting to see because it's quite different from anything that my generation did, for example.

Hendin: When you say you don't think you'd be able to regard what's going to happen with such equanimity, in this particular story it's a kind of doom. At least in a specific city that is going to happen, and in *The Four-Gated City* you prophesy a kind of apocalyptic war. Is that what you see as coming?

Lessing: This story is about San Francisco, of course. There was a program on British television, it must have been about eighteen months ago, and I read an article about the same time, and what fascinated me about this was that the citizens of San Francisco didn't seem to know the situation they were living in, yet one can have programs on British television or erudite articles about it. I mean, the fact that all the amenities are on the San Andreas fault, everything from fire stations to hospitals, and in fact the posts that are supposed to cope with emergencies will be the first to go if there's an earthquake. Well, it was a fascinating thought that the people who were going to be involved didn't know what they were in for. And this just sparked off that story. But I gather that since then things are not really much better. If you write something like that, people send you articles and comments, and I gather that the citizens of San Francisco don't know very much more than they did then. But it's quite freely discussed in other parts of the world, much more than it is in San Francisco. And that is the interesting thing about that, that we don't face the situation that is perhaps intolerable. We decide not to look at it straight. Maybe it's a basic human tendency or something of the kind. This is possibly what's going on in New York, because when I came here in 1969 everything was much sharper, more aggressive, more tense, and the newspapers were much more sharp and clear. But this time, when manifestly the external situation hasn't changed in the slightest, I find the newspapers rather bland compared to the English newspapers, and everything seems to be rather good-natured, from which I deduce that things have been swept under the carpet because it's too painful to look at them. I may be wrong about that. But it's possible at least that that's what's happening.

You asked about the ending of *The Four-Gated City*. I'm not saying that's a blue-print, but I think something of the kind is likely to happen. One doesn't need to have a crystal ball to see that this is what's going to happen. You just have to read [a newspaper]. There's a paper in England, for example, called *The New Scientist*, which is written in language that non-mathematical dopes can understand, you see, like me. You've just got to read that for a couple of months to see that far from the danger of war receding, it's sharpened, that far from our ecological problems being better, they're worse, and so on. When I wrote *The Four-Gated City*, I thought that I was perhaps going out on such a limb that no one would ever speak to me again. By the time it was published it was all old hat, things were moving so fast. But the fact that they're old hat doesn't mean to say that anything's changed very much. The problems that we, I mean the human race, have to solve are every bit as bad as they were. The fact that we're not looking at them, or it doesn't seem to be that we're looking at them, doesn't make them any better.

Hendin: I was wondering how you would write about your idea that things seem to be more good-natured here, with the proliferation of small groups, each of which has their own special interests. I'm thinking in the main of those groups which are concerned with improving the environment, with the great number of women's organizations which want to improve the lot of women in this country, and with the proliferation of various kinds of black power groups showing a spectrum of all degrees of militancy.

Lessing: This kind of bitty approach to these enormous problems is not enough, and what we need is something that perhaps the human race is not evolved enough to do, which is some kind of overall scheme which seizes the problems, and looks at them as global problems, and not the problems of individual countries, let alone of groups. As I say, this is not me talking, because whereas previously, when I had such thoughts that I really thought were quite extraordinary, and indeed, perhaps shamefully pessimistic and so on, it turns out that this is the kind of thinking of people in very responsible positions who, in fact, say extremely clearly things like: "If within ten years we don't do so and so and so and so, the situation will be out of control." Now what they suggest should be done in ten years is usually precisely this ability of humanity as a whole to look at itself as a whole, and to face its problems as a whole. This is in fact what is necessary.

Hendin: Is what you call the "disabling despair" of the young in some way a reaction to the sense that this is not going to be done?

Lessing: This is what some sections of young people seem to do. Do you know, I do find this difficult, when a sentence or statement from a story is quoted to you: "You say so and so," and in actual fact it is out of context.

Hendin: Fair enough. To get back to the context of the story, which is interesting in itself in terms of the form, you describe the situation as it evolves around the visit of creatures from another planet to the Earth. And in a number of your books you've been interested, it seems to me, in

using this—whether as a metaphor or whether you see it as a possibility—
the idea of space travel, and beings from another planet coming here. I
was wondering what significance you felt this had.

Lessing: I don't see why it's impossible. If there were beings from another
planet here I doubt whether we would recognize them. It wouldn't take
very much, would it, some day for intelligent creatures to disguise themselves in such a way that they wouldn't be recognized.

Hendin: I get the feeling sometimes in many of your stories that people
see each other as though they were space travelers looking at aliens on
another planet—that somehow the distance between people is sufficiently
great, or between people and the lives they are leading. The sense of
disillusionment becomes so great that there's a feeling of immense
distance.

Lessing: This whole business of using people from outer space is a very
ancient literary device, isn't it? It's the easiest way of trying to make the
readers look at a human situation more sharply.

Hendin: But somehow it seems to reflect the same sense of distance that
so many of the characters in your books have in relation to themselves
and to the worlds they live in. It seems to be bound up with the whole
sense of estrangement, for example, that Martha Quest has, in so many of
those situations where she's there and not there, and in situations in
which she feels alien, whether as a girl growing up, on this farm in central
Africa or in London, when the disaffection with the Communist Party is at
its highest—a sense of being a part of something which she has no deep
emotional connection to. I was wondering whether or not you didn't have
in mind the idea of being spaced out and yet involved in something. In
"Not a Very Nice Story," you talk about people's sense that feeling is all-in-
all. You say, "We feel, therefore we are."

Lessing: The story was about two married couples who were all close
friends, a set of affairs which continued for years. Two of the people in the
situation have what is known as an adulterous relationship. What I was
asking in the story was, "What in fact is love?" because these two were not
supposed to be in love, or lovers, but they were lovers, but their relationship was extremely cool and practical. This was an anecdote told to me by
someone, by one of the men actually, involved in this foursome, and I was
extremely shocked. He wanted to know why I was shocked. He said that

these two marriages were in fact very successful marriages, and the children were all happy, well adjusted, etc., and so on. I was shocked by the deception. Having listened to him for some time, I asked myself, "All right, why am I shocked?" And out of this question I wrote this story, which simply made a statement. I haven't taken any sides or anything of that kind. I'm still shocked by the situation; yet I still ask questions—about the nature of marriage, which I find hard to admire, the institution thereof. I'm always interested in the patterns that people try to evolve themselves. But this one, please note, nobody consciously evolved. It happened in life, and it happened in my story, much to the surprise of all the people involved in it.

Hendin: I'm tempted to ask what you think the nature of marriage is.

Lessing: Well, there must be something very wrong with this Mum and Dad and two children, or it wouldn't break up all the time. I used to have a great many theories about marriage, sex, love, and all this kind of thing. But everything is going to change. Sometimes I think that maybe some form of polygamy or group marriage would be a good thing. But then, whenever you have thoughts like this, of course, you end up with the problem of the children, because children are the most conservative creatures in existence, and they get very upset if they don't get what everybody else has. One can either say it doesn't matter that it's hard on the children, or you're not going to do it because it's hard on the children, but one has to face the fact that children tend to pay the price for any experimenting that adults do.

Hendin: In *The Summer before the Dark,* you describe the situation of a woman whose children are pretty much grown up, and who, looking back on her life, seems to feel that a great many of the personal questions which seemed at one time so important, whether to love this man or that, whether to marry, aren't very meaningful.

Lessing: When you get middle-aged, which I am, it's fairly common to look back, and to think that a lot of the sound and fury that one's been involved in perhaps wasn't all that necessary. Or you can say this is just emotional middle-aged spread, or something of the kind. But it could also possibly be quite a useful frame of mind to be in. I discuss this with my friends who have reached the same age. There is quite often a sense of enormous relief of having emerged from a great welter of emotionalism.

Hendin: But it's more than that for Kate, a sense that personal relations were not as important as she had thought—that the sense of strength to be derived from feeling at peace with oneself, apart and alone, is what's important. She dreams of carrying a seal through all kinds of misfortunes and protecting it as though the seal in some way is bound up with the most important part of herself, which gets carried through whatever storms occur in marriage, or raising a family, and is preserved intact.

Lessing: I don't think that I'm saying that this woman was repudiating anything she'd done. She'd simply moved on to a different state in herself, which is a different thing altogether, really. You know, we're very biological animals. We tend always to think that if one is in a violent state of emotional need, it is a unique emotional need, or state. In actual fact, it's probably just the emotions of a young woman of twenty-three whose body is demanding that she should have children. It's hard for some people to take, because we're all brought up to have this fantasy about ourselves, that everything we feel and think is uniquely and gloriously our own. Ninety percent of the unique and marvelous and wonderful thoughts are, in fact, expressions of whatever state we happen to be in.

Hendin: Kate becomes friendly with a young girl in that novel, Maureen, who's trying to decide what to do with her life, and she decides that at the end it really doesn't seem to matter whether she marries one man or another.

Lessing: Maureen tends to be more passive than not, and getting married was very much on her plate. A lot of young women think of marriage in terms not of a man, but of a way of living. When young women think about getting married, what they're choosing when they choose a man is often a way of life. Maureen had quite a lot of choices and she wasn't really mad about any of them. I know a lot of girls who don't want to get married at twenty-four. It would be interesting to see how they're thinking at thirty, but that's another thing. But it is interesting the number of young women I know who don't want to get married at all. They don't want to have children. Well, they're trying to cheat on their biology, and as I say, it would be nice to see what happens.

Hendin: Couldn't it also be an alternative to marriage?

Lessing: Yes. When I find a very determined young woman of twenty-four who announces she's got no intention of ever getting married, and looks as if she's going to stick to it, I'm interested because I'm wondering if in fact women are changing their nature or not.

Hendin: In *The Golden Notebook,* Anna or Molly says that she thinks there must be a completely new kind of woman.

Lessing: No, I think that maybe they are not new kinds of women at all. They are women very much conditioned to be one way who are trying to be another, or what they think is something different. But the way we think and the way we feel are usually pretty well at loggerheads for most people. These conversations between women in *The Golden Notebook* and other places are always being taken out and quoted as if they are blueprints of mine or a political program. Well, they're not. They're accounts of the kinds of states of mind women get into.

Hendin: In *Martha Quest,* there's a comment about people coming to books of different kinds for cues to life. Do you think this is the way a great many people have come to read your books?

Lessing: I think people now go to sociological books more than novels for cues of how to live their life. I used to go particularly to novels to find out how I ought to live my life. But, to my loss, I see now I didn't find out.

Hendin: About the way we think and the way we feel being at logger- heads, one thing that always interested me about Martha Quest's life was, why does she do it? Suddenly given her freedom at a certain point, why does she get married to a man she scarcely seems to love, and who she's aware of not being in love with?

Lessing: Well, this was a very general situation about men, and don't forget that that was the war. The more I look back at that war, the more I think that everyone was insane, even people not involved in it. And I'm not being rhetorical. I think that everyone was crazy round about then. And the rest of the behavior that went on was more crazy than usual. I don't want to suggest that human beings are sane in between wars; we manifestly are not, but that was a very terrible war, you know. This is a thing I keep coming back to. We go through a terrible experience, it comes to an end, and it is as if it hasn't happened, or it simply gets pushed off into words. It becomes verbalized. The First World War degraded and demoralized us terribly and the Second World War did it more thoroughly, and we have not got over either of these wars. The children of that war were profoundly affected by it. We tend to ignore this. We get steadily more and more demoralized, and barbarized, by the things we do, but we don't like to really look at this fact. So, if in the middle of the Second World War a young woman, or very many young women, got married somewhat light-heartedly, it's just a very minor symptom of the general lunacy.

Hendin: Well, in what ways do you think the war affected trust in relations and the way people see themselves and each other? Is it the bomb, or simply the accessibility of so much violence through films?

Lessing: No, it's just one very small thing. I remember towards the end of the Second World War, after we'd had four and a half years of horror, non-stop, of the most vicious propaganda from both sides we were still capable of being shocked by the fact that the Russians publicly hanged Nazis. Well, no one would even lift an eyelid now to look at the photographs. Twenty years on, we've become so used to worse. That's the horrible truth. We're just not shocked at anything.

Hendin: The characters, then, in *The Four-Gated City* in particular, seem to be as acute in terms of their ability to sense what's going on about them. Particularly, I think, the character you describe as being mad, being insane, Lynda, and I think in that portion of the book when Martha self-consciously drives herself mad. Do you think they're the only people who remain in touch with these things?

Lessing: The person in that book who has much more of a grasp of what's going on, physically if you like, is a man. He has a kind of a blueprint of what's going on everywhere, separating him off from what he thinks and does, from the others. These people were really into their own experiences with each other. People living together, who know each other very well, form some kind of a whole. They experience things through each other, and what one of them discovers becomes the property of the others usually. But also there are many different layers of ourselves. I mean, we know something in one part of ourselves that we don't know in another.

Hendin: There is a feeling in that book of being collective, not personal and unique. Even when Martha decides to go mad she describes it as being plugged into the self-hater, as though this were some almost universal force, which anyone would encounter.

Lessing: This figure is very prominent in many schizophrenics. That's a word I don't like but these labels will have to do. You'll find very many "mad people" saying: "They hate me. They're talking about me all the time. They want to destroy me." There are endless variations on this particular theme. This figure is common to very many people who are off-balance. I don't think it's very hard to explain either. All you have to do is to watch any mother bringing up her child; from the time this child is born this goes on: "Be a good boy and do this. Be a good girl and do this. You're a bad boy. You're a bad girl. If you do that I won't love you. If you do that so-and-so will be angry." This "conscience" is partly the externalization of what its parents can't stand, mostly its manner. This figure, the self-hater, which mad people describe continually, and express continually as this very powerful destroying force, is this lifetime of conditioning.

It's very easy to send oneself round the bend for a couple of days. I did it once, out of curiosity. I do not recommend it. I'm a fairly tough character, and I've been in contact with a very large number of people who've been crazy, and I know quite a lot about it. I sent myself round the bend by not eating and not sleeping for a bit. There's nothing remarkable about this process. It's a process deliberately used by medicine men and witch doctors in "primitive societies" all over the world. It's a process that can be described, let's say, by prisoners in a prisoner-of-war camp, who've been not eating and not sleeping, and they start hallucinating, or have various kinds of experiences of dissociation and so on, or they discover this figure I call a self-hater. I could go on indefinitely. It's described plentifully in religious literature, both Christian and Eastern.

But what makes a difference is the society you're in, and how this is accepted by the people around you. If in Africa somebody would turn up saying that they felt disassociated from themselves and heard voices, they wouldn't be clapped into the nearest loony bin, drugged silly, and given electric convulsive therapy. Now when I, and I may say I'm not the only person who's done this, deliberately sent myself round the bend to see what it was like, I instantly encountered this figure I call the self-hater. Now since I know, as I say, a little bit about it, I didn't rush off to the nearest doctor and say: "Oh doctor, I'm hearing voices and I hate myself, and the voices say they want to kill me," because I knew what was going on. But it is an extremely powerful figure, very frightening, and I'm not surprised that in this very unsophisticated society, unsophisticated psychologically, somebody experiencing this for the first time is scared, loses balance and goes off to the doctor, and I'm afraid to say, in very many cases is then lost. Because what happens is that a person who turns up at the out-patients or whatever, is slammed full of drugs, and then he's diagnosed as being remote or incapable of contact, or can't be reached, he's slammed full of more drugs, and the end of this can very well be in some ghastly snake pit somewhere. I understand that in this country you have as many as in ours. But what is frightening is not the snake pits, because they're out in the open and people know about them. What is frightening is what goes on in the name of orthodox and general treatment. This is where I think so much damage is caused out of ignorance and stupidity.

Hendin: In the way Martha deals with it, though, she gets quite a bit out of her experience. Whatever she encounters in herself seems to be a source of strength and insight. Do you think that this kind of experience has a positive value?

Lessing: You've put a whole lot of things together there. In the first place, Martha's experience was not an account of mine. But it was similar in some respects. Yes, of course, I got a lot out of it because you learn a great deal about yourself. For one thing, one learns a lot about why some of one's nearest and dearest land in loony bins.

About the *Briefing for a Descent into Hell,* one of the starting off points for that was that it occurred to me that so many of the things described by people who are mad are the same. They use the same phrases. They're fantastically stereotyped in fact, these experiences, and I was trying to think of different interpretations. Now, it is quite possible that this is distorted. It's an attempt to express something which she's trying to get through, from somewhere else. It's probable that there's another dimension, very close to the one that we're used to, and that people under stress open doors to it, and experience it, in a very violent, unpleasant, or dangerous and possibly permanently damaging way. *Briefing for a Descent into Hell* was an attempt to suggest what in fact this experience could be.

Hendin: Going back to Martha's experience in the novel, I always wondered—this experience she has occurs right after she has seen her mother after so many years—since in describing it you mention the reproving voice of the mother of childhood as being bound up with it, do you think in some way the connection between...

Lessing: No, not necessarily. This figure, this reproving "do this, don't do that figure" is internalized, and I don't think it's got anything to do with what time an actual mother turns up.

Hendin: I think that's quite true. But I wonder, in some ways, if to Martha the visit of the mother seems to ruin the time that she's been having in

London, and precipitates a kind of break in her conception of things. Interesting that she sends her mother to her analyst. I thought that was a wonderful scene.

Lessing: I must say, Martha's not the only person to have done that. I've heard about it quite often. It's using your support figure to say to your parent: "She says so and so." It helps one out, I suppose.

Hendin: To move away a little bit from the novel, do you see something in the way mothers and daughters get on together, and the way women of one generation create or help create women of the next, as somehow maintaining some particularly painful bond? In other words, are they self-haters, who feel they must marry, but in some way don't want to, but that it's inevitable? Is this something mothers contribute to their daughters?

Lessing: Well, every one of us has to live through our parents, and ourselves, and come out the other side. I don't know if that makes sense. There's no good sidestepping one's parents.

Hendin: I think that's true. But you've written so marvelously of the friendships between women, and yet mothers and daughters in your books don't seem to get on very well, do they? I suppose that's true in my case as well.

Lessing: Bernard Shaw once said that mothers should bring up sons, and daughters should be brought up by their fathers, because this was the natural bond and the other was unnatural. I'm not saying I agree with that, but it certainly does seem to be quite hard for parents and children of the same sex to get on together. Not always, of course. But it's a problem.

Hendin: Why, would you say?

Lessing: Well, it's biological, again. There's nothing mystical about it.

Hendin: What's biological, the attitude?

Lessing: The daughter threatens the mother and the son the father, in the most primitive and backward and animal-like way. You can observe it in any herd of animals, let alone human beings. Most of our behavior is not very advanced, is it? We like to fancy that it is. You can see the sort of competition going on between fathers and sons and mothers and daughters in any family. It's quite a primitive sort of thing.

Hendin: I think so. I always thought that Martha's mother was one of the most particularly envious and resentful mothers one could have.

Lessing: I think perhaps it was that generation. I don't think that women of this generation are so bad because most of them have work. They enjoy their work much more, whereas it was much rarer for women of that generation to have work. And that's terribly important, not to be out on a limb when you're fifty, without anything to do. It seems to me that every woman should be very careful that that shouldn't happen, and nowadays women are indeed very careful that that shouldn't happen, and that's why things are better.

Hendin: In the beginning of *The Golden Notebook,* Anna says: "The point is that as far as I can see everything is cracking up." Did you have anything particular in mind, or did she, at the time?

Lessing: Yes, it's no more than what we've already talked about. It seems to me that her and our civilization is falling apart. I think that this is what is happening around us, as we sit here. We're on the top of a slippery slide, and what's going to be at the bottom I don't know. Why am I talking of it as if it's in the future? It's not in the future; it's happening now. We're always talking about physical catastrophes. Just before I left England I was listening to the radio, and there was the President of the World Bank, or some such institution, calmly quoting figures of people who are going to die this year, of hunger. I mean there are millions of people, two-thirds of the people in the world, who don't get enough to eat, and will be stunted permanently by this, because as you probably know, if a child doesn't get the right protein at the right time, his brain will be permanently stunted by it. Now this is a quite formidable fact, but they're always talking about catastrophes as if they are going to happen in the future. Perhaps we should ask how bad does a catastrophe have to be before it becomes a catastrophe.

Hendin: In the title story to your new book, *The Temptation of Jack Orkney,* Jack Orkney, the main character, how would you describe him? Well, you do describe him.

Lessing: I use fifty thousand words describing him, don't I?

Hendin: I know. An old guard hero of the left wing, I suppose? No, that's too pejorative. But, at any rate, a dedicated socialist? When his father dies he begins to dream of his own death in a way, and with a peculiar horror and sweetness at the same time bound up with it. But his personal tragedy is played off against the tragedy in Bangladesh, and the protest that he's been having to organize against it. Do you see a relation between the personal loss and the public tragedy?

Lessing: Well, it is in the story, isn't it? Not more than that, no.

Hendin: Well, again, I was wondering. There are two things really. First, the relation between the public and the private, and the way these events shape our dreams, our lives.

Lessing: I don't know that this story is about the relationship between the public and the private, you see. What I'm describing there is the person who has been like a revolutionary or a left-winger all his life, and then finds himself to be a member of the establishment. This happens to every generation, of course. But what has happened, we see it very sharply in England and Europe; I don't know about here. It would be different here because the era of McCarthy made a fairly thorough weed-out of your left wing, but in England and in Europe, you would see in all countries, a group of men and women, middle-aged men and women, who in their prime were revolutionaries of one kind or another. I don't mean to say necessarily Communists. On the contrary. They could have been all kinds. Or not even political. They could have been "world changers," to use a silly phrase. What has happened to them is what happens to everybody— they've become institutions. Now, a set of mental attitudes shared in common by this generation is fairly easy to describe. They're all believers that society can be endlessly manipulated to achieve good ends. I'm not saying "socialists," because they include people who aren't socialists. They were all rationalists and atheists of one kind or another, or most of them were. They tended to have liberal ideas about sex, and so on. Very often their private lives were quite different from their liberal theories. There is a whole series of limited liberal attitudes, shared by all of them. Well, in any place, take one of these men and confront him with the death of his father—because such people tend to be petrified by the idea of death— it's not a fact that can be assimilated easily into their way of thinking. At his father's death he starts to dream, which he's never done before in his life. At the end of the story, this man has turned his back on an opportunity that was offered to him of opening doors on himself, to explore different ways of thinking. In the story he has a door opened for him, even though he doesn't want it; in fact he's going to go on dreaming. It is a pretty important door to have opened, because it's a way of learning a very great deal about oneself, and about this other dimension.

Hendin: Dreams do seem to find more and more of a part in your work.

Lessing: I don't think they play any more of a part than they have always done. In *The Grass Is Singing,* for example, the first novel I ever wrote, they play quite an important part. They've always played an important part in my life, you see. I've found them very useful in my work. In *The Summer Before the Dark,* I built dreams right into the story, so that the way out for this woman was in fact through her dreams of this magical seal that she found on this hillside. I'm doing a lot of research on dreams at the moment, and I read about it when anything comes my way. It's possible that we're not asking the right questions about them, because, after all, dreaming's not a new phenomenon. It's a capacity that human beings have always had and in some cultures used quite consciously. Some people in our culture use them quite consciously. There's a great deal already known about dreams if the scientists would like to look slightly sideways from their straight and narrow path, and read and study what's already available. But unfortunately they do tend to be somewhat hide-bound, many of them, and they're not prepared to consider as evidence material that doesn't fit neatly into their own little boxes. However, I think that even scientists seem to be improving in this direction. So I have hopes. Let's put it this way. I think a lot of research that is interesting is quite a waste because a lot of it we already know. It's already around, and has been for thousands of years in fact.

Hendin: At one point, in describing Kate sitting in a restaurant, you say, "She knew now, she had to know at last, that all her life she'd been held upright by an invisible fluid." Do you think that's true of women in general?

Lessing: Really it's true of everyone in general. But it's certainly true of women because we've been taught to attract attention all our lives. You're taught to be attractive and to dress attractively. For example, I notice that Women's Lib women tend to be attractive and to dress attractively. They don't despise the attention-attracting devices that women have always used. I'm not saying that they should. Far from it. I think a good deal of the depression and the mental breakdown of the middle-aged women are due to the fact they suddenly find they're not able to command attention the way they've always been able to command it. Let's put it like this: an attractive young woman finds it very hard to appreciate what she really is from her appearance, because she has only to walk into a room, or to put herself into an attention-getting situation, to find, in fact, that she can regulate the kind of attention she gets, fairly clearly. You only have to discover the difference between what you really are and your appearance when you get a bit older, which is a most fascinating experience. It really is. It's one of the most valuable experiences that I personally have ever had. A whole dimension of life suddenly slides away, and you realize that what, in fact, you've been using to get attention, or command attention, has been what you look like, sex appeal or something like that. Once again it's something that belongs to the condition of being a young woman. It's a biological thing, yet for half your life or more, you've been imagining that this attention has been attracted by yourself. It hasn't. It's got totally and absolutely and unopposedly nothing to do with you. It really is the most salutary and fascinating experience to go through. It really is most extraordinarily interesting.

Hendin: What do you think of the Women's Movement?

Lessing: Well, I know very little about it because I'm not involved in it. I've met some of the liberation women, and I like them very much personally, but I really do feel that I've said all I have to say about this in *The Golden Notebook,* and some of the things I said about Martha. One can't go on being preoccupied with the same problem, or the same set of problems. I don't want to say I'm bored by it, though that's partly true. It's just that you work your way out of something, and you go on to something else.

Hendin: Many of the women in the movement would feel that way too. But I think they would see working their way out of it in maybe slightly different terms. I have a feeling that you stress a kind of individualistic approach, more than they would.

Lessing: Well, being a writer is a very individualistic thing, isn't it? Anyway, I'm not altogether sure that I hold with all this, the dogma that everything has to be done in groups. This is only one of the ways of setting up one's life or one's politics. It's a new dogma, you know, one has to be in groups, but why?

Hendin: I think some of the most important parts of life are lived alone and apart from everyone, men and women alike.

Lessing: That's right.

Hendin: I once heard you lecture, and you described the situation of a writer having to battle against and confront the world's indifference. Did you find when you first started writing that there was an audience for your work?

Lessing: You're putting it very melodramatically. I put it much more clearly than that. I said that when a writer starts, nobody has the slightest interest in reading what he or she has to say, that a writer has to create an audience. I didn't say anything about battling or anything like that, which I think adds to this somewhat romantic myth about writers being heroic, battling away. I'm always against this romanticizing of situations or people because as soon as you start doing that you lose the capacity to look at a situation coolly, and to see what's really going on. And there's far too much of this glamorization of writers and the writing situation.

Hendin: How do you feel about your own career as a writer?

Lessing: Well, I have right here a quotation which I took off the wall from the wall-newspaper downstairs, and it reads: "The function of art is to make that understood which in the form of argument would be incomprehensible," and that was written by Tolstoy. And that is what I feel about writing.

Creating Your Own Demand
Minda Bikman

Minda Bikman's interview originally appeared in *The New York Times Book Review* March 30, 1980. Copyright © 1980 by Minda Bikman. Reprinted with permission.

Bikman: I found *The Marriages Between Zones Three, Four, and Five* to be a very different kind of novel from its predecessor, *Shikasta*.

Lessing: I can't think of another novel like that one. It's more a sort of legend than anything. It's in that kind of territory, a legend or myth. There's never been a book that I enjoyed writing as much as that one. It was a piece of cake, very unlike most of my books, which are agony. I really loved it. When I finished, I was sad that it was ended. But the relationships between these sorts of stylized men and women—that doesn't strike you as even somewhat comic? Which was my intention, slightly.

Bikman: No, I found the relationships all too real. You described so well the problems men and women seem to encounter, the way people are locked into their perceptions of how things should be. But I found it rather sad that the Queen of Zone Three, the heroine of the novel, had to endure such suffering because her way of living no longer worked for her kingdom. I liked her way of life before it changed; I liked its lightness, its sense of ease.

Lessing: You know, whenever women make imaginary female kingdoms in literature, they are always very permissive, to use the jargon word, also easy and generous and self-indulgent, like the relationships between women when there are no men around. They make each other presents, and they have little feasts, and nobody punishes anyone else. This is the female way of going along when there are no men about or when men are not in the ascendant. I'm not saying good or bad anything. I'm just saying that this is so, whereas the natural male way of going about things is this pompous discipline and lack of subtlety in relations. I've recently acquired a thought—but not too seriously, of course—which is: is it possible that women arrived on this planet from a different planet from men at some point? We have such difficulty in relating, in understanding each other. It's just possible we're different species altogether. Anyway, that was the idea when I wrote the archetypes of male and female.

Bikman: It has been reported that when you started writing *Shikasta* you thought it would be one book but that it expanded into five books. Is it definitely five books? Do you have the next three planned?

Lessing: There's no specific number at all. People have announced that I'm doing three or five. I never had any such thought. What I think is that with this kind of structure, there is nothing to stop me from going on quite a bit until I get bored with it. Because there are all kinds of possibilities. I finished the third one just the other day. It is about a Sirian female offical who's been one for many thousands of years, and the plot, if you can use that word, is that she slowly discovers through those long ages that, in fact, Canopus is a very much more highly developed empire than Sirius [both Sirius and Canopus developed life on Shikasta] because of course Sirius regards itself in many ways equally good. But this is how she learns how much she might still learn. She is very much an official. She is a bureaucrat, and she thinks like one. I made her a female because, after all, female bureaucrats are innumerable now and I haven't noticed that they're all that different from men in operation. Somewhere along the line, female good qualities get lost very often when women are put into positions of certain kinds of power.

I've noticed over and over again in these dominantly male structures that there are usually females tucked away, generally in subordinate positions. In fact, they play an extremely important part which no one recognizes—possibly not even they themselves. And I will quote an example that demonstrates it. A friend of mine got ill in Russia and was in hospital. It was a European hospital, with doctors on top, male and female, and wards and the whole lot, just as we're familiar with. But she was struck more and more by the role played by the ward women, which we do not have in this country. They weren't nurses so much. They were cleaners, and floated around—they brought meals and all that kind of thing. They had an enormous influence, and everybody relied upon them. Yet they were paid nothing at all, and nobody gave them much respect. In fact, it became evident to her that these females were a kind of bastion. Everything depended on these women for a sort of humanity and decency. Whenever I went into a big organization, I would look for these women. They can be anywhere, they can be at the top or the bottom, but they provide a quality without which the whole thing wouldn't exist. That is in fact what I think women do generally.

I don't have the old kind of feminist thoughts that I used to have. I mean, I've lost my moral indignation completely. I certainly try to understand what is happening. That's quite different from trying to think what ought to be happening. The thing is that in trying to find what happens, you come to some very interesting conclusions. And one of mine is that this great suppressed class of women in fact keeps everything going. They are what makes things run. I do so much hate the way women who have children and run homes are put down all the time. Sometimes you meet a woman with four kids and you say, "What are you doing?" and she says, "Oh, I'm afraid I'm only a housewife." It's enough to make you cry when you know the work this woman does, how hard she has struggled with it all. Yet they're so apologetic. They think they haven't done anything. It's awful. There isn't any harder or more demanding job, or one that needs more quality. Middle-aged women, at the end of half a lifetime of working with children and so forth, are the most highly equipped people there are. They can turn their hands to absolutely anything. They can cope with God-knows-what human situations with tact and patience. I used this theme a little bit in *Summer Before the Dark*.

Bikman: In your novels, particularly the first four *Children of Violence* books, you write so incisively of the forces that shape women's lives. Nearly every issue that the Women's Movement in the United States has raised in the past decade is discussed in those novels and, somewhat less centrally, in the last *Children of Violence* book, *The Four-Gated City*. Do you have any idea how you developed those perceptions?

Lessing: It would be enough to say I'm a woman, after all? You know, it wasn't my generation that invented feminism. My mother was a bit of a feminist. In fact, it was born, I think, with the French Revolution. You see, every generation suddenly invents everything.//

Bikman: Did the conditions of your growing up in Rhodesia contribute to your perceptions?

Lessing: I had a very isolated childhood. There were various reasons why I had to develop an extremely clear and critical mind. It was simply survival. Which isn't to say that I haven't in my life been ridiculously emotional. Without boring you with all the psychological details, my position in the family was such that I was very critical, and fairly early on. I had to be, because my mother and father were both in complicated emotional states. I was under terrible pressure as a child, which is true of every child, mind you, but I think it was slightly worse in my case. And then I was in this social set-up, which I disliked, this white-black thing. I can't remember a time when it didn't make me uneasy, even when I didn't know why I was. I think most young people have an extremely clear eye as to what goes on, but women, particularly, tend to lose it when they become adolescents. Perhaps I lost it less than some.

Bikman: So you were able to see clearly the dynamic between white settlers and the black population?

Lessing: I wasn't clearly seeing it at all. It took many years for me to see it. I think it had far more to do with the family set-up. I had to fight every inch of the way against a very difficult family situation. I've got several friends who had a fairly tough childhood, and every one of them has this extremely clear critical eye about what goes on—which is not always a good thing. It can make you very unhappy. You tend to be somewhat bleak, which I am. I think a good many children are born looking at the adult world—because they've been forced into it—with an extremely cold eye. And I had it, or I can't remember any time I haven't had it.

Bikman: Did you know when you began the *Children of Violence* series that it was going to be five books?

Lessing: Yes, I knew almost at once that it was five books, roughly sketched out in my mind. I didn't know how it was going to end, of course. It got less and less realistic as it went on. A good deal of it was in fact autobiographical, but some of it was invented. I think most writers have to start very realistically because that's a way of establishing what they are, particularly women, I've noticed. For a lot of women, when they start writing it's a way of finding out who they are. When you've found out, you can start making things up.

Bikman: The idea of the perfect city appears in several of your books, even as early as *Martha Quest,* when Martha has a vision of a golden city. *Shikasta,* of course, is based on an ideal city that gives rise to harmony and serenity. Before *Shikasta,* the idea seems to have been most fully stated in *The Four-Gated City.* In writing *Shikasta,* did you consciously go back to *The Four-Gated City* and take that moment and expand it into a full-length book?

Lessing: No. You see, the whole concept of a city, four-gated or otherwise, is so archetypal, so in the mythology of all nations, when you start looking. You will find it's nearly always a metaphor for states of mind, states of being. Anyway, my thought is a serious query about the effect the proportions of buildings have on the people who live in them. This is not a metaphorical thought at all. This is a practical thought, which I think about more and more. And I wonder if the violence, the antisocial attitudes we associate with high-rise buildings, the tower blocks [a reference to London's council flats, or public housing], might have something to do not only with the fact that the people who live in them have no real responsibility for the building as a whole—which is what I think the sociologists have decided—but I'm wondering if buildings affect the mentality of people in ways we haven't begun to research. This is my thought. This is my specific thought, not metaphorical. And I've used it in *Shikasta* as a query because I'm not making statements. You know, whenever one writes a book like *Shikasta*, it's a series of queries—to myself, to other people—as ideas.

I think it will turn out that there is a whole science of building that we know nothing about, that we might have lost and that ancient civilizations might have known about. And that is how to affect the minds of people living in buildings. Ordinary people who will regard such a thought as "mystical" or silly will in fact say, "I cannot live in that house, it upsets me." Or they'll say it has a ghost or something. This kind of thought goes on in my mind at the moment. I can't enter a building without wondering what other aspects it may have. But we don't know. Look at cathedrals. They were built in ways which a great many people thought were very specific, to produce certain states of mind. Yet we don't think like that any more.

And this leads me to the other thought. It is a commonplace way of thinking that we are the great high pinnacle of all kinds of sciences, but I think, on the contrary, we have lost a great deal of knowledge from the past. Far from being on a high pinnacle, we're on a very low level indeed, in all kinds of ways. You mention buildings because they run throughout my work. Now you can go through a writer's work and say, "Writer X is fascinated by the symbol"—I don't know, a rose or a seagull. But what is interesting is not that there should be a rose or a seagull or a teacup or whatever, but what use is made of it, how it develops. Because it can be a metaphor in one book and it can be something quite specific in another.

Bikman: Do younger women writers seek you out?

Lessing: Yes, they do, and I like that very much. I enjoy all that. Mind you that I think women writers are pretty independent characters; they have to be. I wish we could stop talking in terms of men and women writers.

Our whole language, the way we think, is set up for putting things into departments. We've got far more in common with each other than what separates us.

Bikman: I had access to a file of reviews of your books. I was unpleasantly surprised to see how often reviewers disliked your novels, especially the earlier ones.

Lessing: A reviewer will write a half-damning review of a book, but if the book turns out to have some lasting power, as *The Golden Notebook* has, they'll forget all about their reservations and talk about how marvelous they thought that book was.

Bikman: *The Golden Notebook*—and you mention this in your introduction to the book—was taken up by many readers as a bible of what you refer to as the sex war.

Lessing: It was, and it was a great surprise to me. It shows how naive I was. I was very nastily reviewed in most countries, in fact. They've now forgotten that. It's become a kind of boring, old classic, sitting there on the shelf. And men were angry. Now I get letters from men all the time about *The Golden Notebook*. But at one time it was classed as a "women's book." You see, people are very emotional. If a book upsets someone emotionally, they will very seldom come out with the real reason why they're upset. They'll deflect it onto something else. They won't say, "I'm annoyed with this book because it described how I behaved to my second wife." They'll say, "This woman is in bad taste. She's got no sense of"—I don't know what, the proprieties or something.

Bikman: I'm also interested in what you said in *The Golden Notebook* about the pressures in relationships.

Lessing: Living with someone is very, very difficult. How hard it is. Solitude is that great, great luxury which you can hardly ever achieve. People don't like other people who are perfectly happy by themselves and don't want to get married and don't want to do the things other people find essential. I get letters from these marvelous women in the States— I've got several pen pals—these naturally quirky, solitary and observant women, and they write me incredible letters, which I adore getting. I don't answer them properly; I just write and say, "Thank you very much," which I genuinely feel. But there's someone living in the middle of America who writes these witty letters about why all her women friends have to get married all the time. It's like a novel that goes on. I don't know why people say letter-writing is dead. There are people writing letters by the ream.

Bikman: I've read that you wrote two novels before your first one was published. So you did start writing novels at a fairly early age?

Lessing: They were very bad. They really were quite appalling. I'll tell you what I learned from it, though. One thing was fairly elementary. It was to type, because the first novel was in longhand and I couldn't read it back. I wrote very fast, and I couldn't read it. I just know it was awful. And the other thing is that I can write if I get into the groove; if I set things up right I can write easily. It's a question of setting the stage or something. You have to learn to set up the conditions that are right for you personally.

Bikman: Aside from the novel you've just finished, which I think would hold a special place—do you have any novel that is a favorite, that you feel a lot of affection for?

Lessing: At the moment, I feel affection for *The Marriages of Zones Three, Four, and Five,* but I don't know how it will strike me in ten years' time. I might not like it by then. In the past, *The Golden Notebook* was the most useful to me personally, as a sort of education. But then, every novel's got a different kind of part to play in your life. Some of my short stories I think are pretty good. But writing short stores doesn't change you the way a novel does, because writing a novel is more of an intensive effort.

Bikman: Can we talk about the craft of writing?

Lessing: You're not going to ask me how many hours a day I spend writing, are you? Time and again I get a novel sent to me which is nearly good; my thesis is that talent is in plentiful supply but people don't stick with it. I send it right back and write, "Well, just do it again." But they don't.

Bikman: So you feel there has to be a tremendous persistence?

Lessing: Yes, persistence. And you have to remember that nobody ever wants a new writer. You have to create your own demand.

Testimony to Mysticism
Nissa Torrents

Nissa Torrents's interview originally appeared in *La Calle* #106, April 1–7, 1980. The following translation was prepared by Paul Schlueter and appeared in the *Doris Lessing Newsletter* 4 (Winter 1980). Copyright © 1980 by Paul Schlueter. Reprinted with permission.

Torrents: It has been said that since 1962, or since *The Golden Notebook,* your work has changed direction, that it has inclined toward mysticism and has changed radically.

Lessing: I don't agree. I recently had to reread all my work for reprinting, and in my first work, *The Grass Is Singing,* all my themes already appear. Critics tend to compartmentalize, to establish periods, to fragmentize, a tendency that university training reinforces and that seems very harmful to me. At first, they said that I wrote about the race problem, later about Communism, and then about women, the mystic experience, etc., etc., but in reality I am the same person who wrote about the same themes. This tendency to fragmentize, so typical of our society, drives people to crisis, to despair, and that is what I intended to describe in *The Golden Notebook.* I always write about the individual and that which surrounds him.

Torrents: Yes, but along the way a person discards choices that don't work, politics, for example.

Lessing: I have never thought that politics resolved anything, nor have I ever defended any definite political position. I have simply limited myself in writing about people who are active politically.

Torrents: Like you yourself. Have you thought of returning to Zimbabwe now that things seem to be on the road to straightening themselves out?

Lessing: I do not intend to return. We served a certain purpose in the 1950s because we insisted on being witnesses to the problem of Rhodesia and to the injustices that were committed there. At that time in England, there was talk of all the colonies except Rhodesia. There was a curtain of silence that ran all the way to the left, which wasn't able to understand African politicians who quixotically believed in honor and were convinced that in England they knew nothing of arbitrariness and repression as practiced by the white colonists. Later African politicians learned that honor has no place in the modern world.

Torrents: Your characters always go looking for new values, renouncing old, traditional values and revealing the gulf that exists between public values and private practice. It's a permanent search for one's own equilibrium.

Lessing: We all do that. Nobody now accepts established values and everyone looks for personal morality. At least, that is, until we weaken and return to the church, or to the churches.

Torrents: I don't believe so. The majority still accepts for the sake of convenience that which was traditionally established. What you propose is to travel perpetually on a tightrope, and not everyone is so brave.

Lessing: Everybody that I know acts like this, including the time when we were Communists and when we maintained a political morality. Personal morality was exclusively private. We questioned everything, especially the male-female relationship, and it's there on the left where feminine liberation began to make this search, through this kind of critical doubting.

Torrents: But this constant exercising of moral judgment leads your characters to complete loneliness.

Lessing: I don't believe that it would be a worse kind of loneliness than that experienced by a married woman. One has to accept loneliness; it's the human condition, and no matter how many parties or churches we belong to, we cannot deny this central truth. Political parties and religions are above all social structures, refuges. One must take risks and not think of the loneliness that awaits us. Otherwise, life is impossible.

Torrents: You're very severe; you push your characters to the limit, toward the point of irrationality where a sense of direction and accumulated experience can't help us.

Lessing: But that isn't a disaster, only a way of seeing things more clearly. We all have extraordinary, non-rational capacities that we use to communicate in a very subtle way. Without these the world would be destroyed. Even physicians, who are the most obstinate in accepting this type of experience, are beginning to work with the metaphysical. The best scientists, those on the highest levels, always come closer and closer to the mystical. Much of what Einstein said could have been said by a Christian mystic, St. Augustine, for example. Science, which is the religion for today, looks for the metaphysical, as with Catholics of old. Hence the boom in science fiction, which reflects this preoccupation and which moves in the world of the non-rational.

Torrents: You've always been interested in that. In *Briefing for a Descent into Hell,* in your exploration of schizophrenia and of the savage treatment that society dispenses to its "crazies," you seem to follow Foucault in considering that treatment to be the central metaphor of social repression.

Lessing: Not entirely. I don't believe, as does Szasz, that mental illness doesn't exist. It does exist, but it's also true that the label corresponds to the discomforts that it causes the establishment. I have read narratives about war in which the protagonists, imprisoned or famished, experienced sensations similar to schizophrenia, and this has made me think that under certain conditions we could all exhibit signs of "abnormality." The dark is in us, and if we lower the barriers it will penetrate us and we'll show the symptoms.

Torrents: Your encounter with Idries Shah and Sufism was fundamental, because it established your interest in the irrational. When did this occur?

Lessing: At the beginning of the 1960s and as a result of the experiences that came to me in writing *The Golden Notebook.* When I wrote that I was a Marxist and a rationalist, but I experienced many things I could not explain. I believe that people try to deny a large part of their experience for fear of those who would call them crazy, but I decided the contrary. I read a book of Idries Shah's, *The Searchers;* I realized that it answered many of my questions, and since then I have studied it sufficiently.//

Torrents: You have complained about the poverty of language as an instrument.

Lessing: Words are contaminated, full of traditional associations, above all in psychology, in religion, in the interior world.// Words such as "the unconscious," "the ego," "the id"... They are few and they're all connected with factions, with specific groups. Hence, I find myself forced to write by analogy, in order to avoid the mundane. *Memoirs of a Survivor* is the direct result of my meditating about the inadequacy of language. I write as in legends or in fairy tales, by means of metaphors and analogies, but it is necessary to be careful, because what is not realistic is slippery ground. One must accumulate enough daily details in order that the reader isn't lost, since he requires the presence of mundane details so that he can then respond to the irrational.

Torrents: Your questions about language coincide with those of the avant garde, which you don't belong to; though they start with different presuppositions in trying to avoid the referential, they end in complete obscurity. Do you believe that your work, increasingly private as it is, can also end up so very obscure because of the lack of a common language?

Lessing: Not a single experience is totally private. What can happen to you or to me can happen to many others, and that is my response to the accusation of bourgeois individualism. Where is this individualism? No one has exclusive experiences or thoughts.

Torrents: Progressive internalization has a surprising result, the appearance of apocalyptic thought. In your most recent works there is evidence of our proximity to the end, to an Armageddon that is very close.

Lessing: We are already living it. The newspapers this past week gave some statistics from the FAO about infantile hunger. Some said that 37 million children will die before they are six months old, others 57 million, and this is without counting those who will die of malnutrition or progressive infirmity. This is the apocalypse, here and now.

Torrents: Can something be done to stop this disaster?

Lessing: I'm not sure. People believe that the situation is controlled, but this is not so. Some individuals can choose, but not groups or nations.

Torrents: You have frequently spoken about the writer's "small personal voice" and of your duty to describe the immorality of the system. Do you still believe that this is possible?

Lessing: Possibly. Now I know that if I write faithfully what I think or feel at a particular moment, then I'll get to the other matters. At times when I write, my obsessions seem to me to be madness, but when I finish a book, it's already almost a common situation, because everything changes so rapidly. One can't choose one's readers; they choose us.

Torrents: But you have enjoyed the great talent of seeing things before they happen, such as collective obsessions and talk about racism, or feminism, or about putting the metaphysical before everything else.... I'd like to ask you about your working routine.

Lessing: Writing is habit. I have disciplined myself to write very fast in short periods of time. It was the only way when my children were small and I could write only when they were in school or playing in the street. If I do not like what I write I discard it. I prefer throwing it away to editing it.

Torrents: I'd like to speak about women and their roles as mates. In your work there are many such women, but they're never successful. Perhaps the only relationship that can work is the fleeting one, the one-night stand.

Lessing: It took me a long time to realize that I was not made for marriage. If I had known beforehand, I could have saved myself much sadness and anguish. As a young woman I believed that to lie down for one night without the heat of a man's body was a monumental disaster, but I have slowly realized that it is not like that and have gone so far as to be self-sufficient, which implies a great loneliness because the majority of men, naturally, don't like this attitude; it's not needing them. I don't believe that it's worth the effort necessary in order to get near a man, in order to intend to form a couple. Men need to be taken care of, to have their egos treated tenderly. They like to be the center and to push the woman to the outside edge. Perhaps the young are different, more flexible. Everything changes so rapidly! I lost much time looking for my ideal man, my match, and now I believe that perhaps my failure lay in trying to make the kind of search appropriate to another historical period and that it's no longer possible. But I have women friends who are attempting that. They treat men as men treat us. They are free, strong. They demand sex, but when they reach thirty the biological urge possesses them. They want to have children and everything is gone, and then they fall into a routine that will completely destroy them if they don't maintain their alertness.

Torrents: Men don't like it that we behave like them. Moreover, certain forms of the Women's Liberation Movement have hardened masculine attitudes in the war between the sexes.

Lessing: The danger is in confusing liberation of one with the submission of another. I have a couple of liberated friends who have simply inverted roles and have husbands as servants. The Yankee model!

Torrents: Can it be that marriage doesn't work?

Lessing: The needs of adults and those of children are different. That which is for us a dried-up institution, institutionalized frustration, is a necessity for the young who require a stable home, a constant relationship. They need their parents in a conventional way, the home and the routine, and the couple that cannot confront those responsibilities shouldn't have children, because the only thing that they get, if they have them, their problem children, is mental turmoil, much sadness.

Torrents: But what you say is terrible, because procreation implies destruction, more or less spectacularly, of the adult and his possibilities, a total sacrifice.

Lessing: That has been my experience. The children who live only with the father or the mother suffer indescribably. We don't have the right to get what we want at the expense of others, but people oblige themselves in continuously seeking happiness as if they had a right to it. Perhaps a happy marriage is possible, but only with a great effort, renewable everyday, and people aren't disposed to make the effort or the sacrifice. We want it all to be simple, on a platter. As with prepared meals, soup in packages, fish without fishbones. They sweeten everything and at the end they all know it's a trick. It's not even necessary to chew! This is the sign of our time—to avoid pain, to accept that which exists, to demand happiness—but we have forgotten that no one owes us anything and that pain and sacrifice are necessary to find the right path, for moral equilibrium.

The Need to Tell Stories
Christopher Bigsby

Christopher Bigsby's interview took place April 23, 1980, and originally appeared in *The Radical Imagination of the Liberal Tradition* (London: Junction Press, 1981). Copyright © 1981 by Christopher Bigsby. Reprinted with permission.

Bigsby: You once said there was a great deal that George Eliot didn't understand because she was moral. What did you mean by that?

Lessing: Well, I think she was a victim, like many of the women of that time, of Victorian morality. Because she was "living in sin" with George Lewes there was a great pressure on her to be good. I noticed the same pressure on myself when I wrote *The Golden Notebook*. I am not being paranoid; you have got no idea of the kind of attack I got. It was really quite barbarous. They said I was a man-hater, a balls-cutter, particularly Americans. I noticed enormous pressure on me to be feminine and to be good and to be kind and sweet. Quite nauseating it was. I notice that other women who have gone through the same pressure confess to the same; they suddenly find themselves thinking, Oh God, I mustn't do that because they will say I am a balls-cutter. Well, this has already gone because Women's Lib has achieved so much. But to go back to George Eliot, I would be very surprised if she wasn't falling over backwards to be good because of the pressure on her. I mean, it was no joke living in that society. It must have been dreadful.

Bigsby: You mention that you were alarmed or surprised by the reaction you got from men with respect to *The Golden Notebook*. Were you equally alarmed by the reaction you got from women?

Lessing: Oh, you are quite wrong in thinking that I only got attacks from men. I got a lot of support from men, from a few men, and the most vicious attacks from women, on the lines that I was letting the side down by revealing the kind of things that were said. I had never thought on those lines at all. Not only had I not thought that I was writing

a women's book but it had never crossed my mind to think anything of writing the kind of things down that I was writing. Women talk
like this. Men talk about women, letting off steam in locker rooms and
so on, but they don't necessarily mean it. And when women sit around
and say these things they don't necessarily mean it either; it is letting
off steam. It never crossed my mind when I wrote all that down, that
it hadn't really been done before. I thought, How is it that I am getting these violent reactions? What have I done? What have I said? And
when I started to look around I couldn't think of any novels voicing the
kind of criticisms women have of men. Almost like breathing, you know,
so deep-rooted.

Bigsby: In an essay called "A Small Personal Voice" which, admittedly, you
wrote quite a long time ago now, you said that the highest point of
literature was the novel of the nineteenth century, the work of the great
realists. You also said that the realist novel was the highest form of prose
writing. What led you to say that then and why did you move away from
that position with *The Golden Notebook* and with most of your subsequent
work?

Lessing: I was wondering myself not long ago why I reacted so strongly—
something must have happened to make me react. I do remember having
that set of thoughts about the nineteenth-century novel. I mean, it was
magnificent, wasn't it? What they had was a kind of self-assurance which I
don't think any one of us has got. Why don't we have it?

Bigsby: Well, you did say that part of your admiration came from the fact
that they shared what you called a climate of ethical judgment.

Lessing: That's right. Well, they did. We don't have anything like that.

Bigsby: On the other hand, you said of George Eliot that she didn't
understand certain things *because* she was moral.

Lessing: Well, there was a kind of womanly certitude in George Eliot
which you would not find, let's say, in Chekhov. There's something tight
there in judgment. I admire George Eliot enormously, I am not saying I
don't. But there is something too cushioned in her judgments.

Bigsby: In talking about a climate of ethical judgment were you suggesting that there is a necessary relationship between art and morality, or that
there should be, that art is a moral force in some way?

Lessing: I don't know if there should be. But if you write a book which you don't see as moral believe me your readers do, and that's something that I can't ever quite come to terms with. Now *The Marriages of Zones Three, Four and Five* I almost regard as outside judgment because it's a legend. It is full of forgiveness. Wouldn't you say it was full of forgiveness? An old warrior of the sex war simply shrugs his shoulders and gives up and laughs; I mean, that is something.

Bigsby: Yes, I think it is, but reverting to this question of why you admire the nineteenth-century novel, why did you yourself move away from that tradition which you wanted to claim early on?

Lessing: Because it's too narrow, that's why, because we have gone beyond it. Let's take *Anna Karenina*. What a marvelous book! It is all about the social problems which existed in a very narrow, bigoted society and which was completely unnecessary. In fact, a good deal of Victorian fiction can be classified like that. Look at Hardy, for example. These tragedies are mini-tragedies because they derive from fairly arbitrary social conditions; they are not rooted in any human nature. When you finish reading *Anna Karenina* you think, My God, here is this woman ruined and destroyed because of this stupid, bloody society and it does make it a smaller novel in my opinion. Because it is Tolstoy it is full of the most marvelous things but in actual fact the basic story is a story about nothing, about a local society, a very local, temporary set of social circumstances. My train of thought was that we now live with our heads in the middle of exploding galaxies and thinking about quasars and quarks and black holes and alternative universes and so on, so that you cannot any more get comfort from old moral certainties because something new is happening. All our standards of values have been turned upside down, I think. Not that I don't think life doesn't do that for you anyway because it seems to me there is a process of losing more and more conviction all the time. I really did have very firm opinions about all kinds of things even fifteen years ago, which I am unable to have now because the world has got too big, everything is too relative. What's true in one society isn't true in another. What is true for one time isn't true five years later.

Bigsby: So in fact there are no fixed moral standards.

Lessing: No, I don't think there can be any fixed moral standards. I mean, you can pay lip service to a fixed moral standard because it saves you trouble, which I am perfectly prepared to do. I have got a different attitude towards hypocrisy, perhaps.

Bigsby: Yet isn't there a strong moral drive in your work, a sense of trying to stop a headlong rush towards disaster by deflecting your reader away from a dangerous path.

Lessing: When you say that, it sounds as though I believe I can do it.

Bigsby: I half-think you do.

Lessing: I think in the past I have had some such thoughts, that if enough writers write this, which God knows we do, if enough writers say, "For God's sake, look at what is happening," things might change. But I have gone back to a thought I had in the *Children of Violence* series right at the beginning. I reread *Martha Quest* recently. Do you remember the passage when she stands at the door and watches the prisoners walk past in handcuffs and thinks that this has been described now in literature for so long and nothing has changed. Well, you know, this is a very terrible thought for a writer to have, and this is another of these complexes I live with because with one-half of myself I think I don't see the point of it, I don't think we change anything.

Bigsby: That is the function of art then, is it, to change reality or to change the way people perceive reality?

Lessing: I think the function of real art, which I don't aspire to, is to change how people see themselves. I wonder if we do. If we do it is very temporary. Let's go back to the Russians. You can say that Turgenev and Tolstoy and all that crowd of giants, in fact, changed how people saw themselves. They did, but to what end? Because look at the Russians now. I have just finished reading a book called *The Russians,* by an American correspondent in Russia, and it is very clear there is very little difference between a communist society and a capitalist society. I think perhaps the communist society is worse, but there isn't very much difference; they have got a new ruling class, a differently based class, but it is a highly privileged class that has got every intention of hanging on to its privileges, and a whole mass of serfs who get very little. And, as for freedom, there is as little of it as there was under the czars. So you ask yourself, I ask myself, if you can have a blaze of marvelous writers, which they had, all shouting the same thing, which they did, in one way or another, and yet they have so little effect, what then?

Now it so happens that I am a writing animal and I can't imagine myself not writing; I literally get quite ill if I don't write a bit. Perhaps that is my problem and not anyone else's.

Bigsby: But I wonder if in a sense you don't compound that determinism. Take a book like *Shikasta*. Contained in it is a version of world history, history as pathology, as degeneration, as movement towards catastrophe. But we discover that that movement is not chance, it is not arbitrary; it is actually the result of intervention, of manipulations by various distant star systems. That being so, aren't you proposing a determinism in which it is impossible to resist this onward movement because it derives from outside of humanity?

Lessing: Well, you see, this is what I think I think, or what I think now. I don't know what I will think in ten years' time. I think, in fact, that we do not have much influence on events, but we think we do, we imagine we do. There is a marvelous Sufi story about the mouse who, through a series of accidents, becomes the owner of a cow. It has the end of a rope which goes around the cow's neck in its mouth and as the cow wanders out across the countryside it cannot control the cow. But as the cow stops to eat some grass it shouts, "That's right, eat up some grass," and when the cow turns left it shouts, "That's right, turn left." Well, this is what I think we're like because it seems to me self-evident. I know that is arrogant, but just look at the course of events. We are continually, and by "we" I am now talking about politicians, suggesting decisions to cope with the results of other decisions which have turned out quite differently from what was expected. We do not plan, we do not say what is going to happen.

Bigsby: And is there a governing manipulative force behind this?

Lessing: No, I don't think so. But I do not see humanity as the great crown of all creation. Let's put it this way: we are sending rockets at this moment around Jupiter. Why do we assume that we are the only people with technological knowhow when the astronomers and physicists talk in terms of planets, many many hundreds of thousands of inhabited planets. I mean, it is not some lunatic novelist who is talking. The novelist now cannot keep up with the physicists in what they say.

Bigsby: Isn't there a danger, though, that if you accept this view you are in fact advising people that there is no point in playing a role in the social world or indeed in attempting to intervene in history at all? You are inviting them to be supine in the face of violence.

Lessing: No, I am not. Certainly I would never have anything to do with politics again unless I was forced at the point of a gun, having seen what happens.

Bigsby: Early on in your work you were interested in the problem of the individual's relationship to the group; that is, you had a conception of the individual as apart from the group and then negotiating his or her relationship with it. But isn't individuality without meaning once you acknowledge sheer determinism?

Lessing: No, I don't see that at all. I mean, this is a very ancient philosophical debate. Can you have free will if God has planned everything? Well, the answers to that, as you know, have been going on for centuries, particularly in the West.

Bigsby: But your view has changed, hasn't it, because even in the *Children of Violence* series at the beginning Martha Quest is very much the focus of the book: things are filtered through her sensibility. But in the last volume, which I presume you hadn't actually predicted when you started writing the sequence, we move through catastrophe to a situation in which Martha Quest disappears from the center of the novel, and she disappears because the situation has changed fundamentally and she exists only insofar as she serves the perpetuation of the race in some sense. It is the sheer survival of the group that becomes the important thing at that stage. The individual has been reduced by the impact of history.

Lessing: But she has lived her life and has influenced events and individuals.

Bigsby: Yes, but in the context of a deterministic move towards catastrophe. In your later books individuals seem to be admired to the extent that they realize that their chief function is to submerge themselves in a generality. You talk about moving from "I" to "we," as though a state of being "I" were in some sense undesirable, something to be transcended.

Lessing: I am really not chopping logic. I think that the individual is extremely important. I think the individual is more and more important in what we are going into, which is horrific. I do think that what matters is evolution. I think that the human race is evolving probably into something better through its usual path of horror and mistakes because when have we ever done anything else, when has history ever shown anything different?

Bigsby: So history isn't pure pathology; it reaches some kind of critical point of regeneration.

Lessing: I don't think like this. I find it very difficult. You keep saying things are different from each other. You see it as either/or. While there is something in me which I recognize is uniquely me, and which obviously interests me more than other things and which I am responsible for, at the same time I have a view of myself in history, as something which has been created by the past and conditioned by the present. And when I die I will have left something, for good or for bad, not because I am a writer but because I am alive. In the mid-'50s I was preoccupied with the relationship between an individual and political groups because all the people I knew at that time, or nearly all of them, were political in one way or another; they were either Communists, or ex-Communists, or Labour Party. Also, don't forget it was just after McCarthy in America and I had a lot of American friends and they were very preoccupied with the way they had either given evidence to the Committee or had refused to give evidence. This whole problem of the individual and the group was very strong at that time and in that particular form.//

Bigsby: There was a time when you accused Beckett and others of making what you called "despairing statements of emotional anarchy": and you said that "the pleasurable luxury of despair, the acceptance of disgust, is as much a betrayal of what a writer should be as the acceptance of the simple economic view of man," and you identified both of these approaches as a kind of false innocence. Is that a view that you would hold now, and what exactly is the writer's function then if that isn't his function?

Lessing: Well, I don't hold those views now. About the simple economic view of man, of course I hold that; that was a specific statement about a communist view of literature. About the other I don't remember. You see I don't remember the emotion that made me write that. I don't remember why I said those things about writers that I admire. So that has gone. What any writer should do is to write as truthfully as possible about himself or herself as an individual because we are not unique and remarkable people. Over and over again I have had the experience of writing themes that I thought were quite way out and I have discovered, simply by the letters I get, or because ideas surface, that I have been on a fairly low-class common wavelength. Over and over again I have written ideas down that shortly afterwards have become commonplace. I am saying it exactly like that because I don't want to make it sound something high class. But I do think I have sometimes a sensitivity to what is going to come in five years' time, and it happened with *The Golden Notebook*, for example, when I didn't know I was writing what I was writing.

Bigsby: When you made that comment about Beckett you also said that the writer must become a humanist, feel himself an instrument for change, for good or bad: "it is not merely a question of preventing an evil but strengthening a vision of good that will defeat evil." That puts enormous weight on art; art becomes an instrument for good in some way.

Lessing: I wouldn't say that at all now because I don't know what good and evil is. I think now that if writers write really truthfully (it is very hard, you know, to be truthful, actually) you will find that they are expressing other people.

Bigsby: You have had a sense that the human mind is changing, or the way that we perceive reality is changing; you were suggesting that this might be a result in part of advances in physics. Does that really filter down to the individual, or in what other ways is our sense of reality different now, being perceived differently?

Lessing: Well, I don't think it is filtering down as fast as it ought, and I think the reason why it doesn't is a fault in the education system. I am not talking so much about the new ideas in physics, but sociological ideas, some of which are quite shattering in their implications. And they should be taught to children. I think the child should be taught that you may easily find yourself in your life in a situation where you can behave as Eichmann did—I am using Eichmann simply because he is a symbol for mindless obedience. Eighty-five percent of all people, it has been proved, can be expected to behave like this. You may find yourself in such a situation and you must now think about it and prepare yourself for such a choice. In other words, give children choice; don't let them be precipitated into situations that might arise. And then there is this whole business about thinking and acting as an individual instead of as a member of a group because we now know that very, very few people, a negligible number, are prepared to stand up against a group they are a part of. This has been proved over and over again, by all kinds of experiments; if you put a certain number of people together, people will do anything rather than stand out against it. And it explains, for example, why certain advances of knowledge get accepted with such reluctance. We have discovered a whole armory of facts about human nature since the Second World War. Because of the horror of the Second World War and what we discovered human nature was capable of, research has been going on in universities all over the world in this field. We now know what we are really like. There is also a great deal of knowledge about how groups function.

Bigsby: It seems to me actually that that is a running theme in your work, the need to escape the definition that has been offered to you as a member of a particular group, a race or a country, or in some sense as a sex—the need to escape the type that is offered to you.

Lessing: We live in a series of prisons called race, class, male and female. There are always those classifications.

Bigsby: But equally, I think, in the most recent books, you seem to be urging the breakdown of divisions within the sensibility as well, divisions between the mind and the imagination, the body and the spirit. Intuition, for example, which is usually treated with skepticism, becomes a real force. To feel something is not presented in your work as in some sense reductive; it actually has meaning. Feeling is a genuine response.

Lessing: It is interesting, you use the word *feeling* to cover both emotion and intuition. Because intuition has been banished from our culture, emotions are spread to include it, whereas in actual fact I think there is thinking and there are emotions and there is intuition which is something quite different. It is fascinating. You see it on television, for example, in God knows how many series. For example, *Star Trek*. Mr. Spock has no emotions and therefore he is handicapped, but the good Earth people have emotions and therefore they are on a higher level. The word emotion has been spread to include intuition and this is how we get round it. Intuition is not the property of women or of sensitives; everybody has intuition but somewhere in the past, probably in the Renaissance, there was an unspoken agreement to banish intuition. But none of us could operate for five minutes without it. I think we all use it all the time.

Bigsby: When you talked about evolution did you mean the intensification of those abilities which have decayed. Are you actually anticipating the restoration of these abilities or the intensification of them?

Lessing: I think any human being can, if he watches and listens, use them now. It takes practice.

Bigsby: Is that the appropriate moment to ask you about Sufi?

Lessing: Yes, it probably is. I became interested in this because I had to recognize that what I had experienced and what I was thinking and feeling had got nothing whatsoever to do with my philosophy. This happened when I was writing *The Golden Notebook*. Writing that book in the form I did forced me to examine myself in all kinds of ways. I was writing about experiences that I had never had. I have had some of them since, let me tell you, but I had to recognize that the way I thought then, my philosophy, was absolutely inadequate. I either had to pretend that I didn't have the experiences I had, or thoughts I had, or admit them openly. I think enormous numbers of people do this. There comes a point where they have to make a choice and a lot of people decide to forget it. When I got to that point and I examined how I was thinking, the whole progressive package (which is shorthand for all the ideas the young people have now as if they are programmed, which they are—they are all materialists, and socialists and semi-Marxists or something of the kind and there is a whole set of ideas that go together). I decided I could no longer live with it so I started looking around. Now the interesting thing about that—I have described that in *The Four-Gated City*—is that I simply read extensively in areas which were regarded then as quite kooky, though they are not so much now because, in fact, they have got quite trendy.

I did an immense amount of reading and I came up with certain basic facts. One basic fact was that our education was extremely lacking informationwise. You could be brought up in this culture and not know anything at all about the ideas of other cultures. We are brought up with this appalling Western arrogance, all of us. This is the reason I am glad I haven't been educated because it seems to me almost impossible not to have this arrogance if you are brought up inside the Western education system. The other idea I came up with was that if I was going to do this seriously, explore this area, it was a dangerous thing to do it without a teacher; people go crazy and they go wandering off. God knows what they don't do. They go off to Katmandu, etc. So I took a great deal of trouble. I am nothing if not obsessive, perfectionist, and boring when I am faced with this kind of situation, and I put a great deal of time and trouble into looking for a teacher. I went through some experiences which were quite interesting, making mistakes, and then I found Sufism as taught by Idries Shah, which claims to be the reintroduction of an ancient teaching suitable for this time and this place. It is not some regurgitated stuff from the East or watered down Islam or anything like that. And I read a book called *The Sufis,* which I knew was on its way. I waited for it and read it and thought simply, This is where I might find what I am looking for because my ideas were there and no other place; there was no other place for them. I did not want to become a Christian mystic. I couldn't possibly be a Christian. I can't be religious; I haven't got the religious temperament in the way it is demanded of you. In parentheses, again, Christianity is a very emotional religion. In Hinduism you do not have to be emotional. But Christianity demands an emotional response, and I couldn't do that. There are other things that demand of you a totally intellectual response, and I couldn't do that. What I have found is the beginnings of a way of looking at things which unfolds as you go on, and if that is an annoying phrase I can't help it. You discover all the time. It is not an easy thing.

Bigsby: You said that you couldn't be religious, but is your outlook pantheistic or does it posit some sort of ultimate being?

Lessing: Is it any help if I say, yes, it believes in God? So what. Do you see the point I am making? Supposing I said it didn't believe in God? What then? Supposing I said it believed in the Devil? These are words, they don't mean anything.

Bigsby: But it does talk about oneness, doesn't it? Is the sense of the oneness, not actually a being external to the self but in a sense the aggregate of the selves, is that what it means by unity?

Lessing: Perhaps I don't know either. I am still at the beginning of it. You start off shedding prejudices and preconceptions. If I say "mysticism" or "Sufism" I don't know what your particular set of associations is, but they are likely to be something like the Maharishi, Mantras, Yoga, chanting, dancing up and down, and Islam, something like that, because that is the culture we live in. You begin by shedding the ideas that you have, many of them unconscious. Let's take the word "teacher." A teacher is someone who stands at the end of the room on a dais and he lectures to you. But you see this is not a teacher as I have experienced it; it is something quite different, but it takes a long time even when you have accepted that intellectually, to translate it into how you experience what is happening, because all the time, unconsciously, you are thinking, Ah, one day the guru will announce, "My child, this is the truth." Now I am caricaturing a very deeply rooted psychological need, and I was quite shocked to find how deep it is. One of the things that Shah says is that we are taught all the time in this culture that we are not conditioned, that we are free, that we have made up our own minds all through our lives about what we believe, and that we are here as a product of various acts of will made throughout our life. He will simply say, "I am sorry but this is not so, and in actual fact you have been programmed to want authority; you want to be told what to do, you want a guru, you want something to belong to, you want rules." Now when he first says this to you, you say, "Oh, come," but then you are put in a situation where you find out that it is true and very humiliating it is, because it is true. I did want all those things. Well, now, please God, I don't. But the thing is you learn to shed all the time, not through an intellectual process at all; all the time you are put into situations where you see the truth about yourself and it isn't at all pretty, actually. It is humiliating.

Bigsby: It seems to me that *The Marriages of Zones Three, Four and Five* is actually suffused with this kind of thought. Isn't it about the breakdown of these kinds of assumptions, the recognition of a determinism?

Lessing: You keep talking about determinism. It is the opposite that I have experienced.

Bigsby: Well, Al.Ith, the princess, receives a summons. It is a summons which really doesn't immediately operate on the conscious mind, but on the subconscious mind. It is a summons which must be obeyed. There is no scope for denial. That is what I mean by determinism; her actions are determined quite apart from her own sensibility. Now isn't that what you were just talking about, the recognition of that determinism? And indeed the recognition becomes a kind of moral act; it is what you pay, it is what you owe, the recognition of an element of determinism.

Lessing: I don't think that *Marriages* is a description of Sufi attitudes, unless what I have learnt has become very unconscious and has come out differently. But I am not at this moment qualified to judge. One cannot judge the processes of sea change until later. In ten years' time I might be able to.

Bigsby: But one thing that Al.Ith has to learn sounds very close to what you are describing. You are saying that the individual has to learn to see himself outside of the group, outside of that set of assumptions. This is what Al.Ith herself has to learn; she has to move outside the group in which she feels so much at home, and for whom she in a sense resonates.

Lessing: I hadn't thought of it in those terms, but I suppose so.

Bigsby: And the marriage which is contracted and the subsequent marriage, as there are two, isn't that the marriage of two people who are themselves being forced out of their set of presumptions? And presumably some kind of new quality is coming out of that, some third thing which pulls those zones together or breaks down the barriers between them.

Lessing: Yes, but let me do something different about this book. It was written out of this experience. When I was in my late thirties and early forties my love life was in a state of chaos and disarray and generally no good to me or to anybody else and I was, in fact, and I knew it, in a pretty bad way. Unconsciously I used a certain therapeutic technique which just emerged from my unconscious. I had an imaginary landscape in which I had a male and female figure in various relationships. And don't forget this was twenty years ago or so and this whole business about what men are and what women are was a question of debate and, of course, it still is. I made the man very strong as a man, responsible for what he had to do and autonomous in himself, and I made the woman the same because I was very broken down in various ways at that time, and this went on for some years in fact. And then I read about it; it is a Jungian technique. They tell you that if you have some part of you which is weak, you deliberately fantasize it strong, make it as you would like it to be. Now the fact that when I wrote it it turned out somewhat differently has got nothing to do with it; this book goes right down into me pretty deep. How and why, I really don't know. This book is the result not of any theories or ideas, but of some pretty close work of the imagination on my experience of the past.

Bigsby: Why did you take so long to get round to writing it down, if it came out of that experience?

Lessing: I suppose it went underground and came out in this form. It was marvelous to write this book. I really enjoyed writing it because it was so easy, and there is a level that I hit and I wrote it out of that level. It will never happen again.

Bigsby: Can I revert to asking you a question about novel-writing and the structure of the novel? The "Free Woman" section of *The Golden Notebook* is a conventional novel, but the book as a whole is about the inadequacy of the conventional novel in that it is about the complexity that has to be rendered down finally into a fixed form. Isn't that reductiveness in a sense unavoidable, whatever technique you are using? In that novel you were drawing attention to the problem, but drawing attention to the problem doesn't solve the problem. Is it a solvable problem? Isn't art always reductive?

Lessing: Yes, it is, but that is why we are all breaking the form, we have to break it. The five-volume or three-volume realistic novel seems to me dead—the family novel. Well, maybe it is not dead, but I am not interested in it. I am much more interested in a bad novel that doesn't work but has got ideas or new things in it than I am to read yet again the perfect small novel. I read somewhere the other day that in 1912 in China when the civil war was all around they were still writing the most exquisite little poems about apple blossoms and so on, and I have got nothing against exquisite little poems about apple blossoms and I very much enjoy reading the small novel about emotions in the shires, but I do regard it as dead.

Bigsby: Is that why you have responded so enthusiastically to science fiction? You said in the introductory note to *Shikasta* that it enables you to be both experimental and traditional, in a way that I suppose *Marriages* is because there is a recognizable traditional element there.

Lessing: I think that is a traditional book. I think it is almost a timeless sort of book, where *Shikasta* is a mess, but at any rate it is a new mess.

Bigsby: *Marriages* is a sort of legend or myth?

Lessing: Well, yes, I have been fascinated with science fiction and space fiction because it is full of ideas. In science fiction the real scientist who writes it will produce some scientific idea and take it to its logical conclusion and say, "Well, if you do this, that will happen," and so on, which I find fascinating, though very often I can't follow the science. And I am sure that this genre of science fiction has educated a whole generation of young people into thinking scientifically, which they certainly don't get where they're taught.

Bigsby: In the prefatory note to *Shikasta* you seem to suggest that the novelist is driven beyond realism because reality itself has become more fantastic. I wonder if that is really the reason or whether, at least in your case, it isn't because you believe that reality is more dense, more profound, more various than we usually assume; in other words, reality has not changed. What has been failing is our perception of the fact that it has been this.

Lessing: This is true, of course, because our view of ourselves changes all the time. Sometimes this view is based on some kind of mythical framework, legendary framework, like people we describe as backward, or it can be based on fact. We like to think of ourselves as based on facts, but the facts are becoming so extraordinary.

Bigsby: I don't know that they are any more extraordinary now than they used to be. For people who believed that the earth was flat it must have been quite a staggering thing to discover that it wasn't. In a sense contemporary reality is much less extraordinary than that. We are now attuned to absorb almost anything within very rapid time. It becomes part of our world view. A few hundred years ago it would take a century to get people to accept things.

Lessing: Yes, that is true, I suppose. Things have speeded up so fast that we can cope with it.... There is a point I want to make about writing, or telling stories. It is a thought that I can't come to terms with: why do we tell stories? What is the function of the storyteller? We never stop telling ourselves stories. It is the way we structure reality; we tell stories all day, don't we? And when we go to sleep we tell ourselves stories because a dream is a story, maybe sometimes very logical and straightforward and sometimes not, but there is something in us that needs stories. I heard someone on the radio the other night say that the dream is a way of reprogramming our minds. This is a theory, but when somebody sits down to write a novel, we don't know what we are doing. Why does humanity have this need?

Bigsby: In fact storytellers play an important part in *Marriages,* don't they? The narrator is a professional storyteller; that is, his cultural function is a storyteller, isn't it? A singer of songs.

Lessing: I wanted one voice so I had to think who was likely to have that one voice. I couldn't have either Al.Ith or Ben Ata because they were too partial, or even my lovely servant, who I adore.

Bigsby: You have an interest in the realm of the subconscious and to some extent what is now called paranormal. Now that is not just as metaphor, is it? You mean that literally?

Lessing: Yes, literally. It is what I have experienced and what a lot of other people have experienced.

Bigsby: Telepathy, for example.

Lessing: Yes, I have experienced telepathy, but then I think a great many people do. I think we are probably at it all the time without knowing it. Ideas flow through our minds like water all the time. But my interest in the paranormal is not as kicks. I used to be terribly fascinated, but now I try to use it in a very quiet, sober sort of way. For example, I keep a diary where I note down the odd events, like coincidences and things, that I think are going to happen whether they do or not. I am quite objective about that, I don't make things up. I use dreams all the time. I have done since I was a child. I use dreams in my work because I get ideas or I get warnings in my dreams about people or situations. I don't know if that goes under paranormal or not, but humanity has been using dreams ever since it was born.

Bigsby: Moving to your more recent books, there are constant images of devastation, but on the other hand humanity seems to come out the other side of that devastation. It was true, of course, of *The Four-Gated City*. But in the latest books you move towards a simple faith, isn't it, in something not fully perceived? Obedience to some sort of cosmic will?

Lessing: I don't know about obedience. Do you choose to have obedience?

Bigsby: But I think you use the word "faith" yourself. That is what finally they are left with.

Lessing: I thought a lot about putting that word in because it has got religious connotations.

Bigsby: What is it they are believing in, then?

Lessing: Since the history of man began, has there been anything else but disaster, plagues, miseries, wars? Yet something has survived of it. Now our view is, of course, that we're onwards and upwards all the time. I just have an open mind about all that. But I do think that if we have survived so much in the past we are survivors, if nothing else, and if nothing else we are extremely prolific. Has it ever occurred to you how prolific we are? We are worse than rabbits. We just breed; the world is full of babies. I like to think some of them will survive, perhaps even better. Also, is it possible that the radiation that we are going to inflict upon the world might make us mutate? We don't know. There is now a theory that the dinosaurs died out not because of a shift of climates, but because of a different kind of radiation. We are bombarded by different kinds of radiation. Neutrons pour through us as we sit here, did you know? Well, you see, we don't know what else pours through us and how we might react to a different kind of medicine.

Bigsby: So this is faith?

Lessing: Optimism.

Writing as Time Runs Out
Michael Dean

Dean: You spent your formative years growing up in Rhodesia with English parents who imagined, at least half the time it seemed, that they were still in England. Was it a happy childhood?

Lessing: No, it wasn't at all. Fighting every inch of the way I was. No, I had to. It was nobody's fault. You have to get to be old like me before you can look back and understand your parents, and now I'm desperately sorry for my mother particularly.

Dean: You were a late developer and had no formal education as we understand it, leaving school at fourteen.

Lessing: That's right.

Dean: Why?

Lessing: Well, it was part of fighting my poor mama. I went off and I was what is now called an au pair girl. I was a nursemaid in fact for about two and one-half years in Salisbury. I didn't mind the work, because I liked looking after babies, but it was an awful waste of time. Then I went back and I wrote a novel or two on the farm, very fast and very bad.

Dean: What kind of novels?

Lessing: //One was a very mannered artificial book about Salisbury social life. I was seventeen.

Dean: Was there a political edge to your writing then?

Lessing: No, it was bad social satire.

Dean: I'm interested to know why and how you became different? I mean, the prevailing wind of that culture which was white supremacy wasn't questioned I should imagine by the people you lived with.

Lessing: People say how remarkable it is that you saw through all that color-bar thing when you were so young. I do not feel that this was due to anything innate, anything on my part at all. I think it was simply that I had to be critical about everything, all my life. I can't remember any time in my life where I wasn't sitting looking at the grown-up scene, for example, and thinking, This must be some great charade they've all agreed to play. I was always seeing through what went on. That was the makings of a critic, you see. Now this is a bad thing as well, because it can be very sterile.

Dean: There's an epigraph to your first novel, *The Grass Is Singing*, which goes I think, "it is by the failures and the misfits of a civilization that one can judge its weaknesses." Have you always felt yourself sitting in judgment of your civilization?

Lessing: You see, this is a very crucial question. Yes, I have, and perhaps it's not much use, but I think it was the way I was brought up. You must imagine my parents who were Tory and admiring Churchill when he was still some pain in the neck, you know, but soon afterwards he became a kind of cherubic saint with a cigar. He was no good, you see, because he prophesied the Second World War and said we should prepare for it and my parents who suffered terribly from the First World War, their entire lives were ruined by it, were torn up, you know. They were anguished by the approaching war and that no one was doing anything about it. Imagine them sitting in the middle of the bush—our nearest neighbors were three, four, seven miles away, listening to the BBC, eight o'clock news and Big Ben and angry because of English politics. I can't remember a time when I haven't heard people discussing politics. This was probably my earliest education.

Dean: You must have read widely and I'm sure voraciously as a child and as an adolescent.

Lessing: I read in Salisbury when I felt myself very shut up there. You know what it's like, this dreadful provincial little hole. I read very strange novels, almost as a deliberate counterbalance, like Proust. There was a time when I think I must have been really quite an authority on Proust. It was such a relief to read something like that. Somebody once said

Rhodesia was a combination of the Wild West and Tunbridge Wells. I would read my way from book to book. I found a book mentioned in one and then sent for it, to England, the Everyman's Library. The excitement of these books arriving after waiting sometimes for six weeks was the marvelous moment in my life, when a new book, a parcel of books came, from England and I could start in. Sometimes they were absolutely useless to me because I hadn't got to the stage of appreciating them.

Dean: I think you wrote once that Africa is an old fever, latent always in the blood. Are you still carrying that old fever?

Lessing: Yes, very much so. And I dream about it all the time with terrible nostalgia and a sort of anguish, because that's finished, I think; and you know, I haven't been allowed to go there, for I'm a prohibited immigrant. Now here my head and my heart are absolutely like this, as they often are, but here particularly, because while my head applauds like this, out goes my heart. I weep like a small child, you see, that I'm shut out of my country. Now when I say this to an African he very probably laughs, and I'm on his side. But there are some things, you see, that you can do nothing about.

Dean: What is it that your heart grieves for?

Lessing: It's a beautiful place, and the Africans, you see. I know it's very suspect for the daughter of a white settler, which is what I am, you see, to talk about Africans in this way, but I see that Van der Post also does, so I'm in good company. I miss the Africans so much; they're such beautiful people. They've got this marvellous grace and good humor and charm, and I miss it.

Dean: I'm going to wrench you away from Africa now rather cruelly. The year is 1949. You're arriving in England, a source of so much of your culture, with the scars of two marriages, I think, and the manuscript of *The Grass Is Singing* in your suitcase. This was post-war London, very austere, very gray. Was it a shock to you?

Lessing: Yes, it was. It was so gray and lightless and grim and unpainted and bombed. It took a lot of getting used to. And of course I had very little money and fairly difficult circumstances. I had a small child. You see, I recently discovered I was a one-parent family, which everyone knows was quite hard.

Dean: Something you wrote that seemed to me to be terribly heartfelt was on experiencing England for the first time: everybody was so kind, so decent, so bloody dull.

Lessing: Well, it was dull. You see the colonies are full of very out-size characters. There's plenty of room for everyone's eccentricities to blossom, and here there isn't space for it. You find people being eccentric behind closed doors. You get to know them, then you find these marvelous maniacs living their quiet, mad lives, but it's not out in the open at all.

Dean: When *The Grass Is Singing* was published and acclaimed, did your life change? Did you earn a lot of money?

Lessing: No, I didn't at all. I had a £150 advance and at that time I had a job as a typist again to earn a bit of money, and I didn't know it was impossible to live on what you earned by writing, so I tossed up the job and sold my clothes—all that kind of thing, chiefly evening dresses. You see, we danced in Rhodesia, in Zimbabwe, we danced; I didn't in London, so I sold all that kind of thing and got on with writing short stories. The publisher Michael Joseph kept ringing me up to say, "We have reprinted *The Grass Is Singing,*" and I said, "Oh good." You see, I thought that everyone was reprinted.

Dean: In the early '50s you published *Martha Quest,* which is the story of a young girl growing into maturity through sex and marriage, disastrously, and coming to grips for the first time with social and political realities. This has the shape and feel obviously of autobiography. Is there much of you there?

Lessing: Yes, some of it; you mean the character. Yes, this pugnacious intolerant character, yes absolutely, of course, that's me. But this whole series gets less autobiographical as it goes on. Don't forget that halfway through the series I wrote *The Golden Notebook,* which completely changed me, you see. It wasn't that I wrote five volumes one after the other.

Dean: How did you come to write *The Golden Notebook?*

Lessing: A friend of mine kept notebooks and they were on politics, psychology, her husband, children, job, and I thought that was the oddest thing. When you're living a life, you don't live in this kind of way at all, do you? It's just inhuman. There's something wrong with someone who thinks like this. So I used this, when I was working out the shape of *The Golden Notebook*. As you know, there's this framework, the absolutely conventional novel. Five bits of conventional novel and all this chaos in the middle. One thing I was saying was this feeling of despair, which every writer feels when they've finished a novel, that you haven't been able to say it because life is too complex ever to be put into words. That's one thing I was saying through the structure of this book.

I'd constructed this whole book on my experience, what I was thinking, what I was feeling, what I knew women were thinking and feeling, but it never crossed my mind that I was writing about feminism or what is now called Women's Lib, because I thought I was doing the opposite. I had thought my way into the conclusion that we all split ourselves off into little bits all the time; there's something in the human mind that makes these divisions. It's something probably wrong with us. Seriously. You smile, but I really do think there might be something wrong with us the way we are always making categories about things that should be like men/women, for instance. Of course there's a great truth there, and I'm not arguing about that, but perhaps we're not all that different where it matters, like in our inner selves.

Dean: How did women respond to *The Golden Notebook?*

Lessing: A lot of them were very angry and wrote me a lot of very bitchy letters on these lines: Why are you betraying us? Why are you giving away our secrets? Really very malevolent some of them were. I got a lot of support from men; you see, my male friends were supporting me all along the way, which is quite interesting.

In *The Golden Notebook*, I really tried to write a book which would capture certain vital ideas that were all to do with socialism in one way or another. The idea was that people might look back in 100 years' time, if they're interested, and find a record of the kind of things people thought about and talked about during these years. *The Golden Notebook* was a failure in a formal sense, because as usual I take on too much. It was so ambitious, it couldn't help but fail.

Dean: But it became a great deal more than what you intended it to be, didn't it?

Lessing: Oh, it spilled all over the place, didn't it? I don't mind because I don't believe all that much in perfect novels. What's marvelous about novels is they can be anything you like. That is the strength of the novel. There are no rules.

Dean: I'm making a mistake as I speak, I know, because inevitably I'm identifying you with the character who writes the notebooks in *The Golden Notebook*, Anna, so I'm probably putting her words into your mind. But when she writes about naiveté as spontaneous creative faith, a kind of innocence if you like, the capacity especially for females to believe in someone or something against all the evidence, isn't there something of you in this? I mean, in your Marxism you believe you're the dynamic of hope, I suppose, isn't this you? Was it you?

Lessing: Yes, it was—an enormous capacity for acceptance. I think I still have it to an extent, but I don't have it the way I had it. I don't know how to put it. Something happens or you meet somebody and you just open your arms and say "right" to an idea or to a person or anything, or any event. But you can't go on like that, you have to learn a different way.

Dean: Were you ever that romantic?

Lessing: Yes, I was.

Dean: And wounded by it?

Lessing: Oh, terribly. Yes, of course, I was. Well, the evidence is in my work, isn't it? But it's an awful waste of time all that banging and crashing around.

Dean: But hasn't it been personally useful to you? Haven't you been quarrying that disturbing kind of experience?

Lessing: Yes, but there was too much, you see. There's no need to go on doing something when you've learnt better. I remember after I had a kind of somewhat informal psychotherapy.
    What I was really doing, of course, although I didn't see it at the time, was buying a friend. I needed someone desperately to talk to and accept me. This is what she did and this is what I needed. Anyway my last meeting with her was when I'd come to grief over some ridiculous love affair and I went to her and she looked at me and she said, "Have I really not taught you any better than that to repeat your mistakes?" Then there was a long silence and she said, "As for me, I'm going to die very soon and I'm totally

occupied and preparing for a good death. Good morning," and threw me out like a kitten into the harsh world, which I thank her for.

Dean: You anticipated Women's Lib. You anticipated, I suppose, a new school of psychoanalysis, the Laing school; I suppose you'd call it, the divided self. And you in a sense anticipated a move towards the mystical.

Lessing: Can I say something about words in this area? There are great gaps in the English language where there are words like "spirit" or "soul" or "unconscious" or "collective unconscious." When you start writing in this area the words are usually the property of some cult or other— "collective unconscious" belongs to Jungians. You might not want to have that association so you're always wrestling with words that haven't got the meaning you want them to have. This is my perhaps biggest single problem. There is not one of these words that you can use, and that is why I've gone so much off into metaphor, like *Memoirs of a Survivor*. Now my impulse behind that was I wanted to write about dreams. I don't know if you've noticed that the word "dreams" is never used from start to finish in that book.

Dean: Could it be that there is a collective unconscious which we're all, and writers especially, plugged into? How do you plug into it, if you're a writer, of your sort?

Lessing: By chance, very often. The time I've done it most purely was in *Marriages Between Zones Three, Four, and Five,* which is the only book I've ever written which from start to finish was on this other wavelength. I don't want to claim too much, to use the word "inspiration." Something happened when I wrote the book. I hit some other level. And is it a legend or a myth or a fairy tale or a fantasy? That isn't the word for what I've written, I think. You see, only I could have written *The Golden Notebook,* but I think Anon wrote this other book.

Dean: When you do get messages from what we'll call the unconscious, your own or a collective mind, how do you discriminate between the nonsense and the good stuff?

Lessing: By experience, living it out, seeing if it turns out to be true or not. I think we are all studio sets with ideas flowing through us, just as neutrons and cosmic particles go shooting through us all the time that we sit here. When I wrote *The Four-Gated City,* I thought no one would speak to me by the time I finished because the ideas were so way out. I was thinking some pretty horrific thoughts about what was likely to happen in the world. I wrote that book sort of like half a page at a time and the rest of the time I was in bed with the covers over my head. That was what I was really thinking and I had to write it. But, as has happened to me so often before, by the time the book came out, these way-out ideas were all commonplace, you see. So this cheers me up every time I decide to write a book that is wild. I don't waste time worrying about what people are going to think about it, because probably all these ideas will be in the newspapers.

Dean: You're no respecter of academic critics. Are you a good critic of your own work?

Lessing: Yes, I think perhaps I am. After a short passage of time, I think I am pretty cool about it all. It's not easy to be detached when you're doing it, but shortly after, it sort of floats away from you and you can look at it.

Nearly all my books have weak patches, but that is because I'm the kind of writer I am, which means I'm always trying things out and I'm very seldom interested in the perfect book.

Dean: Anthony Burgess once criticized you as a writer by saying that he thought that you didn't edit enough. You wrote too much, too many words. Is that fair, do you think?

Lessing: Probably. I've got a terrific, great facility. When I start I can write easily, and he's probably quite right, yes. There is a place for novels that have ideas and shake people up and then die. It's a different way of writing from Jane Austen, you see.

Dean: For someone who's written so penetratingly about the relationships between the sexes and who's written so perceptively about men, it's a surprise to find you living alone now. Do you miss marriage?

Lessing: Well, you see I think I acquired the qualities to be married rather too late and by that time I'd rather lost interest in the whole business of being married. I certainly didn't have any of the necessary qualities. I was much too impatient and always fighting about something.

But no, I don't miss marriage. What I'm interested in now is real friendships, not just acquaintances. You can have thousands of acquaintances, but I think friendship is hard and takes a long time. That's what I'm interested in.

Running Through Stories in My Mind
Michael Thorpe

Michael Thorpe's interview was conducted June 23, 1980, in London and originally appeared in the Danish journal *Kunapipi* in 1982. Copyright © 1982 by *Kunapipi*. Reprinted with permission.

Thorpe: Mrs. Lessing, perhaps we may begin by speaking a little about the relationship between your early life in Southern Rhodesia, growing up on the veld, and what you describe as the gift of your solitary childhood. If I may relate you to your heroine, Martha Quest, in one of your early novels, you describe "the gift of her solitary childhood on the veld" as "that knowledge of something painful and ecstatic, something central and fixed but flowing. A sense of movement, of separate things interacting and finally becoming one but greater. It was this which was her lodestone, even her conscience." I would like to ask you if you would perhaps expand a little upon the sense in which you use the word "conscience" there, because I feel that this may not be altogether clear to many readers.

Lessing: I'm using it in a sense that it is a feeling that you measure other things against. But it's very hard to describe, of course, because what I was describing in Martha Quest was that kind of ecstatic experience that many adolescents do in fact have. It's very common to adolescents, and I think perhaps it's overvalued.

Thorpe: Is it a romantic ecstasy?

Lessing: Oh, I don't know if it's romantic, no, but it's extremely common. You'll find it described in a great deal of religious literature too. It's not an uncommon thing, but it is a reminder perhaps that life is not quite so black and white or cut and dried as we sometimes make it, and if you have had this kind of thing happen to you then it's something to refer back to, if you are about to make things too oversimplified.

Thorpe: May I ask you if this conscience is the individual conscience of which you speak in the essay "A Small Personal Voice" where you speak of

the importance of dealing with the individual conscience in its relationship with the collective. Is that a different conscience?

Lessing: Well, I hadn't thought of relating them, I must say. In "A Small
Personal Voice" I was preoccupied at that particular time—it was the mid-
fifties—with how being a member of political parties or groups or
collectives of various kinds can in fact pervert you and make you tell lies.
Now this was something that not only I, but very, very many people were
thinking about at that time; indeed, all the people I knew at that time
were thinking about it in one way or another. Some people in fact had
suffered very deeply because of it. I lived in England, and I hadn't
suffered, but people from Europe, from the Communist countries, and
from America, where the Cold War was something fairly savage, had done
a lot of thinking, and that got into my essay because I was, and am,
concerned at the way you can sell yourself out under pressure from other
people. It's extremely easy to do, particularly when you think you are in
the right about something. This is the essence of politics. You know that
you are in the right. It's also the essence of religions which are right by
definition. If I were to rewrite this essay, I wouldn't perhaps put the
emphasis now where I did then, but I still think that in a time when we are
more and more institutionalized—because this is what is happening to
us—more and more expected to be group people and members of
collectives, it's extremely important for us to try to decide what *we* think,
what *I* think as an individual. It's extremely hard to separate it, you know.

Thorpe: The individual conscience, then, that you speak of in that essay is
a moral conscience, and perhaps the conscience that you speak of in the
novel referring to the ecstatic experience in childhood is a much deeper
thing. But it seems to me that in your work the two are intimately related,
that the sense in which we use the word "conscience" is perhaps a highly
spiritual one rather than what I suppose many readers would take to be a
matter of political viewpoint or leaning or even the orthodox moral
conscience.

Lessing: You see, I think one shouldn't get these two things confused
because dealing with ordinary life, day-to-day life, in our relationships
with groups or institutions, I do not think one needs to use anything very
high-flown or mystical. It seems to me that the problem there is rather
different. It's a question of the conditioned conscience there, what had
been conditioned into me by society, and what the individual conscience,
as far as we can be aware of it, is saying. This problem of the conditioned
conscience is one that isn't lightly pushed aside; just watch any child

being brought up. From the moment this unfortunate being draws breath it is being told "you are good," "you are bad," "what a good little baby you are"—all this goes on throughout every person's life and it's always a question of what is convenient for the parents or society because every child is some kind of wild animal that has to be tamed; otherwise, no one can deal with it. It has to be, but there has to be a point where any one of us says all my "you-are-good, you-are-bad" comes from society. Now that is the conditioned conscience which, I think, is our biggest prisoner. You see, when you are standing face to face with your group, which happens more and more in this rather unpleasant world of ours, then you have to decide what is speaking, is it "you are a good little boy, you are a bad little boy," that you are brought up with, because the collective and institution always talks to the good little boy or the bad little boy or good little girl. That is the strength of institutions and politics and states and armies and the lot. They can go straight into your childhood conditioning—"Oh, he's such a good little boy, such a good little girl." That is where they get us all the time. And now this other conscience, this sense of something much deeper is something you build on, particularly as a writer. It's something that you allow—I cook a lot—to simmer quietly there so that you look at it from time to time and see what it's getting up to. I am of course talking about the unconscious.

Thorpe: You have clarified an important point for me, and I think it gets to the heart of one of the problems that I think you have felt in the reception of your work. You have been at some pains to stress, for example, that the African stories are not about the color problem and that *The Golden Notebook* is not a trumpet, as you put it, for Women's Liberation. Also I think that perhaps your political affiliation to the Communist Party for a very short time was a personal rather than an ideological matter. Would it be true, then, to infer that the reader is perhaps often so attached to the "ism" for which he is looking that he does not read your work necessarily in the spirit in which it was written?

Lessing: You see, all of these things are experiences I've been through, so they find a place in my work. But, you know, there are about three questions you put into one there. About *The Golden Notebook;* the whole point of *The Golden Notebook* when I was writing it was the opposite of what it was taken to be. I had spent a lot of my time breaking things down into categories and classifying things and making either/ors and blacks and whites of everything, I'd come to realize that it was psychologically, psychically, an extremely dangerous thing to do, and the people that I've known in my life who've done it have invariably broken down and cracked up, particularly in religion and politics. So the thesis of *The Golden Notebook* was the opposite of what it was taken to be. You know, these thoughts that you suddenly have and you can't understand why you never had them before. It was one of those thoughts that prompted *The Golden Notebook*, the thought that there's something in the way our minds are set up, created or conditioned, that makes us think of what divides people. So all of us all the time, if I say black and you say white, will instantly think of what divides the black and the white or divides men and women, and I have been trying ever since then to try not to do this and to try to see in fact what we have in common which is much more important.

Thorpe: Your preoccupation, then, is with unity.

Lessing: Yes, I think it's very important. We've got to learn to think like this.

Thorpe: When you spoke in the Preface to the second edition of *The Golden Notebook* of the necessity for a search for a world ethic, I take it that this is an aspect of that unity that you speak of.

Lessing: I talked about Marxism being an attempt at a kind of world ethic outside religion. Well, of course Marxism, as far as I am concerned, is a religion; it has all the same characteristics. But what Marxism at its best does is to look at the world as a whole and see the different parts of it interacting. That's how it is as a theory, not what happens to it when it's put into practice. And that is very appealing, I think, to young people particularly. Generation after generation falls in love with Marxism, and I think nearly always for the same reasons. It's because looking around at what we can all see, and it doesn't get any prettier, Marxism is presented ideologically as something that sees Man as a whole, and it takes some time, some experience to see that the theory and practice have got absolutely nothing to do with each other.

Thorpe: The practice, then, for a humane novelist is to find a convincing alternative to this very appealing, all-embracing ideology.

Lessing: I don't look for ideologies any more, oh no. What I do think is that the different classes of the world have got to start acting as a whole, or we are going to do ourselves in, politically, but that is not an ideological thought. It's a practical one.

Thorpe: Were you inspired by certain writers?

Lessing: //If I listed them your mind would split with amazement, like Proust, for example. I'm quite sure that at one time I must have been one of the world experts on Proust. I also knew Tolstoy and Stendhal and so on. I can go on indefinitely, so of course I was influenced, but I do not know who I was influenced by particularly. I think I was influenced much more by a kind of largeness of attitude, which is what you find in "great literature," which was the opposite of anything around me. This was Salisbury, Rhodesia, bigoted, narrow, color-bar society where nothing was ever discussed excepting the color bar, or sport, or gossip. Literature was my safety line, something to hold on to.

Thorpe: I was struck by your comments about *The Story of an African Farm*. You speak of its obvious flaws, but then you speak of its quality as a work on the frontiers of experience which redeems whatever flaws it may have of structure and conception. I wonder if you would be kind enough to say a little more about what you had in mind with regard to the quality of that novel.

Lessing: Well, the least important part is the feminism which is the intellectual motivation. Olive Schreiner was bitterly conscious of the position of women in the nineteenth century. (In passing I would like to say that if somebody wanted to condemn me to some vicious prison sentence they could condemn me to live as a woman in the nineteenth century. It must have been utter hell.) While she was fighting this particular battle all her life, and fighting it well, she was also preoccupied all the time with other things. There's a central place in that book where this very clumsy, inarticulate farm boy, Waldo, talks to his stranger— you know they both have strangers, Lindell has her stranger who is half sexual object and, I felt, perhaps not very important—but the real stranger is Waldo's stranger who talks to him of the meaning of life, and that is really the core of that book. It's not a subtle book any more than *Wuthering Heights* is. *Wuthering Heights* is an appalling novel. Have you ever sat down to analyze it? It's dreadful, but it doesn't really matter, does it? And I think the same is true of *An African Farm*, because if you wanted to pull *An African Farm* to bits, you could do a very good job of it. But it's redeemed because of the spirit of the book. All the time she's trying to come to terms with what life is all about. This is what her writing is really about.

Thorpe: I would like to ask a few questions about *The Grass Is Singing*. How did this novel evolve? I have read that you originally intended to center it upon the figure of Marston.

Lessing: It was originally two-thirds as long again. What happened was I wrote—based on a little newspaper I'd kept and I'd kept *that* because of gossip I'd heard as a child about a woman, a farmer on some near farm, and her relations with a cook-boy and the unease of the white people discussing it. Now it was not suggested that this was a straightforward sexual thing. What was suggested was that she was asking for it, with comments like my father's: "There was a French queen who used to dress and undress in front of her servants because they were not people to her." That stuck in my mind. I gave up my job as a typist because I said to myself, "You are always saying you are a writer, but where's the evidence?" I was then faced with writing a novel, and what was it going to be about? A third was the existing novel. There was also a great mass which was social satire, and it couldn't possibly have been any good because I had then hardly been out of Rhodesia, and you have to have some kind of comparisons to make satire. So I just ripped off this two-thirds. The original plot was that this young Englishman, full of idealism—they were always turning up in Rhodesia, they never lasted for one reason or another longer than about a year—this idealistic young Englishman turned up and actually was confronted with this extremely basic, sordid and, above all, enigmatic incident because no one would tell the truth about it, nor bring it out in the open. When discussing this incident, the white farmers and the white farmers' wives on their verandas never said anything like "We can't have a black man screwing a white woman" or anything like that, or "How immoral!" It was always ambiguous and wrapped up. This is what struck me as a child, and this is what that novel came out of.

Thorpe: It has always seemed to me that your treatment of Mary Turner and of Dick Turner is a compassionate one; that you satirized the extreme figures, but not the central figures.

Lessing: I hadn't satirized Mary Turner and Dick Turner at all. No, I satirized the whole of the white community, using Marston as a focus. The satirical part of the book had nothing to do with the Turners. What I had to change was Marston.

Thorpe: May I ask you if the second epigraph which you put at the front of the novel is invented?

Lessing: You know, that I couldn't remember. The thing was I'd written it in a notebook and I hadn't got an attribution and I didn't know whether I'd invented it or whether I'd read it, so I put "anonymous."

Thorpe: But it is of course very apt not only for this novel but for many of the stories that you have written. It seems that in so many of your African stories, as in *The Grass Is Singing,* your imagination is moved by the spectacle not of brutality or insensitivity, but of muddling incapacity to cope. Is this simply an instinctive, intuitive way of dealing with it, or is it really a deliberate looking back?

Lessing: Well, now I can intellectualize it and say I think that this is how most people are, but I suppose it must have been my experience. I was running through stories in my mind as you spoke, trying to think which fitted this description.

Thorpe: One thinks of another woman, like Mrs. Gale, for example, the way in which she is treated when she confronts the young girl who is full of ecstasy and passion.

Lessing: No, that was when I was trying to contrast the English and the Afrikaners, that English kind of cold, upper-class thing and the Afrikaners, who are very simple and direct.

Thorpe: But there is still, it seems to me, in your treatment of the cold and upper-class a sense of the pathos of this crippled sensibility.

Lessing: Oh, yes. Well, Mrs. Gale is a woman in prison; all of them are, aren't they?

Thorpe: Yes, indeed. The figure in *The Grass Is Singing,* I suppose, who attracts the most comment is the figure of Moses, the boy, the African servant. Did you see him not so much as an individual as the essence of the African as the white sees him and fears him?

Lessing: With the anonymity I tried to sum up how the white people would see someone like this because they wouldn't see him very much as an individual at all. If I had made Moses a very particularized individual, that would have thrown that novel completely out; it would have been a different novel. Supposing I rewrote it from his point of view. For a start, I don't think I'd be able to do it, which is another thing.

Thorpe: Yes. In the long story "Hunger" you did in fact do this, didn't you? And you did feel dissatisfied with it.

Lessing: I felt dissatisfied with it because it was too oversimplified. The thing is I wrote *The Grass Is Singing* in Rhodesia as a white person and my contact with the blacks as equals was just non-existent. It was always either as an employer or as a rather patronizing person, simply because that was how you were situated. You couldn't have a really equal relationship with a black person. We did have a kind of political relationship, but they were not equal. If you are meeting black people who have to be home at nine o'clock to beat the curfew while you sit around in the office when they've gone and you can go off to a restaurant which they can't go to, no amount of ideology is going to turn this into an equal relationship; it's just not possible. I'd had no equal relationships with black people. By the time I'd come to write "Hunger" I'd lived in England for quite a long time and I'd known a great many Africans and Jamaicans, and so on, as people. I no longer thought in terms of color. I remember once how I realized that I really was on my way to being cured from color feeling when an Indian turned up in my flat unannounced and asked me to do something. I disliked him as a person, and I said, "Get out" and I thought, My God, I'm cured because it never crossed my mind that I mustn't be unkind to a dark-skinned person.

Thorpe: When you embarked on *The Grass Is Singing,* and in fact on all your African writing, did you have any previous writers about Africa in mind at all? Did you feel this has been done and it must be done differently by me? Did you have a sense of relationship to those who'd gone before you, or did you feel completely alone, as it were, in treating this?

Lessing: You mean with *The Grass Is Singing?* No, I didn't have anything to take it from at all. No, I didn't.

Placing Their Fingers on the Wounds of Our Times
Margarete von Schwarzkopf

Margarete von Schwarzkopf's interview appeared in *Die Welt* May 9, 1981. The following translation was prepared by the editor with the assistance of Heidrun Neth. Copyright © 1994 by Earl G. Ingersoll.

Schwarzkopf: Mrs. Lessing, as an Englishwoman, you carry a famous German name. Where does it come from?

Lessing: My second marriage was to the German Communist emigrant Gottfried Anton Nicolai Lessing, who was not, in any case, directly related to the great German poet. After the divorce, I retained his name as an omen, so to speak, for my own career as a writer. It signifies inspiration and proportion at the same time for me to carry the name of a genius.

Schwarzkopf: In Germany you are known primarily for one book—*The Golden Notebook*. What does this work mean to you now?

Lessing: It seems curious to me again and again that almost twenty years later this book produces such an echo everywhere in the world. I still receive letters from its readers, primarily in Germany and the United States. In the foreword to the ninth edition in 1971, I went into detail concerning this echo and attempted to probe why *this* novel is still exciting so many minds. For in those ten years which had passed since the book's appearance infinitely much had happened and its explosive themes should have lost much of their relevance. What was still considered taboo in 1962 is no longer so today.

But what astonished me even more was that hardly any of my readers has seemed prepared to see the book as a whole. Some have considered it as a challenge to men (which it is not), others have believed it a political confession, while a third group have reckoned that it was exclusively about the spiritual confusion of my heroine, and my alter ego, Anna. Such responses make me anxious, on the one hand, because they demonstrate how far apart the intention of the author and the comprehension of the reader can be. On the other hand, this response also shows me—and this relieved my mind again—that a book is a living thing which can bear many kinds of fruit.

Schwarzkopf: Could you write this book today once again, or at least could you be concerned with a similar subject?

Lessing: No. First of all, as I said, circumstances have changed. Why should another book be written about these two women, very coura- geous—for the circumstances of that time—albeit rather crazy in their experimenting with liberation? Beyond that, writers should not repeat themselves and should not try to use the same theme twice. Many of my readers, even my publisher, have indeed expected me to write "Golden Notebooks" again and again. But a book is like a child. Once it is born and the umbilical cord is severed, you cannot haul it back into the womb to be born again. The subject is passé.

Schwarzkopf: Where do you stand now on the Women's Movement?

Lessing: That is a very complex and for me rather painful subject. *The Golden Notebook* brought me a lot of attributes at the time—from enemy of men to hater of women. I was proclaimed the Saint Joan of Women's Lib, and then I was condemned by the feminists as a notorious despiser of women. In any case, misunderstandings swarmed around the book. Of course, I am for women's equality; of course, I consider women inher- ently equal to men. However, I would never maintain that men and women are alike. They simply are not. Physically, psychologically, and intellectually, they are not—which is not to say that women must be more stupid than men. They have other gifts. No two people in the world are perfectly alike; how can men and women be alike?

What I wish is that women should be independent, neither the slaves of men nor Amazons. In my novel *The Marriages Between Zones Three, Four, and Five,* I attempt to create a woman approaching this ideal: she is free, independent, a loving mother, compassionate but not sentimental, intel- ligent but not overbearing. To be sure, the book is a utopian novel and this woman is an ideal figure. And I harbor no illusions about how women can be. They are not better nor worse beings; they are human beings. That my two heroines in *The Golden Notebook* can be even aggressive and shrill the feminists attacked me for above all, because I say that these attributes are part of their ego—not the result of long-term oppression. If the Women's Movement has gone so far that women cannot be criticized, that the truth can no longer be spoken, then the movement is bad, then it does not serve women well, but instead harms them. Then it is senseless and dangerous.

Schwarzkopf: Are you saying that there is a significant difference between "men's literature" and the literature which women write?

Lessing: A woman sees certain things very differently from the way a man does, yet there are also male writers who maintain they can plumb the depths of a woman's soul. But the reverse is difficult too. A woman can never completely get inside a man's consciousness. For better and for worse. Only in this way can multiplicity arise in literature. I believe, for example, that women act more instinctively than men, that they approach psychological subjects not scientifically but instinctively.

Schwarzkopf: In a reading of your novel *Briefing for a Descent into Hell* and also *The Golden Notebook,* the impression is unmistakable that your approach to psychoanalysis is not very positive.

Lessing: I have been reproached many times for being a declared enemy of psychoanalysis. Now, "enemy" is certainly an exaggeration, but I am actually an opponent of the current fashion of overpsychologizing. This tendency is a very bad phenomenon in a century which seems to have become speechless and in which words seem to be created rather for declarations of war than for declarations of love. Certainly humanity needs psychology too, simply because it suffers from deficiencies in expressing emotions. However, I have continued to oppose the methods of case studies with which human beings are classified and stamped. Each person is a marvelous mosaic of thousands of pieces. Each is unique. Also, if this remark smacks too much of a truism, there is still a fact behind it. And because psychologists often seem to forget this important fact, people have to point out the truism again and again.

Schwarzkopf: What do you believe is the function of writers in our time? What can they do? What should they do?

Lessing: There is no universally valid answer to these questions. There are hundreds of writers, and we are all individuals anxiously intent on preserving our inner lives and our ideas. In my opinion, it is obviously the job of writers, if they take their profession seriously, to place their fingers on the wounds of our times, but that is not enough. Each can find fault in prevailing conditions. That sort of thing can easily become a fashion. In my opinion, the author should be something of a prophet, tracing a thing before it is fully apparent, grasping a subject before it becomes a trend, stretching out one's antennae into the universe to sense its most subtle vibrations.

Schwarzkopf: May, can, should writers express themselves politically in their works?

Lessing: When I came to London over thirty years ago with twenty pounds in my pocketbook and my young son in hand, that's what I firmly believed being a writer means—changing the world. I saw it as my duty to be politically active, to take to the field against injustice, and wherever I went, standing or sitting, to discuss political subjects. But what is politics?

To express it poetically politics is not as the beating of wings. And the writer is nothing but an isolated voice in the wilderness. Many hear it; most pass by. It has taken a long time for me to recognize that in their books writers should distance themselves from the political questions of the day. They only waste their energy senselessly and bar their vision from the universal themes of humanity which know neither time nor space.

Schwarzkopf: You yourself were a Marxist...

Lessing: That's exactly why I dare to comment on this problem. Under the influence of my second husband I became a fervent Marxist. Another factor was my rage about conditions in Southern Africa and later my impressions of the workers' district in London. It was a slow, painful process of disentangling myself. My series of Martha Quest novels, which is extremely autobiographical, depicts my own development toward Marxism and away from Marxism, a process of disillusionment. I have long recognized that the salvation of this world cannot lie in any political ideology. All ideologies are deceptive and serve only a few, not people in general.

Schwarzkopf: Are you—to use the fashionable term—"frustrated"?

Lessing: No, I have just become wiser, if not yet wise. As I returned for the first, but also for the last, time to Southern Africa in 1955—since my "escape" to England—I suddenly became conscious of how superfluous my political somersaults had been. In my journal of this trip back, *Coming Home*, which represented for me the final farewell to my youth, I have written about these realizations.

Schwarzkopf: What do you want to accomplish and what can you accomplish with your books?

Lessing: If I am honest, and this honesty, of course, injures my vanity: not much. But I can still stimulate people to think, I can entertain them and make them aware of things which in the whirlpool of the everyday they might not see or hear. The writing profession is above all a process of give and take. In this way, I myself learn just as much from my readers as they do from me. And with surprise and fear I realize how many problems there are everywhere. Often it seems to me like being in Bluebeard's castle. Everywhere there are doors which I open and behind each closed door sits someone with a ravaged spirit.

Schwarzkopf: How important for you is language itself as a vehicle for your ideas?

Lessing: I don't like to have to express myself in a complicated fashion. A book should be understandable for everyone. For that reason, I treasure parables, metaphors, fables, and allegories, and fall back on literary forms that are simple yet excellent in suiting my purposes of explaining the most profound spiritual phenomena. Above all, I am forced to recognize again and again how fast language encounters boundaries. How, for example, can deep perceptions be clothed convincingly in words? That's where language begins to limp deplorably and realizing this, I plunge sometimes into a creative crisis.

I recognized the limitations of language for the first time when I was searching for the words to depict Anna's dreams in *The Golden Notebook*. The older I get, the more concerned I am with the reality of dreams, which I believe are mirrors and outlets of the soul. I'm fascinated by the way in which symbolism and the multiplicity of the world are represented in dreams. Each morning as I wake I take up my scratch-pad to hold onto my nightly dreams. However, it is infinitely difficult to capture in words the atmosphere of a dream, this mixture of delusion and truth, fog and light. In film or in a painting, all of these can be represented more easily, but in a book? For that reason, I have abandoned, at least for the time being, my long-cherished project of writing an autobiography, which would comprise my dreams of the past ten years. Nevertheless, I will eagerly continue to pursue my dream research. After my garden and my cats, it is my third hobby.

Schwarzkopf: In *Memoirs of a Survivor*, in which the future plays a part in a London completely destroyed and turned into a slum, you have in the end of the novel an older woman and a young girl go through a wall. Has this metaphor been relevant in your own life and your work?

Lessing: Yes, of course. After that novel, I began to occupy myself very intensively with utopian thoughts and was transported from our present-day world to the bizarre world of foreign galaxies. With it, a new period of my work had its beginning.

Schwarzkopf: In recent years you have actually written four science-fiction novels. Have you become an "SF writer"?

Lessing: I wouldn't classify these books as science fiction. They don't have much to do with "science," that is, scientific knowledge and technology. I leave that to my colleagues who really know something about technology. I am skeptical about science as it is practiced today, this shortsighted discipline concerned with tomorrow but not with the day after. No, my novels are fantasies, or utopias in the truest, most precise sense of the term, to be sure, rather less related to Orwell and Huxley than to Thomas More and Plato. They are fables, spun out of what is happening today. Thus, I depict, for example, in the third book in the series, *The Sirian Experiments*, genetic experiments casting what our scientists today call "cloning" into the shade. But despite a certain spiritual and moral superiority over the Earthlings, my denizens of distant galaxies are finally equal to us as human beings again.

Schwarzkopf: Mrs. Lessing, in your books like *Memoirs of a Survivor* and *Shikasta*, in which the earth is ruined by environmental pollution, anarchy, and rebellions, you see a less rosy future for our planet. Are you pessimistic about what the future holds for humanity?

Lessing: I must admit that it has become a bit fashionable to paint the apocalypse on the wall. From childhood on, I've never been a pessimist, but rather I see less occasion at the moment for any great optimism. Wherever one looks, stupidity and chaos. But perhaps a small chance exists that the ship can once again steer clear of the reefs. We have to start with the education of children, to teach them how to accept themselves as complete individuals, regardless of their group or race. Only human beings who are self-assured and do not feel inferior can discuss problems and talk with each other on the same plane. That would be the first step toward reducing aggression and hatred.

As for our politicians, I would not claim, like Plato, that we ought to be ruled by philosophers. But our politicians should be human beings who have somewhat more farsightedness than they actually have, human beings who know, respect, and understand their fellow human beings. Hopes, nothing but hopes, I know. However, as long as the hand is not yet at midnight, I will not give up hope that the earth will last for a while.

Schwarzkopf: There are, it would seem, hardly any subjects left which have not been taken up by one writer or other. Can you think of any subjects still "open"?

Lessing: Sadly, there are only a few lovely, pleasant subjects. I personally am interested in the rapid growth of unemployment among the young. The thought of its possible consequences is utterly horrible. What would happen, for example, if all these unemployed, aimless beings banded together? Or let's take the field of prenatal experience. Will the fetus in the womb be stamped by particular events and emotions? Is the mother's joy transmitted to the unborn, or is it her anxiety? I am very certain that children can be shaped and influenced before they come into the world. Next to my passion for dream research, I spend my time very intensively on these questions. Whether a book will come out of all this, I have no way of knowing.

Breaking Down These Forms
Stephen Gray

Stephen Gray's interview took place in November 1983
and originally appeared in *Research in African Literatures*
17 (Fall 1986). Copyright © 1986 by *Research in African
Literatures*. Reprinted with permission.

Gray: I'd like to start with your early days, when you were publishing your
first short stories, in *Trek* in Johannesburg in 1948 and elsewhere. Some of
these you've not picked up in collections. Johannesburg was your literary
center then.

Lessing: Yes, I remember sending them off. Well, it wasn't only
Johannesburg; there was a Cape Town periodical, but I can't remember
what it was called, where I sent a rather false, sophisticated story, as I
recall. And then there was the *Trek* man with whom I had a very enter-
taining correspondence. But I don't think there were very many stories,
you know.

Gray: About half a dozen or a dozen. Did you at some stage sort through
them?

Lessing: I suppose I must have done. One turned up the other day. It was
published in Salisbury, and I'd completely forgotten about it. But I don't
think any of them are much good, are they?

Gray: Well, you were writing many stories prior to 1950, the year after you
came to London and when *The Grass Is Singing* came out as a fully
accomplished work. Were you always going to be a writer?

Lessing: Well, you must remember my circumstances. I was singularly
beset by everything in Salisbury, as it was then: I had a job for nearly the
whole time, and at best I had a half-time job. I was a kind of typist for
Hansard, and I typed for special commissions. But most of the time I was
working in a legal office. And that was my political era; looking back, I
cannot understand how we didn't all die of overwork. So writing wasn't all

that easy. I wrote those odd stories, and I was continually writing poetry, but very little of it is any good. Perhaps four or five are worth remembering.

Gray: You haven't suppressed those, have you?

Lessing: Well, not suppressed them, but I'd be very happy if they were forgotten. There was a man at Zimbabwe University who wanted to publish them all, and I was appalled because they're not worth publishing. Here is where I come up against academics—I don't see this point at all of preserving second-rate stuff of writers, but no academic would ever agree with me about that.

Gray: As a "Rhodesian," as they were called, what were your early experiences of what was then the Union of South Africa?

Lessing: Well, I never had the money to pop back and forth, but I did spend some time in South Africa. I was there in 1937 for two months—in rich Johannesburg, staying with a family who was with the Chamber of Mines. And Johannesburg was a great shock to me, but I did useful things. I worked in a dress shop for a week, and I worked in a cafe for a few weeks, and I've never been able to understand how anybody can stand it, standing all day and night. I didn't meet anybody, of course, but whites, because one didn't. I didn't start meeting blacks until I came to London. The next time in South Africa was two months in Cape Town early in the war, with my son John—but there's nothing to be said about that because I was in a hotel with no money and a small child—but I did get about Cape Town a good deal. Then I was in Cape Town again for three months in 1946, and among other things I worked for *The Guardian,* the Communist newspaper, in the subscription department. That was an extremely lively lot of people, but I was only a very small secretary or typist. I didn't meet the great gods, as they were then seen; all of them are now here in England. But I did for the first time, in the course of my work, get taken to all kinds of horrible factories and farms, and I saw something that I'd never seen before. I'd not have been able to imagine what I saw: these terribly badly paid factory workers, and farmers who were paid some of their wages in drink. That was all useful because how would I come into contact with that otherwise? I also met quite a few artists in that time, and that was for me—a very raw girl from the sticks—absolutely marvelous. And then I was there again for two or three months on my way out—yet again in Houghton, again in rich Johannesburg. I could write a novel about that because my hosts were Communists! You can't improve on life!

It's so improbable. Then Cape Town again, and in the most amazing boardinghouse, which I've written about in *In Pursuit of the English,* which was incredible, and I often think about it.

Gray: In your fiction you rather generalize about your "Rhodesian" experience and your "South African" experience, blending them into one.

Lessing: I don't think there was very much difference between the Rhodesian experience and the South African experience. *The Grass Is Singing* is very Rhodesian because it was based on the life of the district which I was brought up in, but I'm sure that could have happened in South Africa.

Gray: How do you account for its overnight fame, once it was published here?

Lessing: Well, it was the second book on those parts. The first was Paton's *Cry, the Beloved Country*—that had just come out, and then came mine. I was just extremely lucky in my timing. But it certainly wasn't as simple as that, because *The Grass Is Singing* was bought by a South African publisher, with a very crooked type of deal, although I didn't know it then. Then I was here and sent some short stories to Curtis Brown, and a woman there wrote back and asked did I have a novel. And I said I did, but it was contracted in South Africa, and she instantly smelled a rat. When she saw the contract, she was so shocked she wrote and said they should either let me go or be brought up before some court. The court didn't exist, but they let me go, and she sold me instantly to Michael Joseph. And it was an instant success, but the joke was I didn't know it. I was so raw and green, and in any case I had so many problems at that time, that when they used to ring me up and say we've printed again, we've printed again, I thought that happened to everybody. I was ever so blasé about it. So it did very well.

Gray: It seems to me much sparser than that other work you were doing at the time. Did you edit and edit down?

Lessing: No, that book was only a third of a much longer one. That was a subplot, actually. But the theme which interested me, and still does, was about the idealistic young—usually English—man who arrives in a place like Rhodesia and is appalled by everything, and rushes around for a few weeks saying, how terrible. And then leaves, which they did; or succumbed, and then usually became worse than the locals. Dick Marston was in fact the hero of the original book. But because of my complete lack of experience of England it was very bad. I tore it up, I'm glad to say. But what happened was that this enormous manuscript was going around. This was no joke because it was going back and forth by sea after the war. You know how long publishers take, and they would send back vaguely friendly letters with it. And then I looked at it again, and I saw that a lot of it was awful—and I just had to take *The Grass Is Singing* out of it. The original was supposedly comic in the main part, but I didn't have the equipment to write it.

Gray: Where did you find the remaining plot?

Lessing: *The Grass Is Singing* itself was based on somebody I knew—though I suppose not an uncommon type. Don't forget I was brought up on the veld, and then I came into Salisbury and met people who never put their noses out of town, unless they went on some picnic or other. One of the people I knew was a woman who used to go on a picnic and sit with her ankles together and her skirt down in case some beetle might crawl on her. She hated the veld with such a passion. And I thought, Supposing this woman by some tragedy married a farmer. Then, of course, there was the story that I began the book with. There was this inexplicable murder—I can't remember what year it could have been.

Gray: But the main impact today is the Mary-Moses relationship.

Lessing: You see, if you take a very inadequate, a very psychologically frail woman and put her in an environment like that, of course, she's going to become dominated by a strong personality. It doesn't really matter who it would be, black or white. You know how a novel gets made up from so many different things. And I remember listening as a child to the people talking on the veranda about this woman, a neighbor who allowed her servant to do her dress up the back and to brush her hair. Now this was so—I don't have to tell you—so impossible; I remember now the note in their voices of sheer awe—was she mad, what was wrong with her?—there was a note of doom, horror. I don't remember who this terrible woman who allowed this servant to button her up was. But I don't have to tell you how to them it was impossible. What would this black man have thought? And so the story coalesced around the Marston character, who wouldn't have understood a word of all that.

Gray: Did you approve of the recent movie of *The Grass Is Singing?*

Lessing: I thought it was too sensational. I thought Karen Black was wrong; she's one of the sexiest women in the world, I would say; and there's my poor Mary Turner, who doesn't understand anything about sex or life. But I don't see many moviemakers being honest enough to cast Mary Turner.

Gray: Did you read other local authors like Olive Schreiner a lot before writing *The Grass Is Singing*, and did you feel part of a group?

Lessing: No. Not really. Of course I'd read Schreiner. But I hadn't read Pauline Smith—I didn't know she existed. And I read the Gertrude Pages—the ones that go in for very lush descriptions of landscape. Schreiner's *African Farm* really had an enormous impact on me.

Gray: They deal with the one myth-system of the white person landing in the veld. Then there's virtually the opposite system, in the "Jim Comes to Joburg" works about a tribesman landing in town. In a short novel like *Hunger* you deal with that. Hadn't you read works like William Plomer's novella, *Ula Masondo*, dealing with that?

Lessing: Well, the funny thing is I'd never heard of him either, until I came to London. I read him after I got here. I was very isolated, and lots of things have happened in Southern Africa which hadn't then. There was no feeling of continuity; nobody said you should read Plomer or—whoever.

Gray: Then you were rather self-inventing. But the interesting thing is you've worked myths that many of your forerunners had worked as well.

Lessing: Yes, but who could not write about the African coming to town, because it's such a story.

Gray: But in a novella like *Eldorado* you situate your characters so consciously between London, the metropolitan center, and Johannesburg, the industrial nexus to the south, as if you wanted to see them especially sociologically and mythically.

Lessing: Well, it did have a kind of myth quality—Johannesburg, the wicked city. But a lot of people had come to Rhodesia from the Rand, often because of lung trouble, you see. We got t.b. from London and a lot who'd had other lung problems from the mines. I don't know if this all still goes on; I should think the conditions are better in the mines. But in

Lomagundi, because it's gold country, there were a lot of small miners—running small mines for a time. There was one just across from our ridge called the Muriel, from which we could hear the mine-stamps. So I've met an awful lot of these small miners.//

Gray: How aware were you of a mythical dimension in your early African stories and novellas?

Lessing: There *was* this mythical consciousness about. For example, this wicked city of Johannesburg—it represented something bad, and gold, and disease, with people always coming up with their shot lungs. That wasn't realism at all—it was how people spoke of it. So perhaps I did have this feeling of living through some kind of almost invented world. And don't forget that if you put people on farms, fairly remote from one another—and they have to be a bit peculiar anyway, or they wouldn't be there—they become outsize. Because everything they do becomes known; it's all, as it were, on stage. And fairly ordinary people, even, become amazing, particularly to a child, whom I now see had a particularly strong sense of drama.//

Gray: So the novel became the dominant form for you. And you've dropped the stories as well now?

Lessing: No, I haven't; I'll probably write some more. But now I'm terribly involved in this *Canopus* series, about which there's so much hard feeling. It's the kids who like it; the older people don't like it.

Gray: But even the *Canopus* series derives very strongly from your African past.

Lessing: I certainly couldn't have written *Shikasta* without it because there are whole sections in *Shikasta* that are straight from Africa.

Gray: And *The Making of the Representative for Planet 8* as well.

Lessing: But that's all snow and ice.

Gray: Yes, but there's the memory of a beautiful, warm, pastoral landscape that resonates through it. And the fearful control from an outside system which seems to me is all about colonization.

Lessing: But the whole sequence is based on colonization. This is history, isn't it? All history is the history of empires rising and falling.

Gray: You're at what point in the sequence?

Lessing: Well, I have written other things as well. And I'm not saying I'm not going to write any more short stories; I'm writing one now. But what I'm interested in, you see, is breaking down these forms that we set up for ourselves—you know, you have to have a novel, and there's a poem there, and a short story there, and there's an essay there. Why does it have to be like that? Because some of the great books, for example of the Middle East, are just compendiums of all kinds of things, and they're very rich. In *Shikasta*—I don't know if you've noticed it, in fact, but there are things that are virtually short stories. I would like to have another shot at a work—I'm thinking about it now as a novel—which would have all these different things in it. But it's terribly difficult.

Gray: But wasn't the great watershed for you *The Golden Notebook,* which contained everything in it from the germs of stories to complete stories to parallel stories—and everything else. There you were exploding the novel form open.

Lessing: But it was quite controlled, you know. But one of the things that book was about was the difference between reality and the novel, because the frame of that book was a short, self-contained novel. But what I was saying was that this is what went into that short, contained novel. Every writer's tormented by this kind of thing because we know that as soon as you start framing a novel, then things get left out. But *what* gets left out...it's painful, really, isn't it, because you can never really do it!

Gray: Well, you certainly made an attempt at it. But now you've come back to writing a much less abundant, more allegorical type of writing, and the myth has come back to the surface again.

Lessing: Have you read *The Marriages between Zones Three, Four, and Five?*— that's pure myth, that one.

Gray: But there you're trying to give the essence of form, rather than exploding it.

Lessing: I don't think I've got that kind of energy anymore. You know, I wrote *The Golden Notebook* in a year. I can't believe it now, but I did. But then everything and my life was changing and so, being a writer, it expressed itself in that book. But there's a sense, you know, in which one is surprised by what comes out. You can set a thing up as much as you like, but it's different when you do it.

Gray: But in *The Golden Notebook* you incorporated exactly that; its excitement is that it always seems to be created as one reads it.

Lessing: You see, I had this rough framework. I said I want this tight structure, so I did the structure. But what came out in between was something else, and not always foreseen. It was almost out of control. And I was feeling despair because I couldn't find a way of saying what I then knew about life. I know it sounds ridiculous because it was so late, but it was a very explosive time because a lot of people around me had had their hearts broken politically. Mine, because I'm a cynical soul, was not broken, but I was surrounded by people who were in breakdowns or turning into their own opposites, from being dedicated, 100-percent Communists into brilliant businessmen. It was quite extraordinary to see what was happening. And a lot of Americans and Canadians were in London, who had left because of what can only be called persecution. And I was meeting people who will not at all hit the history books, as far as I can see—that sort of rank-and-file person, fairly dedicated, not necessarily Communist—who were literally driven mad or to suicide by the FBI dropping round once a week, with this steady persecution, but that's another story. Anyway, I was meeting people from all over Europe who knew about the real horrors under Communism, and so that method had been exploded. And in my own life I was at the end of my forties, and my own life was up for grabs. You can't plan this happening; it happens. And I consciously think, if that kind of concentration of psychological pressure and events should happen again, I'd then write another book with that pressure behind it. But until that happens...you can't plan it. So, I'm always listening, as it were.

Gray: But what was your inner need to go into your *Canopus* series, with its immense, many-perspectived scale, using everything from realistic lives to science fiction, which has such a poor public image these days?

Lessing: It may get bad publicity, but let me tell you I'm read in hundreds of thousands by everyone in Europe under thirty, so I can't really complain about my readership.

Gray: But are you just casting off realism as a mode?

Lessing: I had cast it off, hadn't I?—with *The Memoirs of a Survivor* and *Briefing for a Descent into Hell.* And I think *Briefing* is one of my best books. Anyway, what happened was that with *Canopus* I didn't plan a new series; I planned one book. I wanted to write the Bible as science fiction because somebody had said to me that nobody had ever done this very simple thing, which was to read the Old Testament and the New and the Apocrypha and the Koran right through; it's a continuing story, it's the same play, with the same cast of characters. And wow! zap! pow! you think, My God, things just slot into place. Because you have these three religions that tear each other to bits—what nonsense; they're the same religion, in fact, in different installments. And so I thought, supposing I made this science fiction because what they have in common is "messengers" or prophets who come and say to human beings, "You stinking lot of no-goodniks, pull your socks up and do better, or else." I thought, How about writing this from the point of view of such a visitor, or series of visitors? It was only when I got halfway through the book, *Shikasta,* that I realized I'd created a marvelous format which I'd be mad to jettison—the archives. I'd got halfway through when I realized that I was going to use this again.

Gray: Do you have a plan for the entire sequence?

Lessing: No... Well, I've got so many things I could write. But it's not continuous because *Marriages* has got little to do with the others. It's simply an interesting, useful formula that I can use. What the continuity is is that the format releases some kind of energy in me. For example, I waited for years to write *The Marriages,* and I couldn't—I couldn't do it. Then that format made it possible.

Gray: So there will be more?

Lessing: There'll certainly be one more, but I don't know if there'll be any more after that, unless I'm terribly inspired by something. But I really enjoy writing them. I also enjoy what happens to them when they come out because that form provokes the most violent extremes—it's quite extraordinary! There are people who you'd assume are sane and balanced who will scream, "The publishers who published this should be shot!" Or, "Fan as I am of Doris Lessing, I will never read another novel of hers as long as I live!" There's absolutely a lack of proportion.

Gray: As I understand it, in *The Making of the Representative* you have the provocative idea that character and role are not always related, that the role can be passed on and people are really interchangeable. Haven't you detached the individual from a personal destiny here?

Lessing: The idea is that we have functions, and when we do something it's a function that we share with other people who do that. For a long time I've seen "the writer" as a kind of function of humanity; I feel connected with other writers because I feel that in a sense we are one, doing perhaps slightly different things.

Gray: But you're now talking of people in terms of function instead of in terms of the previous individual psyche, which is very far from your social realist mode of thinking.

Lessing: You know, you can't go on writing the same thing. There's a really big gap in sensibility between older people and younger people today. Why is it that younger people, everywhere I go, read this series with such ease? It's a language they understand, and the older people don't. Younger people have been brought up on a bigger perspective about the earth. They don't identify themselves with a town or even a continent; they identify themselves with Planet Earth. The moment you have a shot of the earth from space—a beautifully colored bubble floating in space— then there's a new sensibility; there has to be. And also I'm getting older, and I think that as you get older you get very much less personal about everything. You simply recognize that what you're doing is what other people do, at the same time and under the same circumstances. You don't think that *I*, the laborious, amazing individual, am doing this, and I'm the only person doing it.

Gray: Do you feel any special affinity for writers now working in the same field?

Lessing: I don't feel any more affinity for them than I do for realist writers; just because I used to write a very realistic fiction doesn't mean I've floated away from it. It's all part of the same thing. But what interests me about *The Representative* is that all my speculations in the "who-am-I?" department are in there; you couldn't put those in an ordinary novel, but it's quite easy to put them in that type of book.

Gray: And you couldn't get there with social realism?

Lessing: The convention would only allow that in dream sequences. But I think this is what happens with everybody. You start off with your life and the need to define yourself and this frightful struggle to make this statement of what you are, to find out what it is. Then you do sort of float away from that—instead of being embedded in it, you see yourself from a distance.

Gray: Do you feel yourself a woman writer or a writer who is a woman?

Lessing: I don't feel at all when I'm writing that I am a woman writing. I don't think it's a good thing to do that. I know, you see, that there's this matter of great bitterness among women writers. Their argument is that it's absolutely essential to write as a woman as long as you are persecuted.

Well, I disagree absolutely because I think you may be a second-class citizen, which we certainly are, but it doesn't prevent you from being a human being as well. It's another prison to think I am a woman writing this. It means that you deliberately narrow all your sensibilities. But I do see why women have to do it.

Gray: But you've been given so many labels at different times in your career. Did you ever feel yourself an African writer?

Lessing: No. I've never felt anything but me. First, there was this now-obsolete phrase, I was a "color-bar" writer; that is how I was presented. And then it changed and I was a Communist writer—they didn't say I was a writer about Communism, and those are two very different things. Then there was a whole string of things that I've been—one of them was feminist—that was *The Golden Notebook,* and they hadn't bothered to read it. Then there was the Sufi label, and they've dropped that one, I'm glad to say—oh yes, then mysticism. And now it's the space-fiction label, which really includes everything, so I suppose it's all right. I don't know what they'll think of next!

Acknowledging a New Frontier
Eve Bertelsen

Eve Bertelsen's interview was conducted in January 1984 and originally appeared in *Journal of Commonwealth Literature* 21 (1986). Copyright © 1986 by Eve Bertelsen. Reprinted with permission.

Bertelsen: Firstly, how do you feel about being regarded as an African or Southern African writer?

Lessing: Well, I think it's perfectly right that I should be, because I did after all spend twenty-five years growing up there and that's what forms people. Certainly everything that's made me a writer happened to me growing up in Rhodesia, in the old Rhodesia.

Bertelsen: And you don't object to that as a limiting label?

Lessing: Well, recently in Germany they gave me the Austrian State Prize for Literature for European Writing, because they regard me as a European writer, and that's fine too. The whole of Europe has been involved in colonialism for two or three hundred years. You can't separate Europe from what is now called the Third World.

Bertelsen: In your introduction to Schreiner's *African Farm* you said you read that novel when you were fourteen, and that it had a searing effect on you.

Lessing: I don't think it influenced me in the way I wrote. What influenced me was the fact that she wrote about Africa in a way you could take seriously. Because I had been reading all the English classics of which my parents' bookshelves were full, and it hadn't come home to me that there could be serious literature from Africa. So that was the influence. It started me off thinking about Africa in a new way, writing about Africa. I hadn't read any of the things that I could have read because I was very isolated.

Bertelsen: So it was more the subject matter, taking African material and forcing it into an artistic shape?

Lessing: No, it was Africa, you know. Because literatures all tend to be provincial. There was no suggestion in anything that I'd read that one could write a serious novel about Africa. There were a lot of very romantic and extraordinarily bad novels around, which you've probably never even heard of, and I can't even remember the names of them. I think Gertrude Page was one. And they were all full of a lot of very highly-colored landscape and quite appallingly melodramatic love stories. But I didn't take that serious, you see; I just discarded it. And then suddenly here was Olive Schreiner who was writing about Africa which was an absolute revelation to me.

Bertelsen: Do you feel any kinship with Nadine Gordimer?

Lessing: Well, our careers have been very twined together. I read the other day in an interview she gave that both our stories were published for the first time in the Johannesburg journal, *Trek*. We've always been bracketed together and we've had a lot of similar experiences. I think the difference was that I was brought up on the veld and she was brought up in a suburb of Johannesburg. That is very different, because her first short stories were of that experience and mine were all of the farm. But I think we have a great deal in common in fact.

Bertelsen: I have spoken to several major "Lessing critics" who feel that you've got a tremendous antipathy to the academy, to universities and literary critics generally. I wonder if that is founded, or if you feel they're being hypersensitive?

Lessing: Well, the *Doris Lessing Newsletter* I find acutely embarrassing actually—wouldn't you? I don't like the cult atmosphere at all. Critics are a different phenomenon. On the whole they tend to be extremely set in their own particular way, and I think they all pursue their own particular lines. Which has got nothing to do with writing. But it does interest people in writing, so OK.

Bertelsen: Getting narrower still, Anthony Chennells, at the University of Zimbabwe, has taken you up as a "Rhodesian" writer. He's written a thesis which includes your work, called *Settler Myths in the Southern Rhodesian Novel*—hundreds and hundreds of novels that were produced in Rhodesia up to the '70s. He takes a set of "protomyths"—the pastoral, the open veld, the myth of the noble savage, and looks at how they work in all these novels. He detects the same myths in your work, because they're what set up the Rhodesian mind, but says that you interrogate the myths, expose their limitations, whereas some of the other writers are just led by them, and use them in an unconscious way.

Lessing: Well, I haven't read him. But he's a friend of mine, of course. The thing is I don't see the veld as a myth but a fact. What is mythlike about being brought up on the veld? It's an experience which everyone who's had is changed for life by. So I don't understand the word "myth" in that context.

Bertelsen: I suppose by "myth" he means a sort of cultural organizing idea: people look at the veld and they think about openness and freedom, a sort of Garden of Eden that is waiting for them to appropriate, that kind of thing.

Lessing: Surely the experience comes first and the myth afterwards. It is very academic to think like this. You don't start with a myth. You start with an experience.

Bertelsen: As critics, I suppose, when we oversee a lot of work we begin to detect common themes. And then we start after the fact and suggest organizing ideas. The proposal is that within a specific culture people perceive in patterns they hold in common.

Lessing: Well, the common thing is presumably that all these people lived on the veld. This was the common experience. I'm sorry now I can't remember more of those novels, because I would be interested to read them now.

Bertelsen: What about people like Rider Haggard?

Lessing: Oh, Rider Haggard of course I read. But I don't regard that as Rhodesian.

Bertelsen: Do you know a woman called Hylda Richards who wrote a book called *Next Year Will be Better*, which is a diary of her life in the Lomagundi district?

Lessing: Oh yes, I've read that! I didn't know it was Lomagundi.

Bertelsen: This was the same time, the '20s and '30s when your parents would have been farming there. What interested me is that she talks from an uncritical point of view about "the native and his habits" or the servant problem. These appear again in your work but very much worked over and looked at with a sharp eye.

Lessing: Well, they sent me this book—Hylda Richards's book—and they asked me to write an introduction. And I said I wouldn't because this particular type of settler was very unsympathetic to me. She didn't like anything about the Africans, about the country, and also she was quite extraordinarily incompetent. She was a type. There are very many people who came out from England like this family, who never were successful. They never made a good go of it. They were always bolstered up by money from elsewhere, from "home." Of all the kinds of white people, this is the kind I find least sympathetic, because not even as white farmers did they contribute anything. They were just people who niggled and complained all the time. So I didn't want to be bothered with that one.

Bertelsen: There was one bit that fascinated me. Digging on a kopje nearby the house they find that there were fourteen hundred Shona huts and lots of broken pottery. It made me think that this is the real "chief's country" of your stories, where they are farming on top of an ancient native reserve.

Lessing: Yes, well, you know that the antheap material is very good for building and making bricks and floors. Several times, looking for this material, the Africans would come and say, "We're not going to go on digging there, because we've come on a burial," and there would be the bones and the pot and so forth, because they buried their dead in antheaps. I'd forgotten about that in the book.

Bertelsen: She also talks about the paraffin box furniture and the cretonne, and the mud walls and the ants eating away at things. But she's finally saying, "I endured all this—the British character—ability to endure this insufferable land."

Lessing: You see, everybody coming out from England with very little money did the same things. They nearly always went into pole-and-daga huts, a group of them; we all had paraffin box furniture, or there were African carpenters who made tables and things, quite well sometimes, in fact very well. And we all used a certain thick, white flour sack which made extremely good aprons and things like that. We all had the same contrivances until people got better off. My mother was extremely good at all that, as I recall. It was marvelous what she made with those flour sacks!

Bertelsen: Can I move on to ask about the degrees of generalization that occur when you're writing a fiction about Africa? You've said in several places that your stories were "not about the color problem, but about the atrophy of the imagination," or "the lack of feeling for all creatures that live under the sun." And elsewhere you've said "the states of Southern Africa in their political economy are all one." I wonder whether when you ask the reader to take a general meaning out of the stories you are downplaying the historical particulars—the fact that there were specific policies that caused the suffering and problems in Rhodesia at that historical time?

Lessing: Well, I've written so much about that I can hardly be accused of playing it down! About this color-bar thing: the point I was making was that it's not just the white man's attitude towards the black, but people's attitudes to each other in general—all over the world you'll have a dominant group despising the rest. This is the pattern. This is what interests me more and more. I've found it very limiting when people say, "You are a writer about color-bar problems". I wasn't writing only about color-bar problems. Not even my first volume was only about color-bar problems; there were a lot of other themes in it. I used the background as something to take off from. About the historic thing: South Africa and Rhodesia had a great deal in common, you see, because, as you know, Rhodesia usually passed laws that had been passed in South Africa, shortly afterwards. The whole legal structure of Rhodesia was patterned on South Africa. That became very clear over the Federation business. There was this brilliant idea to federate Rhodesia, Northern Rhodesia and Nyasaland against the will of the Africans. What they were overlooking was that the Africans in Rhodesia were very much more enslaved on the South African pattern than the Africans in Nyasaland and what was then Northern Rhodesia. And the Africans up north certainly did not want to come under the umbrella of Rhodesia, the stronger economically, because they knew that they would become enslaved to the same extent. And the interesting thing was that in this country absolutely not one of the big newspapers noticed this, including *The Guardian* which campaigned for federation (because *The Guardian* is a paper that tends to fall in love with grandiose ideas). And practically nobody in this country—excepting the left, the left of the Labour Party and some Communists and some people who knew Africa—pointed out that this was absolutely unworkable. And of course the thing didn't work. This demonstrated, as seen by the

Africans, how similar to South Africa Rhodesia was and is in some ways still. But what you want me to do is to write didactic novels.

Bertelsen: No, I don't, really! I'm just thinking how, for example, with Conrad's *Heart of Darkness*—did you see *Apocalypse Now?*

Lessing: Yes, I did.

Bertelsen: As the men move up the river you see them burning villages, all the napalm and the violence and the decadence of the soldiers, and as they move up the river these things somehow fall away and you end up with Good and Evil, and it's almost as if you then don't say, "There are real historical forces that can be confronted and perhaps the conditions improved."

Lessing: Well, I don't like that film, you see. I thought the first part was brilliant. I thought they got that experience of war, that kind of hectic mood of war, everybody a bit high on it, very well. But it has nothing in common with *Heart of Darkness* at all as far as I can see. And as for the ending, it was quite appalling and nonsensical.

Bertelsen: I suppose the similarity is that *Heart of Darkness* starts off talking about the scramble for Africa and about ivory and does end up making a mystical statement about "the evil that lurks in the heart of every man," so that then the colonials seem to get off rather lightly because we're saying this is just a universal problem.

Lessing: Well, it is a universal problem! When I was in Zimbabwe last year all the discussions went on as if this was a country isolated from all other countries. They were talking about Southern Africa as if it's not affected by what happens everywhere else. You can't see the race feelings as if they're confined to Southern Africa. For example, India is as full of color feeling, color prejudice, as anywhere. You still have the untouchables system, a horrendous system. I think as long as one sees these problems in isolation, so long you'll not be able to understand them. If you're going to say in Southern Africa that the problem is that the whites want to enslave the blacks and that's the end of it, you're overlooking a great deal else. I can illustrate this by a story which might strike you as somewhat fanciful, but it's true and it illustrates a recurring psychological set. There was a South African young woman fighting for various causes on behalf of the Africans, very idealistically romantic. She went up to Nigeria and found that in Nigeria there was corruption, and it was not a paradise, although run by blacks, and she committed suicide. Now people will say, "Oh dear, how very unbalanced of her," which it certainly was, but it's an extreme illustration of a certain strand of revolutionary thinking, which is when you get a revolution or a change of government and your side gets in, then everything is going to be all right. Everything is not going to be all right because the same—I don't like words like "evil" which seem to me somewhat romantic—the same psychological attitudes will then come into play in reverse. If I were living in Zimbabwe and were black, of course I would have fought as a guerilla/terrorist, whichever word is applicable. I'm sorry to be cynical, but one has to be a little bit. Maybe you can't fight as a freedom fighter without being somewhat blinkered about what's going to happen when your side gets in. I find this kind of romanticism and sentimentality not merely irritating but very *inefficient.*

Bertelsen: Do you think that fiction inevitably is going to find its general application; otherwise, it's just documenting something, like journalism?

Lessing: Well, you're really asking what is the use of literature. There are many different kinds of literature, aren't there? They range from the extremely highly worked and imaginative to some things not very far off fact, like factoids which is a new branch, quite interesting. But my attitude as a writer is, well, critics are bound to say something. Forgive me, but there are vast numbers of critics in the world and my attitude towards criticism is it is of no use to writers and of not much use to readers. It may be of use to other critics. But this kind of argument or discussion—what interest is it to anyone except people who are going to teach literature in universities? None whatsoever! To the people who actually read books and enjoy them, finding use for them, it is quite irrelevant.

Bertelsen: Can we talk about some of the work that you wrote before *The Grass Is Singing*—your stories in *Rafters* and *N.B.* and poems in *New Rhodesia?* How do you feel about that early work? You've never thought of republishing it?

Lessing: No, it's not worth republishing. It's mostly extremely bad. Some of the short stories were quite promising, but they're not very good.

Bertelsen: There's a book of *Fourteen Poems* that I found very nice. There's one called "Dark Girl's Song" which seemed to say in a nutshell so many of the things that you were saying later, catching that whole European in Africa.

Lessing: They're OK, but I'm not basically a poet, you see. Now there's a great difference between the poems of *New Rhodesia* and the poems of *Fourteen Poems.* The first were very bad beginner's verses and I'd be very happy if they vanished from view, because I don't think they contribute anything. There were some short stories which I think have been lost forever, but they'll be no loss I assure you. But some of them are interesting, because they are obviously the work of a writer. But they had a lack of control, and they tended to be overwritten, as beginners' work always is, and they lack simplicity. Why revive something that is not up to much? There's a very great step between those stories and the stories in *This Was the Old Chief's Country.* I suppose the one thing that could be of use to understanding writers is the kind of rawness of the experience. To publish immature work interests scholars, OK. But the experience of that time might be of use. But when writers become well known and have become the property of other people, everything gets tidied up and becomes respectable. Those years, particularly the last years before I left, were quite extraordinarily raw—that's the word for it—painful, blundering, difficult and generally a mess. But in writers' lives these periods always tend to be prettied up and glossed over. So no, I don't really see that it's of all that interest.

Bertelsen: I think, on the one hand, there are always people looking for a completely virgin text to work on. But there is also a real biographical interest in the sort of "intractable material," experience that hasn't really been fully worked. Well, that was before *The Grass Is Singing.* You once said that you wrote *The Grass Is Singing* in a vacuum, that there was no African equivalent.

Lessing: What did I mean by that? I suppose I meant a literary vacuum.

Bertelsen: You said you'd read a lot of English writers, and I find in *The Grass Is Singing* quite a lot of passages that are very reminiscent of *Lady Chatterley's Lover.* Where, for example, Mary comes upon Moses washing himself. This is very similar to Connie Chatterley coming across Mellors, isn't it?

Lessing: Well, I'd read all of Lawrence and Virginia Woolf of the moderns, but it actually astounds me that it's reminiscent of *Lady Chatterley's Lover!* I suppose they influenced me. The thing is I read so much then, you see. Because I was very isolated, I read day and night. Luckily I read very fast. It'd be very hard to say what influenced me and what didn't.

That incident of Moses being seen washing came from something quite real, a similar incident. But I didn't put it in as it happened, simply because I thought and I still think it would have been wrong; it was too directly sexual. My mother sent me to call the "cook-boy" and he was standing naked out the back of the house under a tree. But what I saw, being I don't know how old I was, twelve or thirteen, was this classical sight of a naked penis which I had never, ever seen in my life before, because my parents—that was not the atmosphere I was brought up in, I'd never seen one. The thing is, you see, even as I describe it, it gets too strong for that book. Mary wouldn't have noticed a penis, I'm sure. So that story was written out of experience. One of my "formative" experiences, to use a cliché, was listening to them talking on the verandahs, that is the grown-ups talking on the farm verandahs. And the children, as it were, didn't exist because there was nothing for us, there was no social place for children. We hung around verandahs listening, bored stiff. There were men at one end and women at the other end. And I remember listening to the men talking about a woman, a white woman who had recently come, who allowed her "boy" to button up her dress and brush her hair, which coming from South Africa, I don't have to tell you, is absolutely impossible! I don't know if it's impossible now. It was so impossible then that it stopped your mind dead. The tones of their voices went into that book. I wish I could have a tape recording of that talk now.

When I went out to Zimbabwe last year I had an accident which laid me up on a verandah, my son's verandah actually, for a long time, weeks. And I was listening to the talk, the talk on the white verandahs which, since they're bitterly anti-Mugabe, of course, has got a whole new element. But a lot of it is identical with what I heard, timeless. It's quite extraordinary how the decades can roll by and wars come and go, and they still say the same things in the same tone of voice. Looking back, there was an element that has been lost, though. I remember my father and the white farmers saying things like, "Well, of course in a hundred years they'll all throw us out into the sea, and quite right," they'd say with a kind of unscrupulous chuckle. Now that was, as it were, on a different level altogether from anything they would fight for or say they believed. You've got these different strands going, you see, running in this talk, and the gossip about each other. So much comment and criticism which was never verbalized. But, looking back it's quite extraordinary how few quarrels there were. I can't remember any. I don't think they could've afforded quarrels. But they certainly gossiped and criticized all the time— they never stopped.

In Zimbabwe I find they still talk from morning to night. They get up grumbling and they go to bed grumbling. It's quite appalling, about everything! I mean a lot of things go wrong, I don't have to tell you, but they make everything worse, and they create problems. I'll describe a little scene which you won't find surprising. In Umtali, Mutari, in the bank, I wanted to cash cheques. I arrived there just before the doors opened and already a queue of about four whites stood there bitching about the incompetence of the blacks. They just stood there with these *angry bitter* faces. You think, For God's sake, you're going to kill yourselves with hatred if you don't stop it! Which they are, of course, one way and another. So then, the doors do not open at the stroke of nine, or half past eight I think it was, because if they could see the man who was looking at these faces, and he was thinking, I'll just let them stew, he was thinking, these hate-filled faces! Finally the doors open, and then we sit in a line. There was only one person available; there should have been more, true. He happened to be a very correctly dressed, very proper man. There he was, dealing with everyone with this cold, hard correctness. And they were standing there with these nagging voices—nag nag nag nag nag! Then finally when I get to him, he looked at my passport. His face changed—he recognized me. "Ah," he said, "I've read your books!" Can you imagine? A bank teller—I was so *flattered!* So you see, you get him to chat. And this person is transformed to the most charming, funny, witty man. I don't have to tell you the queue is absolutely *enraged!* And I go out, and I think, If these people were not as stupid as they are, they could be living in a landscape full of charming, witty and intelligent people. It's so very sad, what's happening.

Bertelsen: It seems to me that you were incredibly aware of the divisiveness of the society behind this front of white unity. You know, the different groups—Jews and Greeks and English. In some of your stories the civil service versus the farmers.

Lessing: Oh well, that's so Rhodesian. I don't know if it still exists. In the district I was brought up in the big division was a snobbish one. On our side of the district was roughly the dark red soil, maize-growing soil, and of course, they grew a lot of tobacco. They tended to be nearly all Scottish around us and lower-middle class. I had met them at that time in literature, so I could identify them. They were very frugal, very religious indeed, and they tended to be hard-drinking, the men. And on the whole they were pretty awful with their labor, quite appalling! And they had a very hard edge in their voices when they talked about the other side of the district where that "fast lot" were, who had horses, and were richer, tending to have private income, and went in for wife-swapping. Well, not wife-swapping, but they divorced. They were mostly English, Irish. And so while these two sides would meet at gymkhanas and so on, there was no socializing, or very little. But my mother and father tended to visit with some of them. Interestingly, because it didn't strike me at the time at all, but they'd been in the war as soldiers, and they were all wounded. They'd lost arms and legs and so on, and they were lucky to be alive. So when we went across to the other side we tended to visit people who'd been in the war, and that's what the men talked about, the trenches. It was a very big division.

When I went back I was told that Banket, that's the district where I was brought up, is now known as the rich farmers' area. Which quite amazes me because I can't see it like this. Most people were very poor. Rich, of course, compared with the Africans, but most of them lived with the petrol-box furniture, dyed curtains from flour sacks. This kind of level was terribly common. And what we were seeing was the birth of the big farmer. Of course, the sons have taken over the farms, so presumably they are now these rich farmers. What difference has it made to their lives, if any? I can't see what difference it could make really, except that they have better cars. The Banket of my stories might very well have vanished for all I know. I wanted very badly to go back, but I wanted my brother to go with me. But he said there was no way of seeing where it was. And obviously it disturbed him terribly, the whole experience; he was very upset. So I don't know. On the other hand, he said that he was so upset he wasn't even looking too closely. You know, for all I know there was a heap of rubble that had been the house. But on the other hand, what heap of rubble could there have been from pole-and-daga, from thatch-and-locks, after all that time?

Bertelsen: I was thinking just then about the story called "The Antheap" where you have Dirk and the colored boy making these sculptures that get eaten by the ants. I can't help linking what you're saying with the changes in your style, being quite ready to slough off old forms of looking at things. Does that come partly from this business of living in a pole-and-daga house? Allowing things to just sink back into the land, and not looking for a permanence? Or am I being farfetched now?

Lessing: No, certainly, no, for all I know it did. It's very hard to know. I was certainly brought up with impermanence because you can't live in that kind of house without feeling it. Our entire world was in brackets, in parentheses. Our entire life was a war against insects, particularly ants. The whole kopje was full of antnests and there was no way of abolishing them; you were always digging them up. It was all quite terrible looking back on it, this war that we fought, and how the new tunnels would suddenly appear on a wall. So probably, yes. But I think probably more important than living in a very impermanent house was the fact that I left

Persia to come to Rhodesia. Then we were six months in England. To a child it's an eternity. I remember that six months as going on forever and ever. So you can say that I made two big changes.

And then I was in a place called "Lilfordia" for six weeks while my parents went off to look for a farm, which was one of the most appalling experiences of my childhood. Have you ever heard of Boss Lilford? [A prominent white supremacist gunned down on his farm by guerrillas in 1985—E.B.] It's a very famous name, he's a great white, a man that people said was behind Smith, very powerful. Well, Lilfordia at that time was a group of huts—the beginning of this farm—and they had paying guests, and I and my brother were left there. We came to the country and we were left there with a very cold and unkind girl. She was a twenty-one-year-old Irish girl, and I often wonder what's happened to her, because I've only heard about her through my mother, who disliked her intensely. For all I know she was the most charming person in the world, but I will never know now, I suppose. She certainly had no idea about children, whatever else she had, and I was miserable. I started fighting with my poor mother as early as that, like cutting up all her evening dresses with scissors on the ship, because we were left downstairs when they went to dinner. I can't remember a time when I wasn't fighting with my poor mother. And when she went, I remember a time of fierce and terrible misery that's never been anything like it in my life since. Because they'd just, as it were, vanished—you know how parents vanish—leaving me with my little brother whom I felt very protective towards, with this girl. She was called a governess; she was equivalent of the au pair, I suppose. And we were with a group of older children who bullied us horribly. I'm saying this, because that period, while it doesn't sound like it, for me was another lifetime. And then we went to the farm. So I'd already moved a lot of times as far as I felt it. By the time I got to the farm it was only one more in a long string of places I'd lived in. And I've lived in so many places since. I don't seem able to stay. I wonder how long I'll stay here, for example. I've been here four years and I think, Well, something will happen because it always does.

Bertelsen: To get back to *The Grass Is Singing.* I was thinking how in that story Mary's personality is very much determined by her upbringing, the poverty of the family situation, emotional and economic. There's a sort of determinism in that story which also comes into the early Martha Quest books. Does that come from your political attitudes at the time?

Lessing: No, I would say it was the other way around. My political attitudes at the time came from watching. Mary specifically was based on somebody

I knew who interested me, because at the age of nearly forty she was like a young girl and lived the life of a girl. In town she was this kindly elder sister to everybody, still playing sports, and wearing shorts, and she was one of the girls. And we sometimes used to go on picnics out into various places. And she used to sit on a rock with her feet drawn up. You know when you write a novel you have a lot of ideas floating around in your head, and sometimes they float together and sometimes they don't. Well, I was thinking about this newspaper cutting, which I *did* find, this inexplicable murder. I was thinking about the tones of voice of the men talking about this woman on the verandahs, and I was thinking about this woman I knew. What would she be like if she went out into the veld with that kind of *direct physical contact,* that kind of up-to-your-neck-in-fighting, physically, all the time. What would such a girl do, such a woman do? Well, I couldn't see her surviving, you see. But about determinism. I think that the patterns of people's lives are determined by their society and by their characters and their upbringing, of course. But what I'm interested in in people is not what makes them like everybody *else,* and what you can expect because they had this and that upbringing, but something else that can fight them out of it or make them different.

Bertelsen: I read *The Grass Is Singing* a long time ago. Then coming back to it much later, it strikes me that so many of the themes of your later stories are there. For example, in the opening chapter there's a tremendous sense of what people now call "ideology," the unspoken silences. The English character is feeling his way almost dumbly into that colonial mentality. Was that again just an intuitive description of the kinds of conversation you used to hear?

Lessing: Of course I remember all the things that were never said. It's what is always interesting isn't it, the unsaid thing? But I should imagine there were more unsaid things in a place like the old Rhodesia. Probably in South Africa now things are said more than they used to be?

Bertelsen: Well, I don't know. We've evolved a whole new set of euphemisms. We call people by different labels. I've seen in my lifetime the transition from "kaffir" to "bantu" to "native" to "black."

Lessing: "Munts"—what about "munts"?

Bertelsen: People will still talk about "munts" in unguarded moments. I don't know if because the language changes, those structures of feeling change totally. I suppose they do to some extent. And as the blacks unionize and gain more authority, and their spokesmen are more articulate, a different kind of attitude develops towards black people, I suppose, than when one only saw them as servants or laborers. But about *The Grass Is Singing.*// I was wondering about the epigraph from *The Waste Land.* Had you been reading it quite intensively at the time? Because it strikes me that the dryness and waiting for rain is so much, again, a physical aspect of Rhodesia. April the cruelest of months becomes the Rhodesian October, doesn't it?

Lessing: Yes, well, I was soaked in Eliot and Yeats and Hopkins, but I don't think that I was influenced more by one writer than another. I was certainly influenced by all the Russians because I found so many parallels, in Tolstoy, for example. The kind of talk I used to hear, which used to be more idealistic than it is now, was terribly similar to this kind of talk in Tolstoy about the serfs, perpetual brooding about them. At certain periods we tend to romanticize them, in our case, the African peasant. And black poverty. Which always makes me furious, because I don't see anything romantic about poverty. It's horrible and makes people brutal and miserable, nearly always. It's a sentimentality that goes with being part of affluent Europe. Fascinating. I went to Munich last year, and I spoke to a group of sixth-formers in a girls' school. Now Germany is suffering acute problems, unemployment and genuine hardship. All they wanted to talk about was Africa and Nicaragua. And I kept saying, "How about your own backyard?" The thing was, they weren't interested in it. They were much more fascinated by some romantic peasant. It's that noble savage again!

Bertelsen: Taking a line from the noble savage: in *The Grass Is Singing* there's an identification going on between Mary's darkness, that repressed part of herself, and Moses and the darkness of the bush. And at the end you say, "the bush avenged itself." Aren't you identifying, somehow, Africa and the African with this "darkness," even with the white man's past? This creates problems with Moses.

Lessing: You know I'm not aware of it. There was a long time when I thought that it was a pity I ever wrote Moses like that, because he was less of a person than a symbol. But it was the only way I *could* write him at that time since I'd never *met* Africans excepting the servants or politically, in a certain complicated way. But now I've changed my mind again. I think it was the right way to write Moses, because if I'd made him too individual it would've unbalanced the book. I think I was right to make him a bit unknown. As I was thinking the other day, Why did that probably long-dead black servant kill that woman all those years ago in Lomagundi? For no reason whatsoever, apparently. I mean, well, why did he? He went off to the court saying nothing, explaining nothing. And presumably was hanged. And that was that.

Bertelsen: In a way it's the final white fear, isn't it—this business of "your servants will turn against you" or the black man raping a white woman? Probably rising from guilt that the white in Africa has about black people?

Lessing: What was really extraordinary was that there were all these isolated white farmsteads, miles apart from each other, just houses with the bush twenty yards away with a newly conquered people who were savagely ill-treated. And yet I can't remember people being particularly afraid. They would say to girls, "Don't go walking around in the bush because you'll be raped." But we did go walking around in the bush; it was more of a convention than anything else. There were no locks on the house. Anyone could've raped me fifteen times a night. The doors were unlocked, stood open all night, because I liked the night. This was a very unafraid community in fact! Well, this whole thing was irrational. I can't remember anybody being raped. I don't think any white women ever were raped, were they? They certainly looked in through the windows when the district had parties. There were always a group of black people watching these goings on. And I've now got a very sad, sad story. Somebody, about five or six years ago from what was then Salisbury University, said to the students, "Why do you lie around in the grass and fuck and neck and get drunk and be sick and all this kind of thing? Why do you do it?" And they said, "Well, we've been watching you do it all these years, so why shouldn't we do it? This is civilized behavior!"

Bertelsen: About your stories: you did collect the African stories separately. Was that a publisher's marketing decision, or was it your own decision to have African and non-African story collections?

Lessing: The thing was that I'd got so many short stories going by that time, and they tended to divide into two, so it was convenient. I wanted to have the African stories separate because as they came out they were in volumes mixed up with other stories.

Bertelsen: How do you decide that there's a short story forming as opposed to a longer fiction? Is there a different sort of feeling?

Lessing: Yes, because a novel tends to be a long process and a short story something small crystallizing out. Though I have started off short stories that have become longer, it's a completely different process. Something works itself out in a novel which it doesn't in a short story, really.

Bertelsen: The five novels of *Children of Violence* represent the other extreme—a very long work. Did you at the time see the whole sequence as one continuous *Bildungsroman?* Because in *The Four-Gated City* you mention that genre. Did you project it as a novel of education and experience?

Lessing: Well, it was after I'd written it that I simply reintroduced the word into English criticism, because it wasn't around. A great many novels are, in fact, these long descriptions of somebody learning something, which the Germans have a word for and we don't.

Bertelsen: And of course the Hardy and Lawrence that you talk about were doing that in a way, in Paul Morel and Jude. But what hit many of us in Africa about *Children of Violence* is the way it reads as one's own biography.

Lessing: Well, though I did actually think it was going to be five, there's a difference in tone, of course, after volume three. What had happened was, of course, that I'd had a lot of hard experience between the two, and it gets less and less autobiographical as I go along. After I'd written *The Grass Is Singing* and I'd written the short stories, I wanted to write another novel. And I had all these unbelievably complicated ideas in my mind as I recall, and then I suddenly remember very clearly thinking, Why do all this when I was having this experience which is really quite extraordinary? So why not write more or less? So I had to decide about the more or less, which I know has interest to the critics. But to me, I don't think it's important. I wanted to try to use experience as a framework, and not write too directly about my parents who in fact are pretty, you can use the word, "mythologized." I mean, both their characters are there but they're very broadly sketched actually, both of them, particularly my father, who became dreamier and dreamier as life went on, and began to talk like an ancient sage the older he got, very impersonal he got. But the last two are quite different. What happened in the meantime was that I'd written *The Golden Notebook,* you see, at that point, which really changed me totally.

Bertelsen: So it was dutifully that you returned to *Landlocked?* I mean, you must have felt strange about having to continue that series after *The Golden Notebook.*

Lessing: No, I wanted to write about that time, and I still don't think I've done it right. I wanted to write about that extraordinary time of hanging around in Rhodesia waiting to be able to leave, which was quite the worst time in my life.

Bertelsen: October figures quite a lot in that again, October "like cord-ite." You use that terrible claustrophobia before the rain, which is so geographical and yet has this mythological overtone. And the father and mother in the books: you say they are mythologized to some extent. You use strong images of sleep and numbness with the mother. She becomes an enchantress, telling Martha to sleep, to rest, "holding sleep and forgetfulness in her two hands." These themes come across both realisti-cally and mythologically.

Lessing: Are you interested to know personally what it was? Because I can tell you in a few words: my mother was an extremely talented, very energetic and very frustrated woman who had nothing to put all her energy into excepting her children, which was fairly classical in those days, and I think perhaps it's changed now. Also she was a nurse and she *liked* it when we were ill. This is pre-Freud, and psychology hadn't hit them, you know. I don't think she could exist now, certainly not in the West, not without a certain amount of self-knowledge. She *did* want us to be ill. She had all this energy going, you see, and you had to get out from under it. But all my friends were in the same situation—that was what's interesting. I do not now meet women who've had to fight powerful mothers; it seems to be a phenomenon that's passed. But for my genera-tion of the women I knew, everyone without exception fought a battle against a mother, who also was a victim, of course, because they're very pathetic people.

Bertelsen: So she wasn't at all like the rather useless, frustrated women who were just yearning to go "home" all the time.

Lessing: Well, of course, she wanted to go home, but the thing was she worked very hard. And she did make a good job of an impossible situation, like my father getting iller and iller and the children whom she didn't approve of. My mother's life was a tragedy; she got nothing ever that she wanted, ever. She made this great choice: was she going to be the matron of St. George's or was she going to get married? And then she went to Persia, which she liked. All very jolly—she was very social. That probably was the high point of her life I should think, five years in Persia, which my father loathed every minute of, because he wasn't social. He hated it, you see, all these jolly and musical evenings; he loathed every second. So from then on I think nothing ever went right for my poor mother, including her daughter who was a perpetual misery! I mean, some joker arranged that I should be born to my poor mother; it was really unfortunate for both of us. And then my brother. His way of resisting was to be very passive and smiling and go-and-do-it-anyway sort of thing. So I'm desperately sorry for her, actually.

Bertelsen: The particular atmospheres that you create—the hotel ballroom and the club and the Avenues. I wonder if you can remember very much about those places? I was looking at an old tourist brochure of Salisbury 1950 produced by the Salisbury City Council, and these things jumped out of the pages: Meikle's Ballroom, and a dance at the club with those waiters...

Lessing: The club I'm told is exactly the same. When I went back they said if I went to the club I would see that nothing whatsoever's changed.

Bertelsen: Integrated now?

Lessing: No, apparently it's still mostly white. You know, blacks don't necessarily want to be with us, really; they don't find us the nicest people in the world! I saw such a terrible scene in a restaurant outside Salisbury. All white, in the bar which was absolutely packed, where I was standing with my brother and some friends of his. A black man came in, obviously for the first time, and you could see that he was coming in incredulous that he could. And in spite of himself he was servile and apologetic, and you could see him hating himself for it. And when he asked for a drink the barman was kind and condescending. And he said, "Thank you, boss." That's the kind of scene you see all over Zimbabwe, which some young novelist is writing about, I hope. Well, they're all still there. Meikle's has vanished, alas. It has become a totally anonymous, flavorless modern hotel, and they've got photographs of what it used to be on the walls as "the historic past" which upset me slightly, as you can imagine. The Grand Hotel was pulled down. The Salisbury Club is going on.

Bertelsen: And the houses in the Avenues—do they still look pretty much the same, with their servants, nannies, etc?

Lessing: That hasn't changed. They don't have so *many* servants. In the houses I saw, where they previously had a cook, houseboy, a piccanin, and probably a nanny, and even a garden boy, they will have one who does nearly all the work they all did before. And I noticed on the farms that I went to, they all have at least two, and the second is a garden boy, which I should have thought was a terrific luxury. They don't think it so, of course. But the relationship between the masters and servants hasn't changed at all, absolutely not. The whites *can't* change, you know, the Rhodesians. I'm not talking about the ones that *have* changed, but the ones on the farms, that won't change.

Bertelsen: They still have a lot of clout because they control most of the productive farming in the country, don't they?

Lessing: Well, they do produce nearly all the food, and some of the ones I spoke to are extremely cold about it. They look north to Zambia and say, "There were nine hundred farmers and now there're ninety, and we're going to be like gold dust if we keep our heads down and just wait." There was a marvelous farmer I saw, so inventive. He'd made all these machines out of scrap iron, machines for the farm, everything you could think of, an entire blacksmith's shop made out of scrap. He was a passionate farmer. And his wife. Well, they've gone to South Africa. They can't stand not being bosses! And they're quite prepared to go and take second-rate jobs in South Africa, just to go on being bosses. They're pathetic. Apart from the loss to Zimbabwe, because they need those skills still.

Bertelsen: I wonder if you remember a Labour Party meeting that you describe, apparently a real meeting in the Harare Hall in February 1944, which caused the big split?

Lessing: Well, yes—because the whole thing was impossible, you see! Mrs. Maasdorp was mayor at that time. She made it possible to have a hall in Harare and for white people to go down, it would have been impossible otherwise. And what was actually said at this meeting was so innocuous, I can't begin to tell you. But it was as if the revolution had taken place. And of course, apart from the fact of living in a permanent fog of poison letters and filth pushed through her letter box, she lost her seat, which for her was a tragedy. You see, these characters vanish from history. There was a man called Charles Ollie no one's ever heard of, who ran his own magazine, who was her enemy. He was also a councilor who represented the opposite side. He would write long letters about the blacks having just come down from the trees and all this kind of thing. And he had immense influence. But when I say to people "Charles Ollie" they don't remember anything about him. It's quite amazing! Perhaps they're ashamed. I hope that's it.

Bertelsen: What about the Quest story? You did choose the name "Quest" for Martha.

Lessing: I did that on purpose. I wanted to put a name to some part of the character.

Bertelsen: I was wondering whether, as the series continued, you became more conscious of creating continuity by reinforcing that quest myth as she moves through the various phases of her life?

Lessing: Do you mind me saying that all the time you're talking as if the writer imposes an idea on the material instead of writing from inside!

Bertelsen: But when you're writing a long series like that and things have come between like *The Golden Notebook* and a very sharpened awareness about form and what the realist novel is doing, and then you had to go back and write *Landlocked* and *The Four-Gated City*. Wasn't there a certain necessity to create continuity with the earlier novels? Could you still be writing intuitively?

Lessing: What I was basically trying to do was to get the atmosphere of that particular time, which was intangible and difficult. That was my preoccupation. A very demoralized atmosphere it was—very flat after the war, certainly in my personal life, the personal lives of everybody I knew round about then. But I don't think I had any particular difficulty in it. You just had to think yourself back to that time.

Bertelsen: You were writing about the '40s in Rhodesia from London in the mid-'50s, and '60s, with hindsight. Your attitude towards politics had obviously changed quite a lot?

Lessing: Well, the fifth book was not at all autobiographical. I simply wanted to convey what London was like, and I tried to find ways of doing it. And I also wanted to find a fairly typical English upper-class family. It's surprisingly common to find in them these political differences. You know, you'll find one a Communist or one extreme left Labour or one a Tory or something, within the same family. I've met this several times, so I thought I would use that.

Bertelsen: So you don't think that the hindsight of having been in London for quite a long time affected the way in *Landlocked* and *Ripple* *from the Storm,* you described the political situation in Rhodesia in the '40s? In other words, perhaps you were being more critical, satirical, of it than you might have been if you'd written it directly at the time of having the experience?

Lessing: How could I have written it directly?

Bertelsen: Well, I mean *Martha Quest* and *A Proper Marriage* were written closer to the experience in a way, before you'd been in London for such a long time. So it seems to me that there's a more critical reassessment going on in the next two books because you've actually become much more sophisticated.

Lessing: *Martha Quest, A Proper Marriage* and *Ripple from the Storm* are all pretty critical. There's a great distance between me and what I'm writing about, particularly *Ripple from the Storm,* because that was all about politics at the time I was living through it. I take the view that everyone who goes through that experience is really crazy while they do it. I mean, we genuinely believed, for example, the whole world would be Communist in about ten years' time, or it might take fifteen to create Utopia, things like this. You know, you can't call this anything else but crazy! And also I think in the war people were crazy without knowing it. So I certainly had a very cool and different approach to all that when I came to write it. I was much more interested in *Landlocked* in the atmosphere; I was interested in creating this kind of feeling of disillusionment which follows the elation of wars. It starts obviously in the army, in the fighting forces, and it spreads everywhere. You can't fight without this kind of being slightly crazy, and I think that in war everybody is slightly crazy. Even in remote places like Rhodesia. We went through the war in a kind of elation. It expressed itself in politics and everybody was high on the war, and then all that goes and you're left with the reality.

Bertelsen: I want to pursue the "Quest" story, although you rebuke me, and say I'm finding artificial constructs binding the books together. But it strikes me if one takes something like the image of the Ideal City which occurs throughout the whole series. When Martha first has this vision in the veld in *Martha Quest* it seems to be very much like a Marxist vision of a classless society. Then it moves through being a symbol of personal harmony in those middle books. And by the time we get to the end, we've got London as a final "false city" and Faris Island with the pure notes of the flute being almost a mandala of mystic harmony. That one image both binds the books and changes quite a lot. Would you agree with that?

Lessing: Not particularly. The first one certainly couldn't have been Marxist. You know that Marxism took over a lot of Utopian ideas. Marxism didn't create these ideas of harmony and happiness and equality. It comes from religion. Utopias long predate Marxism. The idea of paradise and heaven comes from Christianity, not from Marxism. So Marxism is in fact structured like Christianity with Hell being capitalism, and suffering redeeming you. It's exactly the same structure. And the idea of paradise in the classless society. It predates even Christianity. It's the old Golden Age theme.

Bertelsen: So where would that sort of dream come from in Martha's life?

Lessing: From literature of course. Her books, her house was full of books. It'd come from the Bible. Not that I read the Bible much.

Bertelsen: I was wondering if the sort of swings of mood that we see in Martha, her lassitude that seems to be reinforced by her mother, and then her energetic imagination and will to action that takes over when she leaves her marriage and moves into politics, and also later when she engages with Lynda Coldridge, are those two parts of Martha autobiographical? Or is this just a common situation for women?

Lessing: I think it's pretty common, the lassitude and the energy. The energy in the war came from, as I say, the elation of the war, and because everyone was high on this release of political belief. It happened all over the place, I discovered, this springing into existence of Utopian groups of one kind or another. We called ours "Communist," but it wasn't terribly Communist. Energy always comes from the undivided; all fanatics have energy. When you're doing any one thing singlemindedly, you have energy.

Bertelsen: I've tended to think of the lassitude having a lot to do with Martha giving in to her social fate, giving in to her mother and the club and all the rituals that society was trying to impose on her. And the energy as something very positive. But you're saying that the energy belongs to the fanatic? Wasn't it the energy that made her pull herself out of that social fate of being a Rhodesian wife in the suburbs?

Lessing: Yes, it was—as if that life had really got very little to do with me. Which sounds quite ordinary, since I was living it rather competently; I really was doing it all very well! This again is fairly common—that young women will go along with whatever they're doing with great efficiency, and then suddenly say, "What am I doing this for?" But talking about energy, this absolutely pure energy which kept a whole lot of us going. God knows, I don't think we ever slept two or three hours a night for a couple of years! It was because of our pure and burning faith with which we, only we and a few like us, were going to transform the world! Well, you know, you've probably lived through it. We were the people who understood everything. We would deal with all that lot out there who were so stupid and didn't know anything. Well, this kind of fanaticism creates energy, and it's certainly very pleasant to live through. There you have a recipe for a lot of hard work and sacrifice. But actual serious living, unfortunately, is usually divided and many-stranded.

Bertelsen: But although you speak rather disparagingly of it, it was that energy that managed to extricate Martha from a typical colonial fate, that criticism of her situation.

Lessing: I wasn't speaking disparagingly. It's a good thing that she left. The only thing is, if you're talking about the two strands in her nature, one full of energy and one divided, I would say the divided state is preferable, because at least you're accommodating a whole lot of different possibilities, whereas that simple pure energy always goes with a narrow direction and a focus on one thing. Which is all right if you want something done. I like to have it if I'm writing a novel. You've got something to do, and you do it.

Bertelsen: Do you find in your own experience that the moods alternate and constantly recur?

Lessing: Well, no. I find that these moods of pure energy occur hardly at all, simply because I am not single-minded anymore. I can't be.

Bertelsen: And when you're writing?

Lessing: Yes, but I live a very complicated life with all the other things going on too. I sometimes watch the approach of such a mood. When I am passionately angry about something, I think that something is terribly wrong and something else is terribly right, and I identify with the right and I can hate the wrong. This produces this pure flame of energy. But it's extremely suspect, and I try to suppress it, because life isn't like that, not at all.

Bertelsen: Is there a certain misanthropy about Martha? She doesn't seem to ever completely ally herself, although she's committed to the Group. Always this critical edge, about Jasmine, about everybody?

Lessing: Well, it's certainly what saved me as a person. The funny thing is that I was discussing this—I still know Jasmine—said she had it too, you see. It's very interesting that people who are apparently total fanatics working twenty-two hours a day, and who never say anything that isn't some dogmatic cliché, have this same disquiet that sort of says, "Well, that's pretty silly!"

Bertelsen: I love the send-off that Jasmine gives at the end of *Landlocked:* "Barricades!" And Martha just looks at her very sardonically. It also interests me that I keep talking about "Martha" and you talk about yourself. Perhaps it's easier that way?

Lessing: Well, it's easier.

Bertelsen: I wonder why Martha couldn't, in the role of mother, accept domesticity, the mothering instinct? And yet when she goes to London and is with people who are outside herself, the Coldridges, she manages to be very useful and mother Lynda and Mark? Is it only possible in a situation where it's not conventionally lined up for her?

Lessing: Well, I suppose she was older. In *The Four-Gated City* various aspects of myself were parceled out between the different characters. They were a fairly interesting map of myself, that roll of characters, actually.

Bertelsen: So Martha isn't a central persona anymore. The style becomes much more complicated. You said *The Golden Notebook* had decentered things?

Lessing: No, I didn't say it had decentered. I said it had got a different tone. What has happened is that the tone of *Landlocked* is flat and heavy and rather disillusioned. It's not decentered, because Martha's still the center of the book. But *The Four-Gated City* is something completely different. There's nothing autobiographical in it.

Bertelsen: So Lynda and Mark and Martha and all the others are parts of a single character really, and people who try to trace an easy narrative line are reading the book wrongly?

Lessing: People like things to be autobiographical. But when I say this is not all autobiographical or it is autobiographical, to my mind this is of no importance. What is important is what I've done with an experience which you say yourself is very common. I mean, there's a lot even in

Martha Quest that I invented, you see. But I don't see that it matters all that much. And it is of no help to the historians of Harare University who say, "What happened? Did this meeting happen?" Well, I can only reply that partly it did and partly it didn't—that's not the point! And about this business of misanthropy. Was I critical of people? I probably was. I can't remember. What I remember and can't get over is the unbelievably social life I led then. So many people all the time. I and my second husband, Gottfried Lessing—our flat was always full of people, the left of various kinds, very mixed. And I used to cook for, God knows, fifteen to twenty people on two hot plates, as a matter of course. Seldom went to bed without someone asleep in the bath or on the floor or somewhere. This went on for years! My poor husband hated it, but that's what I was like then. Far from being a misanthropist, I collected people!

Bertelsen: Perhaps that's a strong word. I suppose being friends with a writer always puts people slightly on edge, because you're not sure whether you're going to appear in a slightly altered light, but recognizable.

Lessing: Well, I've had a conflict all my life about a very social side of my nature and what I need to write. Unlike some of my friends who thrive on social life and writing, I don't. I have to be terribly quiet and preferably solitudinous and, if you like, misanthropic, to write. But on the other hand I love giving parties and having dinner parties or people round. So this has fought in me ever since I can remember. But it certainly wasn't fighting in the period of *Landlocked,* because I don't think I've ever been as social in my life as that time, and the time before that. And the thing is, you know, people like to be in books. Quite amazing, you'd think that they wouldn't but if I say, "But I've never put you in a book," they're furious! In the period of *Landlocked* the outward life I was leading was extremely social. Because while the actual Communist group had dissolved as an entity—people had just vanished in all directions—here were a great many left-wing people around of various kinds, not just Communists. And passionately interested in politics. And our flat was always full of them. There were all kinds of discussion groups and things going on all the time. So it was a very, very social life. Inwardly we were having a very bad time because the marriage was—we knew was not going to last. But that's another thing.

Bertelsen: In *Landlocked* there is a strong sense of outer activity and inner deadness.

Lessing: Well, it was the worst time of my life. Outwardly I was extremely social and energetic; I had a job I was doing. That's the time when I was typing for Parliament. I was writing *The Grass Is Singing,* and God knows what I wasn't doing! But it was in fact a very bad time. People! Full every minute of the day with people! God knows how I ever wrote that book— I can't imagine!

Bertelsen: At the end of *The Four-Gated City* we have this survival after the apocalypse where Martha ends up with the mutated children. I'm skeptical about this idea of a remnant surviving, because in my evangelical background I was brought up to aspire to be one of such a remnant. It seems to be a preoccupation of yours that a group of people with higher faculties will be the ones who will survive and recreate society from its ashes. Isn't there a chance it will just be a terrible abortive mess? Romantics like Coleridge and Lawrence also wanted to take a few carefully selected people and start a new world.

Lessing: At any rate I've been too intelligent to do that—give me credit! Well, we don't know what's going to happen. But it seems to me that human beings are in evolution, and this is what will evolve next. I think we're likely to become more intelligent and more intuitive and so on. That was the idea behind that. And the other idea was that if children are born with greater faculties than ordinary people, we know enough about ordinary people to know they will kill them. I mean, this is what we human beings are like. We cannot stand what's different from ourselves. So if, in fact, such better or more intelligent people are born, for their own sake they would have to be concealed in some way, since the human animal is a murderer, and would do them in. I see no reason why not; everything seems to me to be moving in that direction. We speculate about the mind, what faculties it has, what faculties it could have, what faculties it does have and we don't acknowledge. It seems to be a new frontier.

The Habit of Observing
Francois-Olivier Rousseau

*Francois-Olivier Rousseau's interview appeared in Le Maga-
zine Litteraire in Paris in February 1985. The following
translation was prepared by the editor, with the assistance of Patricia Siegel. Copyright © 1985 by Le Magazine
Litteraire. Reprinted with permission.*

Rousseau: You recently published a book, *The Diary of a Good Neighbor,*
under a pseudonym, and your regular editor turned it down. What did
you want to demonstrate in returning to anonymity?

Lessing: The reason I offered the manuscript under a pseudonym was
that at the time various people who had inspired one of my characters
were still living. There was little chance that they would read the book,
but I didn't want to run the risk. For the rest, I wanted to see what would
happen. It has been an extremely instructive experiment. My regular
editor turned down the manuscript. I later learned that it hadn't been
read by any of the literary editors in charge; it had simply been assigned
to external readers. When the book was finally published, we sent it to
some Doris Lessing specialists who apparently didn't see through the
hoax, even if they had bothered to read this novel of an unknown.
Conversely, other critics who until this time had never paid any attention
to my other books liked this one. Ivan Nabokov, my French editor at
Albin Michel, bought the rights to the book without knowing it was mine,
then called and asked if by any chance I knew the author and if I had
provided her with any help. The book was also accepted in the United
States. In that regard, my agent told me a very interesting anecdote: the
American editor, who liked the book, regretted that his firm would not be
able to do more for the book's promotion; since, he said, the author was
an unknown, he had nothing to sell. That means the book itself wasn't
enough. The public and editors want a photograph, a personality, an
author's "profile" to go with the novel.

Rousseau: What do you think of the literary world in England?

Lessing: There are good editors and intelligent critics, but unfortunately it's a closed world which feeds upon itself, in a kind of unhealthy inbreeding. Everyone knows everyone, and everyone thinks more or less the same thing at the same time. In addition, the publishers' policy is more and more dictated by costs and best-sellers. It's the same in the United States. Now it is computers which decide at what moment a book will be taken off the shelves. They even speak of the "shelf life" of books. It is not an encouraging situation.

Rousseau: *The Diary of a Good Neighbor,* which could be summarized as a kind of apprenticeship in decrepitude and dying, is an extremely trying book, even intolerable at times.

Lessing: I suppose that it is intolerable for someone who never has been confronted by old age or the death of a loved one. Old age and the physical deterioration of others naturally seem to be something repugnant, shocking to us; and we protect ourselves from it with a barrier of disgust. But the real reason for this disgust is fear, the fear that sooner or later we too will be that object of disgust. Unless we are extremely lucky, that's what's facing us, and I think it is best to try to get used to it. That is what my narrator, Jane Somers, did when she took on the responsibility for the old lady. And if I made of her an egotistical and rather inane person at the beginning of the novel it was because I also wanted the discovery of old age and misery to come as a shock for her.

Rousseau: It's tempting to draw parallels between *The Diary of a Good Neighbor,* in which a middle-aged woman helps a nonagenarian in the last months of her life, and *Memoirs of a Survivor,* in which another middle-aged woman observes the development of an adolescent. Are you saying that insurmountable barriers separate the generations making it impossible to understand or communicate with those who are older or much younger?

Lessing: I don't believe in the generation gap. It is only experience or the lack of experience which separates people. Accordingly, in *Memoirs of a Survivor,* it is the adolescent who doesn't understand the older woman, because the adolescent is separated by lack of experience. The woman, on the other hand, figures out the adolescent perfectly, because she has gone through the same phases. Basically this child is herself.

For years I had the project of writing an autobiography originating from dreams. I had to give it up because it was impossible to organize the dreams into a coherent sequence without making the whole work extremely artificial. In *Memoirs of a Survivor,* what the narrator believes that she is seeing behind the wall, that apparent dream world, actually represents her own life, her own childhood. In the tangible world, Emily whom she sees growing up represents the image of her adolescence. Thus, reality and dream, marked off by the wall, complement each other to give an all-encompassing vision to the narrator's past. I have said that *Memoirs of a Survivor* was my imaginative autobiography. Curiously, no one noticed it, as if that precision was embarrassing.

Rousseau: Africa and your colonial experience inspired your first novel, *The Grass Is Singing,* published in 1949. *A Ripple from the Storm* is set in Africa. *Particularly Cats* describes the life of African farmers. At the same time, you were born in Persia, of English parents.

Lessing: I was born in Kermanshah, then we lived in Teheran for two years. My father worked for the Imperial Bank of Persia. At the time the country was divided into several spheres of influence—because of its frontier with the new Soviet Russia—one sphere of influence was English.

It was my father himself who requested a transfer there. He had been wounded in the war; he came out of it, like many veterans, bitter and unstable. He couldn't bear life in England. As a result, he wanted to become a farmer in Africa; he came from a long line of Norfolk farmers.

African agriculture had nothing to do with agriculture in a temperate climate, and essentially it was not a wise decision. In Rhodesia my father sought above all else a refuge where he could live his imaginative life. Earning money did not interest him—that led my mother to despair because she was ambitious. Have you read *The Children of Violence?* It is in large part an autobiographical novel.

Rousseau: Could you talk about the genesis of your books? In *The Golden Notebook* you have your heroine Anna Wulf, herself a writer, say that what distinguishes the writing of a novel from nonfiction is the emotion which writers deliberately provoke in themselves.

Lessing: I no longer remember what I said in *The Golden Notebook,* but I would say now that writing is an act of conscious self-hypnosis. Rather, let me tell you how I wrote the book which I just finished and which is called *The Good Terrorist.* At the outset I was inspired by a couple I knew. She was the daughter of one of my friends, a former juvenile delinquent, a rather admirable girl. Until she was past thirty, she had lived in several fringe groups, doing the cooking for others and assuming the role of nurturing mother. The boy she lived with was a rather antipathetic sort of revolutionary whose doctrine was middle-class exploitation. For several years they lived off my friend until she decided to kick them out. They took revenge by saying that they were going to join the IRA. When I heard the story, I immediately wondered how many terrorists had been produced in the same way by a settling of accounts. Shortly after, Irish terrorists exploded a bomb in Harrod's department store; it was clearly an amateur attempt, and I said to my friend, as a joke, it was exactly the kind of action the two people in question were capable of.

Suddenly the idea came to me to write a novel based on the attempt as it was probably conceived of by a group of incompetent amateurs. I also recalled what a friend with contacts in the American terrorist movements of the '70s had told me. Throughout his descriptions I was struck by a quality of clear self-dramatization, as if the members of these groups were less concerned with the action to be carried out than with the image of themselves they would project to the public. I also remembered my own experience in the bosom of a political action group; we were convinced that we were right and everyone else was wrong. All these experiences and memories fleshed out the story and fed into the book. What fascinated me while I was writing was something that I had never sensed so distinctly: I was in the position of an eavesdropper, and a whole cluster of details from my own life coming back to me were determining the form of the book. I wrote it very quickly, in one year.

Rousseau: In *The Golden Notebook* your heroine who has some of your characteristics and who is made famous by a novel set in Africa during the last war suffers from writer's block. Is that a situation which you too have experienced?

Lessing: No, but the idea seemed interesting to me. For a time I was analyzed by a psychoanalyst specializing in artists suffering from "blocks." She would have loved to see me "blocked." I always disappointed her about it. What I wanted to discover was the origin of this blockage. I know writers who write half of a book, then stop because they suddenly are horrified by what they have done. Is it a sort of paralyzing perfectionism? Is it because in the end the book always seems greatly inferior to the one that they would have liked to write?

Rousseau: Do you share the opinion expressed by your heroine Anna Wulf that the novel today is an outpost of journalism and its function, in a closed world, is to supply one segment of society with information about another?

Lessing: Yes, I believe that more and more. Regardless of its possible literary qualities, a novel supplies us with a fund of information. Novelists have to some extent squared off the world and created an immense store of information. Take Proust, who is one of my favorite great writers. He offers a rather exhaustive portrait of society in his time; he renders, through his characters, the upward mobility of one social class and the decline of another; he shows how a class of parvenus is gradually absorbed by the aristocracy and in turn becomes aristocrats. The same is true of Mann's *Buddenbrooks*. And what would we know of pre-Soviet Russia without Chekhov, Tolstoy, Dostoyevsky, or Turgenev? A friend to whom I made these remarks disagreed, saying that no Russian author of the nineteenth century had mentioned the beginning of the Industrial Revolution, which was taking place, and that the picture furnished by the novelists is historically inaccurate. Perhaps, in that particular instance, but there are novelists who take into account everything. In any case, I read a lot of novels with the aim of informing myself. Good novels and also less good ones. I leave for Australia in a month. Everything I know about Australia I learned through novels.

Rousseau: The Australian novelist best known in France is Patrick White. Who are some of the other major Australian writers?

Lessing: There is Henry Handel Richardson, author of *Australia Felix*, a marvelous early twentieth-century writer, and then in the next generation Christina Stead, still unknown but whose work is going to be re-issued. One of her novels, *All for Love*, admirably describes life in Sidney. But even among more minor writers one finds a valuable and quite precise description of the country.

Rousseau: You've never been to Australia?

Lessing: No, never. I find the idea of a great savage continent with people around its edges quite fascinating. But then in Europe or in the Eastern United States we tend to forget that the Pacific is the new center of the world; the people living down there are completely aware of it, however. On the whole, I don't expect to be very surprised by Australia; I expect that the Australian spirit and life style won't be very different from what I knew in Africa. There is an English colonial style which one encounters everywhere. Of course, I won't say that to the Australians.

Rousseau: You have been a Communist?

Lessing: When I really was a Communist, it was in Rhodesia during the war and there wasn't the ghost of a Communist Party. We invented one for our own purposes, a totally imaginary Communist Party. It was in the bosom of that semblance of a party that I went through the different phases which represent the evolution of party members. Phase I, my eyes were opened, I saw the light, I was right, we were the ones who had the truth, in contrast to the rest of the world. Phase II, total immersion in group activity. Later there was the rejection.

Rousseau: How long did that take?

Lessing: The period of blind faith ended rather quickly. But when I arrived in England in 1949 I moved into the leftist milieu, the Communist milieu, the Labour milieu furthest to the left. I was no longer as active as I had been in Africa where I had taken part in meetings, sold pamphlets, stuffed envelopes. But also my life, difficult at that time, didn't leave me much time to devote to politics. I had no money, I had a child to raise, I was trying to live by my pen.

A little later, I joined a movement called the Colonial Liberation Movement. In retrospect, that was undoubtedly the most useful thing I accomplished. The Movement had its offices in the House of Commons. We forget today, now that there are no longer any colonies, the important role played by this movement in allowing members of Parliament to meet the future leaders of countries moving toward independence, some of whom had just been released from or were about to be sent to British prisons, others on the point of being imprisoned again. The Colonial Liberation Movement, we thought, would help the liberation of Kenya and the settlement of the Cyprus conflict which was a horrible war.

Rousseau: What is the event that made you change your mind about the Communist Party?

Lessing: It wasn't the situation in Hungary; as far as I was concerned, things had been settled for a long time. At the beginning of the '50s, while Stalin was still alive, I shared a house with a woman who was an active party member; our friends, our associates, were almost all party members. That was a very bleak period in the history of Western Communists. We knew what was going on in Russia; we had been dismayed by news of the Prague trials and the famous executions.

I mistrust the natural tendency of hindsight to simplify things; they weren't simple. At the time, despite everything we learned, Communism still seemed to have a future, and we continually sought to excuse what was going on over there—I'm not proud of that now. Arthur Koestler said once that every member of the Communist Party from that period had a personal myth which allowed him to remain in the party. It's absolutely true, and my own myth was that the things going on in the Soviet Union had nothing to do with true Communism, but there were people over there champing at the bit waiting for the moment when they could establish Communism as my friends and I knew it. It was a completely stupid line of reasoning; these people would never have the opportunity to establish true Communism, and for good reason: it was they who might have who were being assassinated as the first victims of the purges.

Then there was the 20th Congress and Khrushchev's famous speech denouncing Stalin's crimes. Many fervent Communists were shocked by that denunciation. I was shocked for different reasons: if that was the best they could do, it didn't satisfy me, it wasn't enough. It was then that I really left the party. My political journey wasn't at all unique, you know. England was full of Communists in the '40s and '50s, who experienced the same deceptions. Some had nervous breakdowns; some launched themselves into business. Former Communists make excellent business-men; it is undoubtedly related to the sense of businessmen; it is undoubtedly related to the sense of organization.//

Rousseau: Do you actually believe that literature changes nothing? Don't you think, on the whole, that it slowly transforms our consciousness?

Lessing: You're undoubtedly right. Literature does help to change things...a little. But you have to take into account that when I wrote *The Golden Notebook* I was in a state of mind which I condemn today—the apocalyptic condition. I believed that things had to change very fast, and if literature couldn't succeed in making those changes why bother to write. It was a sequel to my period of being engagé. When I was struggling in Africa my friends and I were so sure that we would succeed in changing the world in ten years that any effort which didn't contribute directly to that change seemed futile to us. It was an article of our political faith. Today I question that state of mind, something I would never have dreamed of doing in my youth.

When I was young, the attitude of people on the left was that it was better to pass out political tracts door to door than to write. A writer maturing in a politically active atmosphere is often the butt of nasty, cruel jibes. I now know that envy inspired these remarks, because those who made them were themselves for the most part failed writers. That explains the virulence of their remarks. It took me some time to understand that.

I observed this very process again in a young friend who was writing a book. She was very friendly with a group of people belonging to various leftist groups. These people did not restrain their hostile criticism and attempted to influence what she was writing, each according to his own political leaning. It is clear, to anyone from the outside, that these people were angry with her above all for having talent. She wasn't aware of it, any more than I would have been at her age.

Rousseau: What is striking, throughout your novels, is the infinite complexity and the infinite instability of relations between the characters. Do you think this analysis in miniature of human relations is what defines your manner of writing?

Lessing: It's true. I always see things in motion. In life, in reality, nothing is ever static.

Rousseau: Could it be that this kind of confusion of feeling grasped in motion is something you invented in literature?

Lessing: Don't you believe that the aim of a novel is always—I won't say to analyze but—to comment on things in motion?

Rousseau: Is the minute attention you pay to your characters evidence of your experience with psychoanalysis?

Lessing: No, I don't think that has anything to do with it. Besides, I have not really been analyzed. It was only "mild" psychotherapy. I believe rather that it was the result of a difficult childhood, not materially but morally.

I think that children who have had to struggle psychologically have a tendency to be good writers. They are constantly observing. An example comes to mind, that of a little girl I know, who I am prepared to wager will be a writer; you can foresee in her a kind of tension when she looks at what is happening around her, between her parents. It is the habit of observing that makes a writer. For me, it was similar; as far back as I can remember, I observed, I was aware of what was going on around me, and what was not being said. It's strange. When I talk to my brother, he remembers nothing; he has no awareness of anything from our childhood. Something must have happened to me very early, something which I don't remember and which determined this temperament, this vocation of the observer on the lookout, this vocation of writer.

It's very difficult for parents to have a child they do not like. My mother didn't like me. I'm not blaming her for it. It happens that people have children with whom they cannot get along, who are unlovable. That was the situation. In retrospect, I pity my mother, stuck with this incredibly difficult child who never thought or did anything "conventional." Whereas my father, who had a disposition to be critical, was never shocked by anything I could say or do.

Rousseau: You are read all over the world today. Among writers in English you are one of the most famous, and your novels it can be reasonably assumed have a considerable influence. What effect does that have on you?

Lessing: You know, living here, quite secluded, I don't think about that very much. Would you think about it if you were in my place? In any case, if I have any influence, it is a contradictory one, for I have written many very different books. What I would like to be able to say at this point is that someone who has just read a book of mine is incited to ask questions. I am not seeking to influence the reader, to make him think such-and-such a thing as I do. I would simply like to be able to tell myself that I aroused the reader's curiosity, that I made the reader more attentive, more alert intellectually, and that following the little therapeutic jolt that reading represents, he asks questions, regardless of what they are. That is what I'd like to be able to say.

Caged by the Experts
Thomas Frick

Thomas Frick's interview took place in London in Summer 1987 and originally appeared in *The Paris Review* #106 (Spring 1988). Copyright © 1988 by Thomas Frick. Reprinted with permission.

Frick: You were born in Persia, now Iran. How did your parents come to be there?

Lessing: My father was in the First World War. He couldn't stick England afterwards. He found it extremely narrow. The soldiers had these vast experiences in the trenches and found they couldn't tolerate it at home. So he asked his bank to send him somewhere else. And they sent him to Persia, where we were given a very big house, large rooms and space, and horses to ride on. Very outdoors, very beautiful. I've just been told this town is now rubble. It's a sign of the times, because it was a very ancient market town with beautiful buildings. No one's noticed. So much is destroyed, we can't be bothered. And then they sent him to Teheran, which is a very ugly city.// Then in 1924, we came back to England where something called the Empire Exhibition (which turns up from time to time in literature) was going on and which must have had an enormous influence. The Southern Rhodesian stand had enormous maize cobs, corn cobs, slogans saying "Make your fortune in five years" and that sort of nonsense. So my father, typically for his romantic temperament, packed up everything. He had this pension because of his leg, his war wounds—minuscule, about five thousand pounds—and he just set off into a totally unknown setup to be a farmer. His childhood had been spent near Colchester, which was then a rather small town, and he had actually lived the life of a farmer's child and had a country childhood. And that's how he found himself in the veld of Rhodesia. His story is not atypical of that lot. It took me some time, but it struck me quite forcibly when I was writing *Shikasta* how many wounded ex-servicemen there were out there, both English and German. All of them had been wounded, all of them were extremely lucky not to be dead, like their mates were. It didn't strike me at the time, but it's struck me since.

Frick: Perhaps a minor version of the same thing would be our Vietnam veterans coming back here and being unable to adjust, completely out of society.

Lessing: I don't see how people can go through that kind of experience and fit in at once. It's asking too much.

Frick: You recently published a memoir in the magazine *Granta* which, according to its title, was about your mother. In some ways it really seemed to be more about your father.

Lessing: Well, how can one write about them separately? Her life was, as they used to say, devoted to his life.

Frick: It's astonishing to read about his gold-divining, his grand plans, his adventures...

Lessing: Well, he was a remarkable bloke, my father. He was a totally impractical man. Partly because of the war, all that. He just drifted off, he couldn't cope. My mother was the organizer, and kept everything together.

Frick: I get the feeling that he thought of this gold-divining in a very progressive and scientific way.

Lessing: His idea was—and there's probably something true about it somewhere—that you could divine gold and other metals if you only knew how to do it. So he was always experimenting. I wrote about him actually, in a manner of speaking, in a story I called *Eldorado*. We were living in gold country. Gold mines, little ones, were all around.

Frick: So it wasn't out of place.

Lessing: No! Farmers would always keep a hammer or a pan in the car, just in case. They'd always be coming back with bits of gold.

Frick: Were you around a lot of storytelling as a child?

Lessing: No... the Africans told stories, but we weren't allowed to mix with them. It was the worst part about being there. I mean, I could have had the most marvelously rich experiences as a child. But it would have been inconceivable for a white child. Now I belong to something called a "Storytellers' College" in England. About three years ago a group of people tried to revive storytelling as an art. It's doing rather well. The hurdles were—I'm just a patron, I've been to some meetings—first, that people turn up thinking that storytelling is telling jokes. So they have to be discouraged! Then others think that storytelling is like an encounter group. There's always somebody who wants to tell about their experience, you know. But enormous numbers of real storytellers have been attracted. Some from Africa—from all over the place—people who are still tradi-tional hereditary storytellers or people who are trying to revive it. And so, it's going on. It's alive and well. When you have storytelling sessions in London or anywhere, you get a pretty good audience. Which is quite astonishing when you think of what they could be doing instead—watching *Dallas* or something.

Frick: What was it like coming back to England? I remember J. G. Ballard, coming there for the first time from Shanghai, felt very constrained; he felt that everything was very small and backward.

Lessing: Oh yes! I felt terribly constricted, very pale and damp; everything was shut in, and too domestic. I still find it so. I find it very pretty, but too organized. I don't imagine that there's an inch of the English landscape that hasn't been dealt with in some way or another. I don't think there is any wild grass anywhere.

Frick: Do you have any deep urges or longings to go back to some kind of mythical African landscape?

Lessing: Well, I wouldn't be living in a landscape, would I? I'd be living in a reality. It wouldn't be the past. When I went back to Zimbabwe three years ago, which was two years after independence, it was very clear that if I went I would be from the past. My only function in the present would be as a kind of token. Inevitably! But I'm the "local girl made good." Under the white regime I was very much a baddie. No one had a good word to say for me. You've got no idea how wicked I was supposed to be. But now I'm "OK."

Frick: Were you bad because of your attitude to blacks?

Lessing: I was against the white regime. There was a total color bar. This phrase has completely gone now: "color bar." The only contact I had with blacks was what I had with servants. It's very hard to have a reasonable relationship with black people who have to be in at nine o'clock because there's a curfew, or who are living in total poverty and you are not.

Frick: In the *Granta* memoir there's the image of you as a child, toting guns around, shooting game...

Lessing: Well, there was a great deal of game around then. There's very little these days, partly because the whites shot it out, or the blacks came and lived off it.

Frick: Did you have a desire to be a writer in those early days? You mention hiding your writings from your mother, who tried to make too much of them.

Lessing: My mother was a woman who was very frustrated. She had a great deal of ability, and all this energy went into me and my brother. She was always wanting us to *be* something. For a long time she wanted me to be a musician, because *she* had been a rather good musician. I didn't have much talent for it. But everybody had to have music lessons at one point. She was always pushing us. And, of course, in one way it was very good, because children need to be pushed. But she would then take possession of whatever it was. So you had to protect yourself. But I think probably every child has to find out the way to possess their own productions.

Frick: I just wondered if you thought of yourself as becoming a writer at an early age.

Lessing: Among other things. I certainly could have been a doctor. I would have made a good farmer, and so on. I became a writer because of frustration, the way I think many writers do.

Frick: Because you've written novels in so many different modes, do people feel betrayed when you don't stick in one camp or another? I was thinking of the science-fiction fans, quite narrow-minded, who resent people who write "science fiction" who don't stick within their little club.

Lessing: Well, it is narrow-minded, of course it is. Actually, the people who regard themselves as representatives of that community seem now to want to make things less compartmentalized. I've been invited to be Guest of Honor at the World Science-Fiction Convention, in Brighton. They've invited the Soviet science-fiction writers too. In the past there's always been trouble; now they're hoping that *glasnost* might allow their writers to actually come. Actually, it never crossed my mind with these later books that I was writing science fiction or anything of the kind! It was only when I was criticized for writing science fiction that I realized I was treading on sacred ground. Of course, I don't really write science fiction. I've just read a book by the *Solaris* bloke, Stanislav Lem. Now that's real classic science fiction...full of scientific ideas. Half of it, of course, is wasted on me because I don't understand it. But what I do understand happens to be fascinating. I've met quite a lot of young people—some not so young either, if it comes to that—who say, "I'm very sorry, but I've got no time for realism," and I say, "My God! But look at what you're missing! This is a total prejudice." But they don't want to know about it. And I'm always meeting usually middle-aged people who say, "I'm very sorry, I can't read your non-realistic writing." I think it's a great pity. This is why I'm pleased about being Guest of Honor at this convention, because it does show a breaking down.

Frick: What I most enjoyed about *Shikasta* was that it took all the spiritual themes that are submerged or repressed or coded in science fiction, and brought them up into the foreground.

Lessing: I didn't think of that as science fiction at all when I was doing it, not really. It certainly wasn't a book beginning, say, "At three o'clock on a certain afternoon in Tomsk, in 1883..."—which is, as opposed to the cosmic view, probably my second most favorite kind of opening, this kind of beginning!

Frick: You've written introductions for many collections of Sufi stories and prose. How did your interest and involvement with Sufism come about?

Lessing: Well, you know, I hate talking about this. Because really, what you say gets so clichéd, and it sounds gimmicky. All I really want to say is that I was looking for some discipline along those lines. Everyone agrees that you need a teacher. I was looking around for one, but I didn't like any of them because they were all "gurus" of one kind or another. Then I heard about this man Shah, who is a Sufi, who really struck me. So I've been involved since the early '60s. It's pretty hard to summarize it all, because it's all about what you experience. I want to make a point of that because a lot of people walk around saying, "I am a Sufi," probably because they've read a book and it sort of sounds attractive. Which is absolutely against anything that real Sufis would say or do. Some of the great Sufis have actually said, "I would never call myself a Sufi—it's too large a name." But I get letters from people, letters like this: "Hi, Doris! I hear you're a Sufi too!" Well, I don't know what to say, really. I tend to ignore them.//

Frick: Let me ask you one more question along these lines. Do you think that reincarnation is a plausible view?

Lessing: Well, I think it's an attractive idea. I don't believe in it myself. I think it's more likely that we "dip into" this realm on our way on a long journey.

Frick: That this planet is merely one single stop?

Lessing: We're not encouraged—I'm talking about people studying with Shah—to spend a great deal of time brooding about this, because the idea is that there are more pressing things to do. It's attractive to brood about all this, of course, even to write books about it! But as far as I was concerned, in *Shikasta* the reincarnation stuff was an attractive metaphor, really, or a literary idea, though I understand that there are people who take *Shikasta* as some kind of a textbook.

Frick: Prophecy, perhaps?

Lessing: It was a way of telling a story—incorporating ideas that are in our great religions. I said in the preface to *Shikasta* that if you read the Old Testament and the New Testament and the Apocrypha and the Koran you find a continuing story. These religions have certain ideas in common, and one idea is, of course, this final war or apocalypse, or whatever. So I was trying to develop this idea. I called it "space fiction" because there was nothing else to call it.//

Frick: Do you work on more than one fictional thing at a time?

Lessing: No, it's fairly straight. I do sometimes tidy up a draft of a previous thing while I'm working on something else. But on the whole I like to do one thing after another.

Frick: I'd imagine then that you work from beginning to end, rather than mixing around...

Lessing: Yes, I do. I've never done it any other way. If you write in bits, you lose some kind of very valuable continuity of form.

Frick: Do you have a feeling of yourself as having evolved within each genre that you employ? For instance, I thought the realistic perspective in *The Good Terrorist,* and even sometimes in the Jane Somers books, was more detached than in your earlier realism.

Lessing: It was probably due to my advanced age. We do get detached. I see every book as a problem to solve. That is what dictates the form you use. It's not that you say, "I want to write a space-fiction book." You start from the other end, and what you have to say dictates the form of it.

Frick: Are you producing fairly continuously? Do you take a break between books?

Lessing: Yes! I haven't written in quite a while. Sometimes there are quite long gaps. There's always something you have to do, an article you have to write, whether you want to or not. I'm writing short stories at the moment. It's interesting, because they're *very* short. My editor, Bob Gottlieb (who's now at *The New Yorker*) said, quite by chance, that no one ever sends him very short stories, and he found this interesting. I thought, My God, I haven't written a very short story for years. So I'm writing them around 1500 words, and it's very good discipline. I'm enjoying that. I've done several, and I think I'm going to call them "London Sketches," because they're all about London.

Frick: So they're not parables, or exotic in any way?

Lessing: No, not at all. They're absolutely realistic. I wander about London quite a lot. And any city, of course, is a theater, isn't it? Total drama!

Frick: Do you have regular working habits?

Lessing: It doesn't matter, because it's just habits. When I was bringing up a child I taught myself to write in very short concentrated bursts. If I had a weekend, or a week, I'd do unbelievable amounts of work. Now those habits tend to be ingrained. In fact, I'd do much better if I could go more slowly. But it's a habit. People always ask, of course, as if it matters. I've noticed that most women write like that, whereas Graham Greene, I understand, writes 200 perfect words every day! So I'm told! Actually, I think I write much better if I'm flowing. You start something off, and at first it's a bit jagged, awkward, but then there's a point where there's a click and you suddenly become quite fluent. That's when I think I'm writing well. I don't write well when I'm sitting there sweating about every single phrase.

Frick: What kind of a reader are you these days? Do you read contemporary fiction?

Lessing: I read a great deal. I'm very fast, thank God, because I could never cope with it otherwise. Writers, of course, get sent enormous amounts of books from publishers. I get eight or nine or ten books a week which is a terrible burden, because I'm always very conscientious. You do get a pretty good idea of what a book's like in the first chapter or two. And if I like it at all, I'll go on. That's unfair, of course, because you could be in a bad mood, or terribly absorbed in your own thing. Then there are the writers I admire, and I'll always read their latest books. And, of course, there's a good deal of what people tell me I should read. So I'm always reading.

Frick: Could you tell us more about how you put the "Jane Somers" hoax over on the critical establishment? It strikes me as an incredibly generous thing to do, first of all, to put a pseudonym on two long novels to try to show the way young novelists are treated.

Lessing: Well, it wasn't going to be two to begin with! It was meant to be one. What happened was, I wrote the first book and I told the agent that I wanted to sell it as a first novel...written by a woman journalist in London. I wanted an identity that was parallel to mine, not too different. So my agent knew, and he sent if off. My two English publishers turned it down. I saw the readers' reports, which were very patronizing. Really astonishingly patronizing! The third publisher, Michael Joseph (the publisher of my first book), was then run by a very clever woman called Phillipa Harrison, who said to my agent, "This reminds me of the early Doris Lessing." We got into a panic because we didn't want her going around saying that! So we took her to lunch and I said, "This *is* me, can you go along with it?" She was upset to begin with, but then she really enjoyed it all. Bob Gottlieb, who was then my editor at Knopf in the States, guessed, and so that was three people. Then the French publisher rang me up and said, "I've just bought a book by an English writer, but I wonder if you haven't been helping her a bit!" So I told him. So in all, four or five people knew. We all expected that when the book came out, everyone would guess. Well, before publication it was sent to all the experts on my work, and none of them guessed. All writers feel terribly caged by these experts—the writers become their property. So, it was bloody marvelous! It was the best thing that happened! Four publishers in Europe bought it not knowing it was me, and that was nice. Then the book came out, and I got the reviews a first novel gets, small reviews, mostly by women journalists, who thought that I was one of their number. Then Jane Somers got a lot of fan letters, mostly non-literary, from people looking after old people and going crazy. And a lot of social workers, either disagreeing or agreeing, but all saying they were pleased I'd written it. So then I thought, OK, I shall write another one. By then I was quite fascinated with Jane Somers. When you're writing in the first person, you can't stray too far out of what is appropriate for that person. Jane Somers is middle class, English, from a very limited background. There are very few things more narrow than the English middle class. She didn't go to university. She started working very young, went straight to the office. Her life was in the office. She had a marriage that was no marriage. She didn't have children. She didn't really like going abroad. When she went abroad with her husband, or on trips for her firm and her office, she was pleased to get home. She was just about as narrow in her experience as you can get. So in the writing I had to cut out all kinds of things that came to my pen, as it were. Out! Out! She's a very ordinary woman. She's very definite in her views about what is right and what is wrong.

Frick: What to wear . . .

Lessing: Everything! I have a friend who is desperately concerned with her dress. The agonies she goes through to achieve this martyrdom I wouldn't wish on anyone! Jane Somers was put together from various people. Another was my mother. I wondered what she would be like if she were young now, in London. A third was a woman I knew who used to say, "I had a perfectly happy childhood. I adored my parents. I liked my brother. We had plenty of money. I loved going to school. I was married young, I adored my husband"—she goes on like this. But then, her husband dies suddenly. And from being a rather charming child-woman, she became a person. So I used all these things to make one person. It's amazing what you find out about yourself when you write in the first person about someone very different from you.

Frick: Your original idea with the Jane Somers books was to probe the literary establishment?

Lessing: Yes. I've been close to the literary machine now for a long time. I know what's good about it and what's bad about it. It's not the publishers I've had it in for so much as the reviewers and the critics, whom I find extraordinarily predictable. I knew everything that was going to happen with that book! Just before I came clean I had an interview with Canadian television. They asked, "Well, what do you think's going to happen?" and I said, "The English critics are going to say that the book is no good." Exactly! I had these sour, nasty little reviews. In the meantime the book did very well in every other country.

Frick: In your preface to *Shikasta* you wrote that people really didn't know how extraordinary a time this was in terms of the availability of all kinds of books. Do you feel that in fact we're going to be leaving the culture of the book? How precarious a situation do you see it?

Lessing: Well, don't forget, I remember World War II when there were very few books, very little paper available. For me to walk into a shop or look at a list and see anything that I want, or almost anything, is like a kind of miracle. In hard times, who knows if we're going to have the luxury or not?

Frick: Do you feel any sense of responsibility in presenting these prophecies, aside from telling a good story?

Lessing: I know people say things like, "I regard you as rather a prophet." But there's nothing I've said that hasn't been, for example, in the *New Scientist* for the last twenty years. Nothing! So why am I called a prophet, and they are not?

Frick: You write better.

Lessing: Well, I was going to say, I present it in a more interesting way. I do think that sometimes I hit a kind of wavelength—though I think a lot of writers do this—where I anticipate events. But I don't think it's very much, really. I think a writer's job is to provoke questions. I like to think that if someone's read a book of mine, they've had—I don't know what— the literary equivalent of a shower. Something that would start them thinking in a slightly different way perhaps. That's what I think writers are for. This is what our function is. We spend all our time thinking about how things work, why things happen, which means that we are more sensitive to what's going on.

Frick: Did you ever do any of those '60s experiments with hallucinogens, that sort of thing?

Lessing: I did take mescaline once. I'm glad I did, but I'll never do it again. I did it under very bad auspices. The two people who got me the mescaline were much too responsible! They sat there the whole time, and that meant, for one thing, that I only discovered the "hostess" aspect of my personality, because what I was doing was presenting the damn experience to them the whole time! Partly in order to protect what I was really feeling. What should have happened was for them to let me alone. I suppose they were afraid I was going to jump out of a window. I am not the kind of person who would do such a thing! And then I wept most of the time, which was of no importance. And they were terribly upset by this, which irritated me. So the whole thing could have been better. It's done. But I wouldn't do it again. Chiefly because I've known people who had such bad trips. I have a friend who took mescaline once. The whole experience was a nightmare that kept on being a nightmare—people's heads came rolling off their shoulders for months. Awful! I don't want that.

Frick: Do you travel a great deal?

Lessing: Too much, I mean to stop!

Frick: Mostly for obligations?

Lessing: Just business, promoting, you know. Writers are supposed to sell their books! Astonishing development! I'll tell you where I've been this year, for my publishers: I was in Spain...Barcelona and Madrid, which is enjoyable, of course. Then I went to Brazil, where I discovered—I didn't know this—that I sell rather well there. Particularly, of course, space fiction. They're very much into all that. Then I went to San Francisco. They said, "While you're here, you might as well..."—that phrase, "you might as well"—"pop up the coast to Portland." You've been there?

Frick: No, never.

Lessing: Now that is an experience! In San Francisco, they're immensely hedonistic, cynical, good-natured, amiable, easygoing, and well-dressed—in a casual way. Half an hour in the plane and you're in a rather strait-laced formal city that doesn't go in for casual behavior at all. It's amazing, just up the coast there. This is what America's like. Then I went to Finland for the second time. They've got some of the best bookstores in the world! Marvelous, wonderful! They say it's because of those long, dark nights! Now I'm here. Next I'm going to be in Brighton, for the science-fiction convention. Then I won a prize in Italy called the Mondello Prize, which they give in Sicily. I said, "Why Sicily?" and they said, deadpan, "Well, you see, Sicily's got a bad image because of the Mafia..." So I'll go to Sicily, and then I shall work for all the winter.

Frick: I hear you've been working on a "space opera" with Philip Glass.

Lessing: What happens to books is so astonishing to me! Who would have thought *The Making of the Representative for Planet 8* would turn into an opera? I mean, it's so surprising!

Frick: How did that come about?

Lessing: Well, Philip Glass wrote to me, and said he'd like to make an opera, and we met.

Frick: Had you known much of his music before?

Lessing: Well, no, I hadn't! He sent some of his music. It took quite a bit of time for my ears to come to terms with it. My ear was always expecting something else to happen. You know what I mean? It's interesting enough. I don't find it surprising now; I have no problems with it whatsoever. Then we met and we talked about it, and it went very well, which is astonishing because we couldn't be more different. We just get on! We've never had one sentence worth of difficulty over anything, ever. He said the book appealed to him, and I thought he was right, because it's suitable for his music. We met, usually not for enormous sessions, a day here and a day there, and decided what we would do, or not do. I wrote the libretto.

Frick: Have you ever done anything like that before?

Lessing: No, never with music.

Frick: Did you have music to work from?

Lessing: No, we started with the libretto. We've done six versions of the story so far, because it is a story, unlike most of the things he does. As something was done, he would do the music, saying he'd like six more lines here or three lines out there. That was a great challenge.//

Frick: Is the space series going to continue?

Lessing: Yes. I haven't forgotten it. If you read the last one, *The Sentimental Agents*—which is really satire, not science fiction—you'll see that I've ended it so that I've pointed it all to the next volume. [The book ends in the middle of a sentence.] In the next book, I send this extremely naive agent off to... What's the name of my bad planet?

Frick: Shammat?

Lessing: Yes, to Shammat, in order to reform everything. It's going to be difficult to write about Shammat because I don't want to make it too like

Earth! That's too easy! I have a plot, but it's the tone I need. You know what I mean?

Frick: Do you do many public readings of your own work?

Lessing: Not very many. I do when I'm asked. They didn't ask me to in Finland. I don't remember when was the last. Oh, Germany last year, my God! That was the most disastrous trip. It was at some academic institution in Germany. I said to them, "Look, I want to do what I always do. I'll read the story and then I'll take questions." They said, the way they always do, "Oh, you can't expect the Germans to ask questions." I said, "Look, just let me handle this, because I know how." Anyway, what happened was typical in Germany: we met at four o'clock in order to discuss the meeting that was going to take place at eight. They cannot stand any ambiguity or disorder—no, no! Can't bear it. I said, "Look, just leave it!" The auditorium was very large and I read a story in English and it went down very well, perfectly OK. I said, "I will now take questions." Then this bank of four bloody professors started to put questions to me, these immensely long academic questions of such tedium that finally the audience started to get up and drift out. A young man, a student sprawled on the gangway—as a professor finished something immensely long—called out, "BLAH, BLAH, BLAH, BLAH, BLAH." So with total lack of concern for the professors' feelings I said, "Look, I will take questions in English from the *audience*." So they all came back and sat down, and it went well... perfectly lively questions! The professors were absolutely furious. So that was Germany. Germany's the worst, it really is; the end.

Frick: Recently, you've turned to writing nonfiction.

Lessing: Well, I've just written a book, a short book, about the situation in Afghanistan. I was there looking at the refugee camps, because what happens is that men usually go for the newspapers, and men can't speak to the women because of the Islamic attitudes. So we concentrated on the situation with the women. The book's called *The Wind Blows Away Our Words*, which is a quote from one of their writers, who said, "We shout to you for help but the wind blows away our words."

Frick: Did you ever worry about what sort of authority you could bring to such an enormous story, being an outsider visiting only for a short time?

Lessing: Do journalists worry about the authority they bring, visiting countries for such a short time? As for me, rather more than most journalists, I was well briefed for the trip, having been studying this question for some years, knowing Afghans and Pakistanis (as I made clear in the book) and being with people who knew Farsi—this last benefit not being shared by most journalists.

Frick: Your methods of reportage in that book have been the target of some criticism by American journalists, who charge that your trip to Afghanistan was sponsored by a particular pro-Afghan organization. How do you respond to that?

Lessing: This is the stereotypical push-button criticism from the left, from people who I do not think can expect to be taken seriously, for I made it clear in the book that the trip was not organized by a political organization. I went for something called Afghan Relief, set up by some friends, among them myself, which has helped several people to visit Pakistan, but not with money. I paid my own expenses, as did the others I went with. The point about Afghan Relief is that it has close links with Afghans, both in exile and fighting inside Afghanistan, and includes Afghans living in London, as advisors. These Afghans are personal friends of mine, not "political." Afghan Relief has so far not spent one penny on administration; all the fund-raising work, here and in Pakistan, is done voluntarily. To spell it out: no one has made anything out of Afghan Relief, except the Afghans.

Frick: From the tag that you used for the Jane Somers book: "If the young knew/If the old could..." Do you have any things you would have done differently, or any advice to give?

Lessing: Advice I don't go in for. The thing is, you do not believe...I know everything in this field is a cliché, everything's already been said...but you just do not believe that you're going to be old. People don't realize how quickly they're going to be old, either. Time goes very fast.

Living in Catastrophe
Brian Aldiss

Brian Aldiss's interview was conducted in London April 17, 1988. Copyright © 1988 by Brian Aldiss. Printed with permission.

Aldiss: The critics seem to have been offended that you have abandoned the so-called "realistic novel." They're not very well equipped to deal with a novel that goes beyond realism.

Lessing: They're very ignorant people, you know, and they lay down the law. This is what depresses me. I get letters saying, "Why is it that you have turned your back on realism and the truth?" "Why have you *escaped* into science fiction?" These people have never read a word of science fiction, obviously, and they don't know that the best social criticism of our time is in science fiction. And they'll certainly never find out because they're too prejudiced to read it, probably. This kind of thing is really annoying.

Aldiss: Would you like to explain what you feel about the main power blocs in the novels beginning with *Shikasta*—Canopus, Sirius, and Shammat—and how you use parable to deal with real empires, not sterile empires but earthly ones?

Lessing: It's only goodies and baddies, like a game, isn't it? Really, it's like a Western. You've got a good empire, a bad empire, and one that's learning to be a better one, hopefully—the Sirian Empire. All I did was to shift the old story into space.

Aldiss: I think you really do a lot more than that, although I can see the whole earthly pattern of exploitation, domination, and so on. But I'm particularly interested in the people of Canopus. They're keeping a very careful watch on Shikasta. How do you feel about your worthy Canopians?

Lessing: When I started that book, it all came out of the sacred books—if you remember I read the Old Testament, the Apocrypha, the New Testament, and the Koran. I found the similar idea of the warner or prophet, who arrives from somewhere and tells the people they should behave differently, or else! It's in all these books. And I thought, OK, what now? My language is not religious so I did it in space-fiction terms and created a good empire. You might notice that I haven't described it very closely, because to describe goodness is almost impossible for us—we're not good enough to. I shall be very careful never to do it.

Aldiss: You seem particularly interested in language.

Lessing: I hate rhetoric of all kinds. I think it's one of the things that stupefies us—the use of words to stop your thinking. But I didn't set off, actually, to do that. First, I wanted to write social satire, which this is, social satire with two-dimensional characters. As I went along, I kept coming on these good ideas like the hospital for rhetorical disease and I lost my way all through that book *[Sentimental Agents]*. I've never enjoyed anything so much. But quite often people get upset by it. I shouldn't be irreverent, really, about these great sacred things.

Aldiss: You're very hard on words, really.

Lessing: You forget my history. I have had a lot to do with politics, and there's a point at which you feel that if you hear one more speech you're just going to vomit. And it's the truth: you just suddenly cannot stand another rhetorical speech. And you begin to hear nothing but.... You know, any political speech can be reduced to nonsense in about three sentences. They always take off into this garbage. I think that children ought to be taught how to examine rhetoric to insulate them from it.

Aldiss: I think it's a very good idea. I agree with that wholeheartedly.

Lessing: Right, left, and center. And the politicians are always talking on a much lower level than their audience—to my mind. Any ordinary person, talking face to face, is much more intelligent than any politician, talking at them. None of them ever tells the truth as far as I can make out; you can't believe a word that they ever say—any of them. It's a very dangerous situation we're in.

Aldiss: In a lot of your novels, not only the so-called "space-fiction" ones, there is the idea of catastrophe. Ours is, of course, a generation that is haunted by various shapes and sizes of catastrophe. But H. G. Wells said that he thought civilization was a race between education and catastrophe. I sometimes think you have the same sort of feeling, although your ideas of education would be different from Wells's. Do you feel like that about it?

Lessing: Well, look at what the human race has survived. I mean, our history *is* catastrophe. We *have survived.* We were born out of an ice age. We have survived earthquakes and famines and the Black Death, and we will doubtless survive AIDS. In some way or other, we seem to stagger through—of course, through catastrophes that are always unnecessary because we allow things to happen that we shouldn't allow to happen. And you talk about this as being in the future. We're *living* in catastrophe: how many people die of hunger every year, how many children die? There are thirty wars going on at this very moment. Because they're not the big wars, we seem to pretend that they're not important. We're poisoning our seas, and our water supply—we all know this—our trees are dying in various parts of the world. This is a state of catastrophe. We're not very bright as animals yet, are we?

Aldiss: What I actually think is that we kid ourselves that we're *Homo sapiens* and our great glory is our brain. It doesn't really seem very good for thinking with. What the brain *is* good at is producing fantasy. It seems that one thing you try to do in the *Canopus in Argos* series is to use that quality to improve people's lives—which on the whole fantasy doesn't do. The Canopians tell stories that will equip children for adult life. I rather like that.

Lessing: You know, I never thought that this must have a function—this fantasizing and dreaming must have a use of some kind; otherwise, we'd have lost it, evolution would have lost it. From the time that we know anything at all about history we were telling stories to each other. Of course, they were fantastic stories until 400 years ago when they became realistic. Why then, you have to ask, why is the brain organized in this way? And why do we dream? What we're doing when we dream is telling ourselves stories; it's the same pattern.

Aldiss: You know, I always wanted to be a writer, and as a young man I spent four years in the Far East; and that gave me, forever afterwards and still, a sense of exile, a sense of remoteness. You have far more years to claim in that respect. Do you think that that's helped you to write the space fiction—that distancing from the world?

Lessing: Yes, I do. I think actually the biggest influence was sitting outside our house, on the hill, night after night after night, looking at the stars—

with my father and brother and mother, or alone. You automatically start thinking in terms of millions of years if you take that point of view. You have *marvelous* African sky, brilliant, *brilliant* stars—you never see it here. And the stars close down, and all the time the meteors going across, every night, every few minutes.

Aldiss: I remember it like that in Burma.

Lessing: Yes. Well, you see, if you spend a lot of your childhood doing that, space fiction doesn't come as a great shock.

Watching the Angry and Destructive Hordes Go Past
Claire Tomalin

Tomalin: Did you feel constrained by colonial society in Rhodesia?

Lessing: Colonial, small-town life, and a white settler's life, was utterly intolerable. Sometimes I've said, Supposing I'd never left? Well, I can tell what would've happened to me: I would've become an alcoholic within about five years, and I don't think I would've done anything very much else, because you could see all that going on. I was surrounded by women questioning what was going on and not liking it very much. I wouldn't have stood it; I wouldn't have survived it.

Tomalin: I suppose the thing readers like to do is to assume that what you write as fiction is really autobiography. Has this been a problem for you? What is the relationship for you between the autobiographical element and the fictional, in a novel like *Martha Quest?*

Lessing: I don't think you'll ever find a writer who doesn't sigh at this question, because to us it's totally irrelevant. In a sense, everything *has* to be autobiographical, of course; but on the other hand, you can also say that it isn't autobiographical at all, because as soon as you begin writing it changes into something else.

Tomalin: Since you've written *The Golden Notebook,* which gives this picture of women living independently outside an ordinary pattern—earning their own livings, bringing up their own children, living without husbands—I've noticed increasing numbers of young women are living like this. You don't gloss over the difficulties and painfulness. I wonder what you feel about the general movement of young women trying to live like this now.

Lessing: Well, of course, I'm delighted. There *are* many different ways of bringing up children now in this country. I don't know how long it'll be allowed to go on, because I think there are signs everywhere of orthodoxy, of conventional thinking coming back. It's been a very interesting time to live through, hasn't it?

Tomalin: What do you fear might happen?

Lessing: The right is fairly stereotyped and the left is not exactly free-minded. I'm very disappointed in the left, as you might've gathered: I think great opportunities have been lost. The left at the moment are people who ban books in libraries—I don't want to hear all the arguments in favor, because I think it's very dangerous, what's happening—and I think it would take very little for books to be burned in bonfires. It's all there: the unofficial committees are all there, waiting, and this scares me.

Tomalin: Your concern for the future is clear in *Memoirs of a Survivor.*

Lessing: When I wrote *Memoirs of a Survivor,* I said that I was trying to write my autobiography. No one is remotely interested in this, nor ever has been, unfortunately. I was trying to write an autobiography in this form, because at some point in my life I thought it would be interesting to write an autobiography of dreams, in dream form. That is so difficult that I've given up on it—it really would take the whole rest of my life. In part I was writing an autobiography in terms of metaphor—behind the dissolving wall is the most ancient symbol you possibly can find. I always use these old, hoary symbols, as they strike the unconscious.

Behind the wall, there are three different kinds of things going on: the personal memories and the dreams, a lot of which come from my own, and the third is the impersonal.

Tomalin: You seem to be predicting a future of anarchy and barbarism.

Lessing: Don't forget that you're much younger than I am. Scenes repeat themselves over and over again. One of the things that repeats itself, as you get older, is phenomena which once seemed absolutely unending, strong, immovable, just vanish overnight. In my time I have seen go the white regime in Rhodesia, which I assure you seemed at one point impossible; Stalin went; Hitler went. If you lived through the war you'll know that didn't seem likely then. All kinds of apparently everlasting things just disappeared. But what happens is you begin to see these mass movements arising and sweeping across your line of vision, and that's what these bands [in *Memoirs of a Survivor*] were meant to represent—you watch the angry and destructive hordes go past.

Tomalin: What sort of response have you had to *The Good Terrorist?*

Lessing: Of all the books I've ever written, the letters I got afterwards were the most fascinating. I got letters from a lot of people who'd been a part of such groups in various countries, but I think perhaps the most interesting thing was when I went to Rome. I met a woman whose husband had been killed the year before by the latest wave of terrorists. In order to cope with her grief she had taken to visiting the first wave of terrorists in prisons. What she told me was so fascinating that I'm thinking about it 'til this day. She said they were all educated people just like you or me, mostly rather pleasant, likeable people. They had committed unspeakable crimes—all of them. The thing that very much interested me was that all of them had now got over this and were full of remorse, saying things like "It was as if we'd been taken over by something; it was like being in a sailing ship and being driven full speed ahead"—this kind of metaphor kept coming up. They have all more or less recovered from what they regarded as a madness and are now busily writing their memoirs, learning languages, and so forth, in prison. Now this raises so many questions that we never even think about: we never ask what happens when people get taken over like this. What *actually* happens? What's going on?

Another thing she said that really interested me was the terrorists who'd committed the worst crimes and were full of guilt were in 100 times better psychological state than the group who said, "It's not fair. I was just standing by and didn't mean to shoot the gun." This brings you to the ironical thought, Is it better to have been a *real* criminal than someone who is just assisting? The questions that arise from all this are endless, in fact.

Tomalin: May I ask you where *The Fifth Child* came from?

Lessing: I'd been cooking up this book for a long time, and a lot of different ideas went into it. It's always easy to talk about the *ideas* that go into a book, but what the engine is, is another matter.

The first idea was that I'm fascinated by the little people, because every country in the world has legends of the little people, and I've got a thing that they probably existed. There are even some minute skeletons in America which no one's explained yet. The Bushmen and the Pigmies are much shorter, let's say, than the Masai, who are nearly seven foot.

Then I read something by this extraordinary man Loren Eiseley, the American, an essayist and an archaeologist. He described in one of his books how he walked up, in the dusk from the seashore in Maine I think it was, toward a country road on which he saw a girl who turned her head to look at him. Now his mind was full of the last ice age and who had lived here, and he thought, My God, but that's a Neanderthal girl. He walked up to the girl, and she had the flaring eyebrow ridges and funny back to her head. He said that this girl could've lived here all of her life, and nothing would've ever been asked of her. They had a conversation, and this girl walked into the dusk up toward her house, and he thought, What I am experiencing now could've happened anytime in the last 50,000 years. So then I thought, OK now, a Neanderthal girl. Why not a goblin, I thought, going back to little people?

And then there was a letter I read in the newspaper, which is with me yet, the most awful letter. A woman wrote that she had several perfectly satisfactory, marvelous children and then had given birth to this little girl—she used theological language: "this little devil, this horrible little imp, which had ruined the family; she was born evil; she was born wicked and malicious and horrible; and the whole family had suffered." And then she ended: "At nights I'd go in and look at this innocent little face on the pillow and I longed simply to put my arms around her, because I never can when she's awake. I know that what will come into my arms is this horrible little devil." Now this suddenly all coagulated, in the way books do.

Tomalin: For the reader, the effect of the incursion of an evil child, a cuckoo in the nest, a child who's evil before he's born, is like a great blow. Is there some element of parable in *The Fifth Child*?

Lessing: You know, that child isn't evil at all. He's just out of the right place. If he is in fact the result of a gene which has come down through many centuries, all he is, is a different race of being that's landed up in our somewhat complicated society. But what I got fascinated by in writing that book was, how would we cope with it if it happened? And I got more and more fascinated, because my first draft was much softer and I thought, My God, I'm cheating here about what it would be like at all. We don't notice things that we can't cope with: we decide not to see them, or we smooth them over.

Tomalin: There seems to be no good way of coping with Ben in the book.

Lessing: No, there isn't.

Tomalin: Harriet, his mother, wishes to cope, wishes to do what the mother you described in the letter to the newspaper also wishes, to embrace him and love him. But there seems to be no way out and this is why one thinks of him, even if you don't intend him to be, as evil. The *effect* he has all around him is evil, isn't it?

Lessing: Well, he breaks everything up. But then he would have to. You know, what interested me as I was writing it was I don't see how Harriet could've behaved in any other way, and yet she destroyed her family. It's not just Harriet's choice: we have it all the time. If you're a civilized people—let's use the term with a certain amount of irony—then we're committed to certain things. Yet often the things we're committed to have unfortunate effects we don't foresee necessarily.

Tomalin: I found it a very, very bleak, depressing message that you seem to be suggesting, that there is no way of dealing with an alien being. And yet in your essays, *Prisons We Choose to Live Inside,* you seem to be much more optimistic: you seem to suggest that education, the social sciences, literature, and history all can be used genuinely to improve life, to change things.

Lessing: Well, I am fairly optimistic. I think that we have all kinds of ways of looking at ourselves that could save us yet. I do, yes. One thing is the ability to distance ourselves from our behavior and examine it, which is a new thing, actually, and that's hopeful. I don't think 100 years ago nations were criticizing each other for brutal behavior. One can be cynical and say that they're only doing it to make a point, which is partly true, of course. But the idea that we can criticize each other for behaving brutally is a new and very promising thing. And there are a lot of things like that. And the fact that given a chance countries will choose democracy, which is happening everywhere in the world, is another hopeful thing. But you're expecting me to be too reasonable, I think. Being reasonable has nothing to do with being a writer.

Drawn to a Type of Landscape
Sedge Thomson

Sedge Thomson's videotaped interview was conducted
November 15, 1989, in San Francisco. Copyright © 1989
by Sedge Thomson. Printed with permission.

Thomson: Have you been startled by the changes going on in the Communist Party, as it's being dismantled around the world? Are you very pleased when you see yet another dictatorship falling? I wonder what your reaction has been to all these events.

Lessing: Well, like everybody else, I'm absolutely delighted and amazed that it could be happening so quickly. It's a miracle, isn't it? If there has been a nation before, like the Soviet Union in the last several years, which has so dramatically come clean over its crimes—I mean, not totally yet—but still has it ever happened before? It's quite remarkable, isn't it, what we're seeing? It's fantastic. I'm also scared stiff at the idea of Germany reuniting—like everybody from Europe. There's no reason most Americans should feel like this, but I can't believe that there's any European who doesn't have two violently contrasting emotions: one, delight at what's happening, and, the other, apprehension.

Thomson: There have been two major instances of Germany in ascendancy in this century, so you fear a third, then?

Lessing: Well, you have an uneasy moment or two. How could we not, when it's happened twice?

Thomson: You've said that the Second World War caused your two marriages, and I'm wondering what you meant by that.

Lessing: Well, I wouldn't have got married at all, I think, without the Second World War. People got married very lightly during the war. Older people know that in wartime everybody is completely crazy and thinks that what they do doesn't count, for some mysterious reason. And people get married—in the most astonishing way, when I look back on it.

You must recall that I was brought up in the atmosphere of the First World War, which completely messed up my two poor parents. Then there was the Second World War. I would say that these are the two influences in my life—these wars. The older I get, the more I realize just what an influence they have been.

Thomson: Was the second marriage also sort of spontaneous, or didn't really count?

Lessing: No, it didn't count. This was a German refugee, a very clever man, who—you see, if I were to tell you this story, I think I'd probably keep you riveted for about two hours: it's one of these epic, impossible stories; it ramifies all over the world with these amazing events. But I won't. It's a great pity, actually, but I haven't got time. Anyway, Gottfried Lessing was the grandson of one of these nineteenth-century self-made millionaires, an enormous entrepreneur: he made all the horseshoe nails for Czarist Russia, built railways, had tankers—he was one of these people. His children totally despised him because he was a rough man and they spent the money he'd made. My second husband's father was a man who spent his life in a library, living of course off this money, and Gottfried had been brought up a very rich young man in decadent Berlin, in the '20s and '30s, and became a refugee, an unpolitical person, but he fell in love with a very beautiful Communist—you see, I can go on like this for hours—girl who was the daughter of a self-made Welsh millionaire. And she became a Communist, of course, to infuriate her father, and she taught Gottfried to become a Communist. He became a very theoretical Communist, and when I met him—we innocents in Rhodesia were dazzled by all the sophistication, which now of course I would regard as pitiful. However, that's life.

After the war—I'm now skipping many, many chapters of this epic—he went back to East Berlin where he became a very important man in the Communist Party, because he was a very clever man, a brilliant organizer. Well, I wouldn't have married him—I'm skipping why I married him—we married because at that time we were in a Communist group, and since we were all mad we believed that Communism was going to fill the entire world in probably about five years. Everyone was going to be happy in this nirvana forever, and personal lives really didn't count. Look, it wasn't only me. This is a very, very common state of affairs inside political parties, not only the Communist Party but left-wing socialist parties, this kind of lunacy. Gottfried Lessing and I had nothing in common; we never really quarreled—you have to have something in common with someone to quarrel. We treated each other with immense courtesy; we didn't like each other at all.

Thomson: I think that was one of the briefest epics I've ever heard.

Lessing: Well, you see, I've missed all the side chapters which involve—well, Gottfried's sister, equally well brought up, was a Communist too. She was in France when war was declared. She was arrested because she was half-Jewish and put into a French concentration camp. Her young man, who was Jewish, found her in this concentration camp, *by chance*—this is war—got her out, and then they voluntarily went back inside Nazi Germany, because it was their duty as Communists. She sheltered him throughout that entire war in some vast house, in the attic—this is a death sentence many times over—and kept the entire family alive during the hungry part of the end of the war by walking many kilometers every week to bring potatoes from the countryside. She was a tiny, little thing. The whole story goes on like this. I think that's about enough.

Thomson: Let's get back to your "chapter" here, where in 1949 you took your third child Peter with you as an infant to London, with a few weeks' money for rent and this unpublished manuscript of your novel *The Grass Is Singing.* Was that an act of courage to go to London, an act of deliberation...?

Lessing: Well, it was just something that I had to do. It wasn't a question of courage at all. The whole point of that is people expect much more now than we did. The other night out at Stanford some young woman asked in so many words, How long would she have to wait to earn a lot of money writing? Such an idea was never in my mind, you see. Things have changed absolutely. I was totally unconcerned with security. All my lot didn't care about security, or about being respectable. We thought that was extremely bourgeois and utterly contemptible, to worry about consumer goods and that kind of thing. So it wasn't a question of courage; I just had to do it. My guess is that most people go through that stage, when they don't have any money to live on—you know that sort of stew-cum-soup you live on because it's cheap? It's always bubbling away there on the stove and you eat good bread with it because you can't afford anything else. But it never crossed my mind that this is extraordinary. That is the point. In due course, I stopped not earning money, I earned money, and then I earned quite a lot of money. What's interesting about all that is I don't live very much better, except that I live in a house instead of a couple of rooms. I don't seem to spend much money and I earn quite a lot, but I don't seem to know what happens to it. Now this happens to quite a lot of people.

Thomson: I've heard about the taxes in England.

Lessing: Yes, apart from that, it's a very interesting thing about money which no one's ever explained to me.

Thomson: Do you look after your own finances?

Lessing: Lord, no! Good God, it's impossible. I have an accountant, but I do my own accounts with something called B.A.T., which makes me very proud, because I'm so bad at what I still call "sums." But I do this, and every quarter I'm so proud of myself for being able to do it at all.

Thomson: Do you still keep a stew bubbling away on the stove?

Lessing: No, those days are over.

Thomson: You've stepped into a kind of fast-track world, collaborating with Philip Glass on an opera based on one of your *Canopus in Argos* books, *The Making of the Representative from Planet 8.* Did you have fun working with Philip Glass?

Lessing: I absolutely adored it all. It was wonderful, because despite the glamorous ideas people have about being a writer it is an extremely unexciting life, and the opera is a wonderful rest from all this. It was on in four opera houses. The point is that operas are so expensive to put on that there are always several opera houses involved. The opera houses were Houston—which is very brave about putting on new operas—and the English National Opera in London, the Amsterdam Opera, and the Kiel Opera House. It went on in all four of these places, it filled 85% of its seats in all four, which is quite good for a new opera, it got mixed reviews in all places except in London where not one critic had one good word to say for it, but the audiences liked it and gave it standing ovations. It was all very, very enjoyable, so we're doing another one based on *The Marriages Between Zones Three, Four, and Five,* but that is on the back burner: only two opera houses are in on it so far.

Thomson: Did you find your ideas enlarged or diminished by showing up in an opera, or did the collaboration make something wholly new?

Lessing: I think something wholly new. It's very good putting something into a different medium. You know, it's just a different thing. First, the music comes first; it has to. Then, if you're reading, you're imagining things, and on the stage you're seeing them. I never at any point tried to keep what was in the book; I tried to do something completely new.

Thomson: And so if he needed some work with some lines for the singers, how would he collaborate with you? Would he call you up on the phone?

Lessing: Yes. We started off by making a story line, which means throwing out a lot of the book, because you can't get all of that in. Then we worked through scene by scene and I wrote that as a skeleton. When he came to write the music he'd ring up and say things like, I want six lines in there or two lines out there. The interesting thing is that some of those lines are the best bits, you know, the ones that go in to fit the music. It's always interesting what happens if you're compressed.

Thomson: Did you have any musical training yourself that prepared you for this?

Lessing: Well, you know, I come from a generation where girls had to learn the piano, whether they had any talent for it or not. I can roughly read the notes in a score, but that's about it.

Thomson: You've also written a few plays. Are you drawn to the dramatic form from time to time, or is this something you get asked to do and you'll try your hand at it?

Lessing: My career in the theater has not been a roaring success. I am in love with the stage; I mean, I really am. I'm stagestruck. I adore the theater. *But* things seem always to go wrong, and I know this sounds like a terrible excuse for incompetence. For example, for one of my plays the producer talked me into waiting three years to put it on because he wanted a certain star, who I didn't want anyway. Then he and the director went off and cast the other part in a way that made me blush with embarrassment, because it was so awful. And so on. I thought, Why put myself through this misery? I have refused to write plays, but I am terribly tempted from time to time—although I should know better by now.

Thomson: One of the things which is so impressive about your work is the great range of poems, plays, epics, space fiction, and the short stories. I think, probably to your satisfaction, this keeps you from being categorized as a specific kind of writer. But readers are often startled when, if they are used to your realistic fiction, suddenly out comes one of your space-fiction stories. Do you react to this in any way? Do you care about a reader's expectations of your work?

Lessing: Well, you know, there are people who like both. It's not totally separated. It's all so humorous. I remember on the same day some professor from Australia said to me, "I do hope you're not going to waste any more time writing realism," I get a letter from someone saying, "I do so hate all this fanciful stuff you write, when are you going to write . . . ?

I think that something has happened to our imaginations that is very bad. When somebody says, "I can't read imaginative fiction," or whatever it is, it means that they have stopped being able to use their minds as human beings have used their minds for thousands of years, because realism was born very recently, 400 years ago. Before that, storytelling was in a mode of animal stories, magical stories, fables, and parables, but never realism. This was how everybody experienced stories. Now, after such a very short time of realism, there are people who literally cannot use their minds in any way but "Peter Brown was born on the fourth of January in 1967 in Birmingham." Then they feel fine. I think that this is a great loss—that people can't do both.

And it's just as bad the other way. I was invited—I'm very proud to say—as a guest of honor to the World Science Fiction Convention in Brighton, just two years ago. Which is one of the weirdest experiences, for this reason: it was a combination of some of the most advanced thinkers of our time, because all of the scientists go down sometimes, all the scientific writers for the newspapers were there, and the science-fiction writers who tend to be extremely knowledgeable about science, coupled with some of the craziest people in the world, who spend their entire lives going from convention to convention and never meeting a normal person. They would come up to me and they would hiss, "What are you doing here? You're mainline." The extremes are really very terrifying.

Thomson: When you made the shift yourself, what was going on in your life in terms of mysticism, or did you just want to try something new in your writing?

Lessing: Well, it's a question of what you want to say. If you want to write a novel encompassing millions of years, you have to find a new form for it; you can't just have a realistic novel.

Thomson: Someone told me today that your writing in *Canopus* is the kind of writing that will be done in about 2,000 years. You're that far ahead of your time.

Lessing: Well, that's very sweet. I think that this is profoundly untrue and that it's the kind of writing other people are doing now. If you look at what the science-fiction fans call "mainline" writing, it's more and more invaded by influences from across the tracks, from science fiction. There are enormous numbers of non-realistic novels being written as "magical realism," which I think is one of the funniest things I've ever heard. I must tell you that when they were discussing *The Fifth Child* on the radio one critic throughout the entire program was saying, "But you can't categorize this book; you can't categorize this book; it's quite impossible"—as if the most important thing is to categorize something. I think that we should forget about all this putting things in boxes. Why should you?

Thomson: Do many of your writing ideas come from dreams?

Lessing: Yes, quite a few of them do. But I wouldn't say directly. I don't have a dream and think, Oh well, that might come in useful and file it away.

Thomson: Do you keep a dream journal by your bed?

Lessing: I write down my dreams every morning in my diary. But most dreams are pretty ordinary. I think that only occasionally do you get a dream from a deeper level.

Thomson: The last time I spoke to you, two years...

Lessing: Have I been contradicting myself?

Thomson: No, no, no. I was going to tell you another dream story. About the same time, Salman Rushdie was in town, and he told a story about dreams. When he's writing a novel—and he was writing his famous one—he said, "I have very ordinary dreams." But when he's not writing, his dream life is wild and fantastic and out of control. Does your dream life vary in that same way?

Lessing: I think it depends on the kind of book I'm writing, because if you're writing a very ordinary, realistic book, then it hasn't got much to do with wild dreams, has it? I mean, if you're writing *The Good Terrorist*, I don't think that would have much effect on what I'm dreaming, because I'm simply using a different part of my mind, for detail, detail, detail.

Thomson: Let me ask you about the detail of a book like *The Good Terrorist*. How do you research a book like that?

Lessing: You know, everybody says this: How did you research *The Good Terrorist*? Why should I *have to* research *The Good Terrorist*? You tell me.

Thomson: Well, presumably it's filled with detail of a cell that wants to go around and wreak a little bit of havoc and your character the housewife has to bring her organizing skills to bear. Now I suppose you could imagine it all and maybe just read how these things are done through the newspapers.

Lessing: You're talking about "squats"? I've known a lot of people who've lived in "squats" and I've been told about others. What has struck me was the preoccupation with money all the time, understandably: I have been told that most conversations are about money. Which is quite humorous in a way.

Thomson: Much of your writing has to do with mothers and children. There's a story in the *New Yorker* a couple of years ago called "The Womb Ward." You've written *The Fifth Child*. There was a story in *Ladies' Home Journal* this past April about a mother and her daughter Shirley. Shirley was a real iconoclast who didn't behave like the woman's other daughter who was normal and was more like her.

Lessing: Oh yes, that was "Among the Roses."

Thomson: This is a theme to which you're continually drawn. I'm wondering why.

Lessing: Well, "The Womb Ward" wasn't really about mothers and children. It was something that I'd watched. I was visiting a friend in a North London hospital and I observed exactly what I described in "The Womb Ward": this woman, with her husband, weeping like a child of three, because she had never, ever been separated from him, and he was surrounded by women, who were widows, who had divorced, who had had every kind of calamity, who had never married. I thought of the immense power, the privilege—everybody had to dance to this spoilt baby. So I wrote the story.

Thomson: And the story "Among the Roses"?

Lessing: I can't remember why I wrote that. I don't remember it, honestly.

Thomson: There was a line in *Martha Quest,* where you described her in the agony of adolescence suffering that misery peculiar to the young that they are going to be cheated out of the full life that every nerve in their bodies is clammering for. There was a fair gap of time between when you wrote *Martha Quest* and your own adolescence. Did you draw on a lot of memories or on observation to describe the young Martha Quest?

Lessing: Memories. Now, of course, I could draw on what you see every time you meet an adolescent, because every adolescent is like every other adolescent.

Thomson: Your book *The Summer Before the Dark* dealt with a middle-aged woman who had an affair with a younger man to help her reaffirm her identity. Is there a book dealing with getting older that you'd like to write?

Lessing: I probably will, since I tend to keep up with what's going on. But that one wasn't based on me. I was watching what you see so very often: a woman who has not had a job and whose children grow up and she has to come to terms with the fact that she has no function. Which is a very terrible thing to watch, particularly if this woman is a close friend of yours. That's what that came out of.

Thomson: The book that you wrote under a pseudonym, *The Diary of a Good Neighbor,* was the observed life of an elderly woman. You wrote the book in part as a way of showing that unless writers have a big name they are not taken seriously in the publishing industry?

Lessing: Well, I don't want to make it too black and white. I don't want to say that I think a novel with merit won't get published. The writer might have to go through several publishers. Every publisher I know will tell fairly self-critical stories about the ones that got away. Every publisher has got a list of the ones they turned down. But I do think young writers are terribly patronized—that's the worst thing. It so happened that I saw the readers' reports for *Jane Somers,* and it was very interesting to have to go right back, to see this note of patronage—you know, Dear little thing, she ought to do better if she tries. It was salutary, you know, and very good for me. I knew it was going to happen.

Again, I had fascinating letters about the book—one of two kinds: one was a very funny letter, like, for example, from the romantic novelist who'd written sixty-nine novels, I think. They all sell millions of copies, they're never reviewed, and she's amazingly rich. She said that she'd got very bored with all this, and sent her sixty-eighth in to her publisher under a different name. Her publisher wrote back, "I'm afraid this is simply not good enough for our list. You should try to do better." Then she sent the same novel back under her own name, and they said, "How absolutely marvelous, darling. How absolutely wonderful, as usual!" I got quite a few of this kind of letter, which was one of the reasons I did it.

But I also got letters and manuscripts from people who'd been hawking around the same book for years and years, and they were simply not good books. And what is astonishing is that these people couldn't see that they were not good books. This is the surprising thing. They were full of anger and convinced that the publishers were not recognizing true merit. Unfortunately, publishers never say, and they ought to, "Look, this is no good." What they do is to say, because they don't want to upset people, "I'm afraid that this is not suitable for our list." That means this writer is left feeling that the next one is going to like it, and they've gone for years and years and years like this. The advice should be: "Throw that away and write another one." This is the kind and good advice.

Thomson: Do you still get rejection slips?

Lessing: No. I couldn't get rejection slips because too much money's involved. Do you know what I mean? It wouldn't matter what I wrote; they're going to make money on it. *I* have to be very self-critical.

Thomson: Just because now it has your name on it, they'll accept it in a magazine.

Lessing: Oh, not necessarily just in a magazine. But then I don't go through that course, because I have an agent. You can't do that; you don't have time.

Thomson: A lot of your novels have an apocalyptic view of the world, and there are a number of events like the Greenhouse Effect and planetary warming that are going on. Do you feel, Yes, this is something I would expect we'd be doing to our planet, or are you surprised that we're polluting our own planet, destroying rain forests—are these themes that engage you when you open the morning paper?

Lessing: No, because I was writing about them a long time ago. You know, I wasn't equipped with some amazing prescience, because all the scientists were talking about this a long time ago. Can I point out that nobody foresaw the hole in the ozone layer? Nobody mentioned AIDS. I mean, some of the worst calamities nobody sees. We don't seem to be very good at foreseeing our crises, in fact. Do we?

And also they come in extraordinary forms. I've just been in Zimbabwe, twice, and like other countries in Africa—I'm talking about this in San Francisco because it's an AIDS town—it's an area in which AIDS never has had anything to do with homosexuality or drugs. This is extraordinary. It's a rampant and dangerous and awful disease that hasn't got the same form at all as it has in any of our cities. We just don't know what to expect anywhere or what form anything is going to take.

Thomson: Some writers have said that the presence of AIDS would change the way they would write their books or the way they would describe relationships between men and women. I'm wondering how you would cope with it. Would you include it in a novel? Would you set your novel pre-AIDS?

Lessing: Well, I don't see how you can ignore it. My young women friends starting out with their sexual lives have a completely different attitude from us lot. I think that my generation, roughly speaking, was probably the luckiest *ever*, because we'd been liberated from what our mothers had to worry about, which was fear of pregnancy. We were liberated more or less, not as totally as with the Pill. I don't remember worrying desperately; I mean, it was a thing I kept in mind. And I can't remember *ever* worrying about any venereal disease; no one had ever heard of things like—I've forgotten what they call it—all these things that people get like thrush.

Thomson: They're called "sexually transmitted diseases."

Lessing: Yes, well, there is a whole lot that we'd never heard of, *ever*. So there we were, liberated from what my poor mother had to suffer, and all her generation, and we were very romantic and free and all that. And now these poor girls downstairs can't go to bed with anyone without worrying about AIDS, and I think it's awful, and I'm desperately sorry for them.

Thomson: Do you talk to them about it?

Lessing: Yes, of course, we do. You know, the scripts are written for us all: I'm in the role of an elderly advisor about not taking stupid risks, you know.

Thomson: And what do they say back to you?

Lessing: They say things like "You know, it's very difficult to be very sensible when you're in love." Which God knows is true. Well, you know what I'm likely to say. I make sensible remarks of the kind you'd expect me to. Which I won't repeat here.

Thomson: I wonder if you could talk about the influence of Persia in your life. You were born there, and different Persian words have shown up from time to time in your books. I'm wondering if you're drawn to that particular landscape where you were born.

Lessing: I'm not drawn to that particular landscape; I'm drawn to that *type* of landscape. When I went to Granada in Spain, I suddenly remembered the mountains around Kermanshah, where I was born, a town which is now, I'm told, battered flat by war, a very ancient trading town, which is now in ruins. It is a landscape which is high, dry, and dusty. That is, in fact, the landscape I had in Zimbabwe—sorry, in the old Southern Rhodesia.

I can only remember the odd incident; but I think the important thing is the amount of moving I did. I think it's extremely good for children to have a lot of experiences when they're very young, and parents should encourage them to travel and see a lot of things, to have a lot of different impressions. It makes them very flexible later on. I moved from Kermanshah to Teheran when I was just over two. I can remember that, driving in some ancient car over this extraordinary landscape. Then we were the first family to travel through the Soviet Union. That was 1924. No other tourists or normal travelers had gone on that route up from the Black Sea to Leningrad. The trains were still battered by war, and there were crowds of starving children without parents on the platform. All that made a great impression. Then I was in England, which I remember very clearly as a place I hated, because it was cold and wet and gray. Now, of course, I adore it. And then I traveled on a very slow boat, on a *German* boat, which was important, because of the First World War, to Africa and then on a very slow train to what was then Salisbury and then on an ox wagon that you people would see in your films of the Wild West to the farm. All of that before I was just five and a bit. Now *that* was what influenced me! And I am very grateful for it.

Thomson: What was the influence that you've carried with you?

Lessing: Well, that one culture is very different from another, and that the absolutes of one culture are just valuable for that culture. It's all relative, and we don't have to take anything seriously of that kind. Which is very valuable for a writer.

Thomson: You've lived in London now for forty years. Do you still consider yourself an immigrant there, or in exile?

Lessing: No. I've been back to Zimbabwe recently twice, and it's the landscape, the country physically that I belong to, as I did then. I never could stand the old society, and I'm not mad about it now for the same reason. It's an extraordinarily provincial place. It's immensely exciting in the rate of change and the fact that everybody you meet is totally absorbed in making Zimbabwe work. That's absolutely marvelous. You haven't been there twelve hours before you're absolutely absorbed 100% in the place. But what is terrible is that just as in the old Southern Rhodesia, nothing exists outside Zimbabwe. And you start suffering from the most dreadful claustrophobia, and you can't wait to get out where you suddenly start this great shout of argument and discussion and information, which in Zimbabwe is just cut off, as it used to be in the old Southern Rhodesia. It's a very boring place after a short time, because of that.

Thomson: You've also felt that when you have finished books they're "lies," that you can't get enough life into them.

Lessing: That's true. I've never yet met a writer that wasn't disappointed by not being able to capture it, not really. At this very moment I'm working on a certain book in my head and I'm watching very wryly how this raw thing is going to take shape. There's nothing to be done about it, because it has to.

Thomson: Do you maintain this sort of detachment while you're writing?

Lessing: Yes, sort of; no, I'm terribly involved in it, but you have to be detached a bit. You have to write cold. You can't write hot; otherwise, it's no good.

Thomson: But you wrote *Fifth Child* out of a rage.

Lessing: No, that was the fuel; that's a different thing. Yes, the "fuel" is the accurate word, for the fuel for that book was frustration and rage—the total intransigence of our helplessness in the face of terror and horror.

That theme got into *The Fifth Child* at a remove. We're very helpless. We're in a conspiracy, I suppose so that we don't tear ourselves up, that we are in control of events. I don't think that we are remotely in control of events. But we like to think we are; otherwise, we wouldn't be able to stand it, I suppose.

Thomson: I was speaking with someone else about the Martha Quest books and she said she found them so real and so full of life that she felt drawn into them in a way which was almost more compelling than the world that was going on outside the books.

Lessing: That's a wonderful compliment. I met someone yesterday or the day before who said *A Proper Marriage* was the funniest book she'd ever read. In Zimbabwe a close friend of mine who teaches at the university said two extremely rich young Americans had come through the university and had read *A Ripple from the Storm,* which is a fairly sardonic book about politics, and they were so inspired by the book that they'd gone off to join the Communist Party. So there's no accounting for what's going to happen as a result of your books.

Thomson: In one of your books you talk about our planet's being out of alignment—that it was lacking SOWF, the substance of we feeling.

Lessing: Well, I don't know, of course; I just deduced that it could exist—for the purpose of the cosmology, you understand. Earlier, you asked about Persian words. It's simply that I have a very vast Persian dictionary, and I think I'm probably not wrong in saying that many people do not know Persian and if I take words from it they're not likely to recognize them. I also use the Greek myths or the lesser known figures in Greek mythology for names, and people always read much more into this than the writer ever intends. You know, you might be choosing a name because it *sounds* right for a character and that's the only idea you have in your head. Yet theses will be written about this. I don't know any writer who isn't continually astonished at what we're supposed to be up to. It's never crossed our minds, you know.

Thomson: Books are like children, though. Once you've released them into the world, they take on lives of their own.

Lessing: Absolutely.

Thomson: But it still astonishes you how they turn out in other people's minds.

Lessing: Well, what would you feel if you'd written *The Fifth Child* and in marches a young woman who sits down and says, "*Of course*, this book is about the migrant labor problem in Europe"? I mean, wouldn't you be surprised?

A Writer Is Not a Professor
Jean-Maurice de Montremy

Jean-Maurice de Montremy's interview appeared in Paris in the April 1990 issue of *Lire*. The following translation was prepared by the editor, with the assistance of Patricia Siegel. Copyright © 1990 by Jean-Maurice de Montremy. Reprinted with permission.

Montremy: In *The Golden Notebook,* almost thirty years ago, you depicted adults concerned with being "free." They analyzed themselves, drank, fought, made up, took up almost all the current philosophical and theoretical problems, confronted each other—men against women—while being observed by their rather confused progeny. In *The Fifth Child* everything is the exact opposite: Ben's parents appear stable, full of good will. Their child, on the other hand, behaves like a psychological bomb, destroying their dream of a happy family. Do you get pleasure out of sailing against the wind? Unsympathetic toward rebellion when rebellion is in season. Unsympathetic toward conformity when it comes back into style.

Lessing: I am a writer: I would like to say *only* a writer, a person of the present day, not the priestess of a Great Project. When I wrote *The Golden Notebook* I was forty. I wasn't writing a treatise on feminine stereotypes of the '60s. To the very end, I wanted to tell a story which neither political positions nor sociological analyses were capable of exhausting. That would be the case with all my books, including *The Fifth Child:* I manage as I can, in a given period of time, with the problems that nearly everyone faces at that time. I don't believe, furthermore, that the writer's role should be to forecast, to condemn, to proclaim, etc. Or not necessarily. A writer is not a professor.

Nevertheless, I am undoubtedly wrong to speak of the writer in this way, as though there were a general rule. Let us say, in my case, I never wished to offer a program of ideas or behavior guides. If I had been in possession of such programs I certainly would never have written. I would have proclaimed that women were such-and-such, that relationships with men—who are, after all, a tough problem for women—ought to be henceforth like this or like that, that our children ought to get such-and-such education, that government ought to promulgate that particular law, that the events in Berlin signify this and not that, that the future of Outer Mongolia, Nicaragua, Mikhail Gorbachev, or Mrs. Thatcher ought to take such-and-such a direction. What would I know?

In fact, I don't think very much about these subjects in the first place. I know the problems of the hour which the whole world knows. The fact of having written novels doesn't give me any more clairvoyance than the average television viewer.

Montremy: All the same, you were a member of the Communist Party.

Lessing: Absolutely! For two or three years in the '50s. It's a matter of the *British* Communist Party. I mean, a very, very British party. We talked; we had tea. If I had participated in a meeting of the French party, I would have had an experience of your inexorable logic and your impressive theoretical coherence. That bears little resemblance to the English C.P. The French C.P. embodied Jacobinism.

The English C.P. formed, instead, a sort of nonconformist club. It represented, with a certain effectiveness, our protest against the terrible class system of castes and pigeonholing people, which is characteristically British.

A system—let me say in passing—still well entrenched today and of which *The Fifth Child* bears the deep imprint. But I was a Communist, I called myself one, well before my taking up residence in London. I was even more irrepressibly so in Rhodesia—where there was no Party—than in England.

Then I was aware that we were pretending to be Communists. Each party was only "communist." We were waiting for Communism, something which didn't in fact have anything to do with any particular party.

Montremy: You have also been held up as someone who "speaks well for women." In a certain manner, you have passed as an analyst par excellence of this "tough problem," as you term it, of the relations between the two sexes.

Lessing: Insofar as I'm a writer, I don't know. Is it possible to write books in order to analyze the problems between men and women? I'm not so sure. I've said instead that there *are* problems between men and women, and that my books consequently reflect these problems. They deal with forces, raveling and unraveling affairs, in which the two sexes do not have the same point of view. They grow out of certain concrete situations, including *The Fifth Child* in which the husband and wife disagree about how to deal with Ben, their child. But I don't believe that they represent a true argument on this subject which I am supposed to have made my "specialty."

Let's say that I begin with an observation, with a feeling which bothered me for a long time, without my ever knowing how to settle on a definitive response. Why does a woman always risk losing her identity for good when she loves a man? If it goes bad, she hardly recovers from it. Whereas after spectacular shipwrecks men are able to find their places again quickly. Yes, why can't women, in the depth of their being, do without men? Whereas men, once they regularize the sexual problem, manage quite well in the end: the job, ambition, metaphysics, sport or automobiles allow them to keep aloof in their relationships with a woman (or women).

As time passes, moreover, I see one source of feminism in that fixation of women on men. In the end, it is something that could be labeled grotesquely as feminism.

Montremy: Which is to say?

Lessing: Which is to say, there is an absolutely indispensable feminism: one which has given, still gives, guaranteed working conditions, equal pay, and autonomy to women. On the other hand, feminism which consists of women getting together to palaver endlessly about the short-comings of men who are not present and to keep trotting out among themselves all sorts of griefs can only inflame the dependence of which I just spoke: it's the modern version of the prattling of good women. I believe that excessive feminism becoming an end in itself, when it ought to be merely a tool—I believe that such feminism reflects a total fascina-tion with men. I'm not really sure, for example, that Simone de Beauvoir really liked femininity or really wished to encourage it. In many ways one gets the impression that for her the ideal of womanhood was called Jean-Paul Sartre.

What I have just said, however, hasn't a lot to do with writing. A good many others, I believe, have in their own ways had that experience. Life has certainly taught me this point more than my books have.// I came to understand that I was undoubtedly made to be unmarried. Etc., etc. We are a long distance from books.

Montremy: Isn't it possible, all the same, to see the majority of them, especially the *Children of Violence* series, as very close to your own youth, putting down their roots into it? One finds there colonial Africa, the great estates, the revolution ...

Lessing: To be precise, let's say that my books have perhaps allowed me to fasten upon the world and the sentiments which they evoke. I am not a person who "cracks" or falls apart. On the other hand, I could often become ossified, giving myself up to the illusion that I would have some theories, as at present I have many critiques. Take, for example, *The Golden Notebook;* it's out of date. I started it thinking I was a Marxist, a progressive. Then I discovered that stripped away the whole texture of ideas, remarks, themes. It's possible to have many more or less interesting ideas on many things. It's possible to have passions, political enthusiasms. But to tell stories, to read them, to create them, that operates in a completely different mode. I wanted to say: physically. Not intellectually, not ideologically.

Montremy: You have sometimes been reproached for having a great indifference to particular literary problems, the technique of the novel, the development of narration, etc.

Lessing: I am in that respect self-taught. With a few exceptions, until I was thirty, I lived in colonial Rhodesia. One couldn't imagine a world further removed from literature, theories, schools. There was countryside, animals, plants. And the most narrow of societies into which I was never able to fit. The blacks themselves didn't exist, according to the law: their world remained hermetically sealed off from us.

I started to write all on my own. I found my way in my own fashion: the Russian writers, Proust, Stendhal, Thomas Mann. Or the great English writers like Dickens, Thomas Hardy (who described nature so well), Virginia Woolf, Richardson, Defoe. I never learned to write, and I am still persuaded, moreover, that literature is not learned. One simply encounters, in that realm, people or books, which suddenly speak to you, show you what you have needed to hear or see. And you go on, pragmatically, by trial and error. Contrary to what is sometimes said at present, I believe the novel has never known a more favorable time. For it is a complete hybrid, full of influences (film, myth, music, pictures), prodigiously adaptable. I know very well that the critics and the professors have their theories about it, but I think there is nothing to them. The novel is whatever each author makes of it. There are no "tricks." It simply exists— tries to exist in what is being written. That could take the form of a vast architecturally complex composition or a simple linear novel in accordance with whatever is happening at the moment in which it's being written.

Montremy: Then you don't like theories.

Lessing: When I was in the Communist Party years ago, everything was pushing me toward what was called "the great problems of the hour." But I sensed that in my books it was also a matter of another thing, a phenomenon deeper and more mysterious.

Montremy: Let's take the case of *The Fifth Child*. One can see in it a critique of the naive return to traditional values. It's the story of model parents, worn out by a child. One can see in it a reflection upon the abnormal. It's the story of an atypical child in an oh!-so-model family. One can see in it an analysis of the fall into delinquency of middle-class children. It's the story of a tough who becomes the leader of a gang of thugs.

Lessing: Oh, it's even simpler. All that you described would appear as a matter of course because I wrote it in the heart of the '80s, capturing the imbroglio of the moment. To begin with, I contented myself—as always— with the need to imagine a story, to talk to myself. I received a bizarre letter from a reader. She complained, in quasi-religious terms, of a fourth child who resembled the devil, an extraterrestrial, dangerous. That bothered me. It seemed to me to be a matter of the old myths, dear to stories, of the "changeling"—the monstrous child that the fairies substituted for the real child and brought about misfortune with it. I started with that theme. It is actually a theme rather characteristic of England: I don't think there is a good translation of *changeling* in French. But I'm afraid that I won't convince you: everyone thinks that I wanted to make a point about education or the tyranny of the English middle class.

Montremy: What do you mean by that?

Lessing: That there is a system, very specific, very powerful, of the middle class in England, especially of women in the middle class in England, terribly competent people, terribly active, terribly efficient and perfectionist. With the single great idea to mark off the compartments, to delimit the zones, to indicate differences, hierarchies, etc. Since childhood and the day I left school (I was fourteen; I found the plants, animals, and countryside in Rhodesia more interesting than classes), I have been struck by this fact: we never think about what we have in common.

We see only oppositions, the yeses, the noes, the whites, the blacks. So we busy ourselves and consider ourselves well turned out by affirming for ourselves, as I said, the marking out of the territory. We live in essentially the same manner; we encounter pretty much the same questions, the same difficulties. And I believe that it is important to me as a writer to attempt to find what it is that divides us.

When I was working on *The Golden Notebook* around 1960, I didn't claim absolutely to be doing a thesis on the feminine condition, on the couple, or on the construction of the novel. I was simply trying to understand what was happening to us, to all of us, who refused to live according to "conventional morality." And who all encountered, nevertheless, many difficulties, submissive to the point of absurdity in our need to proclaim our freedom. Just like others, moreover, timid conformists, or traditional males, who didn't live very much better than we, they too prey to their inconsistency, their burdensome great principles, their need to distinguish themselves.

Montremy: You think that the great movements which have successively crossed your path have in general been only a farce? Communism, throughout the '50s. Then feminism. Then, at the end of the '70s, the mystical, Eastern quest, evident in your books from the late '70s: *Memoirs of a Survivor,* or the science fiction of *Shikasta.* They all amount to the same thing?

Lessing: No, I am not cynical, nor opportunistic. I just take conflicts as I find them. Those which are evident in "Marxism" in the '50s, then in "feminism" in the '60s, and then in "Orientalism" in the '80s, perhaps today in "ecology." I use inverted commas throughout in order to indicate that each of these movements carries with it something which is good and is generally shared by people on all sides. I am simply intrigued by this need that we have to choose a camp, even though we share the same difficulties. It is the well-known story of women in control, popular leaders and fervent anti-feminists opposed to free women, agitators and those who very much lead men around by the nose. All the books that I have written indicate, sometimes in spite of myself, the existence in us of an inexpressible dimension stronger than the theories through which we may attempt to channel it. In a certain way, we are complete fools and act as if it were nothing.

Montremy: Writing should be a form of psychoanalysis then?

Lessing: Psychoanalysis makes it possible to put things in inverted commas, I suppose. I don't believe that we can hope to explain the figure of Ben, in *The Fifth Child,* by an analytic theory or by classical psychiatry. When I was about thirty, I experienced a state of extreme tension. I encountered a woman, a bit ordinary—the Mother Sugar of *The Golden*

Notebook—who put me through a sort of therapy. The varieties have nothing to do with mine, even today: she was a Jew who converted to Catholicism because of her adherence to Jung's theories! But within that ideological-intellectual structure (on the other hand, I can recognize it, the Stalinism of Freudians) there lived a genuine personality. It was the contact, incommunicable, inexpressible, which helped to bring me out of my difficulty. I had encountered someone; someone irreducible to manuals, theories, and treatises.

Montremy: Is that why, about 1964, you chose a Sufi master?

Lessing: Yes, in as much as he, like Mother Sugar, was not a guru. Just a spiritual master. Someone who didn't impose any dogma or mystique. He let me make up my own mind about what God represents, without imprisoning me in a religion. I am absolutely, childishly, allergic to religions—even though I have the greatest respect for our nature, which is profoundly religious.

The Older I Get, the Less I Believe
Tan Gim Ean and Others

Questioner: What motivates you to write?

Lessing: Writers are born, like painters and architects. What motivates me
to keep on writing is that I have earned my living from it for the last forty
years. I'm a work animal. When they bury me, I will probably be
scribbling. That's my epitaph.

Questioner: What have you been working on lately?

Lessing: I have completed a book of fifteen short stories called *London
Sketches* which, hopefully, will be brought out by HarperCollins next
April or May. The idea started when I kept hearing people say how
terrible London is. I like the place, so I decided to write about its
pleasures.

I've also finished a book on Zimbabwe. I lived in Southern Rhodesia
from age five to thirty, but under the white rule, I was a prohibited
immigrant for thirty years. I have been back three times since black rule
and the book is my selected memories about how things used to be and
are now. It's called *African Laughter* and should be out next year. I'm also
writing the film script for my book *The Marriages between Zones Three, Four,
and Five* (1980). It could turn out to be a disaster.

Questioner: Do you plan to do more stories with an African background?

Lessing: I don't have plans, but you never know. If you've lived in a
country for a long time but haven't been back, there is such a gap. I don't
think I could write a proper short story, although I could probably write
sketches. Life is continually flowing and nothing is shut up forever.

Things people say seem different but, actually, are related. There is a great mingling of improbabilities. It's like people you hate at sixteen turning out to be best friends at forty-five. This overlap—everything is part of everything else—is a fundamental trend of Eastern philosophy.//

Questioner: Besides your childhood, what other factors influenced you to write?

Lessing: I had a facility for writing. My mother was an able woman but a frustrated musician and she wanted me to be one. She wanted me to do well, but in her own way.

She used to tell my brother and me stories, long epics which she made up. I think the best thing a parent can do for her kids is to tell them stories. When I look back, those are the most vivid memories.

We also had a library at home and I read everything I could. It never crossed my mother's mind to censor them. After school, I rolled around a few years not knowing what to do. But I could write.

When I wrote my first novel, I was very clearminded about it: this was something I could do. I even thanked the Lord because I was not an artist, as then I would need money to buy materials.

Questioner: You only wrote one play, *Play with a Tiger*, in which the lead characters have a love-hate relationship. Why not any more?

Lessing: The characters of *The Golden Notebook* came from *Play with a Tiger*. When the play was done by feminists, they played it as a great blast against men and the humor was lost. It's very embarrassing when the play is done as a shriek of hysteria and I don't want to know about it.

Play with a Tiger was staged in the West End in 1962. I believe if they had done it in a smaller theater it would have succeeded. It was also badly cast—the male lead was a sexist stud.

That's the agony of being a playwright. Why should one go through this humiliation and torture when you can write a novel and get it printed the way you wrote it?

Questioner: Why do you choose to write science fiction every now and then?

Lessing: I've only written two unrealistic stories, *Briefing for a Descent into Hell* (1971) and *The Memoirs of a Survivor* (1975), and I'm unaware they are science fiction.

I wrote the first book because a friend said nobody sat down to read books about Judaism, Christianity, and Islam. I wondered what would happen if a prophet figure turned up now. So I got the idea of using elements common to the three religions in my story.

I'm surprised readers term them "science fiction." They're more "space fiction." Science fiction should examine some scientific idea, exaggerate, even those not born yet. I would love to be able to write real science fiction.

Questioner: Are you conscious of being influenced by other writers, or influencing others yourself?

Lessing: Any writer would be influenced by others. You have to read the great and the good to get a sense of value. I am influenced by them all. Sometimes, I recognize flashes of myself in others' work. So what? At one stage, I was totally in love with literature. It put me in a state of ecstasy that for a few bob I could get so much. I enjoy reading and it continues to be a great adventure. A novel is so unpredictable; it comes up with so much. You don't know what new writer or country is going to turn up next.

In my seventeenth year, I wrote two novels which were unbelievably bad. I tore them up and wrote other novels... more semi-bits and half-novels.... A writer should read a lot if he's tempted to think he's good. You only need to read a page of good writing to see where you stand.

A year ago, I was going through a phase where I had no energy. It's one of those cosmic jokes, I think. I know friends who just couldn't get out of bed. I wrote the book on Zimbabwe based on three visits back. I knew it was not good, but I refused to believe it. I put it away because I was appalled at the lack of energy... the whole thing was dead. I had to rewrite it three times. After that, I wrote a novel that wasn't any good. I'm using those two books to push myself back again.

Questioner: Are you going through a writer's block?

Lessing: No, I won't say it was a writer's block. It wasn't that I didn't know what to write... it was more a lack of energy. I couldn't see any point in writing or in getting out of bed. After a paragraph, I went back to bed.

Questioner: What advice do you have for young writers?

Lessing: Young writers tend not to do enough work. You get stories that show talent but are not nearly as good as they could be. Perhaps this is linked to the unconscious belief that you need so little to be a writer—just pencil and paper—and that it's easy.

Literary talents are common, as we live in a literate society. Reading turns you into a good writer. Many writers are nearly good, but they don't sit on it or keep at it. When you write, you must put it aside and be prepared to tear it up. I have rewritten copy four times and each time, it gets better. Every writer has to create his own market. You have to create those readers who want to read you. How? The only way is to write absolutely honestly about your own experiences and not think about it. A truthful book.

Questioner: Do you have a timetable for writing?

Lessing: I write when the spirit moves me...when I go out to the garden for a walk. I usually write from 8 a.m. to 1 p.m. and 4 to 6 p.m. It takes me a year to write a book.

No woman writer I know has a timetable. Only men have timetables because they have mothers, wives, and sisters to manage their lives. We have to fit it in. Sometimes we get angry about it. If you're childish, you think it's unfair.

I use an old-fashioned typewriter for the simple reason that I've done so since sixteen. But I'm also terribly afraid of disrupting the brain process, the flow between my brain and fingers. My friends who use the word processor haven't improved.

Questioner: What is your philosophy in life?

Lessing: Give me a break. I don't think I have one. The older I get, the less I believe. I will be surprised when I die.

Unexamined Mental Attitudes Left Behind by Communism

Edith Kurzweil

Mrs. Lessing's remarks represent part of her contribution
to the conference "Intellectuals and Social Change in
Central and Eastern Europe," held at Rutgers University
in April 1992. They appeared in *The Partisan Review* in
Fall 1992. Reprinted with permission.

Lessing: I think people from East Europe and Central Europe will recognize that in what I am going to say, I will be talking as a Western European. I'm going to make half a dozen points, each one, of course, oversimplified. All of them illustrate the fact that while we have seen the apparent death of Communism, ways of thinking that were born under Communism or strengthened by Communism still govern our lives.

The very first point is language. It is not a new thought that Communism debased language and with language, thought. There is a Communist jargon recognizable after a single sentence. Few people have not joked in their youth about concrete steps, contradictions, the interpenetration of opposites and all the rest. The first time I saw that mind-deadening slogans had the power to take wing and fly far from their origins was in the '50s when I read a leader in the *Times* and saw them in use: "The demo last Saturday was irrefutable proof that the concrete situation..." Words that had been as confined to the left as corralled animals had passed into general use and, with them, ideas. One might read whole articles in the conservative and liberal press that were Marxist, but the writers didn't know it.

There is an aspect of this heritage that is much harder to see. Even five or six years ago *Izvestia*, *Pravda*, and a thousand other Communist papers were written in a language that seemed designed to fill up as much space as possible without actually saying anything—because, of course, it was dangerous to take up positions that might have to be defended. Now, all these newspapers have rediscovered the use of language. But the heritage of dead and empty language these days is still to be found in some areas of academia and particularly in some areas of sociology, psychology, and some literary criticism.

Recently, a young friend of mine from North Yemen saved up, with much sacrifice, every bit of money he could to travel to that fount of excellence, Britain, to study the branch of sociology that teaches how to spread Western know-how and expertise to benighted nations. It cost him 8000 pounds, and that was five years ago. I asked to see his study material, and he showed me a thick tome, written so badly and in such ugly, empty jargon it was hard even to follow. There were several hundred pages, and the ideas in it could have easily been put into ten pages. This kind of book is written by people who were Marxists or have been taught by Marxists. Students come from "backward" and closed countries to be taught how to write in this debased language. I have seen people, in Zimbabwe this time, introduced to the English language in this pedantic, empty jargon. They will believe that this is the English language and that this is how they should write and speak it.

Yes, I do know the obfuscations of academia did not begin with Communism, as Swift, for one, tells us, but the pedantries and verbosity of Communism had their roots in German academia. And now it has become a kind of mildew blighting the whole world. One may spend a morning in the kind of bookshop that sells student textbooks and only with difficulty find books that are fresh and alive. How to stop this self-perpetuating machine for dulling thought? For sometimes I do see it as one of those mechanisms set to revolve forever inside a vacuum within a sealed glass case. How to break the glass and let in the air? Perhaps this will turn out to be the ideas themselves concealed in the dead language, for they can be useful and full of insights from the research departments of universities—where, as I pointed out before, work is being done that could, if we let it, transform our societies. Full of insights about how the human animal actually does behave instead of how we think it does. These are often presented for the first time in unreadable language. This is one of the paradoxes of our time.

The second point is linked with the first. Powerful ideas affecting our behavior can be visible in brief sentences or even a phrase. All writers get asked by interviewers this question: "Do you think a writer should...?" The question always has to do with a political stance. Note that the assumption behind the words is that all writers should do the same thing, whatever that may be. There is a long history behind this. Let us go no further back than the nineteenth century in Russia, where there were great critics: Belinsky, Dobrolubov, Chernyshevsky, and the rest. They wanted writers to be concerned with social problems. All the great writers that we now describe as the golden tradition of Russian literature had to endure criticism from this point of view, some of it on a very high level. Yesterday, Donald Fanger explained that the Russian novel contains in itself all areas of sociology and social criticism. But I do believe that this is because this is what the writers were like and not because of what the critics were saying. As we say in Britain, "the proof of the pudding is in the eating." In all these great writers' work there is no moment when there is that dull thump that comes when writers have been writing because they felt they ought to. All these writers continued to write from a much older tradition than their critics. If a writer writes truthfully out of individual experience then what is written inevitably speaks for other people. For thousands of years storytellers have taken for granted that their experiences must be general. It never occurred to them that it is possible to divorce oneself from life or to "live in an ivory tower." It will be seen that this view of storytelling ends the interminable debate about form and content that still bedevils literature in some provincial universities. If these writers in Russia had not claimed their right to an individual conscience rather than a collective one, we would not now be remembering and reading Gogol, Tolstoy, Dostoyevsky, Chekhov, Turgenev, and all the rest of that dazzling galaxy.

We saw what happened when this formula, that writers must write about social injustice, took power in 1917. It became socialist realism. Anyone who had the misfortune to read through a lot of that stuff, which I did in London early in the '50s for a Communist publisher, knows that socialist realism created novels written in a language as dead as the books already mentioned as a product of academia. Why? Writers know instinctively that a recipe for writing dead books is to write because you ought. This is because you are writing out of a different area of your mind. I shall never forget an exchange between a writer and an interviewer on television. The interviewer said, "Among the influences that shaped your work, would you say that Heidegger was the most important?"

The writer replied, "You don't understand. When you describe a scene, let's say at the breakfast table, you have to know what your hero is eating. Bacon and eggs? Pancakes? Is it a cold morning? Is the sun shining in? Is there a smell of burning leaves? Did he sleep with his wife last night? Does she love him? What color shirt does he have on? Is the dog there waiting for tidbits? You have to know all this even if you don't describe it because this is what brings the scene to life."

"Oh, I see, then you describe yourself as a realist?"

Never the twain shall meet. And they can't meet because it's two different parts of the mind speaking. One is the critical part; the other one is the holistic part which is probably situated somewhere in the solar plexus. Two parallel lines: the writer is talking about "the fine delight that fathers thought," in Hopkins' wonderful phrase. The critic is talking out of the same spirit that pervaded socialist realism and before that the nineteenth-century Russian critics, and since I am sure the mind sets of Communism were patterned by religion, Christianity and the dialectics of Judaism. A biography of Cervantes tells us he had the Inquisition breathing down his neck all his life. The questions: "Should a writer...?" Ought writers to...?" have a long history that seems unknown to the people who so casually use them. Another is "commitment"—so much in vogue not long ago. Is so-and-so a committed writer? Are you a committed writer? "Committed to what?" the writer might ask.

"Oh well, if you don't know, I can't tell you," comes the reproof, full of moral one-upmanship. A successor to commitment is "raising consciousness." This is double-edged. The people whose consciousness is being raised may be given information they most desperately lack and need, may be given moral support they need. But the process nearly always means that the pupil gets only the propaganda the instructor approves of. Raising consciousness, like commitment, like political correctness, is a continuation of that old bully, the Party Line.

A very common way of thinking in literary criticism is not seen as a consequence of Communism, but it is. Every writer has the experience of being told that a novel, a story, is "about" something or other. I wrote a story, *The Fifth Child*, which was at once pigeonholed as being "about" the Palestinian problem, genetic research, feminism, and anti-Semitism, and so on. A journalist from France walked into my living room and before she even sat down said, "Of course *The Fifth Child* is about AIDS." An effective conversation-stopper, I do assure you. But what is interesting is the habit of mind that has to analyze a literary work like this. If you say, "Had I wanted to write about AIDS or the Palestinian problem, I would have written a pamphlet," you tend to get baffled stares, such an unfamiliar thought has it become. That a work of the imagination has to be "really" about some problem is, again, an heir of socialist realism, of the infamous Zhdanov. To write a story for the sake of storytelling will not do; it is frivolous, not to say reactionary. Whole literary departments in a thousand universities are in the grip of this way of thinking, and yet the history of storytelling, of literature, tells us that there has never been a story that does not illuminate human experience in one way or other. The demand that stories must be "about" something is Communist thinking and, further back, comes from religious thinking, with its desire for improving books as simple-minded as the messages on samplers. "Little birds in their nests agree." "Good children must, good children ought, do what they are told, do what they are taught." I found that on a wall in a hotel in Wales.

If, for example, a writer should timidly remark, "My book, *Eternal Springs*, is not at all about water shortage in the Middle East," the reply is that the writer has no idea at all of what he or she is "really" writing about. A great deal has been said and is being said about political correctness, but I think we might usefully note that this is yet again self-appointed vigilante committees inspired by ideology. Of course, I am not suggesting that the torch of Communism has been handed on to the political correctors. I am suggesting that habits of mind have been absorbed, often without knowing it. There is obviously something very attractive about telling other people what to do. I'm putting it in this nursery way rather than in more intellectual language because I think it is nursery behavior, very primitive stuff. Deep in the human mind is the need to order, control, set bounds. Art, the arts in general, are always unpredictable, maverick, and tend at their best to be uncomfortable. Literature in particular has always inspired the House committees, the Zhdanovs, the vigilantes into, at best, fits of moralizing, and at worst into persecution. It troubles me that political correctness does not seem to know what its exemplars and predecessors are; it troubles me a good deal more that they may know and do not care.

Does political correctness have a good side? Yes, it does, for it makes us re-examine attitudes, and that is always useful. The trouble is that, as with all popular movement, the lunatic fringe so quickly ceases to be a fringe; the tail begins to wag the dog. For every woman or man who is quietly and sensibly using the idea to look carefully at our assumptions, there are twenty rabble-rousers whose real motive is desire for power over others. The fact that they see themselves as antiracists, or feminists, or whatever does not make they any less rabble-rousers.

Political correctness did not invent intolerance in universities, which is an evident child of Communism. If intolerance, not to say despotism, governed universities in Communist countries, then the same attitude of mind has infected areas in the West and often sets the tone in a university. We have all seen it. For instance, a professor friend of mind describes how when students kept walking out of classes on genetics and boycotting visiting lecturers whose points of view did not coincide with their ideology, he invited them to his study for discussion and the viewing of a video that factually refuted such ideology. Half a dozen youngsters in their uniform of jeans and T-shirts filed in, sat down, kept silent while he reasoned with them, kept their eyes down while the video was shown and then, as one, walked out. The students might very well have been shocked to hear that their behavior was a visual representation of the closed minds of young Communist activists.

Again and again in Britain, we see in town councils and in school councils, that headmistresses or headmasters or teachers are being hounded by groups and cabals of witch-hunters, using the most dirty and often cruel tactics. They claim their victims are racist or in some way reactionary. Again and again, an appeal to higher authorities proves that the campaign tactics have been unfair. This happened to a young friend of mine in Cape Town, whom the fanatical Moslems and the hardline Communists joined forces to expel. They had done the same to her predecessor, and doubtless they are now at work on her successor. The victims were white. Were they racists? They were not. Unlikely bedfellows? Not at all. I am sure that millions of people, the rug of Communism pulled out from under them, are searching frantically, perhaps without even knowing it, for another dogma. Some have already found a home with the fanatical Moslems.

The next point seems to have on the face of it little connection with the others, but I think it underlies them all. It is excitement, pleasure in strong sensations, a search for ever-stronger stimuli. What could be more pleasurable when in one's twenties—the age when millions of young people have tortured or murdered others in the name of the forward march of mankind—than the excitements of being the only possessors of the truth? Revolutionary politics, the House committees, the vigilante slogans, are intoxicating drugs. In Spain not long ago I met a youth, of the same stuff as Byron, who said it was the great regret of his life that he was too young to have been in Paris in '68. I asked why—when that revolution had been a failure? He was amazed I could ask. It must have been so exciting, said he. Bliss in that dawn to be alive. Bliss being the point, being turned on, getting a buzz, a high, a thrill, a fix. This set of mind was summed up by one of our political commentators thus: he was talking about demonstrations that seem to have little point, that is, from the point of view of actually achieving something. He said: A large part of left-wing politics these days has nothing to do with ends. The ends are not the point. The means are the point.

There must be hundreds of thousands of people, now middle-aged and in positions of authority, whose most vibrant experiences were the events of '68. Like a war for soldiers, '68 was a high point of their lives. No, Communism did not invent demonstrations, riots, marches, petitions, or even revolutions. The nineteenth century was full of them, 1848 being only part of it and before that the French Revolution, that great mother of so many of our mind sets. We can't really blame Jean Jacques. He didn't invent sensation and excitement and bliss; he didn't invent the worship of sensibility and elation. He merely mirrored these ideas in books that are still instructive. Exciting ideas have always swept across countries, nations, the world. There have always been people high on ideas. They used to be religious emotions, a fact we might usefully keep in our minds. (They still are religious in some areas, and spreading fast.) But in all our minds are patterns that govern our behavior which we do not examine.

It was, at least until very recently, taken absolutely for granted that revolution is a nobler thing than the ballot box. It was and often still is taken for granted that the right place for a serious young person is with the revolutionaries in Cuba or Nicaragua, with dissidents, or protesting the suffering of the underprivileged, or on a picket line anywhere at all. We have watched successive waves of young people from the West traveling to the scenes of new revolutions, to Gdansk, or Czechoslovakia, or Berlin at the fall of the Wall—anywhere at all where there is strong popular emotion. If half of a certain stratum of youth has been off seeking thrills on the road to Katmandu, then the other half has been getting high on a revolution somewhere or other. The last thing they ever think of is staying at home and working for the good of their own country— even to say it bores them, inspires a yawn. For one thing, their own countries are judged as being beneath contempt and not worth their attention. Thus arose the paradox that countries, like those of Western Europe, seen by people suffering under Communism as unreachable paradises of freedom and plenty, were continually being represented as unendurable by young Westerners in search elsewhere for the good and the truth. Because of this unrecognized need to experience suffering, persecution, oppression, successive political movements have invented or exaggerated the oppression in Western countries.

This phenomenon has been analyzed, but I wonder what are the psychological mechanisms underlying the need to denigrate one's own country and seek eternally for paradises somewhere else? I think one reason is that few people on the left—and far beyond the left—have not been soaked in tales of persecution from other countries. Many have spent happy years fantasizing about being in prison and enduring it all with fortitude and heroism, being tortured by interrogators and outwitting them—being clever enough to immediately identify the good and the bad interrogators. Yet these are people who will never be in prison for political reasons, unless they work really hard at it. The secret minds of these Walter Mittys of revolution are landscapes of disaster, tyranny, torture, prison, car bombs, Semtex, and heroic suffering. I personally believe that these hidden landscapes have and do contribute to the continuation of torture and oppression; that they are the reason why ordinary social or political effort in peaceful and democratic countries have proved so uninviting to so many young people. They yearn for the madder music and for the stronger wine of revolution.

My next point is a development of the last. It is that a great many people love violence and killing. Of course they have always existed and always will, but I think under ideal conditions only as a minority. One result of our history of two centuries of revolution, that is, of violence sanctified by high motive, is that there are many people you would not expect to identify with killing and torture who do. In Europe that type of person classified by the sociologists as "tender-hearted"—who hates capital punishment, flogging, bad prison sentences, and the sufferings of the underprivileged, and who continues to agitate against these things—often accepts terrorism for a good cause. The romance of violence, which began in our time in the French Revolution, was enhanced by the Russian Revolution, and then the Chinese Revolution, and means the left wing and liberals—millions of people—have schizophrenia. You can see it easily in the tolerance, not to say worship, of the I.R.A. murderers or in the Red Brigades in Italy. Few people of a certain age group in Italy have not had friends in the Red Brigades, or even for a time were not themselves in the Red Brigades. It was the chic thing to do. Hundreds of young people with the highest possible motives supported murder for political reasons. Most of the Red Brigades were not deprived people. What they all had in common, of course, was the war just behind them. Granted it was a bad and ugly war in Italy, though we tend to forget that, and war brutalizes all of us. But these were the "tender-hearted," dreaming of gentle, fruitful and noncorrupt futures. Those that remained in the organization became merciless and brutal killers, even if most have now had reverse conversions and become good citizens. They were and are still sometimes admired precisely for their brutality. There are people on the left who still defend them. Why? I think the reason is, again, revolutionary romanticism.

And now my last point, but I am leaving out a dozen other ways, of which we are hardly aware, in which I think our minds have been set by Communism. I think that the left wing, the social, even liberal movements of Europe have been terminally damaged because the progressive imagination was captured by the Soviet experience. The Russian Revolution, the Soviet Union, was a paradigm, whether seen as a success or as a failed experiment which we could better. For decades, for half a century, for three-quarters of a century, all the "tender-hearted" people longing for better things were preoccupied with the Soviet Union. With its history of murder, mass murder, show trials. A history, and this I'm sure is the important thing in the long run, of failure. The entire "progressive" movement of Europe has had its imagination in thrall to the Soviet experience, an experience in fact irrelevant to Europe.

It would easily be possible to make an alternative reality, a history of Europe that had made a decision to develop socialism, or even a just society, without any reference at all to the Soviet Union. We must remember, I think, that because of the Soviet Union it has been impossible even to consider creating a just society that is not either socialist or Communist. We did not have to identify with the Soviet Union, with its seventy-odd years of logic-chopping, of idiotic rhetoric, brutality, concentration camps, pogroms against the Jews. Again and again, failure. And, from our point of view, most important, the thousand mind-wriggling ways of defending failure. I think the history of Europe would have been very different. Socialism would not now be so discredited, and above all, our minds would not automatically fall into the habit of "capitalism or socialism."

The story of the Soviet Union in the last eighty years has been a tragedy, for the Russians and the other Communist nations now free. It has also been a tragedy, on a somewhat smaller scale of course, for Europe. Europe has been corrupted by it in obvious and not so obvious ways, to what an extent it is too early to say. It has been corrupted because we've allowed our imaginations to be totally preoccupied with other peoples' experience and not with our own, for one reason or another. I think that it has been suggested here at this conference, many times, that there are reasons that have not yet been examined. My conclusion is that until we know the patterns that dominate our thinking and can recognize them in the various forms they emerge in, we shall be helpless and without real choice. We need to learn to watch our minds, our behavior. We need to do some rethinking. It is a time, I think, for definitions.

Kurzweil: At the beginning of your talk, you spoke about the use of language, the political implications of controlling it. Do you think we can learn from the experiences of Eastern Europeans and from South Americans who lived through dictatorships—many of whom have remarked that Westerners, especially Americans, are very naive about our government, whether we are criticizing or just dissenting.// It appeared to me, in talking with people who have lived through very different types of dictatorships, that virtually none of them took their government's word at face value, whereas in the United States, it is exactly the opposite. Almost everyone here takes what the government says at face value, and there are only a few who are critical or even question it.

Lessing: I think that it is felt not only by people from Eastern and Central Europe. In Western Europe, too, Americans are regarded as being too uncritical of their rulers. Possibly it is because we in Western Europe are on the whole rather skeptical. We're cynical; we don't really believe what we are told, except, of course, at election times, when everyone gets a bit feverish. Why is it that Americans, every time they have a new president, expect everything from this person—who is inheriting exactly the same situation his predecessor faced? Realistically, not much can change, you know. But every time they elect a new president, Americans talk as if a new age is about to begin. I have absolutely no idea why they do this!//

Kurzweil: The inflation of the values of Communism by Western intellectuals, which you spoke of, and the disparagement of their own values and those of their own cultures came out of a bad conscience of some sort. Do you agree?

Lessing: For some reason in the West there has been an expectation of some kind of ideal or much better society than we've got. I don't know where this has come from, and I've spent a lot of time thinking about it recently. Why are we so terribly dissatisfied with a society that, however imperfect, is actually pretty good for most of its citizens? Where does this dissatisfaction come from? Sometimes it arises from contempt and loathing for the countries we live in. Until recently people here thought that the grass was greener in the Communist countries, or if it wasn't greener, then it was going to be.// It certainly leads to extraordinary paradoxes. Young people in Britain, for instance, go out from fairly privileged positions to work in Third World countries because they are Communists. I'm talking about Zimbabwe. They find the most appalling conditions, and their hearts break. They see yet again that paradise does not exist. But why people expect it to exist is the point.

Reporting from the Terrain of the Mind
Nigel Forde

Nigel Forde's interview was broadcast May 1, 1992, on BBC Radio 4. Copyright © 1992 by Nigel Forde. Printed with permission.

Forde: How was growing up in Rhodesia important to you?

Lessing: From my point of view the most important thing was the space. You know, there was practically nobody around, and I used to spend hours by myself in the bush. My mother was a very remarkable woman, very tough, very brave. I remember seeing her holding my father's 1914–18 army revolver at the head of a cobra which had emerged from the flowerbed. She was such a brave woman and so resourceful. All of that was, of course, wasted on a much too small arena for all the talent she had.

Forde: Did you think of it as a harsh life? I mean, it was more harsh, much more conducive to independence than a childhood in Britain, for instance.

Lessing: Yes, that was the great benefit of it, because not only as a child did I have more independence but as a girl I did things that no girl of that time would have done in Britain, or in Europe. We had a kind of freedom and independence which now I marvel at—that I was so lucky to have had it.

Forde: You were sent away to school. Was that a happy time for you?

Lessing: It was awful. It was a convent school in Salisbury, and it was a horrible place, and I was desperately and miserably homesick. I look back at it now as the worst time in my life. Most of these women were peasant girls from Germany who'd become nuns because of the economic conditions in Europe. I've never forgotten one night. I was very young, seven or eight, and in the sickroom where so often I was. A young nun, who I then thought of as an old woman but she was probably eighteen, was weeping and weeping and weeping out of miserable homesickness for Germany, and, of course, she would never go back. How could one blame these girls? They were ignorant, uneducated peasant girls, very cruel, not meaning to be, and it was very, very bad for me. The whole thing was terrible.

Forde: So it was one of the pressures of your childhood?

Lessing: Yes, it was. It was very bad... People become writers because they've had a very pressured childhood, and that doesn't necessarily mean a bad childhood. I don't think an unhappy childhood makes a writer; I think a child who has been forced to become conscious of what's going on very early often becomes a writer.

Forde: Have you used that part of your childhood creatively? I mean, is that something you close off from yourself now, or is it something you've actually been able to explore?

Lessing: I don't think I've directly used it, but I think it's contributed to a certain dark view of life which I now try to examine.

Forde: I understand that you came to London in 1949 with the manuscript of *The Grass Is Singing*.

Lessing: I didn't know it was impossible to live on what you earned by writing, which everyone said it was. I just didn't have very much money. Nowadays there's a very real difference between writers—our lot and this lot. This lot care passionately about money, as far as I can make out, and success, I think, much too soon. I think they should get on with what they're doing and let the success look after itself.

Forde: Is that easy for you to say now, because you had terrific success with that first book, didn't you?

Lessing: Yes, I did. I had very good reviews, and I had enough money to keep me going for a bit, but I certainly was extremely short of money, quite often. I remember walking in Kensington and weeping—I'm not a crier, you know—weeping because I literally did not have one penny. A man stopped me in the street and asked, "What are you crying about?" I said, "I haven't got any money." He said, "That's all right, because you'll have some next week, won't you?" I thought, He's quite right.

Forde: He didn't give you any money, though. He just said you'd be all right next week.

Lessing: You know, he was very abrasive, and that was rather good.

Forde: You've been unhappy with the response to *The Golden Notebook.*

Lessing: It annoyed me very much when *The Golden Notebook* came out, because I thought it was a fairly complex book. I had wanted to say something in it, which was that it was a great mistake to put things into boxes and separate them off from each other, because that leads to craziness of one kind or another. That's what I thought I was saying, but I now understand what happened. That was an intellectual statement. But *The Golden Notebook* was written in such a blast of energy that something else came across, and that is what affects people. So I don't get cross at all now. I just get on with it. I went to Sweden, and a woman came up to me and said, "Well, of course, I only read the blue notebook." I said, "You know, as the author, I do feel a bit bad about that. It's got to do with you, and it's got to do with me." What am I supposed to do about this, issue a manifesto, or just laugh?

Forde: All of your fiction depicts an increasingly "marvelous" view of the world, one which insists that what we accept as normalty just may be a habit of mind. Human beings may have extraordinary faculties.

Lessing: You see, I think everybody has them, and this culture suppresses them, because we're scientific. I think that probably if we had a different attitude toward them a lot of people would discover they had them. But on the other hand, it's very easy to make them more important than they are, because a great many people who have these experiences complain that they are so petty. And they are. It's as if we are tuning in very clumsily and inadequately to something very big.

Forde: Do you know what we'd be tuning in to? Do you have a concept of God, or a Mind, or Something which is in creative control of what's going on?

Lessing: I think "God" is a word—what is it D. H. Lawrence says? "Me and God is a bit uppity"? I always thought that was one of the most sensible things he said. Look, we are very biologically limited, with our senses set to absorb only what we need as animals. You've only got to look at a picture of the sun that a camera can take to see that it looks different from what we see. What our senses see is a very small, brightly colored world. Our minds are set to take in very little, really. It is a fact; we don't have to invent it. So what is it that we're not seeing? What could we see, if we were different?

Forde: Is that what your novels are doing? Are your novels being for our minds what that camera is being for our eyes in seeing the sun?

Lessing: I would like to think that some of them might be a bit. I'm not in a position of any superior information, you know. But I do think a lot of writers, when they write, are much cleverer than when they are not writing, because I do think you tune into ideas, or sensations of some kind.

Forde: You just returned from a conference in America on the demise of Communism. Are you optimistic about the future?

Lessing: I think we imagine that we've in control of events, and we're not; we're all trailing along behind them usually. We can affect things a little bit, this way or that, but what usually happens is that something enormous occurs that we hadn't foreseen. It's happening all the time, and then we adapt ourselves and go on again. The only difference now is we are aware of this, it seems to me, and we try to be more intelligent. That is the great new thing, which is encouraging—that we do know that we are polluting the world, for example. We begin to get a concept of the world as a whole and that we're citizens of the world and not just our own country. That is a great new sensibility, which could save us all yet.

Forde: And yet you still seem aware of a dark strain in your own imagination.

Lessing: If you take certain stories, like fairy stories or magical stories or teaching stories, and visualize what the stories say, and watch what your mind does, you learn a very great deal about yourself. Now I noticed in a certain story that meant a great deal to me there was an old man who couldn't get into his own house, and the voice said, "Put down what you have and follow me. And if you need enough and don't want too much, you will have delicious food." So I made this old man follow the voice. Now I noticed that I could not make this old man walk around the side of this mountain on a smooth path. There was always the most dreadful chasm. My mind did this. I had to throw bridges across it; I had to take him a long way round it. This was a pattern in my mind that I would never have discovered if I hadn't written this story. Somewhere or other, there is a pattern of disaster. So you have to ask, Where did it come from? Is it in all our minds? Is it because of the war? Which is what I think. So it's in my mind. I don't like it very much.

Forde: But you haven't got rid of that. You still see those images, and you still feel that difficulty of the uphill struggle and the chasms that are always around us?

Lessing: I try to tell what's going on in my mind with a story: what's going on with this cliff, this chasm, this sudden collapse of the terrain? I have to report that it's better than it was.

Voice of England, Voice of Africa
Michael Upchurch

Michael Upchurch interviewed Mrs. Lessing in Seattle, Washington, in November 1992. The interview appeared in *Glimmer Train Stories*, Issue 7, Summer 1993. Copyright © 1992 by Michael Upchurch. Reprinted with permission.

Upchurch: Why so much travel?

Lessing: Well, I do a lot because I like it. In northwest Argentina, I went because I was told that it was my kind of landscape—semidesert and mountains, very high. You can go up to 17,000 feet—and that was enough. It's very beautiful. I recommend it. And the air is so clear that you can see miles of the sky at night, garnished compared to anywhere else in the world. So, I adored that. And, well, I'm here! As far as I'm concerned, the northwest states are quite exotic.

Upchurch: Have you been here before?

Lessing: Not Seattle. But I have a friend in Victoria, B.C., just up the road. She took me up Vancouver Island. I don't have to tell you of what the logging companies are cutting down. What do these people think they're doing, cutting down trees on mountains? This is absolutely criminal, just from the erosion point of view.

Upchurch: In reading *African Laughter* I was struck by the life-or-death concerns in it that are bound almost to overwhelm a young person: degradation of environment, AIDS, a kind of disenfranchisement through lack of information or sheer inability to process that information. It seems hopeless. And yet you came of age in a time of total war which can't have been any better. Have you ever reflected whether you'd rather be twenty-three in 1942 or twenty-three in 1992?

Lessing: I never even thought about it. I think in 1942 there was a lot of optimism around in spite of everything, whereas I think people at the moment are absolutely overwhelmed by the problems because we don't know how to cope with them, really. The worst one, of course, is the degradation of the environment. You read these little items in the newspaper, sort of tossed away, that there's a good chance of another accident like Chernobyl happening. We seem to be powerless to stop that kind of thing. Maybe things will be better when you've got a younger president.

Upchurch: Before I'd read *African Laughter*, I'd given thought to civil unrest in Africa, but I hadn't closely considered environmental concerns.

Lessing: The big question mark is the drought. That's the Southern Africa drought which is a once-in-a-hundred-years drought. But a couple of good rainy seasons could put it right again. It's not the first time that this part of the world has had bad droughts. But it's done an immense amount of damage. One figure, the most horrific figure I heard, was that of 800 hippos down in the low veld on the Sabi River, eight are still alive. And they've been kept alive. They're hosing them down and feeding them alfalfa. It's just one easily remembered statistic. If you imagine that with all the animals! The crocodiles and the pigs, they're the most vulnerable. The birds! I saw something on the morning I left—I was there just recently.

Upchurch: So you've been back since you wrote the book?

Lessing: Yes. It could easily have been five visits, only it was too late for that. I went just to check up on my facts and things, and I watched a couple of hornbills. In the early part of the year they eat berries off the cypress tress because they're soft. I watched these hornbills trying to eat these berries like wooden bullets, taking them into their beaks, letting them fall, taking them, letting them fall. You know, they're desperate. And then they flap very slowly off to the woods where there are a lot of dead birds from hunger. The other thing, of course, is the soil, which is being badly damaged by the drought. It's a frail ecosystem, not a robust one. And it's got too many people on it. When the whites went in—this is something most people don't realize—they reckon there were 400,000 or 600,000 blacks in that entire terrain. And now they think there are 11,000,000. And this is on this fragile land. The population started to explode as the whites came in, but nobody knows why. There are a lot of different theories. But the fact is that there are now 11,000,000, and most of the population of Zimbabwe is under the age of fifteen. Now that is a thought to conjure with. It means that the history has disappeared from their minds, because as far as the older blacks are concerned, the

Liberation War [the civil war which ended with a black nationalist victory in 1980] is the great fact. But none of the children care about that, of course, because kids don't care about the wars their parents fought. So there's a kind of gap in the cultural continuity there.

Upchurch: *African Laughter* and *The Real Thing* use a straightforward, I-am-a-camera approach to give a lucid depiction of time and place.

Lessing: *African Laughter* is mostly straightforward reporting, of course, with lots of little bits from my notebook, the bits that I found amusing or interesting. I think I have a lot better chance at covering Zimbabwe than many of the people living in it because there is absolutely no contact, or hardly any, between most of the remaining white farmers and the blacks and ordinary people. They're full of the most ridiculous prejudices about each other. So that was a sad thing. And I can go at once into the university circles and the people teaching out in the bush, and all this kind of thing. I really do cover the ground when I go out.

Upchurch: What was the origin of the fleeting, slice-of-life stories in *The Real Thing?*

Lessing: I'll tell you how it happened. My old friend [and former editor] Bob Gottlieb remarked, absolutely by chance, that the *New Yorker* had a great backlog of already-bought stories. The thing that surprised him was that there wasn't one under 5,000 or 6,000 words. And he asked rhetorically, "Doesn't anyone ever write the same length as Maupassant once used to, or O. Henry, or Chekhov?" So I wrote some very, very short stories, partly as a discipline—because you do spread yourself around. The other motive was the people who live in London are always knocking it, saying what a ghastly place it is. I can't imagine why. It's an extremely pleasant place to live, if people actually use their eyes. That's true of every city. Why, it was just a week ago on a busy main street, I saw a person walking down the street dressed as a cockerel. Nobody took any notice! You wouldn't ever get that in a little country town or a village anywhere, because people would instantly have to know all about it.

Upchurch: Why was *The Real Thing* retitled for its American release?

Lessing: It was called *London Observed* in London, but they thought here that people would take it as a guidebook. So they changed it to *The Real Thing*—which, of course, is an advertisement for...what is it? Guinness, or something?

Upchurch: Coca-Cola! It's the "real thing"!

Lessing: And it's also a Henry James short story. But there you are. That's what they wanted.

Upchurch: You've gone in so many different directions in your writing. Are there books of yours that are favorites or any you wish you could drop from the opus?

Lessing: I have dropped one—but I'm not going to tell you which. Unkind people come up and say, "I've got that book that you tried to suppress." Because I don't think it's any good; I should have written it differently. But no, I think writers regard the whole thing as kind of a process. You try this and you try that. Sometimes you're quite surprised yourself at what you've done. I was surprised at *The Fifth Child*, which was very pleasing. It certainly came out of a very murky layer in my unconscious.

Upchurch: Do you have overt political affiliations now?

Lessing: No. I'm not interested in politics. Wait, that's not true. I'm fascinated by politics. But I don't believe anymore in these great rhetorical causes. I'm much more interested in smaller, practical aims: things that can be done. There was a wonderful cartoon in the *Independent* when the Social Democrats were a new party. It had two farmers leaning over a gate. One says to the other, "Well, Giles, what do we stand for?" And the other one says, "Let me see, Bill. Yes, now, we stand for democracy, freedom, justice, equality for women, abolition of poverty..." It went on like this, right? Like the mouse's tail in *Alice*. And I think that's what I'm not interested in.

Upchurch: There is a line in *The Golden Notebook* that says a novel should have "a quality of philosophy." That's Anna Wulf, your protagonist, speaking. But it seems very much your voice.

Lessing: No, it isn't really. I can't remember the context. I do think a novel should have that quality that good novels do have that makes you think about life. Forgive me for the clichés, but it should enlarge your mind and not narrow it. If that's philosophy...

Upchurch: Anna also seems to have a fundamental distrust of her medium as far as what words can do. Your sheer output would seem to refute that distrust. And yet you voice her concerns, her scruples, with such urgency that I wondered where you stood on that. And if you had that distrust, how did you overcome it?

Lessing: Well, I've never had a writer's block. I gave her a writer's block because I was making dramatic that concept, the situation writers find themselves in if they are political. They're always being told they're much better off putting pamphlets through doors than writing. All writers get that. That is, if you happen to be in a movement of some kind. There is something else very basic there. There was this great explosion of the realistic novel, which does inform us and does do all these things we know a good novel does. But you sometimes ask yourself, What does it change? And that is depressing. Perhaps it changes a little bit here and there...

Upchurch: You grew up very much wanting to change a lot of things.

Lessing: Yes. I hated what I saw around me. I was a part of this white oppressing elite. I didn't like what I saw. And I was brought up in a household that discussed politics day and night, because my parents did. So that gave me a natural leaning toward politics which I have now as an—I don't know what. An attitude of the mind. I find the whole political thing one of the most astonishing theatrical performances! What a drama goes on! What about the whole business of Mrs. Thatcher's end? Could Shakespeare have done any better than that? A cliff-hanger for three days. It was wonderful. All that is very exciting. And this election of yours— there's so much hanging on it, apparently. But in the end, I'm coming more and more to the conclusion that, in fact, we—I'm talking about the human race—are always running along after events, pretending that we're controlling them, running like mad, trying to catch up with the escaping horse. Because we always come to apparently understanding a situation when it's a cliff-hanger. It's always just too late to do anything about it.

Upchurch: I'm very taken with some of the humor in your work.

Lessing: I'm glad you said that because I think people have always chosen to overlook it. I think some of it's quite funny. That note of dry irony.

Upchurch: How important do you think humor is to your fiction?

Lessing: Well, I don't know if it's important. I find a great deal comic, I must say. I find myself laughing during the day because I can't believe I actually heard what I have heard on the radio or something. Newspapers are really funny because they're ridiculous half the time. I'm talking about the political parts of the newspaper...the immense pomposity of them. If I actually read the gutter press, I'd find it even funnier because we have the honor of having the worst gutter press in the world.

Upchurch: When I was much younger, I had a friend who attended Antioch in Ohio, where they seemed to have whole courses on Doris Lessing at one point. And the feeling I got at the time—and it's the reason why I came to your writing late, I think—was: No men allowed.

Lessing: Well, that's nothing to do with me.

Upchurch: But you were very much identified with feminist literature twenty years ago.

Lessing: The feminists claimed me for one of theirs, which made me very angry because I don't like this separation off into sheep and goats. And I've never written specifically either for men or women. But it was interesting about *The Golden Notebook* because there was a time when I only got letters from women—violently emotional ones. But for a long time now, I've got just as many letters from men. They're interested in other things, like the politics, or things I've had to say about people being crazy, and so on. But so many things change. There was a time when, if I came to the States and talked, ninety percent of the audience would be women. That hasn't been true for a long time.

Upchurch: Have your books been available in Zimbabwe? Were they banned under the Smith regime?

Lessing: I was never formally banned, but they couldn't get my books. They just weren't in the bookshops, or they were under the counter. I was very much a baddie, you know. Really. But now, no one can afford to buy books because of the exchange rate. The English pound to the Zimbabwe dollar is nine-to-one, which means that this book [*African Laughter*] would be nine times seventeen pounds, whatever nine times seventeen is.

Upchurch: I'll do some math later.

Lessing: This is somebody's wage for a month. And the local books are also expensive. And the tragedy is—and I'd love you to put this in just in case someone sees it—with these ridiculous Aid people spending money on the wrong things. If somebody wanted to do Zimbabwe a good turn, they would arrange books, mobile libraries, or libraries in small towns and villages, because these people are desperate for books. And they can't get them, can't afford them; they're not there.

Upchurch: There's this problem with a tariff at Zimbabwean customs that you mention in *African Laughter?*

Lessing: I myself have sent books, and other people have, too, to libraries—the Harare and Bulawayo libraries. And they've asked us not to send them because they can't afford to pay the customs on them. Now, this is such a criminal business. The only thing that has changed is that the University of Zimbabwe may now get books without paying customs. But you know the University of Zimbabwe is one place, and nothing to do with the libraries.

Upchurch: The university isn't in a position to distribute books? You can't use it as a conduit?

Lessing: No, no. Every time I come back, I get so depressed because every person I've met—every black person, every white person—is desperate for books. There are so many unemployed, they're getting an inadequate education... It isn't like here, where nobody gives a damn about books. They're starving for books. They don't have television—or they do, but it's not very good television, not like the kind you take for granted in England, with the Open University. They don't have videos. Their cinema is not very good.

Upchurch: And I gather the radio isn't very good, either?

Lessing: At the school I wrote about in *African Laughter*, the radio depended on batteries which people couldn't afford. They had no telephone. Can you believe it? Their electricity was intermittent, but they usually had oil lamps. It goes without saying there was no television or video. And inadequate textbooks. Why aren't these people with all their *Aid* money using some of it intelligently, and not funneling it to Harare?—because that's the way to get it all spent by crooks of one kind or another. They sit there waiting for the *Aid* agencies to give them money.

Upchurch: AIDS is running rampant in Zimbabwe. It has certainly affected my life here. I gather Europe is not in quite such bad straits—yet. Apart from the devastation of the epidemic itself, there is also this new situation where the kind of sounding of the self through sexual adventure that is described in *The Golden Notebook* is accompanied by far too many threats to be quite as blithely engaged upon as it once was. Have you thought of what the repercussions of this are?

Lessing: Well, let's deal with Africa first. There's a big fact that nobody realizes about AIDS in Africa: it's a heterosexual disease. Everyone assumes it's a homosexual disease. It isn't. No one's ever given me an adequate explanation of why it should be so, but it is. And it's rampant. Nobody knows how bad it is. In some parts of Uganda, whole villages have been wiped out. And they think that might happen in Zimbabwe. The difference is they've got a very lively propaganda campaign going on [in Zimbabwe], and there are condoms. But the men don't like to use them. And, because of the terrible poverty, a lot of women are sleeping with men for a bit of money. They're described as prostitutes, which seems to me wickedly unfair because they're trying to get shoes on their kids' feet and send them to school. Right, so back to sexual adventure. Until they find a cure for AIDS, that time is over, isn't it? I don't see anything else. I think that our generation was an enormously lucky generation, sexually, because we didn't suffer with terrible fear over getting pregnant. People now laugh at the Dutch cap, but it worked. And condoms, and so on. It wasn't like our grandmothers who were tormented with terror of getting pregnant—their whole life was ridden by it. And we went in for romantic love, and not what one of my friends called a "horizontal handshake." But now, you see, that's gone. I wonder when it will come back again. Things always go in cycles. It's bound to come back in a different form somewhere.

Upchurch: In *The Good Terrorist*, you describe a kind of grubby underground communal life. What is your connection with that life now?

Lessing: It still goes on, people squatting. At one point, the London Town Council had a policy of letting people squat provided they paid rates and gas. I've always known people who squat. My granddaughter's been squatting recently. The same business—the relentless battle over detail with officials. She's doing it, of course, out of curiosity. She doesn't have to. And then the psychology: there's very little difference in the psychology of an amateur Communist group and the beginnings of a terrorist group. I didn't formulate it as clearly as that until I got letters from a lot of people who had been in terrorist groups, particularly the Red Brigade, which was interesting. And they all said, "What you have described in *The Good Terrorist* is how the Red Brigade initially started before they became well-organized murderers." And one of them used the phrase, which I've thought about ever since, "They got taken over by the language they used." If you've ever been political, whether right wing or middle or left, they use the most ghastly language. It's dead: set clichés and phrases, which have a very bad effect on the way people think.

Upchurch: What's the subject of your talks in Seattle and Portland?

Lessing: The pressures on literature at the moment that make it all the time worse than it used to be. They range from the commercialization of the publishing houses, which I don't have to go into, to political pressures like political correctness and positive discrimination, and so forth. And then the pressures on the writer to spend more and more time promoting. It gets very heavy as a chore, promoting. The short stories, *The Real Thing*, sold twenty thousand [in the U.S.] without my doing any promoting at all. Which is a lot for short stories. And I tried to get the publishers to see there might be a message for them somewhere in there; like you don't have to have the author out there selling. But they don't see it like that.

Upchurch: Is the pressure to do book-promotion tours as great in England as it is here?

Lessing: Yes, very much. The thing is, I've got no solution for this situation.

Upchurch: You've mentioned the dangers of "political correctness." Can you tell me what you mean by that?

Lessing: Well, I can oversimplify it by saying I think the whole thing is a continuation of Communist Party doctrine. It's the same attitude—the need to control literature by an ideology. But the interesting thing is the people who are politically correct don't seem to recognize this. It's all the same attitude! And they haven't, as far as I can make out, taken the trouble to find out what terrible results it's had in the past, like destroying literature all over the Communist world completely, except for a few people who rebelled.

Describing This Beautiful and Nasty Planet
Earl G. Ingersoll

The following conversation took place July 9, 1993, in Mrs. Lessing's home in London, and was first published, in a slightly altered form, in *Ontario Review* 40 (Spring/ Summer 1994). Copyright © 1994 by Earl G. Ingersoll. Reprinted with permission.

Ingersoll: I take it you don't much like interviews.

Lessing: Well, the basic fact is that there are extremely few very good interviewers. But the point is that readers, when they read interviews, never realize that writers can only answer what they're asked. They don't see that this interview is really the mind of the asker of the questions, not the answerer of them. You can't really make this point every time you give an interview. I have given whole interviews where not one question has interested me in the slightest. The other thing, of course, is that you always answer the same question, over and over and over again.

Ingersoll: Is this because your interviewers don't do their homework and don't look at the kinds of questions that have already been asked?

Lessing: No, they don't. Never. I can't remember what year it was, some time in the early '80s, I was traveling; I went to a lot of countries in that year. I think that it was the year I went to Japan and Italy and Spain and Scandinavia. It occurred to me that in every country I had been asked the exact same questions. And what is emerging is a kind of international literary mind. Which is a bit terrifying, really, when you come to think of it.

Ingersoll: Like the inevitable question about your being a Marxist and about your interest in Sufism—I've sensed those repetitions myself in going through the interviews... What are you working on now?

Lessing: Well, I'm currently writing my autobiography, the first volume, where I'm trying to write about my involvement in politics. That is extremely difficult because it is impossible not to write from where you are now. A kind of world-weary tolerance creeps in, which is not at all the mood you were in when you were twenty-four. In fact, the novels, I think, give more of the flavor of that time. I wrote a book once called *A Ripple from the Storm*, which was not only the most autobiographical kind of book I've written, but it really does give the flavor of that time. So I always recommend that to people; if they want to know, they read that. It was about 1942, '43, '44, which is a pretty short time, with that particular lunatic flavor.

Ingersoll: And this is volume one of the autobiography?

Lessing: Yes, it goes to 1949. And I don't see how I can possibly write volume two.

Ingersoll: When can we expect to read volume one?

Lessing: It will be out next year. I'm just tidying it up now and it'll be going in to the publisher's, probably in October. It's going to have photographs, which always makes a book slower to produce. It'll be interesting to see what happens because from time to time I say to myself, I'm writing a book about a little country that nobody gives a damn about now, nobody gave a damn about then. Why do I assume that anyone's going to be interested?

Ingersoll: Any influence of the autobiography on other writing you're doing? Do you feel that by going back to that early experience you're tapping into anything?

Lessing: No... It's very strange, because the first thing is, why do you remember what you remember? Why aren't you remembering other things? This is the first question, and it seems to me the central one, which we take for granted. For everybody, there are whole stretches of time, months perhaps, when you can only remember—I don't know what—a rainstorm or a cat crossing the street. Why?! The other thing, of course, is that as you get aged and tolerant, you soften things up. Everything's very abrasive in life, you know. Later, you just want to laugh gently. But that isn't how it was when you were living it.

Ingersoll: You've told earlier interviewers how depressed you are when your fiction is read autobiographically.

Lessing: The first volumes of Martha Quest are the most autobiographical. I put it in my autobiography what is and what isn't. It's certainly true about the emotions—these abrasive, adolescent emotions. They are all truer than anything I can possibly say now. But the facts are not necessarily true, because I change things around. *Proper Marriage* is more or less true, with differences, and I've said what the differences are. *Ripple from the Storm* is very autobiographical—of course, people are always fitted together to make a composite. And after that, no, it just all shreds apart. I don't really think it's useful for me to say this or that is autobiographical. I know people get terribly upset about Martha Quest when I say such-and-such things are not autobiographical because they like to think they are.

Ingersoll: Really, then, the watershed is about *The Golden Notebook* and *The Four-Gated City*.

Lessing: The watershed was before *Landlocked*. And that is very true in atmosphere, that sort of feeling, but not necessarily fact...You have to ask what they mean when they say "autobiographical"? If I say, Well, I changed Gottfried Lessing, who was my second husband, and borrowed someone else's husband—I was bringing up his son at that time and he was still alive then—but the fact of the matter is that the two men were very similar psychologically. And there were parallels, so I could say, It's not autobiographical and it is autobiographical with equal truth.

Ingersoll: One of the things that fascinated me about the *The Four-Gated City* was the way it anticipates what comes after it. You even use the term "space fiction." And that came out in 1969, and the first of your space fiction didn't appear until 1979. I found that very interesting. You have a writer in it, Jimmy...

Lessing: Jimmy Wood, the space-fiction writer.

Ingersoll: Yes. In his book *The Force Dealers* there are "warners" who try to alert human beings to the activities of energy vampires among them, and it turns out another planet is actually intent on sucking up our planet's energy. You even have Martha in that novel interviewing Jimmy Wood and asking questions: "What effect does this material, these ideas, have on you, the inner Jimmy Wood? Do you think that at some point three, four hundred years ago, science threw out a very important baby with the bath water?"

Lessing: In the '50s I once had an experience which I wish now I'd paid more attention to. Somebody said, "There's a group of science-fiction writers that hang out at a certain pub; you should come meet them." I remember the fascination of meeting these people, who wrote this wild stuff. They were the most ordinary, quotidian, flat, limited people, and none of the ideas in their heads seemed to have lines out into life. It was as though their world was completely and hermetically sealed off, and you couldn't talk to them. Admittedly, I was a woman in that pub and they don't like very many women in that pub.

Ingersoll: And there weren't all that many science-fiction writers who were women at that point.

Lessing: There weren't any as far as I knew; there certainly weren't any in that pub—not one. It was a rather working-class pub. They were very, very defensive, the way science-fiction writers were, and sometimes still are. It never occurred to them that one might be interested in the implications of what they wrote.

Ingersoll: In *The Four-Gated City* you have Paul take Lynda and Martha to the Cafe Royal, and the narrator asserts: "They looked as if they were characters from two different novels; Lynda, he thought, had a look of *Women in Love*, while Martha looked like a New Woman from Bernard Shaw." The reference to *Women in Love* indicates that Lawrence was still part of your consciousness at that time. What was there about him or his work that was useful to you as a writer or a thinker?

Lessing: Well now, I started reading him in Southern Rhodesia before I'd even left the farm. He was among the first of the modern writers I read. His writing had an enormous effect on me because of the vitality of the man. I've just reread *Sons and Lovers* and *Lady Chatterley*, and I cannot recall now the enormous pleasure and shock of that prose. It was so vivid! That was the main thing. Everything comes alive when he talks about it, doesn't it? That's his great quality. And a book called *Aaron's Rod*. I never read him for his ideas, you know; I don't think that's his virtue. I read him for his vitality—unforgettable scenes, one after another.

Ingersoll: Even *Aaron's Rod*?

Lessing: Yes. Do you remember these humorous scenes about the narrator being fairly drunk? It's so funny! And there's "hills that prowl like tigers around the horizon." Anyway, I think some of his ideas are absurd.

Ingersoll: I was surprised that you mentioned *Aaron's Rod*, because that's not a novel that women I know care very much for. They think it's rather anti-women.

Lessing: I never thought of it as being anti-women. Well, he left a wife, if that's the objection. Men often do, don't they? Well, for that matter I left behind two children—who am I to complain? No, you see, I don't approve of this way of looking at Lawrence. I don't see the point of it. I think you should look at what a writer has to offer and take what is offered—not complain that he's not doing something else.

Ingersoll: Something that you want him to do, rather than what he wants to do.

Lessing: Yes... People complain that he has a very amateur attitude toward sex—he certainly has. But his basic attitudes toward sex, I like: he has got an enormous reverence for sex; he doesn't dismiss it and diminish it and make ideological pornography of it. Which is a nice change these days. But the technicalities of his love-making—I feel one might put them on one side and forget about them. But I'll never forget the excitement of reading him, the pleasure of this man. I mean, this Australian book—I don't know if you've ever read it. It was the same excitement.

Ingersoll: Oh yes, *Kangaroo*.

Lessing: Yes. That continent, I will never be able to see it in any other way, and it's really this wonderful, wonderful vitality in the man.

Ingersoll: That's interesting because in the States he is judged so politically incorrect that one can often go to a conference and find no papers on Lawrence because some people don't want to admit they read him.

Lessing: Well, you know, he's had an enormous influence. You can see it in all kinds of people's writing. This political correctness business—I think that it's so silly, most of it, and it's bound to pass. Probably I shouldn't say this, because I'll be lynched, but your country is intellectually an extremely hysterical country. The great movements arise and disappear over the horizon, and I think this one will too. In the meantime I think it's doing a lot of damage, because literature shouldn't be treated as a kind of blueprint for a better way of correct thinking. This isn't what literature is about at all.

Ingersoll: To go back to Lawrence, do you feel some degree of sympathy in the sense that your readers have had the arrogance to try to tell you how to write. I know that you get these responses from people like, Why don't you go back to writing in the realist mode? Why don't you give up this fantasy, this "space fiction"?

Lessing: Well, you know, there are people who will say to me, Why do you waste your time writing realism? What I object to is the narrowmindedness of both sides. I don't see why people shouldn't enjoy both equally. People get into entrenched positions. I think—and I'm sure I don't have to tell any academic this—people take possession of something like an attitude, and they may defend the position and what they own so that after a bit it ceases to matter what the writer is trying to say because it's more important to defend a position. And this is particularly true with political correctness.

Ingersoll: So that writers and their work become the possessions of people who have some vested interest in reading them in a particular way.

Lessing: Yes, I think it happens all the time. The idea that one can get pleasure and excitement from reading has disappeared somewhere. And most I think you should get from the writer what is there. How do I put this? Well, *you* know this, a book is a great offering of some kind to the human spirit, to the human mind. You should look at that first, get that first. If you want to criticize, you can always tear anything to pieces.

Ingersoll: It's rather like being invited to a dinner party and criticizing the hostess for not having dishes you would have preferred.

Lessing: Yes. And Lawrence has had this immense effect—he has, for better or for worse. But when he was first writing, his ideas certainly had some currency, because a lot of people had them. He wasn't the only one to be slightly in love with what we now call Fascism. A lot of them then admired strong men—it was fashionable. A lot of people had mild anti-Semitism and didn't criticize each other for it. But I'm sure that a lot of people—well, I know this because I know them—have read Lawrence with benefit. They've never read him because they admire his ideas, as far as I know—all this sacrificing of women on altars in Mexico—but what a book about Mexico! His travel-writing is superb. So he's flawed, that's all.

Ingersoll: *The Real Thing*, as it's called in the States, or *London Observed*, the collection of stories and sketches which recently appeared, is a surprising work to me.

Lessing: Not really. Why?

Ingersoll: You have a sketch called "In Defense of the Underground," and I think the collection could be called "In Defense of the City," or "In Defense of London," because you obviously love this city.

Lessing: Yes, I do.

Ingersoll: And that's surprising, because there's been so much city-bashing in our time.

Lessing: There's a kind of fashion to knock London. You know how these fashions go. It's fading a bit now, but it's impossible to read anyone saying anything about living here without an obligatory sentence or two saying how ghastly the place is—from people who I happen to know have a wonderful life. You know, it's just the fashion. They have beautiful houses, nice gardens, wives and children they like or don't like, or husbands; they go to the theater, the opera, and have a life of peaches and cream. And yet they knock this city where they choose to live. I find it so despicable and so tedious, so I thought I would come in on the other side.

Ingersoll: Good for you! I like that.

Lessing: It really is a wonderful city to live in. Last weekend I was in Regents Park Theatre with a young friend of mine; I took her to see *Romeo and Juliet*, and what bliss! Which we take for granted. There it is and anyone can go anytime.

Ingersoll: You say in one of the sketches that London offers you a tremendous feast of possibilities.

Lessing: All the time. All the time. Obviously the people who knock London have never lived in a small town like Salisbury, Southern Rhodesia, or they wouldn't knock it.

Ingersoll: That seems somewhat unusual, because you grew up out in the bush.

Lessing: I went into the city at the age of eighteen. That's when I really left the country behind. Since then, I've been living in cities.

Ingersoll: But your childhood was spent...

Lessing: ...out in the bush. Yes.

Ingersoll: I was impressed when you said that the experience was the making of you as a writer—I don't mean to be putting words in your mouth—in that it allowed you to grow up independently as a young woman in ways that you could not have elsewhere.

Lessing: Not then, anyway. I think it's changed so much now everywhere. But when I met English women of my generation I suddenly recognized how extraordinarily lucky I'd been. Not least, because I was out of the English class system, which is such a killer. It really is! Out in Southern Rhodesia, this kind of thing didn't exist. That was a great benefit. Also, women were much freer, even then. Women used to go off in cars, with men, into the bush, and I can't remember anyone ever saying they shouldn't or raising an eyebrow. Women farmed by themselves—there were quite a few of them—all these things which were taken for granted. I was very lucky.

Ingersoll: In your earlier interviews, you seemed to be really struggling against the interviewers' efforts to make you say that Ben in *The Fifth Child* represented some embodiment of evil. I didn't see him that way.

Lessing: There were two things I was fighting against in those interviews. One was that Ben was evil, when he is merely someone who's in the wrong place, because if he'd been in a forest somewhere 20,000 years ago he wouldn't be "evil" at all. The other thing is what this book is supposed to be about. People instantly say, Well, it's about...I don't know what. Make it up—genetic discovery, or mutations.

Ingersoll: I've been amused by your story of people coming up to you and trying to tell you what *The Fifth Child* is "about." Someone like the woman who comes in and announces that it's really about AIDS, or about...

Lessing: Yes! A French woman came in here and before she even sat down said, "Well, this is obviously about the Palestine problem." I said, "Wait a minute." The energy for that book came from my anger about Afghanistan. It was a blocked fury that translated itself into that book. Writers understand this instantly. Sometimes people say, "Oh, is that about the Afghan problem?" No, it isn't, it was fueled by Afghanistan.

Ingersoll: In the Michael Dean interview, you say: "There is a place for novels that have ideas and shake people up and then die." Can you give an example of that kind of book?

Lessing: Yes, I can tell you one right away, which I've just been writing about. My mother and father used to keep talking about an early H. G. Wells book called *Joan and Peter.* I'm sure you've never heard of it; it's a very bad novel. The point is that it is full of ideas about the upbringing of children, how ridiculously they were brought up then and how they were badly taught and so on. It had an enormous effect upon that generation of parents. Who's ever heard of it now?

Ingersoll: We started out talking about interviews and interviewers, and you've said that we interviewers always ask the same kinds of questions. What kinds of questions don't we ask you that you wish we did?

Lessing: I was in Denmark, and I'd been answering questions for three weeks in various countries. Suddenly the woman who was interviewing me said, "Clearly the most important influence in your life has been the First World War." I could have wept with pleasure and relief that someone had noticed this obvious fact. But this doesn't happen very often. Anyway now I've written about it in my autobiography so no one will be able to say I haven't spelled it out. I'll be curious to see what happens when the autobiography comes out. What is going to be disappointing is that there are two different voices: one, when you're writing a novel, but this one is another. If you're writing a record, a personal history, you're really writing from a different part of yourself, very much more detached, and people are going to find that disappointing. I'm sure of it. I don't know if you remember in *The Golden Notebook* there are two different parts where a group of people go down to a place I call Mashopi. When I'm writing autobiography I come to this, and I write some things about the people. When I end that chapter, I read *The Golden Notebook*. And all I can say is that fiction has it over the "truth" every time.

Ingersoll: I especially liked those scenes; they're very powerful: the scene with the insects and the pigeon-shooting scene.

Lessing: It's very much better than what I've just written in my autobiography, because it's more developed. You can't do that in an autobiography. When you think about it, there's been a lot of life when you reach seventy-four.

Ingersoll: You mentioned in an earlier interview that you'd just reread *Martha Quest*. Do you often reread your own work?

Lessing: Sometimes. I must go back and read *Four-Gated City* again. I haven't done that for a very long time. Last time I read it, I rather liked it. I find that my first two Martha Quest books have got a great, exuberant, rather crude vitality, which I don't have anymore. They were much too black-and-white. You get all full of *ifs* and *buts* as you get older.

Ingersoll: One of the things I liked about *The Four-Gated City* was that there's so much comment on the literary scene.

Lessing: Is there? Good. I shall have to go back and read it.

Ingersoll: Yes. A lot about writers and academics and literary scholarship. There was a writer who was rather hard-up for money...

Lessing: Oh yes, I remember.

Ingersoll: ... and had typed a novel because that was his way of working...

Lessing: That was true.

Ingersoll: That was true? You knew someone like that?

Lessing: Yes.

Ingersoll: ... and then went back and did a handwritten manuscript, complete with erasures and revisions.

Lessing: Well, that was true, because that was the golden age of selling manuscripts to America, and this writer was so hard-up that he did this to keep his wife and children fed.

Ingersoll: You don't seem to have had very much patience with us academics.

Lessing: I don't know. I seem always to be meeting academics and visiting with them and going to their universities and quarreling with them. What more do you want?!

Ingersoll: OK, but you told one interviewer that you don't even think literature should be taught in universities.

Lessing: Yes, but the point is if it isn't taught what's going to happen to poor literature? I've come to the conclusion that universities have become the equivalent of medieval monasteries where learning is being preserved, because look what's happening outside. I keep getting letters from universities in what we call the Third World, saying that they cannot afford to buy my books, can I send them some? And I do. And don't you think that's terrible? Because that means that nobody can afford to buy any books. Poor people can't afford them, and the libraries can't buy them. Having their writing taught is the price writers have to pay so that academics will help to keep it alive. *You* know how I think literature should be taught. It shouldn't be taught in such detail. But it's no good saying that, because that's the way it's taught.

Ingersoll: It shouldn't be taught in such detail?

Lessing: Well, I don't like all this nitpicking.

Ingersoll: The analysis?

Lessing: Yes. I don't see what it's got to do very much with the literature... Well, there are two things here, aren't there? One is interesting young people in literature, where it should be taught differently, and I have no doubt about that. It should be taught in such a way—and it's much harder to teach like this—where they're encouraged to flit their way from flower to flower. That's what I think. And not be made to write detailed essays about something, because it puts them off. That's one aspect of it. The other is that I know there are whole university departments staffed by people and this is what they do. I mean, what's the good of quarreling with it? It's what goes on. I see it rather as the price one has to pay for having all this interest kept alive in literature.

Ingersoll: A good deal of what goes on in the classroom is often talking about how the novel is put together, and students themselves often say, "You've taken it apart and I can see how it's working, but I like it less than I did when I read it before class. Your taking it apart has killed some of my joy in just reacting to it."

Lessing: There's the story about the scientist who dismembers a butterfly and then asks, "Where's the butterfly gone to?" What I feel is there's no point my saying this, because by now there are two or three generations of people in literary departments who've been trained to do this kind of thing. And between people who think like this and writers truly there is a gulf, because we don't understand each other at all. When I go to lecture, sometimes I'm asked questions which I literally don't understand. I've no idea what people are talking about. And it's the same with most other writers I know. What's happened is that the process has become an end in itself, I think. OK, that's fine, but I just don't want them putting young people off enjoying literature, which I've enjoyed so much in my life, and still enjoy so much.

Ingersoll: You get a lot of mail from your readers, don't you? Your non-academic readers.

Lessing: Yes, I do. When I've had a book out, I'm always interested to see what will come in. I've had a lot of letters about *African Laughter*, of course.

Ingersoll: I was interested in the response you got to *The Good Terrorist.*

Lessing: Oh, I had such a lot of letters, some of them from people who by the grace of God had not been swept up into the Red Brigades. And one or two fairly sardonic ones from Ireland. Well, more than one or two, describing people who lived as if they were revolutionaries. One said, "I don't know if you realize it, but if you set up a style as a revolutionary you need never after go to a meeting: you have an identity, you have clothes, you have a vocabulary, and that can be it for the rest of your life." And of course you meet them everywhere. But they're lucky then if they don't get swept up into something bad.

Ingersoll: Your readers who write you letters then give you a sense of audience?

Lessing: They're obviously very different, you know. I mean, the people who liked *African Laughter*. In New York, for the first time in my life, I had this experience. I was in this very prestigious place, and it was packed up. I was talking about *African Laughter*, and about ten minutes after I started, people were walking out. Quayle and Gore were coming on TV in an hour, and I got the feeling I was in competition there. But at the end of that lecture—and I cut it short because people obviously were bored— one woman came up to me and said, "When are you going to talk again about yourself?" On the other hand, when I went to Washington I had the most wonderful audience I've ever had—packed full of people who knew all about Africa and wanted to hear me talk about Africa. But, you see, these people might not have read anything else I've written. I mean, why should they? I don't expect everyone to have the same interests.

Ingersoll: As I say, I am interested in how writers develop a sense of an audience, because as you're writing here in this house you have to be aware there's a world of people out there who are going to read what you write.

Lessing: Well, if you write a book like *African Laughter,* you have to be aware. If you write a book like *The Four-Gated City,* you don't think about what's out there, because it spoils what you're inventing.

Ingersoll: An earlier interviewer, who read the file of your reviews at the *New York Times,* commented on how negative some of the earlier ones were.

Lessing: Very. Particularly of *The Golden Notebook.* Particularly the ones done by women.

Ingersoll: I was wondering whether that sense of those negative, early reviews went into the writing of the Jane Somers books?

Lessing: Not really, no. I was interested in writing under another name to see what would happen.

Ingersoll: Writing under a pseudonym was very risky, wasn't it?

Lessing: I haven't been forgiven for it here. The books did very well in other countries, particularly well in France, of all places. Would you have expected that? They did very well in Scandinavia and in Germany. But they did not do well here, or in America.

Ingersoll: When Minda Bikman asked you about the *Canopus* series, you told her that "there is nothing to stop me from going on quite a bit until I get bored with it." You did stop. Are you going back to the series?

Lessing: I want to write the last one, which will be fairly difficult because I've dispatched my hero off to Shammat. The trouble with that is Shammat is extremely like Earth, and I have to find ways to make it different. There's nothing to stop me, if I live long enough, going on indefinitely. I mean, it's easy for me to describe this nasty planet—this beautiful and nasty planet. I want to write volume six, but I always seem to get sidetracked into something else.

Ingersoll: You obviously love to write.

Lessing: I have to write: it's a neurosis. It's true. I get out of balance, you know, if I don't write.

Index

II. GENERAL INDEX

Praise for END MEDICAL DEBT

End Medical Debt confronts an important, sad truth: No one asks to be sick. It's hard enough being poor; it's hard enough being sick. But being poor and sick becomes a death sentence for some, a life sentence of indentured servitude for others. The bills are almost beyond belief. I went into the hospital overnight with chest pains, and the hospital bill was $25,000. It's time to lift this yoke off the necks of some of the most vulnerable and defenseless members of society — and that is precisely what *End Medical Debt* does.

Alan Grayson
Former U.S. Congressman (D-FL)

End Medical Debt does more than describe the unsustainable structure of our current health care system. The book demonstrates what was always the solution: People helping people, voluntarily and without coercion. The current healthcare system has created a debt-enslaved class with few options. Necessity will produce many solutions, but in the meantime, *End Medical Debt* is offering hope from those willing and able to pay forward their success. Humanity at its best.

Ernest Hancock
Publisher, FreedomsPhoenix
Talk Show Host, "Declare Your Independence"

End Medical Debt explains that among all the developed countries, only Americans risk the probability that medical treatment will be financially inaccessible or that a family will be made destitute from a serious injury or disease. The sacrifices families make for medical care of loved ones is heartbreaking. The experience and wisdom of authors Jerry Ashton, Robert Goff and Craig Antico have resulted in the system presented in their exciting new book. Their charity, RIP Medical Debt, may well help us to turn the corner on this major problem facing quality medical care in America.

Nancy A. Niparko, M.D
Diplomate, American Board of Psychiatry & Neurology
Attending Neurologist, Children's Hospital Los Angeles

While care providers fight to make ends meet and corporate interests seek out profit margins everywhere, politicians struggle to strike a balance as more and more Americans are compounding their serious health issues with unprecedented and unmanageable medical debt. Meanwhile, a small self-appointed group of experts from the world of health care finance are seeking solutions for consumers, providers and a broken system. Where there are no acceptable answers yet, people are creating them. Jerry Ashton, Robert Goff and Craig Antico are putting lifetimes of experience to work in *End Medical Debt* to spread the word that medical debt is a personal and national crisis. More so, they are offering answers that are gaining national attention.

Kevin A. Cahill
New York State Assemblyman (District 103)
Chair, Assembly Committee on Insurance
Member, Assembly Committee on Health

End Medical Debt is exactly what is needed to jumpstart the much-needed national discussion about our current dysfunctional for-profit health care system, and what to do about it, so patients like me don't have to experience the financial and personal hardships caused by medical debt. We are a forgotten, disposable, invisible universe of people. There are millions of us. This book explains with passion and honesty the nightmare of medical debt.

Joel R. Segal
Former senior legislative assistant, U.S. Congress, 2000-2019,
Co-author, HR 676: "Expanded and Improved Medicare For All"

END
MEDICAL
DEBT

*Of all the forms of inequality,
injustice in health is the most
shocking and inhumane.*

— MARTIN LUTHER KING, JR.

END
MEDICAL
DEBT

Curing America's $1 Trillion Unpayable Healthcare Debt

Jerry Ashton
Robert Goff
Craig Antico

Founders of RIP Medical Debt

Edited by Judah Freed

Kauai, Hawaii USA

END MEDICAL DEBT

Publisher Website: HokuHouse.com
RIP Website: RIPmedicaldebt.org

Editor, Cover & Book Designer: Judah Freed

Published by Hoku House, Kauai, Hawaii
Printed in the United States of America.
eBook in mobi and epub formats.

Cloth Hardcover:	ISBN-13: 978-0-9892241-0-9
Trade Softcover:	ISBN-13: 978-0-9892241-2-3
eBook:	ISBN-13: 978-0-9892241-1-6

Please contact the publisher at HokuHouse.com for special orders.

The opinions expressed by each individual author are not necessarily those of the other
authors, RIP Medical Debt and its supporters, or the publisher.

This book contains information intended to help readers become better informed consumers
of health care and citizens active in public discourse. The book is not intended as a substitute
for the advice of a licensed physician or certified financial counselor. The reader is advised to
consult with a trusted professional for all matters relating to personal health and finances.

First edition published on December 7, 2018.

Library of Congress Control Number: (Pending)

Cataloging-in-Publication Data:

Ashton, Jerry, 1937 —
Goff, Robert, 1952 —
Antico, Craig, 1961 —
    END MEDICAL DEBT
    Curing America's $1 Trillion Unpayable Health Care Debt

195 pages with 11 Chapters.

    1. Contemporary Affairs. 2. Personal Finance.
    3. Politics/Government. 4. Health 5. Economics.

Dedication

For all who struggle with medical debt
and for all who care to abolish it.

An institution or reform movement that is not selfish,
must originate in the recognition of some evil that is
adding to the sum of human suffering, or
diminishing the sum of happiness.

— CLARA BARTON

END
MEDICAL
DEBT

Table of Contents

Acknowledgements

The three authors of *End Medical Debt* each have great people to thank for helping them to create this book.

Jerry Ashton: My fullest expression of gratitude goes to my co-authors and the publisher, without whose efforts this book and the success of RIP Medical Debt would not have happened. First in line after them is my wife, Kate Coburn, and my wonderful daughters, Andrea and Alexandra, for their unfailing support. They have been my anchor in every storm. The magnetic center of influence in my personal and professional growth has been Occupy Wall Street and my experience with its famous "Rolling Jubilee" experiment in debt forgiveness, which inspired our charity. Occupy was the petri dish in which many ideas and solutions could develop and mature, RIP being one of them. Here's to all you Occupiers, past and present, who caused me to be aware and then motivated me to put that awareness into responsible action. *End Medical Debt* is dedicated to your continuing and important influence in America

Robert Goff: My contributions to the book would not be possible without my immersion for over 45 years in the American healthcare system. Nearly 20 years with the University Physicians Network gave me insights to practitioners of the art and science of medical practice with care and compassion. Such leaders as doctors Stuart Garay, Sol Zimmerman and Paula Marchetta are examples. I'm grateful for a decade of collaboration with Edward Ullman to create and operate one of New York's earliest HMOs, trying to offer both quality and affordability in health care coverage. The variety of roles during my career contributed different perspectives. My wife Jinny and my son Blake's experience as healthcare consumers have kept me grounded in the actual patient experience within the disjointed healthcare non-system. I also want to acknowledge my co-authors, Jerry Ashton and Craig Antico, for their energy and creativity in forming RIP Medical Debt, whose mission this book seeks to support.

Craig Antico: I wish to thank: Jerry Ashton, progressive activist and gadfly (my balance) turned partner, friend and wise mentor; you haven't changed; but, thanks to you, I have. Jessica, spouse of great sacrifice, giver, cheerleader, loyal best friend, an intelligent, caring, conservative influence. My uniquely caring sons Erik, Clark, Alex, Connor, and Chad. My optimistic and well-read father, Al. Mother Barbara never gave up on me! Andy Goldstone, using TransUnion data for good through RIP. Albert Handy, an unselfish supporter, idea creator, inspiring me to build the most compassionate, life-changing, unbiased, impactful donor-led charity platform for good ever funded, designed and implemented. Fergus Cloughley and Paul Wallis: true partners and friends, inventors of data flow science. Dan Love, pastor, nurturing my faith in God, compassion for community. Robert Goff, storyteller and teacher. Matt Maloney. Bill York, visionary, networking communities for wellness. Judah Freed, our sagacious editor. Researchers Francis Wong, Ray Kluender, Wes Yin, and Neale Mahoney for rigorous, evidence-based insight.

Judah Freed: I thank my wife Melissa Mojo, all three authors, the RIP team, publicist/ally Ilene Proctor, ProofreadingQueen, and Scott Hutchins. I also thank *you* for actually reading acknowledgments!

A Meeting of Minds

Judah Freed, Editor

Have you ever heard the one about the progressive, the moderate and the conservative who walked into a charity? They forgive medical debt, and they wrote this book on how the U.S. healthcare system has created *$1 trillion* in unpayable medical debt. They agree on the economic causes. They disagree on the solutions. Well, all the solutions save a simple act of charity: Abolish uncollectible medical debt by buying it and forgiving it!

All three authors of *End Medical Debt* are medical debt industry insiders. Together they began RIP Medical Debt, a tax-exempt charity that locates, buys and forgives unpayable medical bills.

They see debt forgiveness as necessary but not sufficient, our best interim solution until we can agree on a better financial structure for the U.S. healthcare system. This book is a step in that direction.

End Medical Debt presents a clear "big picture" of medical debt with pragmatic insights on personal and national solutions.

The authors bring deep expertise to the problem of medical debt. **Jerry Ashton** has more than 40 years of experience in the credit and collections industry. **Robert Goff** recently retired from 40 years in healthcare management. **Craig Antico** has 30 years in collections, debt buying, outsourcing, and consulting.

This trio together created RIP Medical Debt. Craig is co-founder, chair and CEO. Jerry is co-founder and Executive Vice President. Robert is RIP's founding board member.

Offering 40 years in journalism, I serve as the book's editor and publisher at my Hoku House. For friend Jerry, I published the 2016 book he wrote with Robert Goff — *The Patient, The Doctor and The Bill Collector: A Medical Debt Survival Guide.* That book led to RIP appearing on the HBO series, "Last Week Tonight with John Oliver." The rest is history, part of which is told in these pages.

When "Obamacare" survived a Senate vote, I suggested updating the book. Jerry wanted to write a new, more current book. Robert wanted to speak more freely than he could when still a healthcare administrator. Craig felt a passion to express his own insights. So, here we are. *End Medical Debt* is the fruit of our collaboration.

You need to know only two more things.

First, each author agreed to write his chapters without seeing the others' work, waiting to read the full book until the layout was done. The views of each author are his own. Balancing their distinct voices has been my distinct pleasure as editor.

Second, Hoku House pays the authors *85 percent* of all the book revenues (opposite of most book deals where authors get a pittance). ***The authors donate ALL their royalties to forgiving medical debt!***

— JF

END
MEDICAL
DEBT

*Debt, n. An ingenious substitute
for the chain and whip of the slavedriver.*

— AMBROSE BIERCE

CHAPTER 1

Seeing Through the Tears

Jerry Ashton

One of the most difficult tasks we at RIP Medical Debt face on a daily basis is reading entreaty emails from people around the country who beg us to relieve their medical debt burdens.

Here's a sampling of the heart-moving postings at our website:

"I'd appreciate it if you would help me pay my medical bills. I am unemployed at this time. Between the student loan and medical bills, I cannot make it anymore."

"I need help! I am $30,000 in debt and having a hard time keeping up with payments. They keep calling me to ask for the money."

"It's hard to sleep now, hard to find some emotionally peace of mind. I owe so much. I'm just tired of being harassed, but no one listens to me."

"I feel like I am drowning. I am trying to clean up my credit, and all I have is medical debt. My health is not cooperating, but I do not want to incur more bills. I honestly do not know what else to do."

"Two major surgeries in past 12 months. Cannot pay the copay. Have been denied disability twice. Lost my job. Losing my insurance next month. Don't know what to do."

"I managed to make monthly payments and pay some of the doctors in full, but my well is empty, and so is my stomach. I have $2 in my bank account until my Social Security check is deposited. It's getting a bit difficult going on like this."

"My husband was diagnosed with cancer, and he is buried in medical debt since then with no relief in sight."

"My wife and I have both have taken on extra work outside our full-time jobs, just to try to pay down the debt. At the beginning of the year, we drew up a budget to again try and tackle this debt. We realized the only hope was to go bankrupt. It has become impossible. I'm feeling more and more depressed."

"My husband was laid off last year and has not found another job. His unemployment runs out next month.... I got a medical bill for a one-night hospital stay. We have gone through our savings, 401(k) and an inheritance, but I'm determined not to let our credit be destroyed. I called the hospital and went on a five-year payment plan at $100 a month. That may not seem like much, but I'm the one who deals with all the finances, and I'm breaking down in tears on a daily basis from dealing with all of this."

The tears of such suffering people evoke our own. You may cry because of their severe financial straits. I personally weep because the medical debt forgiveness charity I helped start still lacks sufficient means to help all who desperately need debt relief.

Medical Debt: The Hidden Problem

Our nation fervently debates the nature and future of the health care system. Whether one favors or opposes the Affordable Care Act (Obamacare), concerned people across the political spectrum agree something must be done about the growing numbers of Americans who are uninsured or underinsured. Health coverage is the topic. The national conversation has overlooked medical debt.

Let's start with seven evidence-based (ergo, indisputable) facts, not political opinions, concerning the impact of unpaid medical debt on individuals, families, communities, and society itself.

NationalBankruptcy.com reports that:

1. The United States spends more per capita (per person) on health care than any other country on earth.

2. About 1 in 10 adults delay medical care because of its cost.

3. An unexpected $500 medical bill is too much for many people to pay, let alone pay in a timely manner.

4. One in five, or 20 percent, of all working-age Americans with health insurance have trouble paying their medical bills.

5. More than 60 percent of insured Americans with medical bills will deplete most or all of their savings to pay these bills.

6. About 60 percent of the people with problems paying medical bills were contacted by a collection agency in the past year.

7. Health insurance annually has become less affordable since 2015, when the Affordable Care Act went into effect.

Based on our research at RIP, I'll add that 43 million Americans now have about $75 billion in past-due medical debt on their credit reports. We estimate the total of reported and unreported unpaid medical debt in America at about *$1 trillion over ten years.*

How can this be happening in one of the world's most robust economies? Well, a major reason is that our economy values profits. Whether that's good or bad, it's a fact. You may or may not be a fan of "capitalism," but it drives our economic system.

As a result, while we do not burden our population with high taxes for health care like so-called

Our national conversation has overlooked medical debt.

"socialist" nations, dollars saved in taxes instead are siphoned off by insurance premiums, copays, out-of-pocket medical expenses, and insurance policies that do not cover us fully or not at all (if we have insurance), plus deductibles that can run into thousands annually.

Everybody up and down this chain of pain profits from medical care, even my own industry of debt buyers and collection agencies. Everybody profits, but not the patient.

Our medical care profit system may not be so bad if we're getting our money's worth. Are we? In the September 2018 issue of Managed Care, Joseph Burns challenged Americans, saying, "Hey, big spender! Why does your quality lag so far behind other countries?"

The USA in 2016 spent $10,348 per capita on health care, almost double the average ($5,198) from 11 comparable nations. Citing statistics showing these other countries do much better in a number of health categories, he asked, how do we solve our gap in care?

Adding injury to insult, Americans do not really live longer than citizens in countries with universal healthcare. Economics professor John Komlos wrote in a "PBS News Hour" column that in 2015, the average life expectancy in the United States was 79.3 years, less than in Canada at 82.2 years. Canadian babies can expect to live three years longer than babies born south of the 49th parallel.

How much would it be worth to you if you could live three years longer? Who cares what you label a healthcare system if it delivers a better product? Forget "alternative facts." Look at the hard evidence of costs and inefficiencies in the U.S. healthcare system.

The Five Stage of Healthcare Grief

In my mind, facing the enormity of the personal and national financial costs of the broken U.S. healthcare system is like facing the five stages of grief identified by Dr. Elisabeth Kubler-Ross: *Denial, anger, bargaining, depression;* and *acceptance.*

Kubler-Ross dealt with *sanely* grieving the death of a loved one. Does that apply? We see enough of healthcare in nations that have mandated free or universal coverage that we may sanely feel grief for what we do not have here in our country. In real ways, we Americans turn out to be the healthcare have-nots.

The USA stands alone among 33 highly developed countries by not having universal healthcare coverage. The USA ranks among such poor nations as Afghanistan, Cambodia, Chad, Gambia, Haiti, Iraq, and Zimbabwe, which also do not offer free medical care or universal healthcare. This is not a good thing, in my eyes.

Americans turn out to be the healthcare have-nots.

Let's now explore the analogy of Kubler-Ross' five stages of grief. Seeing through our tears may be a life-affirming resolution for going forward as a much more complete person and healthy nation.

Denial: Think about the many plays on that word — denial. Ever had a claim denied? Ever watch a politician deny any culpability for keeping in place an economically crippling healthcare system? Ever looked at a hospital bill and exclaimed, "This can't be true!"

"Denial helps us to pace our feelings of grief," says Grief.com, "There is a grace in denial. [Denial] is nature's way of letting in only as much as we can handle." Denial is the first step in unwittingly beginning the healing process. "As you proceed, all the feelings you were denying begin to surface."

Some deny the brokenness of our current system, or the value of universal healthcare, by claiming our profit-centered system yields the best health care in the world. Or if our care isn't the best, at least we don't have to wait in line to get it. Factually, that's not so.

Among eleven major nations, U.S. healthcare ranks last.

The U.S. does not have the best healthcare system on earth. In fact, The Commonwealth Fund rates the USA worst among 11 high-income nations. As reported by Newsweek on July 14, 2017, we rank last or close to last in access, administrative efficiency, equity, and care outcomes.

"The U.S. rated especially poor in equality of coverage," stated Newsweek. The magazine reported that 44 percent of low-income Americans have trouble gaining access to coverage compared with 26 percent of high-income Americans. The numbers for the UK are 7 percent and 4 percent, respectively. The UK's National Health Service was deemed the world's best healthcare system, actually, just as it was in 2014. In contrast to the USA over the past decade, the report said, "The UK saw a larger decline in mortality amenable to health care than the other countries studied."

Why deny denial? Feel grief for what we do not have.

Anger: The shift from tears to anger was exemplified in 2017 by late-night talk show host Jimmy Kimmel when he pilloried Rep. Bill Cassidy (R-LA), who'd vowed to replace the ACA with a law that passed the "Jimmy Kimmel test."

"I don't know what happened to Bill Cassidy," Kimmel told his live audience. "He said he wants coverage for all, no discrimination based on pre-existing conditions, lower premiums for middle-class families, and no lifetime caps." Kimmel paused. "Guess what? The new [healthcare] bill does none of these things."

At the time, Republican town halls nationwide erupted in voter cries for "repeal and replace," but the ACA replacement bill did not pass, thanks to one "no" vote by the late Sen. John McCain.

Psychologist Jeremy Dean asserts that an upside to anger may be gaining attention and raising awareness. We simply need to do a better job of harnessing anger for constructive purposes as we engage in the urgent national debate over healthcare.

Bargaining: In the case of healthcare, is this a bargain with the devil? Threatening a government shutdown in early 2018, the GOP leveraged the Children's Health Insurance Program (CHIP), which provides low-cost coverage to children in families earning too much to qualify for Medicaid but not enough to buy private insurance. In some states, CHIP covers pregnant women, too. For me, such "chips on the table" for politicians are a losing game for the public. Over the years, many a "grand bargain" has been cobbled together only to fail. Propositions ardently loved and championed by one side were automatically hated and reviled by the other.

Can such conflict qualify as bargaining? Political bargains require members of the opposition to be consulted and worked with openly. Not in today's Congress! The gulf widens. Positions solidify.

Depression: The most obvious definition is that people enter a really unhappy mental state. As Grief.com declares, "Empty feelings present themselves, and grief enters into our lives on a deeper level, deeper than we ever imagined." While depression from grief feels as if it will last forever, such depression is not a sign of mental illness. It's an "appropriate response to a great loss."

I can and do feel the depression and the hopelessness out there. Here are a few depressing emails we get at RIP Medical Debt:

"I had a heart attack and two cardiac procedures in the last year. My husband had a heart attack two years before."

"I've had cancer for three years. Unpaid bills are in collections."

"I'm on a fixed income, struggling to pay my past-due bills."

"I have no money to my name, and I fear becoming homeless. I'm not sure where else to turn."

Acceptance: People stumble with this word. For some, it implies passive surrender to unthinkable brutality. For others, it symbolizes giving permission to hostile forces to do as they will, or accepting that we no longer have a choice. I subscribe to the Reinhold Niebuhr approach, as adapted into the Serenity Prayer: "God, grant me the serenity to accept the things I cannot change, the courage to change the things I can, and the wisdom to know the difference."

In the case of our healthcare system, as I see it, acceptance means coming to realize, "It is what it is." I accept that fuming and raging about it draws attention, but it changes little or nothing. I accept that bargaining does not produce a satisfying resolution. I accept that depression is an emotional trap ensuring no energy is left to search for viable solutions, let alone try to apply them.

Let's say we face the facts as we understand them and accept the things apparently beyond our ability to change. The next requisite step is to find the courage to change those things we can. This book cannot alter the facts, but we can help you understand the situation and educate you on those things that can be changed.

With a prayer for the wisdom to know the difference between the possible and impossible, we can find serenity by seeing clearly what can be changed and what may never change. We then can put our wisdom and knowledge to work. That's our goal here.

Awareness, Compassion, Education, Action

Perhaps the first time you heard about medical debt was in 2016, when HBO's "Last Week Tonight with John Oliver" did a segment on debt buyers. To show how ridiculously easy it is to buy and collect old debt, LWT spent $60,000 to buy a "portfolio" of unpaid medical billing accounts with a face value of almost $15 million.

Rather than collect on that debt, John Oliver in the live studio pushed a big red button to signal donating it all to RIP Medical Debt, our startup charity, which then forgave the debts of nearly 9,000 people in Texas — the largest giveaway in American TV history. His viewers were enthralled. We were thrilled.

Overnight, RIP became a "hot" news story. Overnight, donations began flowing in (plus debt relief pleas). In the prior two years since Craig Antico, Robert Goff and I launched RIP, we'd barely brought in $50,000. That was eclipsed in one day. RIP can buy debt at about a penny on the dollar, so the big surge let us forgive more millions in medical debt. We call this impact "The John Oliver Effect."

RIP began receiving proposals for debt forgiveness campaigns by community groups, trade unions, churches, veterans, high school students, and others As a result of such activity, by the end of 2018, RIP will have abolished close to $1 billion in medical debt!

Awareness of medical debt is only the first step to a cure.

Awareness: After all this exposure, we realized public awareness is only a first step toward curing our national scourge of medical debt. It's not enough. At least three more steps are needed.

Compassion: We cannot control anyone's willingness to care, but compassion is crucial in gaining public support to abolish medical debt. The dictionary defines compassion as "sympathetic pity and concern for the sufferings or misfortune of others." The John Oliver piece did not resonate with all TV viewers, but more than enough responded compassionately to make a big difference.

This book aims to make you aware about how and why medical debt exists. If you resonate with the pain of the unfortunate people who suffer from often-involuntary medical debt due to an illness or accident, we will give you grist for your compassion mill.

We hope that feeling empathy leads you to take the next step toward actually solving the social problem of medical debt.

Education: Perhaps you seek ways to resolve your own medical debt? Perhaps you seek to end what many see as a national disgrace? We learned that John Oliver's viewers wanted to educate themselves about medical debt and RIP's work. How do we know? Our website crashed from all the traffic. People wanted to know more.

Action: We believe that awareness, compassion and education lead to the fourth necessary step — action! Now that you've become aware medical debt is a huge problem in America, now that you've been touched by others' tears and troubles, now that you've begun educating yourself by reading this book, you may more clearly know what cannot be changed, and what can be changed. We will ask you to act upon whatever wisdom you gather.

Based on our work at RIP, here is how it may be for you:

Awareness	=	OMIGOD!
Compassion	=	That's not right!
Education	=	I need to know more.
Action	=	I must do something about it!

People respond strongly to hope and silver linings if there's proof. For evidence, let me leave you with two more emails:

"When I think of all the challenging issues facing us, it's easy to feel helpless. However, when I found out about RIP Medical Debt (from John Oliver), the world seemed to brighten. You have shown us that great ideas and hard work can really make a big difference. I know not everyone will get one of your [yellow] debt forgiveness letters in the mail, but

Awaken your heart, educate your mind and choose to act.

your organization is still young. I'll spread the word on social media and say that making a donation in honor of somebody is a great and noble gift. I'd also love to be a volunteer."

Another posting on our website truly made our day:

"I just saw a story about you on 'NBC Nightly News,' and I must admit I am in the same exact boat as you once were in. I'm a debt collections analyst, and today I almost cried while on the phone with a person I called to ask for a payment that I know he just can't pay. He only collects Social Security checks at age 71, yet he has well over $10,000 in medical debt. I literally wanted to transport through the phone and give him a hug to tell him it will be okay. So, I have to say the news segment inspires me, and it gives me hope to see that people are helping, that people out there have a good heart."

In future, the only tears we want to see through are tears of joy. We hope you take action, whatever your favorite solution, and work with others to end medical debt in America — for good!

The first wealth is health.

— RALPH WALDO EMERSON

CHAPTER 2

Medical Debt Is the Enemy of Everyone

Robert Goff

Medical debt is the enemy of the patient as well as the physician, the hospital, the community, the state, and the nation.

When we think about the debts of others, we generally think of such debts as their responsibility. If they are unable to pay that debt, it's *their* problem. (We make it a *You* problem, not a *Me* problem) After all, society tells us, isn't a problem with personal debt a direct consequence of bad decision-making, bad personal financial habits, profligate spending, or living beyond one's means?

We may think the consequences of debt are rightly visited on a person. Whatever the impact — canceled credit cards, low credit, wage garnishment — it's on them. Personal responsibility.

Is this true? In the big picture, we individuals and society both bear the costs and burdens of our personal "bad debt."

For any individuals who fall into arrears in their payments, who cannot pay their past financial obligations, unpaid debt means their ability to purchase goods and services is curtailed or perhaps ended. If new credit is not extended, the person must live on cash.

For any business, debt that cannot be paid by the customer who created it becomes a cost to the enterprise that extended credit. The business may recoup a loss by raising prices for products or services. The business may stop a loss by not providing goods or services to a debtor, which disciplines those failing to pay their bills.

In such cases, the consequences of unpaid personal debt fall on the debtor *and* on the creditor, usually ending there.

This does not apply to medical debt. *Personal debt created by an inability to pay for necessary medical services is called medical debt.* The consequences of medical debt extend beyond individuals and service providers. Medical debt ripples outward, adversely affecting physicians, hospitals, communities, the nation, perhaps requiring government intervention, which impacts the taxpayer — you.

The Debt Daisy Chain

Medical debt is not like a debt incurred by buying a big screen TV one cannot afford. It should not be treated the same way.

Medical debt is largely the result of an unplanned, involuntary event, often an illness or accident. It is not a choice. Illness is never chosen. Sure, certain lifestyle choices, personal habits and emotional habits can lessen chances for good health. Smoking, drinking, illicit drugs, unhealthy foods, or other risky behaviors are private choices. However, no one consciously volunteers to be ill. No one volunteers for a personal injury accident, either. Medical debt is not about living beyond one's means. Medical debt is about staying alive.

If people are unable to take personal financial responsibility for the economic results of medical efforts to restore (or try to restore) them to good health, medical debt is incurred. Having medical debt impacts access to medical services, when the only care available is a hospital emergency room — the care location of last resort. An ER is the most costly and least appropriate for non-urgent care.

Unlike other sellers of goods or services, medical providers do not cut off a debtor from all care. Medical debt will impact the care a debtor receives, and where, but medical services are to be available in some form. Physicians take an oath: Do no harm. Healers cannot ethically let people suffer.

For individuals, medical debt is a barrier to good health.

Among all of the medical care providers, the physicians and the hospitals bear the most economic burden from medical debt. Their patients' unpaid bills impact the rest of the healthcare system.

Unlike commercial enterprises, hospitals and physicians do not routinely recover losses by increasing prices for those patients who *can* pay their bills. In today's U.S. economic environment of private health insurance and government health insurance, the majority of payment rates are controlled by contracts or regulations.

Medicare and Medicaid reimbursements to medical providers, are based on formulas tied to the costs of delivering care, not the true business costs for delivering that care. Insurance plans pay the lowest rates possible, based on competitive fiscal factors. Physicians, hospitals and other care providers cannot simply increase their fees to cover their accumulating losses from unpaid medical debts.

For individuals, medical debt is a barrier to good health. Poor health means a loss of job productivity, maybe less income, which lessens contributions to family wellbeing, reducing contributions to the economics of society through employment taxes.

For medical providers like hospitals, the unpaid costs of medical care can reduce their financial viability. Some seek taxpayer support through government programs to stay viable. Any taxpayer support translates into higher taxes for a locality or state. Businesses tend to avoid expanding or relocating in high-tax areas. Higher local taxes reduce an area's desirability for future economic growth. A higher proportion of medical indigents in a community reduces the area's desirability as a place where physicians wish to practice. Less health care cuts a community's desirability for workers, and for business, so there are fewer jobs, further depressing the local economy.

Back to individuals, medical debt — and a fear of incurring more medical debt— drives the calculation of care vs. cost. When medical costs outstrip an individual's and family's economic ability to pay, the resulting medical debt gets between a patient and vital medical care as needed. "Should I go to the doctor?" becomes "Can I afford to see the doctor?" "Should I fill this prescription?" becomes, "Can I afford to fill it?" Too often, cost wins over care.

Consider the full human costs in desperate situations. In Boston on July 4, 2018, UPI reported, a woman's leg was caught between a subway car and the platform, ripping her flesh to the bone. Crying in agony, she pleaded with her rescuers not to call an ambulance. "It's $3,000," she wailed. "I can't afford that!"

Consider the interconnected social daisy chain of medical debt. What impacts one impacts all.

Gaps in Medical Care

When medical insurance is lacking, or has gaps in coverage that limit protection against dire financial hardship, economics weigh heavily on a personal decision whether or not to seek medical care. If care is sought, insurance coverage, or its lack, affects the decision to follow treatment plans or to fill prescriptions.

Health insurance gaps, such as ever-higher deductibles, coupled with the increasingly byzantine rules for insurance coverage, impact those struggling with health decisions. One in three Americans delay seeking medical care for themselves or family members due to the cost of medical care, according to a 2014 Gallup poll reported in The Daily Caller. That percentage has risen since 2010 enactment of the Affordable Care Act (ACA). The sad increase in delayed treatment primarily can be attributed to the raising of insurance deductibles. *Higher deductibles tend to add to medical debt.*

Failures to follow recommended treatments, such as not taking prescriptions, is not solely due to costs. A 2015 National Center for Health Statistics study found only eight percent of Americans don't take their medicines as prescribed because they cannot afford them. Nearly 20 percent of all prescriptions never get filled.

Delayed or missed care can raise costs by increasing illness. When put-off care at last is sought, the medical costs are inevitably higher, the outcomes predictably poorer. The economic impacts of more extensive and expensive care add to medical debt burdens on everyone.

The economic impacts of more extensive and expensive health care add to medical debt burdens on everyone.

The poor or near-poor are not the only ones who delay care due to cost concerns. Gallup reported that following the first year of the start for the Affordable Care Act, aka "Obamacare," about 38 percent of middle-class people delayed medical care due to cost, up 33 percent over the prior year. Gallup surveyed households with annual incomes between $30,000 and $75,000. Among households earning above $75,000 annually, about 28 percent told Gallup they delayed care, more than the 17 percent in 2013. So, roughly a third of all "affluent" Americans delay care regardless of the costs to themselves or society.

Economic impacts continue once treatment starts. The Cancer Support Center, reports USA Today, found more than 20 percent of cancer patients skipped recommended treatments, fearing high out-of-pocket costs. Almost 50 percent said their costs were higher than expected. Their cost concerns delayed screening tests, which ment delayed treatment. Such non-compliance from cost concerns reduces the effectiveness of treatment. In cancer care, early detection and treatment yields the best outcomes. Fear of medical debt caused later disease discovery, later treatment, and less favorable outcomes. We face gaps in care.

Medical Debt Poverty Trap

For individuals, the ultimate economic consequence of medical debt could be impoverishment. After personal and family resources are exhausted, if impoverished, they are eligible for publicly funded medical insurance, like Medicaid, or maybe charity assistance.

Medicaid benefits tends to be as complete as commercial health insurance coverage, often without deductibles. Medicaid limits the choice of providers, and it carries negative social connotations. Still, the coverage is often better than employer-provided insurance. To receive Medicaid, though, you do have to live in poverty.

Comprehensive insurance with high deductibles contributes to delayed care from money worries — increasing illness and depleting financial resources, making one eligible for Medicaid.

Medicaid or charity assistance is not an escape. Such help comes to the rescue only after the patient or the family has "spent down," depleting their financial reserves, perhaps due to limited or absent insurance coverage. *Seems to me bitterly ironic that families must be economically destroyed before they are eligible for the care that would have avoided the harm in the first place.* Medical indigence can trap individuals and families into actual poverty.

Medicaid or charity care is not an escape for patients.

The hard truth is that access to medical charity comes only after a patient or family is deemed insolvent or in poverty, too often from medical debt. Most charities, unlike Medicaid, do not cover any medical debts accumulated prior to entering their programs.

Costly care depletes family resources, which extends out into the community of taxpayers. The involuntary physical burden of an illness or accident stays with the individual and family, yet the wider economic costs are borne by the entire community and the nation as a whole. Medical debt affects the economic ecosystem.

Taxes fund state and federal government healthcare programs. The ACA, Obamacare, dramatically increased the number of people eligible for Medicaid on a state-by-state basis, including those near the poverty line and below it. In many states, legislatures provided hospitals with funds for the indigent. Same as with Medicaid, state hospital support programs are financed by taxpayers.

When hospitals provide charity care, under current rules, costs may be offset by higher fees to their patients' insurance companies. Charity care is offset by higher premiums paid by those who are not charity cases. Where a hospital cannot pass on its charity costs, when Medicaid payments are insufficient, additional government financial assistance may be needed to keep the hospital's doors open. As a vital community resource and major employer in a community, hospitals too often must rely on taxpayer-financed rescues.

Public resentment at growing tax burdens has severely restrained Medicaid reimbursements. This means Medicaid is not an attractive payment source for providers, so only a fraction of any local medical community participates in the program. Inadequate reimbursement for indigent care by Medicaid means patients often are limited to public or charity clinics or episodic emergency room care. A stable physician-patient relationship or "continuum of care" is lost.

Low Medicaid reimbursements in some places attract only care providers with less-desirable training or talent, not those able to earn a living with payments from insurance or affluent patients.

Poorer care for poorer people costs all the taxpayers more. The medical-gap trap impacts everyone in American society.

Insurance Is No Protection

People who have health insurance are wise not to feel too secure in their coverage. Insured people are at risk of medical debt.

Employers mitigate their health insurance premium increases by decreasing coverage and increasing employee deductibles (amounts employees pay out-of-pocket before insurance kicks in).

> Employers mitigate premium increases by decreasing coverage and increasing employee deductibles.

CBS News "Money Watch" reported deductibles had surged 67 percent since 2010, yet workers' earnings increased only 10 percent. By 2016, found CBS, about 51 percent of all workers with insurance had deductibles greater than $1,000. Deductibles considerably higher than $1,000 are increasingly common.

At the same time, employers pass along to employees more of their costs for higher insurance premiums. From 2010 to 2016, finds a Kaiser Family Foundation study of health benefits, workers' contribution to health premiums increased 78 percent. Still, worker earnings rose only 10 percent, a net loss for them.

A separate 2015 Kaiser Family Foundation study found that:

• 62 percent of those stressed by medical bills have insurance.

• 75 percent of those insured say insurance copays, deductibles, or coinsurance are more than they can afford.

• 46 percent of insured workers face annual deductibles of $1,000 or more for single coverage (up from 41 percent in 2014).

• 39 percent of large firms that offer employee health insurance have plans with deductibles of $1,000 or more.

• 20 percent of those with health insurance say paying medical bills has caused serious financial disruption in their lives.

• 11 percent of insured workers end up seeking charity aid.

Simply put, higher health costs are eating more of workers' pay, leaving them exposed to more costs and more medical debt.

Most health insurance is tied to employment. What can keep any working person awake at night is the reality that the coverage he or she has could disappear in the morning with a pink slip. The loss of employment, like from an accident or illness, can quickly move a middle-income family into medically induced poverty.

That's not what's supposed to happen.

COBRA Costs

In the event of job loss, federal law protects workers' ability to keep employer-sponsored health insurance. Called COBRA (from the Consolidated Omnibus Budget Reconciliation Act), such health care coverage costs more than when employed.

Under COBRA, a former employee may pay up to 102 percent of a former employer's own insurance premium. If an injury causes disability, COBRA coverage can be extended, but at a higher cost — up to 150 percent of that employer's whole premium.

The average annual premium for employer-provided coverage in 2017 was $18,764, according to the National Conference of State Legislators. Faced with the loss of income from lost employment, who can sustain the added pressures on the budget from COBRA? Adding to the disaster, even if you can afford COBRA, it's limited to 18 months while job hunting. After that, too bad, so sad. You're on your own. Try to find coverage you can afford.

The designers of COBRA saw coverage as a temporary stop-gap as workers find other jobs with health insurance. No consideration was given to the fact an illness or accident leading to unemployment may preclude re-employment. COBRA mandates the availability of coverage, not affordability, and this assumes a new job has health insurance. Unreal. The Kaiser Family Foundation in 2016 reported only 55 percent of all U.S. employers offer health benefits. The other 45 percent? Voila! New candidates for Medicaid.

Taking Unfair Advantage

Employees paying high payroll deductions for health coverage often share a false sense of security.

After the deductible, they think, the insurance is there to protect my financial wellbeing. Not so.

All coverage has "rules" limiting protections. Intended to keep down insurance premiums, the rules may come as a shock to workers when reality hits: They need coverage for an illness or injury.

Many insurance plans refuse to pay for care, even if medically necessary, when it falls outside their own self-dictated restrictions. Emergencies may not be covered if they require pre-authorization. Out-of-network service providers may not be covered except in proven life-threatening emergencies.

Insurance policy rules may stop an insurer from accepting fiscal responsibility for paying your medical bill.

Much to our detriment, we Americans seldom invest time to understand the limitations of our insurance coverage, the nuances. If a family member or ourselves gets ill or injured, feeling urgency, we may get care without realizing the financial consequences.

Unethical care providers may exploit ignorance of plan coverage. They'll misrepresent participation in any plan to "capture" a patient and the associated revenue.

> We seldom invest time to understand the limitations of our insurance coverage.

Phrases like "participating" or "will bill insurance" or "will take insurance" may be reassuring to the patient, but none of these terms guarantee what the patient thinks they mean.

A confident patient who receives care may get a nasty and costly shock. When their insurance company unexpectedly denies a bill, the patient finds a physician or clinic is not covered by the insurers' contract. Patients suddenly find the bill is their own responsibility. Patients must fight hard for any insurance coverage.

Some patients find themselves on the short end if the physician cuts a deal to accept whatever the insurance pays. No mention may be made of others in a procedure who are not covered. The patient gets a nasty and costly shock. The New York Times in 2014 told of a patient getting a $117,000 bill from an assistant surgeon who was not covered by the patient's plan.

Aetna, the health insurance company, has taken an aggressive stance against enticing patients into financial traps. In New York, they filed a lawsuit against two doctors, in-network Dr. Ramin Rak and out-of-network Dr. Shuriz Hishmeh. Dr. Rak used Dr. Hishmeh as his co-surgeon on procedures. Dr. Rak got $183,294 in-network. Dr. Hishmeh got more than $1.1 million out-of-network. Crain's New York Business reported the patient was liable for all costs for out-of-network surgery above Aetna's allowable rates.

Even if the insurance steps up to protect patients by paying the bills, the cost of financial abuse by out-of-network billing inevitably results in higher health insurance premiums for all.

Some physicians take unfair advantage of unwary patients by providing services in settings that are not covered. A physician may participate in a patient's health plan, for example, but influences a patient to do a procedure at an ambulatory surgery center where the physician has an ownership stake. The non-participating center, unfettered by contract limits, may not hesitate to send a medical bill, a large one. If the bill is not paid, it's medical debt.

Patients may be liable for all out-of-network care charges.

Medical costs can be tricky. A non-contracted or out-of-network private ambulatory surgery center in New York used a contracted, participating doctor for a medical procedure, and the center billed a patient $42,000. Insurance would have paid the participating center about $3,000, and the patient's in-network cost would have been just $1,000. This "double jeopardy" meant that the physician was paid for professional services and then paid again separately as an owner of the ambulatory surgery center, enjoying a portion of all the profits earned out-of-network.

For unwary patients "captured" by non-participating providers, the economic exposures can be tremendous. The impacts include a higher deductible, higher cost-sharing, and being held responsible for the total bill, the totally outrageous bill.

Fiscal Risks of Hospitalization

Hospitalized patients are among those most victimized by out-of-network situations. The breach may be aided and abetted by the very hospital where they sought professional quality care.

If admitted to a hospital, you are dependent on the institution's care structure. You are reduced to an account number, occupying a bed, incurring charges. During your hospital stay, you are subject to a fees structure that may put your economic health at risk. Your body may recover, but your finances may not.

Few people realize that hospitals do not control the health plan participation of physicians granted privileges to use the hospital for admitting and treating patients. This applies to most physicians in community hospitals. Even if a hospital hires the physician directly, it may not take steps to assure the new physician employee contracts or participates in the same health plans as the hospital.

Without your knowing, one or more of your hospital caregivers may not be covered under your plan, such as a physician consulted on your case. The New Jersey Record reported an egregious example at a New Jersey hospital where a patient was billed $56,980 for a 25-minute bedside consultation by a non-participating physician.

Some hospitals make it worse by contracting exclusively with certain physician groups for staffing, but then do not require these groups to participate in the hospitals' health plans.

For example, hospitals often contract with physician groups to provide anesthesia services or to staff the emergency department. These groups agree to provide 24/7 staffing in return for exclusive rights to provide those services. However, the hospital may place no requirements on them to participate with set health plans, claiming participation is an independent business decision of that group.

Some hospitals grant groups sole monopolies over essential care services, and monopolies tend to price monopolistically. Hospital services often granted to monopolies include radiology, pathology, anesthesiology, cardio EKG, and ER department physicians.

CNBC in 2016 reported that out-of-network emergency room doctors, on average, were paid 2.7 times more than in-network ER doctors were paid for doing the same exact services.

Health plans must pay a non-participating physician for care in a life-or-limb emergency visit. Few patients question the insurance participation of the anesthesiologist or radiologist, rarely in elective admissions. If a hospital participates with my insurance, then all the physicians there must participate, too, yes? Not necessarily.

Hospitals and physicians are consolidating into "systems" with the avowed benefit that care is coordinated by providers who all are part of one organization. However, a 2014 Los Angeles Times article confirmed that "in system" may not mean "in network." To cite an extreme example, an out-of-network California pathologist charged $81,000 for a tissue exam while Medicare pays only $128.

The Guardian in 2018 told a compelling story about the birth of three sons to Stella Apo Osae-Cwum, insured, who was driven near to bankruptcy by the out-of-network physician charges at an in-network hospital. She and her husband did it all by the book, used an in-network hospital and obstetrician. When her triplets were born prematurely, a bill came. The hospital's out-of-network neonatologist charged $877,000. Her employer-provided insurance covered most of the bill, but she was responsible for $51,000.

The financial risks to any patient while a "captive" of the hospital can be financially stressful, to put it mildly.

The Costs of 'Free' Hospital Care

Some people go to the hospital without paying. Is their care truly free? According to the American Hospital Association, community hospitals' uncompensated care — including free, discounted, and unpaid care — increased from $35.7 billion in 2015 to $38.3 billion in 2016. The AHA "Uncompensated Care Fact Sheet" reports such care represents 6.2 percent of annual hospital expenses.

Hospitals recover lost revenues with higher charges to paying patients, higher charges to health insurers (who increase insurance premiums), and with government assistance using our taxes.

Medicare and commercial insurance companies largely restrain "cost-shifting" — raising prices on other customers to cover shortfalls in payments from those of limited means.

Is this system just? Perhaps. Consider the impacts.

A great oddity in hospital finance is how uninsured individuals are charged. The patients *with* insurance are charged the discounted rates of insurance carriers. Patients *without* insurance fall into the "self-pay" category. They must fund the full costs of their care.

Uninsured patients, those least likely to have the means to pay the cost of their care, are charged the maximum rates set by the hospital. In the hotel business, how many guests pay the "rack rate" or full price for a room?

'Self pay' patients must fund the full cost of their medical care.

A hospital's uncompensated care adds to financial pressures on the institution. The facilities most disadvantaged serve areas with weak local economies. Hospitals in poor and near-poor communities provide the most unpaid care. Hospital closures caused by unmanageable financial losses happen most often in less well-off communities and neighborhoods.

The ripples from a hospital closure are less access to care, loss of a positive economic force for jobs, and the community being less desirable, thereby worsening poverty in the community.

Becker's Hospital Review reports 57 hospitals closed from 2010 to 2015, with 21 closing in 2016, and 10 in 2017. All of the acute-care hospitals closing their doors cited financial pressure as a reason, or even *the* reason, for their closure. Medical debt is not the sole source of hospitals' fiscal distress, yet it certainly does contribute mightily. As a last resort to avoid closure, hospitals seek bailouts from states and municipalities. That cost is borne by us taxpayers.

The Impact on Physicians

Physicians in private practice lack the benefits of a local, state or federal governmental program to offset the impact of bad debt. As patients' debts rise, if a physician is unable to absorb the revenue losses, hard choices must be made. Physicians' responses to excessive medical bad debt, even if ethical, often are unpleasant.

Physicians rarely disengage from a patient over a financial issue. By law and custom, they cannot abandon a patient under their care. If this means providing unpaid care until a patient can find another caregiver, or can be referred away, then so be it.

Patients causing unsustainable financial losses for a physician may be discharged from a medical practice. A discharge may be self-imposed by a patient, embarrassed to owe for past care, who quietly stops making or keeping appointments. They exile themselves.

The physician, sensitive to a patient's fiscal hardship, may refer a patient to another medical resource, such as a community health center or public clinic. The continuity of care is lost.

Physicians face a stark financial reality. They must earn enough revenue to sustain themselves and their practice. Bad debt rarely can be replaced by raising rates. Physicians' rates are fixed by insurance and government rules. Time and resources are expended to extend care. Must doctors absorb the loss? Unfortunate yet understandable collection efforts can ruin a physician-patient relationship.

Insurance and government rules ensure doctors must absorb unpaid patient bills.

A primary care physician may refer the patient for specialty care. The patient's stressed finances may prompt skipping care or the prescriptions. A more ill patient returns to primary care, unable to pay bills, or the patient goes to the more costly hospital ER.

Medical debt, ultimately, may prompt physicians to close or relocate their practices out of the communities they serve. They do not abandon a community they love for callous greed, but for self-survival.

Uncollectable patient bills produce an uneven distribution of good physicians in our communities, creating "healthcare deserts." Given a choice, few physicians locate practices in distressed areas, where the need is greatest, unless fulfilling a duty of their medical education.

Some programs forgive physicians' medical school student debt if they agree to practice several years in an underserved community, like working for a clinic or hospital in a rural area. Their service usually is short term unless lasting bonds form within that community.

The institutions supporting temporary local physicians rely on government financing. Such "supported" medical practices add to the ways medical costs and related debt become financial obligations for the whole community of taxpayers.

The structure of medical insurance coverage virtually assures physicians in private practice have unpaid bills. Reliable data for their medical debt is hard to locate because most medical practices use cash-based accounting (recording income when received and expenses when paid). Bad debt is not counted as income or expense, so it's missed. Some studies indicate that bad debt can run between

5.9 percent and 14 percent of any physician's billings. A 2013 Kaiser Family Foundation study found that private office-based physicians provided more than $30 billion in uncompensated care.

If a physician closes an office due to bad debt, the patients suffer disruption of their care, and the community loses a caregiver. The impact spreads outward into society.

The Impact on Patients

The ACA was supposed to solve health care issues by removing financial status as a barrier to obtaining medical care. It didn't work. Medical insecurity continues as Congressional and court activities put the ACA benefits in doubt, such as full coverage for pre-existing conditions, for preventive care without copays or deductibles..

ACA theory and ACA reality do not match.

The ACA's failure to cut the costs of delivering health services contributes to the upward spiral of premiums, which translates into higher payroll dedications or increased deductibles. More than ever now, ACA theory and reality do not match.

If health is restored and people can return to the workforce with paid insurance, they remain liable for *all accumulated prior debt*. To pay off old bills, they often skip or skimp on needed medication and follow-up care. This is especially true (and most troubling) for those with chronic diseases, like diabetes, where skipping treatment can rapidly deteriorate health, resulting in far higher care bills.

Not filling a prescription can be costly and deadly. ProMed.gov compared patients who follow instructions to those who don't take medications as intended, including for financial reasons. They risk hospitalization, re-hospitalization and premature death 5.4 times higher in cases of hypertension, 2.8 times higher with dyslipidemia, and 1.5 times higher in cases of heart disease.

"Putting it off" is no solution. Studies report people who delay or forego care are less likely to report "very good" or "excellent" health. They have lower quality-of-life scores compared to those who do not delay necessary medical care.

According to a 2013 University of Chicago/AP national survey "Privately Insured in America: Opinions on Health Care Costs and Coverage," among adults from ages 18 to 64 with private insurance, 19 percent not visit the doctor when sick, and 18 percent go without preventive or recommended care.

An unfortunate impact of all the byzantine rules for coverage is patients' confusion on benefits and concern for costs, which keeps them from early detection and treatment of their ailments.

A short-term savings by skipping a cancer screening may yield a later identification of more advanced cancer. It's a classic scenario of "pay me now or pay me later." If cancer is identified too late for successful treatment, patients may pay with their lives.

Being wise enough to seek medical treatment, but not being able to pay the medical bills, creates its own set of challenges.

That 2015 Kaiser Family Foundation study found nationwide averages for how people handle high costs for medical care:

- 77 percent cut spending for household purchases or vacations.
- 63 percent use up most or all of their savings.
- 42 percent take an extra job or work more hours.
- 38 percent increase their credit card debt or max out the cards.
- 37 percent borrow money from family or friends.
- 14 percent change their living situations.

Even with insurance, millions of Americans are living only one accident or illness away from potential economic disaster. Could you and your family handle a serious illness or injury?

Medical debt from medical care is the great equalizer. According to Kaiser, about 44 percent of those with employer-provided health insurance shared nearly identical consequences by paying medical bills as the 45 percent paying for their healthcare without insurance. Medical debt is an equal opportunity destroyer.

Collections and Bankruptcy

If people do not pay their medical bills, collections begin!

Aggressively pursued medical debt is destructive to individuals' and families' stability and security. Bill collectors compel debtors to choose between paying rent, food, transportation, childcare, or other overdue bills. To satisfy bill collection demands, those with limited means may be forced to miss a mortgage payment or not put tires on their car. Some may give up on even trying to be a "responsible" person, refusing to answer the phone or open the mail.

Bloomberg News in 2014 ran a story on a William Piorun facing an impossible choice between paying for his mortgage or paying for his medications, which cost $20,000 a month. He had coverage, but his copay was more than $1,000 per month. How does he live?

Urgency increases when any professional bill collector enters the scene. Their aim is singular and purposeful: Collect monies owed to their health-provider clients, regardless of the grim consequences from the life decisions they force patients to make.

Adding more injury, many employers now verify credit reports on prospective employees before hiring them. Any medical debt on a credit report can deter or prevent employment.

Glassdoor in 2018 reported that as many as 60 percent of all employers do credit checks on their job prospects. The presumption is that those under financial stress, or who have difficulty managing personal finances, may be less responsible or more likely to commit white-collar crime, so they are less desirable as employees.

With credit scores integral to hiring decisions, medical debt on a credit report narrows folks' job prospects, hurting their economic recovery and financial stability. Bluntly, medical debt can prevent earning the money to pay the medical debt.

NerdWallet Health in 2013 cited medical debt as the number one cause of bankruptcies in the USA, outpacing credit card debt and unpaid mortgages. Further, NerdWallet indicated that about 56 million adults — 20 percent of the population between the ages of 19 and 64 — struggled with

> # Medical debt can prevent earning money to pay the debt.

paying care-related bills that year. They have not updated their report, but I believe it's greater today.

Bankruptcy releases debt, but it stays 10 years on a credit report. Credit is denied people, negatively affecting reconstruction of their lives. Forget about a mortgage or a car loan, and that's for starters. Even after all the debt is discharged, enduring punishments from personal bankruptcy are anything but a "clean slate."

If you think the ultimate consequence of unpaid medical bills is bankruptcy, a 2017 story in the Miami New Times reports medical debt in South Florida is the leading cause of homelessness. It beat out mental illness and drug use as the top reasons. Medical debt even beat out job loss as the primary cause of Miami homelessness.

Personal Responsibility

Personal responsibility matters, yet debt from necessary medical care is innately different than debt from living beyond one's means. Survival not vanity is the real cause of medical debt. Whether or not the economic impacts are noticed, medical debt affects us all.

Healthcare is an interconnected system. Medical debt drives up our insurance premiums and deductibles. Medical debt drives up our taxes for Medicare and Medicaid, drives up our taxes for saving local medical institutions. Personal medical debt does not stop with the debtor. Medical debt ultimately gets paid by the taxpayers.

All of us pay for medical debt, if not our own, then the medical debt of others. As rising medical costs outstrip individuals' ability to pay, the impacts go beyond the amount of any medical bill. We may argue about the costs of health care. We may argue about solutions. Debate is good but not enough. *Medical debt is the elephant in the room nobody wants to talk about.* We cannot get around it.

Commercial insurance, Medicare, Medicaid, and charity care promise protection and relief from medical impoverishment. But the social safety net has gaping holes for individuals, and communities pay the price, as does our entire nation. Medical debt is the enemy of everyone. That's not what we expect here in America.

CHAPTER 3

Debt Mountains Cause Healthcare Deserts

Craig Antico

W e all bear the costs of medical debt, as Robert says, so why are we ignoring and allowing material hardships from mounting debt to fall upon certain identifiable groups of people? If these people are inordinately burdened by medical debt to the point it negatively affects their psyche, behavior and wellbeing, have we not a collective responsibility to right this wrong?

How does medical debt affect individuals' health and wellbeing? What about such *social determinants* as isolation, income insecurity, transportation insecurity, education level, access to healthcare, and living environment? We're now finding out.

Researchers at the economics and public policy departments of UCLA, UC/Berkeley, University of Chicago, and MIT have released the preliminary finding of an economic impact study to measure the effects of medical debt forgiveness by RIP (see Chapter 8). The findings shed light on how medical debt affects people's wellbeing. We hope these findings influence public policy.

I believe insurmountable "debt mountains" may determine our wellbeing when we behave as if we're living in "healthcare deserts," when we choose not to access needed healthcare, even if available, from fear of the costs and stress resulting from medical debt.

Who all is buried on debt mountain? Those in poverty and with limited public support and resources. Youth in their late twenties. Those with severe diseases (like cancer, mental illness or addiction). Forty million working-class Americans earning an average of $12 an hour with no company-provided health insurance. The veterans denied VA coverage. All are buried on debt mountain.

Hardship, Poverty, Poor Health

What percentage of people do you believe experience poverty, poor health or material hardship each year?

The Centers for Disease Control and Prevention reports only 7.6 percent of people in the USA are admitted to the hospital overnight every year. Such a relatively low usage of the healthcare system contributes to a common misperception that medical debt doesn't affect that many people. Look closer.

According to a three-year study by the Robin Hood Foundation and Columbia University Population Research Center, 63 percent of the residents studied in a community experienced an economic hardship in one year. Specifically, this 63 percent experienced one or more of the defining criteria of being disadvantaged — poverty, hardship and poor health.

Those without savings are the most vulnerable to medical debt.

Poverty: Financial assistance programs pay attention to income levels in determining financial assistance, but "income poverty" can change rapidly by finding a job. A job is not enough. About 69 percent of Americans have less than $1,000 in savings, 49 percent have less than $500, and 34 percent have no savings at all. Those without savings are the most vulnerable to medical debt.

According to a recent Federal Reserve survey, almost 50 percent of all Americans cannot come up with $400 for a sudden bill. They would have to sell off an asset or borrow the funds.

Households with medical debt have 70 percent more credit card debt, plus more debt overall. Sean McElwee in Demos reports that, on average, medically indebted households have $8,762 in credit card debt — compared to households with $5,154 in credit card debt that does not stem from medical bills.

Americans borrow from friends and family to the tune of $55.7 billion per year, Olivia Chow reported in Finder. The disadvantaged rarely have friends and family with that kind of money. They turn to crowdfunding, where 36 percent of all money is raised to pay for medical expenses or its residual debt.

Hardship: The most persistent disadvantage is the inability to pay your bills. For example, the Columbia study found only nine percent of people who entered a year in poverty were in poverty at the end of that year. However, 23 percent of those entering a year in material hardship were still there at the end of the year.

Poor Health: Traditional healthcare interventions account for only 20 percent of a person's health — 80 percent is due to factors like physical environment, health behaviors, and socioeconomic conditions. Changes in income, work or family dynamics are the top three causes of stress, and these drive 75-90 percent of all health care visits and related medical debt. The migration patterns in and out of poverty, hardship and wellbeing need to be better understood by our healthcare system. (RIP uses consumer credit data with social determinant data to assess who qualifies for debt forgiveness.)

Medicaid in the Debt Terrain

Debt mountains are geographically concentrated in states with limited Medicaid coverage. AARP interviewed hundreds of people earning less than $40,000 a year. No one on Medicaid had medical debt. In states that expanded Medicaid coverage under ACA from people earning 100 percent of the poverty level up to 138 percent, we at RIP see fewer requests for debt relief. A gap from 138 to 200 percent of the poverty level still needs to be filled.

We learned by working with the AARP that there is a problem for middle-class spouses who need Medicaid to provide services for a loved one. Once the loved one dies, Medicaid stops paying, and debts mount. It's devastating for me to see a proud, independent person who just lost a spouse to have all their savings clawed back. This debt mountain stays unseen unless the people buried by debt are willing to speak up and be heard.

Uninsured and Underinsured

The Commonwealth Fund considers people "underinsured" if their deductible equals more than 10 percent of their gross income. They comprise most of those who are underinsured. For those who earn less than two times the Federal Poverty Level (FPL) guidelines, if their deductible passes 5 percent of their gross income, they also are called underinsured. The Commonwealth Fund reports that 68 million people in our county are underinsured or uninsured.

Middle Class: The underinsured include people making poor health care choices from being uninformed about medical services, from not understanding what their health insurance actually covers, and the out-of-network providers. They often are in the middle class, earning from 200 percent to 350 percent of the FPL. Despite a good income, they spend at least five percent of their gross income on out-of-pocket medical costs.

68 million people in our county are underinsured or uninsured.

About 20-25 percent of the debt we abolish at RIP is for people in the middle class. They qualify for debt relief by large percentage of their gross income paying for out-of-pocket expenses and debt service. They are more likely to have high out-of-network bills since they want the best care and will "pay" for it, even if the doctor or service is not fully covered under their health plan. That "sensible decision" can be costly,

Working Class: About 44 million people in America are in the "working class," and almost none of them receive health insurance from their employer. Under the ACA, they may purchase health insurance on their own through a government portal.

Youth: The youngest, healthiest workers in their twenties often opt-out of health insurance, or they pick the lowest-premium plan with the highest deductibles. This is why, among all the age groups, 27-year-olds have the most medical debt on their credit reports.

Seniors: Elders often have limited income, and so have high levels of medical debt. As the U.S. population ages, there will be fewer and fewer "free" caregivers. AARP says that in 2018 more than 40 million caregivers will provide at least $470 billion worth of free care-related "hours of service." A 2017 Indiana University study found that tallied $377.6 billion for Medicare and Medicaid, and $410 billion for care donated by individuals, foundations and corporations.

Ailments Atop Debt Mountain

For almost every age and class, mountains of debt keep growing. Those with serious ailments of body and mind too often end up buried on debt mountain. Two examples suggest the scale.

Cancer: As you may know, or someone close to you may know, a cancer diagnosis is devastating. Next, you start getting and paying the bills. A study in the Journal of Clinical Oncology confirmed the bills increase stress and increases early mortality.

More than one-third of the cancer patients with insurance pay more out-of-pocket for treatments than they expected to spend. A Duke University survey found patients in the study were paying an average of 11 percent on out-of-pocket costs for cancer treatment, said lead author Fumiko Chino, M.D, at Duke Health. Patients in the study who reported the most financial distress were spending 30 percent of their household income on health care.

Mental Illness and Addiction: Few health plans cover mental health or addiction treatment services, and these rarely to the extent deemed medically necessary by consumers, caregivers, and doctors. The bills may not show up anywhere in the medical debt statistics. Costs may be paid by friends and family, from savings, credit cards, or by selling a house. Mental health care is a major out-of-network cost because providers want to be paid upfront, or else you or your loved one might not get the help needed.

Kaiser Family Foundation analysis of suicide and intentional injuries,82 percent have more than $1,000 in out-of-pocket expenses (OOP), and 16 percent have OOP expenses over $5,000. The mental health conditions associated with the highest OOP expenses are suicide attempts, psychotic disorders and dementia.

This cost burden is disconcerting. Nearly one-fifth of our total adult population report mental health issues. An insured employee with mental health spending may have out-of-pocket costs passing $5,000, double that of the average health condition. Research by RIP through Definitive Healthcare calculates that out of 35 million inpatient visits to U.S. hospitals, at least 38 percent of them present psychosis as a primary or secondary diagnosis.

Few are comfortable talking about how mental illness, addiction and medical debt are debilitating America and our families.

Out-of-Network Surprises

America's Health Insurance Plans, the industry trade group, has found that about 12 percent of all U.S. health claims were for care services obtained from out-of-network providers.

AHIP studied 18 billion claims for the 97 most common health services. People who got treatments from doctors and facilities not covered by insurance plans, said AHIP, received bills ranging from 118 percent to 1,382 percent higher than what Medicare would pay for those same services.

Health Affairs reports almost 20 percent of inpatient hospital admissions starting in the ER lead to unexpected bills. New York's Department of Financial Services told CNBC that surprise bills from out-of-network radiologists in 2012 averaged $5,406, of which insurers paid $2,497 on average.

Consumers were on the hook for the remainder.

If you live in a rural area, call now to see if your hospital has any ER doctors on your health plan. Most of them are not, so they would be deemed out-of-network. Do the same for anesthesiologists.

Laboratory work is huge out-of-network bill waiting to happen. Ask your insurer for which labs they cover, and demand that all of your lab work goes there.

If a doctor ever says, "I'll take whatever your insurance pays," go to another doctor because this is illegal. You could get a big bill you don't expect yet be legally obliged to pay. Such debt is unfair.

> # Lab work is a huge out-of-network bill waiting to happen.

Hidden Medical Debt

Medical debt is only one type of what we call "debt of necessity." This is an unexpected expense to meet unexpected emergencies and living expenses. Such debts could include payday loans for replacing worn-out tires on the car or for putting food on the table.

More than 50 percent of our fellow citizens in this great country chronically have at least two of three criteria RIP uses to determine debt forgiveness: Low earnings, zero net worth, high out-of-pocket medical expenses as a percentage of gross income.

We wonder how people get by. Well, a lot of them don't. Some 15 million people annually lose their life savings because of medical debt. When it comes to medical bills, thanks to our broken system, crowdfunding has become the insurance policy of last resort. How often can we appeal to our friends and family to rescue us?

VA-Covered Veterans

Heaven forbid that a veteran does not pay for any non-covered benefits and winds up owing the VA! The federal government has collection powers that far exceed anything banks or creditors have as enforcement tools. The "right of offset" means that, regardless of hardship or ability to pay, tax refunds may be garnished to pay off any federal and state liabilities still due.

As for bills veterans owe to the Veterans Health Administration, the government can and will offset not only a tax refund but also monthly benefits. They can offset a medical bill, for example, even if that leaves a veteran with only $25 to live on for the month.

VA members account for more than two million visits a month at non-VA hospitals. Their VA insurance, just like everyone else's, covers only so much. All remaining balances are called "self-pay." If these cannot be handled, the next step is the bill collector.

RIP is concerned about more than $8 billion in medical debt that VA members owe over the last five years from ambulance and ER bills denied for payment by the VA. We learned this by visiting the House Committee on Veterans' subcommittee on health. Denied VA benefits, the claims fall to veterans to pay. If not, the ambulance service or hospital must absorb a loss or pursue collections.

About 90,000 veterans a year are denied coverage by the VA's "prudent layperson" standard. For example, the VA may rule that an ambulance trip and hospital ER visit wasn't really an emergency. An audit found many denials are due to inconsistent application of policy and standards. The denials save the VA about $3 billion each year, burying our vets in mountains of debt.

Remove Material Hardship

What if paying for medical bills was not so stressful, if it did not result in material hardship or financial ruin, so high medical costs do not destroy us and our citizens? Research shows that any person paying more than 2.5 percent of their gross income for out-of-pocket medical expenses feels hardship. At least 20 percent of us are in hardship with medical debt on our credit reports.

This means we don't have to wipe out medical debt completely. We have to remove the material hardship tied to it. Reducing hardship to maximize wellbeing is

Any person paying more than 2.5 percent of their gross income for out-of-pocket medical expenses feels hardship.

what RIP seeks to do by wiping out unpayable medical debt — debt of necessity brought on by injury, illness or violence.

We are now learning how to do it better through an academic randomized control trial of the economic impact of medical debt and debt relief. *Does debt forgiveness actually improve wellbeing?* We are researching that presently. Foundations and policymakers are awaiting the findings in 2019.

People who have not suffered hardship, poor health or poverty might think medical debt is the "fault" of its disadvantaged people. The evidence points elsewhere. Medical debt can happen to anyone, any strata or race, no matter how many assets you have.

Firsthand Material Hardship

Over the first five years of RIP Medical Debt's existence, my family has experienced prolonged poverty with major out-of-pocket expenses due to illness and material hardship. Medical debt has had a major impact on my own family's finances.

Two years after Jerry Ashton and I started this charity in 2014, my spouse asked me a simple question: "Why are we going into debt and hardship to get people out of debt?"

The answers I gave my wife were not an explanation based on logic or self-preservation. I had to seek advice from friends to help resolve this in myself. My determination to keep going was against my family obligations as a provider. My pastor helped me with my dilemma. I'm grateful my family persevered in tough times.

From the stress of three years of financial uncertainty, my wife entered the hospital. We hocked all of her family jewelry and silver. (I am glad to say I could return my wife's precious family heirlooms after them being gone more than a year, thanks to RIP attracting a better cashflow after John Oliver.) We used up all of our savings. We borrowed tens of thousands from friends and family.

To withstand my not having income for almost three years, we sold our home and used the proceeds. We rented for half of what we were paying for the mortgage. We incurred "debt of necessity" equal to three times "our" income (my spouse's teaching assistant income). At least we still had health insurance. My credit report rating fell because of one missed payment — yes, missed by one day — and we could not get parent-PLUS student loans that year for our college-age children. Two of my sons put their college education on hold. One dropped out from all the stress of rising early to work in the cafeteria at 5 a.m., before classes, to pay off an exorbitant installment loan agreement.

> # Two years after starting RIP, my wife asked, 'Why are we going into debt to get people out of debt?'

Can you imagine the hardship of living on your spouse's income, below the poverty level, with a family of six, for over two years, with no more savings, and you are in your mid-fifties?

By RIP's criteria, the Antico family was qualified for RIP's debt forgiveness! (RIP can't yet forgive individuals' debt.) Our income fell to below two times the poverty level. We were insolvent. We had out-of-pocket medical expenses or debt equal to more than five percent of the family gross income.

This is not a victim story. It's my own narrative of what it took for RIP to exist and start to flourish. Compared to the tales of illness, poverty and hardship we read in letters and emails arriving daily, the Antico family had it easy. (Don't tell my wife I wrote that!)

Was putting my family in jeopardy for RIP the right thing to do? No. It was what I *had* to do. Jerry made his own sacrifices as RIP lived on his credit cards. We both went into personal debt. Why? We could not in good conscience walk away from all those with medical debt that we were uniquely equipped to help.

Where else in the world could you ever hope to find two former collections industry executives willing to reverse their career course, deciding not to collect on medical debt but to forgive it?

More than two years in, by the time of the John Oliver show, we had reached a level of forgiving almost $40 million in medical debt for 30,000 individuals who otherwise could never pay off those bills. We could not and would not stop. Our personal finances stank, but we were hooked on abolishing medical debt. For good.

CHAPTER 4

The John Oliver Effect

Jerry Ashton

R IP Medical Debt is being brought to you courtesy of comedian
John Oliver.

RIP first came to America's attention in June 2016 through his
satirical lambast of the debt buying and collections industry, aired
on the HBO series, "Last Week Tonight with John Oliver."

The experience ever since for Craig Antico, Robert Goff, and me
bordered on being surreal, and this continues today.

Overnight, after two years of basic survival (the venture funded
by personal debt), our little startup charity was no longer struggling.
Overnight, people heard about us, got involved, and we grew.

I want to tell you that story.

Thanks to John Oliver's very public introduction, thanks to the
generosity of thousands of donors since his HBO show, thanks to
our hard work pulling together a passionate and dedicated team, by
the end of 2018, RIP has been able to purchase and forgive almost a
half billion dollars in unpayable medical debt. A quarter of a million
Americans have experienced unexpected freedom from medical debt
they thought would never be paid. We hope to do more.

John Oliver on LWT routinely exposes the flaws and absurdities of politicians, extremists, miscreants, and industries whose practices appear unhinged from ethics or common sense. His "Debt Buyers" segment revealed (to many for the first time) how personal debt is purchased and collected, including debts more than ten years old or out-of-statute. He ridiculed the states that do not regulate or license debt-buying companies.

To make his case, he showed an old video of a known "bad apple" in the collections trade. Oliver poked fun at the collector's brazen attitude and his shady tactics. The audience laughed, yet they also cringed.

John Oliver was aghast at his unfettered access to personal data for sale as medical debt.

Becoming a debt buyer himself, once inside the industry, John Oliver was aghast at his unfettered access to thousands of people's personal data for sale as medical debt.

The show's "hook" was to "out-Oprah Oprah." In 2004, Oprah Winfrey had famously given a studio audience nearly 300 brand new cars, valued at more than $2 million. ("You get a car! You get a car!") To surpass that record, Oliver's team set up an elaborate plan to buy and give away $15 million in medical debt.

At the climax of the live show, Oliver pushed a giant red button and glittering confetti came streaming down. He lifted his arms and rejoiced, "I am the new queen of daytime talk!"

John Oliver lampooned a shadow finance industry while freeing about 9,000 people from financial hardship by RIP forgiving their medical debt. To pull it off, he employed two former bill collectors, Craig and me. That irony made the fun all the more delicious.

How did this life-changing event come about?

A Deal Was Done

To show how easy it is to buy and collect debt, LWT producers created a debt-buying company and purchased a batch of Texas debt for about $60,000. Their intent, for comedic and ethical purposes, was not to collect on the debt but to forgive it. How?

The HBO team sought help from a healthcare attorney, Michele Masucci, a partner at Nixon Peabody. She responded to questions about ways to dispose of the debt. ("No, you can't do that, or that, either.") So that the forgiven debt did not count as taxable income, she said, they needed a tax-exempt charity with the expertise to meet the HIPAA "permissible use" rules for medical accounts.

On her desk was a copy of *The Patient, The Doctor and The Bill Collector,* by Robert Goff and me. Robert is RIP's first board member. As her client, Robert had gifted her the new book a few days before. Michele turned to the chapter, "Got Medical Debt? Let's Abolish It!" She said to HBO, "These are the people you need to see."

HBO called Robert, who referred them to Craig and me. We met at HBO's Manhattan offices. All the right people sat around a table. All the right questions were asked and answered. After the flurry of due diligence, all the right things proceeded to happen.

A deal was done.

LWT would donate to RIP Medical Debt its almost $15 million debt portfolio plus sufficient funds to process the accounts and mail the forgiveness letters. The broadcast would air in two weeks.

Mum's the word.

The night of the show, June 5, 2016, my wife and I sat before the TV in our apartment. Two glasses and a split of Champagne sat on a table before us, just in case RIP's name was even mentioned. In the climactic moments, behold, RIP's logo appeared over John Oliver's right shoulder. He pointed to it, acknowledging RIP as the charity chosen to abolish the debt. We popped our cork!

Our website was not prepared for the surge of visitors generated by the show that night. It crashed! The server was overwhelmed by visitors wanting to learn more about RIP. The contact form flooded with praise for RIP, offers to donate, cries for help. Overnight, our tiny two-person venture was compelled to transform from a charity "just getting by" into a credible and recognized organization.

The John Oliver Effect Begins

Despite our readiness glitches, several thousand dollars quickly flowed in along with commitments for more. Most unexpected was the flood of interest from organizations, companies and academia desiring to partner with RIP in our work.

What we later called "The John Oliver Effect" had begun.

RIP was initially contacted by Francis Wong, a doctoral student in economics at the University of California at Berkeley. "I was really impressed by what I saw on that TV show, and my department would like to know if we could work with you to create an economic impact study of the impact of abolishing medical debt."

His offer was immediately and enthusiastically accepted.

A week later came a second call, this time from Ray Kluender, a doctoral student in economics at MIT. He made a similar request. In response, we happily introduced him to Francis.

A month later, Craig and I were invited to the North America conference of the Abdul Latif Jameel Poverty Action Lab (J-PAL), the MIT-based global research center working to "reduce poverty by ensuring that policy is informed by scientific evidence." We were asked to present an explanation of RIP's work and mission as it relates to reducing poverty.

J-PAL asked us to explain RIP's work and mission.

After our session, we were approached separately by Wes Yin, Ph.D., associate professor of public policy at UCLA, and by Neale Mahoney, Ph.D., assistant professor of economics at the University of Chicago. Francis and Ray, meet Wes and Neale!

The four academics decided to team up to conduct a study titled "The Burden of Medical Debt and the Impact of Debt Forgiveness." RIP now found itself affiliated with four outstanding academicians at four major universities, partnering with us for serious evidence-based research on the impact of medical debt forgiveness.

We felt excited, but we still had no clue of what lay ahead.

Technology Allies Appear

One/Zero Capital founder and CEO Vishal Garg felt intrigued by the John Oliver segment and reached out to us. Finding our work congruent with his corporate mission, he invited RIP to share desk space at their offices in New York City. Any office space at all was a big step up for us. We'd been working out of coffee shops and our homes, Craig in Rye and me in Manhattan.

One/Zero connected us to the TheNumber management team, who provided a data platform to use in locating and buying medical debt, plus a way to process large batches of accounts for forgiveness. Their technology, data scientists and manpower relieved us from all the manual processing that Craig and I had been doing. Suddenly, we gained the infrastructure to forgive a lot more debt!

Paul Wallis and Fergus Cloughley at OBASHI then contacted us, offering the next essential technology to be added to the RIP charity. OBASHI (Ownership, Business processes, Applications, Systems, Hardware, Infrastructure) is a method of data process modeling and mapping for enterprises, developed in Scotland by Paul and Fergus. Their solutions addressed RIP's need for data security and control.

How did they hear of us? You already know the answer.

The data integrity we'd gained with OBASHI, Craig and I saw, could transform RIP's ability to forgive medical debt, accelerating the volume of accounts we could process. Our charity could develop new ways of working with debt buyers, hospitals and associations. We could better leverage donations to abolish more debt.

Upstreaming and Health Begins

We next attracted the attention and partnership of a respected Southern California physician, Rishi Manchanda, M.D, known for his TED talk on "upstreaming." He sent us this email:

"Like many others, I imagine, I recently learned of your work through the John Oliver TV show. I am deeply interested in the intersection of health, financial security/literacy, and medical debt, especially for working families. I am active in advocacy and policy efforts to transform healthcare at local and national levels."

Dr. Manchanda encourages doctors to consider the "upstream" social and environmental conditions that contribute to sickness, and likely to medical debt. He introduced Craig and I to the idea that "social determinants" affect health.

What are *social determinants*? "Resources that enhance quality of life can have a significant influence on population health outcomes," states the U.S. Office of Disease Prevention and Health Promotion. These include such resources as safe and affordable housing, access to education, public safety, the local availability of healthy foods, local emergency and health services, and safe local environments that are "free of life-threatening toxins."

He explained to us how social factors benefit or damage health. Poverty often means an inability to afford adequate shelter, good food and quality medical care. Even if people are fortunate enough to afford healthy groceries, they may live in a "food desert" where fresh produce and unprocessed foods are simply not available.

Dr. Manchanda told us of his suspicion that owing medical debt is a social determinant of poor health; thus, he contacted us a month after spotting RIP on the John Oliver show.

The doctor was then working as Chief Medical Officer of a large, privately owned and self-insured Southern California employer. In managing two employee clinics, he was seeking innovative ways to positively affect employee health "upstream" to deter the incidence of illness. He said that in talking with his ailing employee patients, many times, too many times, the issue came up of oppressive debt. He heard woeful tales of being chased by bill collectors.

> Dr. Manchanda told us of his suspicion that owing medical debt is a social determinant of poor health.

Dr. Manchanda tested the efficacy of RIP's intervention by having his company fund a purchase of $2.1 million worth of medical debt in the geographical area where lived most of his rural patients, migrant farm workers. The campaign was not a "proof of concept," but it was a breakthrough for RIP — the first time we'd applied our "random act of kindness" to a specific locale and population, but not be the last.

Dr. Manchanda subsequently left his employer to launch Health Begins, based in Studio City. He circled back to RIP and its tools. In February 2017, Rishi used RIP to buy another $2 million in medical debt for the people of Los Angeles and Ventura counties.

He organized The Campaign to End Medical Debt, a nonprofit coalition of clinicians, advocates and academics. They raise funds to bring public attention to the importance of medical debt forgiveness as a "downstream" intervention to reduce and prevent poverty.

If we cannot easily remove people from poor areas where there is a mountain of medical debt, we realized through his campaign, at least we can begin to remove the mountain.

Pensacola Debt Sharks

At about the same time, two Florida high school students, Samir Boussarhane and Falen McClellan, wrote to say they had decided to emulate John Oliver and raise funds to abolish medical debt in their hometown of Pensacola. Could we help them? Of course!

Craig negotiated project terms with their high school to provide teacher oversight and ensure their efforts would fit the requirements of their special International Baccalaureate (IB) Program.

The Pensacola Debt Sharks, as they called themselves, sought to raise the $10,000 needed to abolish $1 million in local medical debt in the Pensacola-Mobile region. With pizza sales and after-school game nights, they earned local publicity (and a Huffington Post blog by me), which motivated an anonymous donor to make a generous contribution. All in all, the pair raised more than $30,000 to abolish $3 million in unpaid medical bills.

Their efforts earned the pair a George Washington Community Award from the Freedoms Foundation at Valley Forge.

Economic Impact Study

Six months after the HBO show, in January 2017, the university team came to New York City for a "mini-summit" we convened for them with RIP's technology, legal, and data scientist resources. We helped them formulate the practical structure needed to conduct a randomized controlled trial (RCT) for the economic study.

RIP's newest partner, TransUnion Healthcare, agreed to perform data analytics for the study. RIP and TheNumber would handle debt forgiveness tasks. J-PAL and others would fund the research.

The goal: Provide credible evidence of the economic and social impact of medical debt forgiveness.

Craig's and my years in the debt industry, and two years at RIP, had convinced us that medical debt hurts people. (This book details these impacts.) Still, does debt relief improve lives? To what extent does medical debt adversely affect people's financial wellbeing? Do people's lives really improve when their medical debts are forgiven? What are the indisputable facts? Now we could find out.

The research is both topical and urgent. In the USA, 44 million Americans show an aggregate of $75 billion in medical debt on their credit reports. If we add all the medical debt that never shows up on credit reports, we estimate $1 trillion in U.S. medical debt.

Does debt forgiveness actually matter in an individual's life? We are seeing at RIP that medical debt locks people into a "debt trap." Are they fully liberated by debt relief? A balance sheet that compares income to medical debt does not tell the whole story. This academic study will document a range of impacts from medical debt and debt forgiveness. (A list of the outcomes being measured is in the online research registry at the American Economics Association.)

The goal: Credible evidence on the economic impacts of medical debt forgiveness.

The evidence-based study was launched in 2017 with a projected completion in 2019. An initial report was delivered at RIP's second medical debt summit in November 2018.

UC Berkeley's Francis Wong described the study methodology. The researchers record the impact from $150 million in "randomly allocated debt forgiveness" for a group of 70,000 people. Financial outcomes in three waves of forgiveness are tracked on TransUnion credit reports. A control group of an additional 70,000 people does not get forgiveness; their debts stay in collections. Phone and mail surveys, six to 12 months after each wave, track identifiable health and quality-of-life impacts for both study groups.

The study will help RIP better target its debt forgiveness efforts to the populations that most need debt relief, he said.

There may be a more crucial byproduct from the team's work. Francis Wong cited the Oregon health insurance experiment that studied the impact of the 2008 Medicaid expansion. Those findings influenced healthcare policy nationally. The medical debt forgiveness study sample is twice the size of the Oregon study, he said, so the 2019 findings on medical debt will hold significance, and may similarly influence public policy nationwide.

Let Me Count More Ways

Other surprises came our way from the John Oliver effect.

The Better Company: GetBetter.co, a San Francisco Bay Area startup, in 2018 proposed a multistate debt forgiveness campaign, still ongoing. Better will donate to RIP revenues from the app they developed to help patients and care providers having trouble getting out-of-network claims paid by insurance companies.

Intending to "out-Oliver John Oliver," Better pledged to donate $70,000 to RIP to buy $16 million in medical debt (as compared to Oliver's $60,000 spent to buy $15 million in medical bills). Their cross-country marathon campaign will conclude in New York City, where they plan to proudly relieve John Oliver of his crown.

DvM Communications: The "Last Week Tonight" exposure also landed RIP one of the best partners we could imagine in the field of media relations — Dini von Mueffling of DvM Communications.

She and her team have launched and overseen debt abolishment campaigns in communities across the nation, generating buzz and at least $100 million in aggregate debt forgiveness. They are still going strong. Their community efforts resulted in RIP Medical Debt being named one of Town & Country magazine's Top 50 Philanthropists for 2018. Enhanced credibility!

KIRO-TV: DvM facilitated our first taste of TV news investigative reporting on medical debt and debt forgiveness, starting with Seattle's Jesse Jones on KIRO-7. The station followed up his exposé of medical debt collections in the region with a $12,500 donation for us to abolish $1 million in medical debt for folks in the area. KIRO's viewers stepped up with $40,000 more in donations to dissolve an additional $5 million in local debt. Soon after, other radio and TV stations contacted us.

> # KIRO viewers stepped up with $40,000 in donations to dissolve an additional $5 million in local debt

NBCUniversal: Media trade reporting about KIRO caught the attention of NBCUniversal, which proceeded to donate $150,000 to abolish $15 million in medical debt through its 12 local NBC-owned stations: Boston, Chicago, Dallas/Fort Worth, Hartford, Los Angeles, Miami, New York City, Puerto Rico, Philadelphia, San Diego, San Francisco, and Washington, D.C. Much like KIRO's Seattle viewers, NBC's local viewers stepped up by raising another $150,000 for RIP to forgive another $15 million in medical debt. NBC Nightly News featured RIP in a May 2018 "Inspiring America" segment. Anchor Lester Holt interviewed Craig and reported that by then RIP had forgiven medical debt for 60,000 Americans.

Oh Ye of Great Faith

An example of good creating more good came through an email in March 2018 from the Covenant Church in Carrollton, Texas.

"I represent Covenant Church, a North Texas church with many campuses. We recently saw an NBC-TV5 News story where they partnered with RIP Medical Debt to pay off medical debt in the area. We are interested in partnering with RIP in a similar manner to forgive medical debt for families in North Texas."

> '**Good News' forgiveness of $10 million in medical debt was announced from the pulpit Easter Sunday.**

A few back-and-forth calls and emails followed to clarify how RIP by now can locate debt geographically and by need. Proposing a $50,000 donation, Covenant instead donated $100,000 to abolish $10 million in Dallas debt. The "Good News" forgiveness of $10 million in medical debt was announced from the pulpit by church pastor Stephen Hayes on Easter Sunday.

Pastor Hayes told NBC-5 News that the church invests $100,000 annually in mailings to attract new members for their growing and diverse congregation. "Historically, a lot of churches have done it — where you spend upwards of six figures to send out a mailer. I don't think it's a wise investment, so we decided this year for Easter to send a different kind of mail. This [RIP] letter may not go to as many people, but it will have a much greater impact."

NBC-5 taped Hayes telling the congregation, "The $100,000 you invested in Covenant has paid off a total of $10,550,610 in medical bills. These families will get to celebrate in their homes." Referring to the debt forgiven at Easter, he rejoiced, "The bill is finished. It's been paid. It's forgiven. Gone, gone, gone, done!"

Soon after, RIP began to hear from houses of worship across the country proposing local debt forgiveness campaigns. Miracles!

I'll Drink to That

A very different and more secular website inquiry arrived in late December 2016, which opened a new realm for us to explore.

"I work with Melvin Brewing Company. We're launching a new beer next year, and our team wants to have some of the proceeds go to help pay medical debts. We're looking to raise about $300,000 and drive a ton of awareness around the issue. We've realized that we have a very loud megaphone and hope to use it for good."

We had never been "adopted" as a charity before. Craig and I do enjoy a cold one now and then, in moderation, so how could we not accept an invitation by CEO and founder Jeremy Tofte and his crew to visit their headquarters near Jackson Hole, Wyoming? Melvin brewed a special batch of the pale ale and agreed to donate 2 percent of each can sold to RIP Medical Debt. Melvin's contributions by the end of 2018 have forgiven at least $30 million in medical debt within their distribution areas from California to Massachusetts.

Our partnership has evolved. Melvin sponsored a booth for RIP at the 2018 Great American Beer Festival in Denver. They attended our second medical debt summit in New York City to provide after-summit beers for the attendees. We toast their generosity!

(In case you care to forgive medical debt, it may be useful to note Melvin first tried to "do it ourselves" by setting up their own charity. As business people, they soon realized that John Oliver had the right idea: Let RIP go through all the hassle of creating a charity, going to the debt industry to buy debt, and handling data analytics to ensure only truly needy people receive those welcome yellow envelopes.)

Community Pilot Project

A foundation friend in 2018 connected us with 2-1-1 San Diego, a nonprofit operating 24 hours a day, 365 days a year. It's Southern California's most trusted resource for access to community, health, social, and disaster services — all by dialing "211." The call is free, confidential and available in more than 200 languages.

Most relevant to RIP, 2-1-1 San Diego provides access to 6,000 services, resources and programs through an online database. If 211 callers can be identified as deserving medical debt forgiveness, RIP can put to work its analytics and forgiveness services.

We're now planning a first-of-its-kind pilot project with 2-1-1 San Diego. As envisioned, RIP will use TransUnion-based analytics to enable two participating area hospitals to automatically, instantly qualify and verify former and current patients for acceptance into a charity care program or a financial assistance program.

Once the system is in place, when a person calls 2-1-1 San Diego, they will immediately be identified (by cross-referencing both debt portfolios and hospital records) to see if they need debt forgiveness. RIP will access and search millions of accounts to locate any older debt owned by debt buyers. If we locate debt, RIP will automatically apply donor funds to buy and abolish that individual's medical debt. This will be done for free.

At first, debt forgiveness will occur sporadically, and later in real time. The pilot project is a pivotal step by RIP toward being able to forgive individual medical debt on

> This pilot project is a pivotal step toward being able to forgive individual medical debt on request.

request. We long ago created a free Debt Forgiveness Registry at our website to prepare for a day when the capacity is in place. This pilot project may bring individual debt forgiveness closer to reality!

The Second Summits

In early November 2018, RIP convened two major summits on medical debt. On Friday we covered the status of U.S. medical debt. Saturday concentrated on military and veterans' medical debt.

A diverse collection of attendees came from across the nation to study the problem of healthcare debt and work towards solutions. They represented health insurance, collections, medical debt buyers, credit reporting agencies, health technologists, Consumer Finance Protection Bureau (CFPB), Congressional Healthcare Task Force, lobbyists, veterans, economists, and healthcare practitioners.

Both days were magical. The attendees put aside their industry labels, "positions" and agendas, so everyone could work together to resolve problems without defending turf. Our open conversation let everybody listen, speak and be heard with respect.

All returned to their organizations with agreements to support the varied teams formed to continue their summit work. On Sunday, the RIP contingent marched in the New York Veterans Day Parade. This year we had a small float. My heart filled with hope.

A Quarter Billion in Debt Relief

A married couple of substantial means saw us on John Oliver and considered making a donation. They checked us out through their C-Suite connections in Silicon Valley. Has anyone heard about this RIP Medical Debt? Are these guys legitimate?

Like an unexpected billiards bank shot, their confirming source was a Better Company investor who enthused all about how RIP was fulfilling our role in their campaign. Thanks to this reference, RIP got the thumbs-up. We engaged in a lively phone conversation with the couple and secured a small contribution, starting a relationship. And what a relationship it's been!

This fine couple, choosing anonymity, in November 2018 made a seven-figure donation to RIP that empowered us to purchase and abolish a quarter of a billion dollars ($250 million) in medical debt during the last two months of 2018. Unprecedented!

Rolled out in stages, the first $150 million of debt was eliminated in early November, including $50 million in veterans and military debt. Another $50 million in debt was forgiven at Thanksgiving, and the last $50 million was abolished during the December holidays. No one expected our yellow envelope!

The campaign was the most ambitious medical debt abolishment in U.S. history, affecting nearly 100,000 individuals and families in practically every state in the country.

The Ultimate Oliver Effect

The ultimate results of the John Oliver Effect, and what amazes us all every day, are the blessings we provide for all the people whose debts have been forgiven since the LWT episode in 2016.

All the press coverage has not gone to our heads. We never forget that forgiving medical debt is our reason for being. We accept that we are merely a vehicle through which generous donors make a real difference in the lives of thousands of random people whose debts our donors let us forgive. For all this joy from being of service, we at RIP are as thankful as the recipients of debt forgiveness.

The mission driving RIP Medical Debt since 2014 is unchanged: Locate, buy and abolish $1 billion in medical debt. Amazingly, as I write, we are halfway toward that goal. We can visualize reaching it by 2020, given the energy and passion of our partners, donors and fans. When we reach that goal, we will set a new one.

The experience for us is akin to standing in front of an old-style pinball machine, replete with flashing lights and ringing bells, trying to control a careening silver orb. We have learned a little about how to use the flippers to control the direction, to hit a few bumpers to earn extra time and as many points as possible. You might say that we are becoming pinball wizards (with a salute to The Who), but we do not presume to pretend we have true mastery.

Much like a pinball machine, the debt forgiveness game appears to have a mind of its own at times. Our little speeding ball bounces from pillar to post, lighting up whatever it encounters, including us. It certainly has lit up our future as a charity.

A deeper truth is that no matter how awed we feel by the open generosity of astounding friends, RIP Medical Debt and random debt forgiveness cannot solve all the economic and social problems of medical debt. We want to help transform healthcare itself.

Meanwhile, we do our best to draw attention to the issue of debt, hoping to stimulate the creative juices of governments, corporations and foundations to agree on solutions. This is how public policy gets formulated, we're learning. (If you happen to be one of these "major players," well, we'd love to be invited into the conversation.)

RIP continues to evolve as a charitable organization. We've now grown from three founders to a distributed team of twenty, working though our office at Serendipity Labs in New York. As we forgive our first billion in debt and start on that second billion, we will continue being profoundly grateful for the blessings of the John Oliver Effect in the lives of those struggling with unpayable medical bills.

NOTE: Craig Antico contributed to this chapter.

What can be added to the happiness
of a man [woman] who is in health, out of debt,
and has a clear conscience?

— ADAM SMITH

CHAPTER 5

Debt is in the Details

Craig Antico

When I co-created RIP Medical Debt in 2014 with my partner and now co-author, Jerry Ashton, our purpose was and has always been to achieve a forthright, audacious goal: Raise money to buy unpaid and unpayable medical debt, and then forgive that debt to benefit the neediest debtors.

On the surface, simple enough.

In performing this service, we have learned the truth of saying, "The devil is in the details." It exactly fits our work and our mission. That simple. That hard. People tell us they love the goal of removing medical debt burdens from distressed people who need and deserve charitable debt relief. Our donors, partners and sponsors naturally want and need to understand the details, as may you.

Precisely what does RIP Medical Debt do? How do we go about locating, qualifying and forgiving medical debt? Where and how is medical debt located? Who owns someone's personal medical debt, and how does that come about? When does medical debt enter the "secondary debt" market? Why is so much medical debt still owed? Does medical debt ever go away? Is it really a hardship? Why?

To answer these questions, I first need to provide more history. We knew early that RIP needed a clear business case that resonated with donors: Forgive as much unpayable medical debt as we can.

As two former collections industry executives, we are uniquely positioned to raise public awareness about how medical debt harms millions of Americans and our nation as a whole.

People agree that medical debt is a wrong that needs correcting. They hear about us and then say, "Tell me more." They discover that healthcare costs are the leading cause of personal bankruptcies, causing 15 million people and their families to go insolvent yearly. The more people learn, the more they want to help.

This is how and why, as of publishing this book, RIP is almost halfway to our initial goal of abolishing $1 billion in healthcare debt. Is this big news? It's a drop in the bucket. Can we do more?

Well, let's get into those devilish details.

Does Medical Debt Ever End?

If you owe a relative or friend money that you promised to pay back, do you think that debt ever goes away? Fifteen years from now, any unpaid debt lingers between you, so you may isolate yourself from that person. You might feel anxious, guilty, ashamed, upset, or disappointed that you couldn't, wouldn't, didn't know how, or have been plain incapable of paying them back. From a legal standpoint, the debt is still owed, even after the statute of limitations expires. Ethically, the debt remains due. A promise is a promise.

Exchange your friend for a hospital or another medical provider. Does a bill you owe ever go away? No. You have four options:

1. You or another can pay the medical debt in-full or settle it.
2. The provider can issue a credit to cure the debt or forgive it.
3. The debt can be "discharged" by a U.S. bankruptcy court.
4.. The debt can be "extinguished" by law, a voided contract.

Those are your four options. Unless one of those events occurs, you still owe a debt until the day you die, but then only if your estate is insolvent, or if you don't live in one of nine U.S. states where debt is inherited. Generally, medical debt never goes away.

What if a hospital told you they wrote off your bill as bad debt? What if they changed their billing system and stopped sending you statements? What if a doctor agreed to take whatever your insurance company pays? What if that bill is 15 or 20 years old?

Sorry. In all likelihood, your medical bill is still owed.

Is this ethical or morally right? Realistically, can any debt be valid when those owing it, no matter how hard they work to be personally responsible, can never pay it back in their lifetime?

This is the reality with medical debt.

Whom can we blame for the egregious injustice and burden of medical debt? Do we blame the "healthcare system," the creditors, care providers, or loan originators? Do we blame the patients, blame the victims? For me, laying blame does not solve the problem.

To eliminate that onus, in my view, some unpayable debt in the health care system should be canceled, extinguished, as if it never existed in the first place. I hope for a day when medical debt does not persist in America, but getting to that point is a debate!

Until that remote day, debt is debt. Until that day, RIP will keep contacting medical debt owners to locate all the debt we can buy and abolish by forgiving it. This is our "fairness doctrine."

Companies call RIP offering to sell us their "receivables" or "assets," which is what your debts are to them. Knowing debt never dies and government constantly shifts the playing field, they call us to protect their patients, their

In all likelihood, your medical bill is still owed.

customers (or themselves) from liability for future collections. They know that if a company goes bankrupt, a trustee has superpowers to demand payment from all debtors, no matter how old the debt.

Ever hear the term "zombie" debt? In our industry, this is a debt that bounces from agency to agency, debt buyer to debt buyer, and never seems to go away. Too often, a third-party debt collector

'Zombie' debt never dies or goes away.

convinces a hospital or provider to place their oldest unpaid accounts with them, promising they will only charge a collection fee for those bills if they collect. That old debt gets new life. Patients who thought their bills were dead suddenly start getting collection calls.

What if you pay all or part of your medical debt with a credit card, bank loan or payday loan? What if you default upon that creditor? Once they exhaust all their collection activity and mark you as a loss, they may formally forgive the debt or settle it in part. Whew! You think the debt is no longer owed, but there's a catch.

The government considers the amount you did not have to pay as ordinary income. The creditor sends you a 1099-C "Cancellation of Debt Income" (CODI) with a copy to the IRS. You must pay taxes on that "income." For instance, the government annually forgives $110 billion in student loan debt. If you are so "lucky," watch for a 1099-C in the mail. You may owe taxes for income you never saw.

Unintended Consequences

This book could aptly be named "End Medical Debt Hardships" because medical debt never goes away, not legally, ethically, or as a burden on people's minds. Medical debt is a hardship. That is why we seek to buy and forgive as much medical debt as we can (what we call "debt of necessity"), no matter its age or legal status.

To show what we deal with at RIP, take the statute of limitations (SOL). States have an "out-of-statute" time limit on when a creditor can collect money owed through a lawsuit (or the threat of one). The SOL can range from two or three years to more than 10 years. Many think after the statutory time limit is over, collections stop, and the debt is extinguished. That is a common misperception.

Some states go further to protect the consumer. Mississippi has strengthened SOL rules, so now debts are automatically extinguished after three years. If this becomes the law elsewhere, we expect to see sharp changes in the ways hospitals charge their customers and how quickly they collect those medical bills.

If government consumer protection laws or regulations limit the time creditors can collect accounts, the inevitable "unintended consequences" might be disastrous.

If we end people's ability to pay credit (medical debt) over time, and demand payment upfront in cash, expect access to healthcare (or any service or product) to be severely impacted.

This could result in a complete "outsourcing" of care financing away from care providers to disconnect patient-doctor relationships. Outsourced medical bills then would be owed to a finance company or bank, not the provider, just as if you used a credit card. If you had pay medical bills up front, most will use credit cards, yet consumers are warned against using credit cards to pay medical bills.

Imagine what would happen if hospitals were "forced" to bring credit finance companies into their hospitals. It's possible patients would owe banks at least $800 billion a year.

Only 10 percent of medical debt is reported to credit bureaus, tallying $75 billion. That would change. Banks, by law and industry standards, would be required to report all that $800 billion to credit bureaus. This would appear on reports as "other" consumer credit, not as medical debt. Credit cards buy big-screen TVs and vacations, right? Not so! We estimate at least 20 percent of the almost $900 million owed on credit cards is for medical OOP expenses.

People with medical debt on their credit reports already have about 70 percent more credit card debt than those without medical debt. Wisconsin's experiment, just as any finance company or bank takeover of medical billing, suggests the unintended consequences from the most well-intentioned healthcare regulations.

Uncollectable Medical Bills

Hospitals that cannot collect on accounts owed by individuals who are qualified for charity care or Medicaid (but did not sign up) are vexing to both the hospital and the collection agent.

Hospitals collect unpaid bills internally if they have the means to do so, but accounts are often placed for collection to comply with regulations. These accounts likely will become "bad debt."

To keep a 501(c)(3) status, hospitals needs to meet Community Benefit Requirements. A hospital must show the U.S. government they're supporting the needy and those in hardship. My experience, however, shared by others in the medical debt industry, is that more than one-third of the accounts assigned for collections should have qualified for charity care. A hospital's "account misclassification" problem becomes an unintended consequence of the regulations intended to protect healthcare consumers!

Hospitals cannot sell to debt buyers the accounts that collection agencies declare as uncollectible. Hospitals must take the "hit." That hardly resolves the debt problem for patients. They enter purgatory. Although the hospital appears to have stopped collecting on the old debt, the patients still know they owe the amount.

Such debt makes up the lion's share of all the medical bills owed by consumers that are now in third-party collections. This is where we come in at RIP as debt buyers and forgivers.

How Is Debt Bought?

To understand how we can abolish debt for good, you first need to understand how it's bought by investors to make money.

Medical billing accounts you owe, like mortgages, can be bought and sold. At a profit, of course. Collection executives recover money for a living. The debt-buying executives who invest in debt portfolios need to buy debt at a price where they can profit, expecting to collect two to three times the amount they pay. If they buy a portfolio of debt for $10,000, they expect to collect $20,000 to $30,000.

All hospitals and most physicians use collection agencies to help collect money owed by their patients after the insurance company has paid its portion. Hospitals staff their collection departments so each collector has 8,000 accounts to handle at any one point in time. Staff overwhelm leads to unpaid accounts being placed with third-party collection agencies. The Association of Credit and Collection Professionals International says there are 100,000 bill collectors in the USA, and more than half of them collect medical debt.

Suppose that some debt buyer uses the same collection agency as a hospital. The question becomes, "Why wait for a collection agency to collect before we get our part?" A business needs cash to operate. "Accounts receivable" are not cash unless or until collected.

Half of all bill collectors now collect medical debt.

Debt buyers bring needed capital to debt sellers, so these creditors need not wait two, three or four years to finally get their money, if ever. Debt buyers are sophisticated, with strong dispute resolution skills and respectful collection practices. There is no room in their world for unethical practices, not like what we hear about. The debt industry has shifted toward treating debtors with respect.

Debt bought from hospitals is seldom bought for pennies on the dollar, as RIP pays. Prices are closer to five, 10, 15 cents or more on the dollar, depending on the billing accounts' age, the likelihood of successfully contacting patients and the likelihood of collecting from them. As a business, debt buyers take on such risk, aware they might not collect two to three times the amount they paid.

If a debt buyer pays $50 for each $1,000 bill owed, for example, they have to collect $150 to $200 per $1,000, on average, to make an acceptable return for the risk assumed by them, their bankers and investors. They may collect on "fresh" accounts fairly quickly, yet it can take three to 10 years to collect from the remaining accounts — three to 10 years of phone calls, letters, and even lawsuits.

More than seven percent of all workers in the USA have income garnishments. Most are for child support or alimony, yet more than 25 percent of those garnishments are from medical debt judgments, often in cases filed by debt buyers.

We at RIP can cost-effectively buy portfolios of accounts from medical providers and debt buyers because we research the accounts deeper than they do. We are debt buyers who are not economically constrained by profit. We care only about the social profit.

Which Debt Is Bought?

Our strategic partner, TransUnion Healthcare, believes in what we are doing — using their information for good. We use their data, plus publicly available data, plus purchased social determinant data, for identifying the portfolios to buy. We try to get the best possible picture of patients in the context of their debts and situations. With this data, we can better value a portfolio, measure the impact of debt forgiveness. We do this not to ensure that our donors don't overpay, but to ensure people who most need help most get our debt relief. We become, essentially, debtors' second-chance safety net.

Once we identify debtors needing our help, such as where a local group does a community debt forgiveness campaign, our next step is buying their debt. At this point, we may seek a medical provider willing to sell us their unpaid debt at a charitable price. More likely, we go into the *secondary medical debt market.* There we locate debt and run it through our data analytics, so we are confident of buying only accounts that qualify for our charity work. We then negotiate a price for a portfolio and take possession by paying for it.

As the legal owners of a debt, we can legitimately extinguish it.

What we do with debt differs from what collection agencies do. Penniless accounts, for collectors, are nuisances they place on credit reports on the chance one day a debtor will get a job or inheritance, so monies appear to pay it, plus interest and charges, just to clear the debt from credit reports and be done with it.

We buy account portfolios from debt sellers at a steep discount off the amount originally owed to a medical provider. From the date of debt purchase, *our work is the reverse of a collection agency.* We abolish the debt in full, no strings attached. We make sure the credit blemish is removed — all within 90 days of buying that debt.

Such debt purchases can only be done in volume. If RIP tried to buy one account at a time, we'd have to pay 50 times the $5 to $15 for each $1,000 account we pay now.

> # RIP buys debt at a steep discount off the amount owed to a medical provider.

That's too much for us. This why our charity cannot forgive debt for any individuals on request. Not yet. Maybe someday. We created a Debt Forgiveness Registry for that future day we figure out how.

Our success comes only in partnership with donors and debt sellers (maybe you). Medical debt forgiveness occurs when we join with those who want to free fellow humans from undue destructive circumstances. No judgment, no pity. Just a gift from one stranger to another. Our role is to facilitate that affirmation of care.

Also required is a hospital, doctor or debt owner willing to sell or donate accounts to us rather than continuing to collect internally or park bills at a collection agency. Imagine the pleasure of a hospital or provider after donating, or selling for pennies, something of little value in return for changing a patient's life for the better.

We and our donors —"social investors"— agree: A collection process that takes three to 10 years to complete is too long and too socially destructive. We aim to remove hardship from debtors by taking the investor and the bill collector out of the picture, generally after the second or third year of a bill. We work through the market pricing system, not through legislation. Our business careers help us to pay below-market rates to take medical debt off the street.

Community Benefit Requirements

Charity care is only one required community benefit a hospital offers its patients in return for state and federal tax exemptions. On average, hospitals spend about six percent of their revenues upon improving the health of their community.

A tax-exempt charitable hospital can receive significant benefits if they comply with IRS and state regulations. Part of meeting their role in providing community benefits is demonstrating initiatives, activities, and investments they've undertaken to improve health in the community. Hospitals can also lose their federal tax exemption if they do not comply with the rules.

Within these requirements awaits an opportunity. As distilled from Plante Moran, here is an overview:

• The hospital must conduct a local "Community Health Needs Assessment" (CHNA). and adopt an "implementation plan" that addresses the needs. This must be submitted every three years. The strategic plan must be adopted on or before the 15th day of the fifth month after the year a CHNA is conducted. A $50,000 excise fine curbs non-compliance.

Hospitals can lose their federal tax exemption if they don't comply with benefit rules.

• The hospital must create a Financial Assistance Policy (FAP), publicized in the community, and an emergency medical care policy on providing care without regard to FAP eligibility.

• The hospital must limit amounts charged under the FAP to no more than the amounts billed to individuals who have insurance.

• The hospital is prohibited from collection actions against an individual without reasonable efforts to determine FAP eligibility.

Tax-exempt hospitals report four items on their Schedule H to document how they benefit their communities:

1. Financial assistance and means-tested government programs.
2. Community building activities.
3. Medicare shortfall fiscal report.
4. Bad debt attributable to charity care.

Meeting community benefit requirements in 2011 was worth $24.6 billion, noted Julia James at Project HOPE. That tax exemption (state and federal) was shared by 60 percent of 5,500 U.S. hospitals.

What if hospitals could count bad debt for eligible charity care as meeting their Community Benefit Requirements? As calculated from hospitals' Form 990s in 2013, this could exceed $67 billion.

With more than $30 to $40 billion at stake in the tax exemption, is health care leadership ready to act? Here is an opportunity!

A culture of care and charity starts from the top. The CEO, CFO, CMO (medical officer) and governing boards can make change happen. Is the business of health care distracting them from their main mission of helping people? Should regulations prevent hospitals from abolishing indigents' bad debt?

RIP provides an effective and sane way for hospitals to rid their books of medical debt, a "safe harbor" to end intractable problems from medical debt. The potential is evident on the Schedule 990 H publicly filed by tax-exempt hospitals — at least $25 billion!

Everyone know the bad debt is still owed. Letting debt "sit on the books" doesn't make it go away, nor does it grant healthy peace of mind to those owing medical debt they cannot pay.

Community hospitals are not equipped with the cost accounting systems, analytics and reporting to provide reliable evidence that they do provide care for the needy. We are certain hospitals provide this community benefit, but they have a hard time coming up with systems-generated evidence to prove it.

Working in partnership with RIP's analytics and leveraging our tax-exempt charity status, hospitals can provide their communities with the miracle of medical debt forgiveness. The only "debt details" left to manage will be how to identify those accounts and ask RIP to put yellow debt forgiveness letters in the mail.

The cure for medical debt is in the details. For goodness' sake.

CHAPTER 6

Margin Over Mission:
Head vs. Heart

Robert Goff

The healthcare industry is a huge part of the American economy. Along with spending on services, the healthcare industry is the largest source of employment in the nation.

All the trillions spent on healthcare are spread across numerous enterprises, yet it's concentrated in two components — physicians and hospitals. The American Medical Association reports these two represent just under half of all healthcare spending.

Physicians and hospitals are the most familiar to us. Hospitals are those large, imposing buildings that have been there forever, fixtures in our communities. Physicians are honored for knowledge and compassion, each a reincarnation of Marcus Welby, M.D.

While we think of them as linked, hospitals and physicians are different and separate economic units. How each is compensated has determined how they've evolved, and how they evolved greatly impacts healthcare costs. All of these costs outstripping the ability of patients to pay is what creates medical debt.

The Urge to Merge

Consolidating economic power is increasing healthcare costs.

The structure of healthcare delivery is a vestige of 19th and 20th century concepts and limits. If care required more than a physician, the hospital played a critical role as a hub of sophisticated services and technology, such as surgical services, radiology and laboratory. Before immunizations, hospitals also protected communities from communicable diseases.

Hospitals continued this local role while the world around them changed. Isolated communities were linked by roads and bridges. Populations shifted. Advances in medical science and technologies reduced the need for hospitals' core service — inpatient beds.

Hospitals survived by adapting. Between 1975 and 2015, about 1,500 hospitals closed their doors. Eliminating beds and hospitals did not slow spending. Statista reported hospital expenditures rose from $27.2 billion in 1980 to about $1.2 trillion by 2018. Said one administrator, "There is no mission without a margin."

The hospital evolved from a community charity with a mission of service into a business enterprise.

The hospital evolved from a community charity with a mission of service into a business enterprise. To meet the public benefit mission, hospitals were licensed to guarantee competence. Licenses let hospitals become monopolies or oligarchies in their service areas. Hospitals used business techniques to control how the healthcare dollar was spent. Their license let local hospitals dominate inpatient services and then control outpatient and physician services. Hospitals became profit centers.

Hospitals next merged with other hospitals and other sectors of care delivery, like urgent care and ambulatory surgery. A "system" was created that not only dominates delivery of care but exploits it economically. Hospitals grew at the expense of communities that the hospitals' founders had pledged to serve as a mission.

Hospitals are compensated for services provided. The more the services, the greater the revenue. Hospitals are paid formula-based rates for Medicare and Medicaid. Hospitals are paid more for both Medicare and Medicaid services than independent providers.

Commercial insurance plans negotiate hospital service payments. A monopoly or oligarchy hospital system negotiates from a position of strength in the local geography. Pay the demanded rates, or don't do business with that local healthcare system.

Press releases for nearly every merger promise cost savings. After a merger, Forbes reported, prices rise upward to 44 percent.

Not every hospital dominates the local market. Hospitals with favorable Medicare rates (Medicaid rates are rarely profitable), plus a solid volume of commercially insured patients, can expand their profit margins by negotiating increased payments from insurance companies. Higher insurance payments get passed on to patients, of course, as higher insurance premiums.

Downstream Revenues

Hospital systems dominating health care delivery often feed their business interests by capturing downstream revenues. They seek to capture every healthcare dollar spent in their service area. Disney World may seek to capture every vacation dollar spent in Orlando, but hospitals do not run a risk of people vacationing elsewhere.

Profit margins are good in business. Health insurance companies in 2017 ran margins between 4.0 and 5.25 percent, says Investopedia. The American Hospital Association's TrendWatch reports hospitals enjoying 6.4 percent operating margin yet suffering negative profit margins of -23 percent. Seven of the ten most profitable hospitals in 2013 were not-for-profit institutions. Gundersen Lutheran Medical Center in La Crosse, Wisconsin, had $302 million in profits.

Hospital systems use profit margins from their "medical mission to serve" to grow bigger and dominate even more.

Health insurance companies, by law, must spend a percentage of premium revenues on healthcare services or refund policyholders. Hospitals have no such obligation to use profits for reducing their charges or for community betterment, so few do.

Profits go toward acquiring more and more medical providers, like physician practices and urgent care facilities. Hospital mergers and acquisitions tallied 115 transactions in 2017, reported RevCycle Intelligence, and the tally increased 11 percent in 2018.

Venture Capitalism

Hospitals also are entering the venture capital business. Indeed, hospitals are a new source of financing for new ideas and businesses. Forbes reported that in the first half of 2017, more than $6 billion of hospital money financed startup business ventures. Hospital systems investing in new businesses risk mission-driven revenues for future potential economic gains. The adventure can be perilous for a hospital's economic stability.

One area of investment is going head-to-head with the insurance companies. Hospital systems know healthcare best, after all, so they figure, "Why not cut out the middleman and create our own health plans? Why not capture insurance margins as our own?"

The reality is different than expected. A 2017 Allan Baumgarten study, funded by the Robert Wood Johnson Foundation, found that only four of 42 hospital health plans were profitable in 2015. Some reported significant losses, and five went out of business.

Becker's Hospital CFO Report noted that Northwell, based in Long Island, absorbed significant losses from their health insurance startup, CareConnect. Losses on a second insurance plan Northwell owned pushed the entire health system into the red by $36.2 million during the first quarter of 2017. This does not include the loss of all investment capital to launch CareConnect.

Should hospitals increase their charges and their costs to invest in risky ventures?

Premier Health in Ohio, said Dayton Daily News, shuttered its insurance plans after a three-year effort with losses of $40 million. Unable able to find a buyer, their return on investment was zero.

Some hospital systems are still pushing ahead with their health insurance ventures, plowing in hospital revenues to fund deficits. Other systems are pulling the plug, divesting themselves of losers, as did Catholic Health Initiatives in Englewood, Colorado, and Tenet Healthcare in Dallas. Such economic losses reduce the resources for the organizations providing direct health care.

I will not say if these investment strategies are good or bad. The question I raise is: Should hospital systems be able to increase their charges to private and government payers, and increase costs to the patients, to invest their resources in risky business ventures?

Private business hopes for a high return on investment (ROI), no guarantees. If a venture fails, the hit is taken by the investors, the shareholders. However, a not-for-profit hospital system has no such shareholders. Investment losses, if big enough, endanger a hospital's critical medical services. Must a community bail out a local hospital because of its appetite for investing in new ventures?

Should higher health costs, higher premiums, plus higher taxes for Medicare and Medicaid. fund a protected monopoly's attempts to expand domination over where our medical dollar is spent?

Regardless of how hospital systems use their fiscal resources, the public is expected to pick up any added care costs. Hospital systems increasingly invest revenues in self-aggrandizement — advertising. Becker's Hospital Review reported that U.S. hospitals spent an estimated $4.9 billion for local advertising in 2017.

HealthLeaders Magazine has defended marketing expenditures, saying, "Hospitals need to advertise to maintain or enhance revenue flow. Even nonprofit hospitals need to market to insured patients and promote high-grossing service lines, so that they are able to continue to care for the uninsured."

Same rationale: There is no mission without a margin.

Employed Physicians

Hospital systems grow by adding physicians as employees. How? About 80 percent of U.S. healthcare spending results from decisions made by physicians. Influence or control that care decision, and you control a significant amount of revenue. Employee physicians yield a regular flow of patients referred to ancillary services owned by the system. System-owned services are paid more than independently owned services, so boosting patient volume assures the system's overall costs for health care will rise.

Laboratory Economics reported that a UnitedHealthcare in-network hospital lab in New York charged 23 times more than did local LabCorp for the same tests ($384 versus $16.25).

Medical Economics has reported that Medicare paid $188 to an independent physician for a level II EKG without contrast. The same EKG in a hospital's outpatient setting cost 140 percent more ($452,89) when charged by the employed physician.

Costs from hospital-employed physicians are a fiscal drain on Medicare. Modern Healthcare Magazine in November 2017 ran an analysis of U.S. costs for four procedures at hospital outpatient services and independent locations. Employed physicians generated 27 percent more Medicare costs ($3.1 billion) than did the independent physicians. Employed physicians were seven times more likely to provide services in a more costly hospital outpatient setting.

An Empire BlueCross executive said the cost of care provided by an employed physician is 20 to 40 percent higher than the cost of that same care by a physician in independent practice.

> Influence or control the health care decision, and you control a significant amount of revenue.

Hospitals' employment of physicians is increasing dramatically. Between July 2015 and July 2016, hospitals acquired 5,000 physician practices, reported Healthcare Dive. Separately, FierceHealthcare reported that hospital-owned practices increased 100 percent in the four years ending in 2016. Nationally, 38 percent of all physician practices are now hospital-owned.

Independent Physicians

Local independent physicians are fighting a rearguard action.

Independent physician practices may be a vanishing breed, but individual physicians in small practices remain the providers of choice for most of the frequent medical care people receive.

Independent physicians face a greater economic burden than those employed by hospital-owned practices, and they have far less flexibility in revenue generation. Regulations don't favor them in atttempting financial creativity and "revenue maximization."

A 2012 American Medical Association survey of physicians shows that despite the shift to hospital employment, 53.2 percent of physicians were self-employed, and 60 percent of these in practices wholly owned by physicians. Most independent practices are in the medical specialties directly affecting the lives and wellbeing of their patients, such as family practitioners, obstetricians/gynecologists, internists, and internal medicine subspecialties like oncology.

Beyond their responsibilities for the delivery of medical care, the independent physicians must also endure the pressures and concerns of any small business owner. This includes the staff payroll. A Kaiser Foundation report, "Professional Active Physicians," estimates that small practices employ more than five million people. Each physician pays for a median of six employees. Other business costs include rent, supplies, telephone, and computers with specialized apps for all patient

Independent physicians must endure the pressures and concerns of any small business.

records and billing, plus one expense other small business owners do not have in their budgets — malpractice insurance.

Their source of revenue is the sale and delivery of professional expertise and specialized knowledge, generally sold in units of time. Time is a finite resource. The physicians who spend extra time with their grateful patients, in reality, put their practices at risk.

An online video, "The Vanishing Oath," narrated by Ryan Flesher, M.D, gives us a clear sense of the financial realities of the "average" physician. The average compensation for independent physicians in the USA is $146,000, three times the national average for household income. However, when you factor in overhead and working hours, physicians' take-home pay averages less than $28 an hour. It's above a minimum wage of $15 an hour, but not by much.

The average charge from more than 200 million visits paid by Medicare in 2012 was just $57, less than a plumber charges to fix a broken toilet, says Nancy Nielsen, M.D, Ph.D., a past president of the American Medical Association, as reported by MedPage Today.

Another factor in a physician's life is the burden of debt from a medical education, Student Debt Relief estimates medical students graduating in 2018 had $190,000 in debt. This affects where they choose to practice, whether they are independent or employed.

In communities where a population is economically challenged, private practice physicians are in short supply. Practice costs cannot be met through a high volume of low-paying Medicaid patients, not without the quality of care suffering. Therefore, physicians tend to congregate in high-income suburbs or upscale urban neighborhoods. Where and how physicians practice medicine becomes more about lifestyle and economics than meeting a community's needs.

Healthcare Values vs. Costs

Probably the greatest challenge facing physicians is the value that Americans place on healthcare compared with its costs. In general, healthcare costs are perceived as too high and the quality as too low. Patient satisfaction and customer service levels? Even lower.

Physicians are easy targets for efforts to control costs. They're on the receiving end of bureaucratic rules alleged to improve quality. Employed physicians have hospital resources to lessen bureaucratic burdens. Independent physicians are on their own.

Unlike other small businesses, physicians' income is largely out of their control. Businesses adapt prices to cost and competition.

Patients are learning to match their care to their coverage.

The physicians' reimbursements are now dictated to them. Medicare pays fixed rates to physicians for seniors, the largest consumers of health care services. Each state sets its Medicaid rates. Physicians agree to accept the fixed rates from private health plans in exchange for plan participation.

Physicians in a hospital practice benefit from their monopolistic hospital assuring that its physicians are paid higher rates, but independent physicians have little leverage when negotiating with commercial health plans. For private practices, plan participation is a take-it-or-leave-it proposition.

Unique in medicine is that physicians' compensation is tied to a service or procedure, regardless of the physicians' experience, which improves the quality and efficiency of the care delivered. A surgeon removing an appendix is paid the same regardless of whether she or he is a veteran of thousands of appendectomies or a recent graduate with the ink still wet on the license. While patients want the most experienced physician, is the physician's experience being valued or respected by insurance and government plans?

Despite the perennial cry, "The sky is falling!" physicians are not dropping out of Medicare in droves. The Centers for Medicare and Medicaid Service (CMS) say that 90 percent of practicing physicians accept Medicare patients. Kaiser Health News says that 69 percent participate with Medicaid. These numbers are holding steady.

Physician participation in the commercial insurance plans is increasing while benefit coverage is shrinking or being eliminated for health services provided by physicians who do not participate with commercial plans. Patients are learning to match their care to their coverage to avoid higher out-of-pocket costs and to avoid a lack of coverage for care provided by out-of-network physicians.

Insurance companies have been less than generous in sharing their increasing premium revenue over the last ten to twelve years. MD Magazine reports on the discouraging slide of payment rates to physicians since 2001, saying they have declined or remained flat almost every year, a trend likely to continue.

Payments to physicians from commercial plans are now running less than Medicare. Between 2006 and 2013, payments dropped by about 43 percent. Medscape calculated that payment for the most common office visit is 39.8 percent less than what Medicare pays.

Patients need to understand that their physicians, all physicians, sell their time. Time remains a limited resource.

For independent physicians in private practice, their constrained reimbursements are falling behind their costs to stay in business. From 2002 to 2012, Medicare fee-for-service (FFS) rates increased 9 percent, while the cost of operating a practice — as measured by the Medicare Economic Index (MEI) — increased 27 percent, reported the Medicare Payment Advisory Commission (MedPac). The MEI includes everything from physician and staff compensation to rent, exam room tables, postage, and computers. During that very same period, the overall inflation rate was 33 percent — a net loss.

Physician-Patient Relationship

The physician–patient relationship is a unique business model. A physician is expected to provide specialized knowledge with a high degree of compassion, which is what the vast majority of physicians do, yet it poses a challenge for business viability.

A compassionate connection with patients induces independent physicians to write off unpaid bill balances, putting their practices at risk. Employed physicians' compassion for patients is the same, but they largely have removed themselves from business operations; their institutions pay other people to maximize revenue. Employed physicians traded independence for a more secure income.

Independent physicians must sustain their practice as a business, compensating their staff well enough to retain them, yet still derive a decent income themselves, so they can be there for their patients. This difficult, sometimes impossible challenge is why the number of independent physicians is diminishing.

Independent physician participate in insurance plans to support their patients. Their participation lets patients obtain the maximum coverage possible with fewer dollars coming from patients' pockets. Participation builds the patient-physician relationship by limiting fiscal pressures on that relationship. Plan participation means less income for physician, subtly straining relations with patients.

Lawrence Casalino, M.D, Ph.D., Weill Cornell Medical College, studied physician's practices and found their total cost for dealing with insurance plans was $31 billion annually — 6.9 percent of all U.S. expenditures for physician and clinical services. For patients with limited insurance coverage, or no plan coverage, considerably more time gets spent on patient–physician financial arrangements.

Time spent on insurance could be spent on building up the patient-physician relationship.

The Commonwealth Fund found physicians devoted three hours a week, three weeks a year, interacting with insurance plans. Nursing staff spent 23 weeks per year per physician. Clerical staff spent 44 weeks. This time could be spent on building up the patient-physician relationship.

With care reimbursements fixed, payment sources reduced and expenses increasing, "cost-shifting" has been largely eliminated for independent physicians. Employed physicians' costs get subsidized by hospitals through referring patients to costlier ancillary services. For the independent physician, there are fewer options, and no one to help with the expense of that patient relationship.

For those with health insurance, the patient–physician financial relationship is undergoing a major change. Low copays and limited deductibles (if any) are disappearing. TransUnion Healthcare has reported that patients' average out-of-pocket costs increased 11 percent in 2017, rising to $1,813. About 39 percent of patient visits to physicians incur out-of-pocket costs from $500 to $1,000.

Origin, a healthcare analytics company, reported that the patient financial responsibility for insured individuals increased 47 percent since 2009. About 40 percent of care revenue is at risk due to patient bad-debt. This harms the physician-patient relationship.

Obamacare Impacts

The Affordable Care Act, Obamacare, increased health insurance coverage while increasing its economic burden. Obamacare added to the intensity of the patient–physician financial exchange.

The debate over "health reform" turned into a plan for getting all Americans covered by health insurance. We talked a lot about the cost of coverage but little about what it cost to obtain that coverage. Coverage did not cover everything from the first dollar onward. To get the broad coverage of the mandated benefit plans, patients had to accept higher deductibles. In theory, this would "engage" patients in realizing that care is not free, so they are judicious in its use.

In reality, cancer patients would be happy never to need services, but they have no choice. High deductibles sting the necessary users of medical care as well as the unnecessary users.

There was much talk about premium costs, how there would be tax credits for businesses to offer coverage. There would subsidies to provide for individuals to purchase coverage, and the "essential benefits" that had to be included. What it all would cost patients to access care received short shrift in the conversations.

With subsidies cushioning the economics of purchasing coverage, with essential benefits like "free" preventive care, the sticker shock of deductibles only hits us when there is an illness or injury. That's when the out-of-pocket costs can decide whether people actually choose to keep themselves or their family members healthy.

The Physician's Dilemma

High deductibles and copays become "account receivables," bad debt for physicians and medical debt for patients. Affordability is not academic for physicians in their practice. For them, it's a real challenge to their fiscal survival as well as to their ability to provide proper care for their patients.

Given the fixed or declining care reimbursements from insurance, given increased operating costs, our independent physicians face a conflict between the doctor-patient relationship and the patient-doctor financial exchange.

Physician-patient relationships give physicians more knowledge of patients' situations than the usual business transaction. This intimate knowledge of individuals' personal circumstances creates tension.

> Physicians face a conflict between doctor-patient relationship and the patient-doctor financial exchange.

The patients who need the most physician or other medical care and services often have the most economic issues, perhaps caused by illness or injury, or as a consequence of the stress. These patients frequently cannot work, or they're restricted in their ability to work, requiring time and attention by family members, who may decide care giving takes priority over producing income.

The physician's dilemma: With limited time to care for patients and yet produce revenue, with fixed reimbursements that limit their income, how can they balance the economic needs of their practice with a compassionate response to each patient's situation?

Head vs. Heart

Physicians in private practice must generate sufficient income to cover expenses of their practice and still support their family. When payments from insurance are insufficient, due to poor coverage or limitations on coverage, the patient is fully responsible.

Physicians know in their heads that any heart-guided write-offs of patients' debt can spell financial ruin for the practice. This struggle between the head and heart is rarely faced in other businesses.

"Hard core" bill collections against patients, who likely have both medical and financial problems, are contrary to most physicians' personal values and sentiments. Physicians will add to patients' debt load, not out of desire, but out of economic necessity.

With their heart, physicians feel an urge to forgive the debt. With their head, they know that they cannot absorb rising loses at a time of increasing expenses, nor can they risk administrative sanctions (or worse) from the insurance carriers.

What should independent physicians do? What would you do?

The easiest course is removing oneself from the business of medicine to be an employee of a large organization or institution. Free yourself to practice medicine, unburdened from the challenges of business administration, billing and collections. Turn over those distasteful tasks to your institution's financial experts. However, doing so means your patients will not be treated with your level of compassion, as billing for the services you provide go into a system designed to maximize revenue.

Billing and collections on behalf of hospital-employed physicians tend to follow the processes and programs of that institution. While every hospital has a policy for charity care, there is little outreach to ensure wise use of the funds. In fact, since the advent of the ACA, with more people being covered under Medicaid, the use of charity funds by hospitals has gone down, according to an analysis by the Advisory Board, to less than 2 percent of their operating costs.

Under Obamacare, as plan deductibles rise, the middle class suffers a gigantic increase in medical debt. This economic demographic, which mostly has insurance, just does not think of seeking charity care from local hospitals, especially at the time of service. Only when the bills arrive do the gaps in their plan coverage become evident. Only then are the tangible burdens of medical debt understood.

> Independent physicians who choose mission over margin, put heart over head, do so at their fiscal peril.

By then, a patient is out of the hospital. That sign in Admissions, welcoming inquiries for charity care, is not remembered. Hospitals do not go out of their way to promote charity care. A bill or demand for payment seldom offers relief by contacting the hospital.

Independent practices that sell their medical debt are few and far between, and fewer ask an agency to pursue collections in court or report bad debt to credit bureaus. However, hospital-owned medical practices, following a hospital's practices, regularly file legal action and regularly report bad accounts to credit bureaus.

Another twist causing medical debt is that the hospitals which do provide charity care, if barely, could seek better compensation rates, or community support to fund charity care. However, not-for-profit hospitals instead focus upon raising money to provide new services that increase revenue, which then increases medical debt.

Independent physicians lack institutional or community support for a heartfelt approach of absorbing the medical debt of hardship patients. There is no support for any increase in their rates, so they cannot afford to provide charity care, but many do.

Absorbing the medical debt of patients who need care but can't afford it, bluntly, is another reason to abandon private independent medical practice to join a hospital-owned practice. That choice for personal survival by independent physicians results in higher costs for health care, increasing medical debt in a community.

Independent physicians seek to provide for their patients, their employees, their own families, and their communities. They choose mission over margin, choose heart over head, yet they do so at their fiscal peril, and they alone are expected to pick up the tab.

Hospital systems tend to choose profit margin over missions of service, put mission in service of margin. Despite all the compassion of hospital leaders, institutional needs compel them to choose head over heart, to exploit every opportunity for market dominance. Our society is expected to pick up the tab. Is this sensible?

I attribute my success to this:
I never gave or took any excuse.

— Florence Nightingale

CHAPTER 7

Fanciful Healthcare Financing

Robert Goff

Speaking only for myself, I believe insurance is the wrong way to finance the healthcare needs of Americans.

I come to this belief honestly, only after decades in management for medical billing and collections. I do not expect you to share my opinion, yet I want to offer insightful facts, ones persuasive for me, so you can reach your own conclusions.

To understand why I say insurance is the wrong way to finance the healthcare needs of Americans, I offer here a brief education on how insurance actually works, in practical terms, and a brief history of health insurance, tracing back to war and tax policies.

Insurance is a financial device to absorb economic consequences of rare events. Insurance provides money to the policyholder to restore physical damage from a covered incident. Property insurance works well for homes and autos, so I'll use it as an example.

The financing of insurance is relatively simple. A company offers to provide coverage for these rare events. The risk is spread over all the policyholders, allowing each to pay a small amount on a regular basis toward a fund to pay any policyholder should that rare event occur. Policyholders, essentially, fund one another's losses, and the insurance company holds funds not paid out. Insurance companies, in general, prefer to be paid than to pay.

To avoid those rare events that must be covered, or to mitigate the impact, insurance companies promote safety. Policyholders are encouraged to conduct themselves in ways that reduce risk.

Insurance companies offer policyholders financial incentives to reduce claims, such as discounts for vehicle features that reduce the risk of theft or accidents. Likewise, they offer discounts for home security features, such as smoke and burglar alarms.

Policyholders assume part of the financial impact from a rare event through *deductibles*. Homeowners or car owners who become "high utilizers" of insurance coverage, or potentially high utilizers — like living in a flood plain or having a poor driving record — may find obtaining insurance coverage unaffordable or unavailable.

Lastly, homeowners' insurance policies and auto policies contain "caps" or limits on their coverage. Because homes and automobiles have market values, which can be established, insurance companies do not want to overpay for coverage. Therefore, limiting the liability of the insurance carrier is accepted in the law.

Health Care Insurance Business Model

Applying property insurance concepts to financing health care, in my view, is simply wrongheaded. An individual's need for health care is not a rare event. The need for health care is expected, perhaps predictable. Illness and injury are commonplace. Few mothers give birth today without intervention from medical services.

Health care is lifelong. A childhood rite of passage are preventive services like immunizations and checkups. In adolescence, HPV vaccinations for both genders are advised to protect against cervical and throat cancers. For young women, upon reaching maturity, a Pap test for cervical cancer is an annual ritual, as are mammograms for older women. As men mature, PSA prostate cancer screening is routine. Colonoscopies at age 50 are advised for everyone. A routine annual physical is an opportunity to screen for common measures of less-than-optional health, such as diabetes or high blood pressure. Good health insurance covers such usual and expected events in life.

> Covering rare events, the business model for other forms of insurance, does not fit for lifetime health insurance.

The business model of covering rare events, as expected for other forms of insurance, does not fit health insurance. Unlike with a car or house, we cannot put a market value on human life.

As you age, your statistical chances increase of developing one or more chronic conditions, As medical science improves, your chances rise for living through an acute illness like appendicitis or pneumonia. Cancer treatments have now made that killer survivable for many. Cardiac surgery is considered safe and routine. Americans now live through episodic health crises that in past generations would have ended life. As we live longer, we live long enough to develop and live with chronic illnesses. We expect health insurance to cover it all.

Yes, unfortunate catastrophic and rare illnesses do occur, but 45 percent of the population, or 33 million Americans, have at least one chronic disease, reported the Partnership to Fight Chronic Disease. The Clearing House Advisory Committee calculated that chronic diseases account for the vast majority of health spending, totaling

$2 trillion in 2005. Total health care spending in 2016 surpassed $3.4 trillion. Close to 99 percent of Medicare and 83 percent of the Medicaid expenditures are necessary for chronic care.

The healthcare financing model is designed to provide financial assistance for rare events, but the system instead is expected to fund health care needs that are no longer rare, to fund needs that are not only predictable but expected. Such financing is fanciful.

High Health Insurance Premiums

The rising cost of health insurance premiums gets bashed in the healthcare debate. Critics vilify insurance company profits, big CEO salaries and wasteful administration. Often forgotten is the fact that premiums largely reflect the hard costs of medical services, the unit cost of each service, and the volume of services utilized.

Now add the cost to operate an insurance company, including claims payments, marketing, and efforts to influence utilization of services, plus a margin for profitability.

Health insurance premiums follow a simple equation:

Medical costs + administrative costs + profits = premiums.

America's Health Insurance Plans (AHIP) in 2011 reported basic industry profitability at 4.4 percent, far below the public perception that profits are in the range of 10 to 25 percent. (The average profit margin for an S&P 500 company in 2017 was 11 percent.)

To hold down their policy premiums, health insurance companies mimic the devices of property and casualty insurance to limit or mitigate their risk of claims. They encourage people to adopt healthy habits. They want us to be well.

Prior to the Affordable Care Act (Obamacare), health insurance companies often reduced their risks of medical claims by excluding coverage for pre-existing conditions. They imposed waiting periods before coverage began. They excluded individuals and small groups,

Medical costs + admin costs + profits = premiums.

requiring enough policyholders to spread the risks. The business case set coverage limits.

No health insurance company can survive or provide coverage for anyone if the only people who buy policies are those who require medical care. Similarly, no auto insurance company can survive selling policies only to people with poor driving records and have had lots of accidents.

Such fiscal pragmatism is the basis of the ACA requirement that everyone must purchase coverage. As the "individual mandate" fell under the Trump administration, health insurance companies felt compelled to raise premiums to remain viable.

Health insurance emulates property insurance on deductibles, so it set limits or caps before care services would be covered, like caps on the coverage for homeowners and auto insurance. Lifetime caps or limits on health insurance of $250,000, $500,000 and $1 million were not uncommon. The ACA banned lifetime caps and limits. Insurance companies now must pay all these claims without any end in sight. This stresses their business viability.

Before the ACA, deductibles were a disincentive to preventative care. The ACA requires insurance companies to cover preventive care services without a copayment or coinsurance, even if a patient has not met the annual deductible. The rule requires an outlay by health insurance companies, but since the individual mandate was repealed, the risk can't be spread out among many anymore .

You may or may not agree with the individual mandate, but in practical terms, its repeal has added to the reasons health insurance companies are raising premiums to stay in business.

Insurance Funds Medical Advances

Health insurance, for all its criticisms, should be complimented for dramatic improvements in the sophistication of health services. All those dollars paid by insurance companies become the income for health care providers. Health insurance let medical caregivers end their dependency on charity, replacing pleas for donations with a dependable source of funding.

Reliable funding from health insurance has been a stimulus for expanding medical research and transferring research to practical use. Reliable funding allows medical device makers, pharmaceutical companies, and research hospitals to develop new lifesaving medical technologies that otherwise would lack funding.

Consider the 1972 expansion to Medicare, which covered those suffering End State Renal Disease (ESRD) kidney failure. Before then, there was limited investment in dialysis machines and services, mostly at the academic medical centers. Limited time allocations were decided by committees that selected who would receive life-continuing treatments. Access to funds meant access to care.

> Reliable funding from insurance has been a stimulus for expanding medical research.

Due to Medicare expansion, more patients with ESRD began to survive. The U.S. Renal Data System in 2016 reported close to 350,000 people having a primary diagnosis of renal failure. In 2013, Medicare reported its costs for treating patients with chronic kidney disease (CKD) surpassed $50 billion — 20 percent of all the Medicare spending for those over 65 years old.

Patients surviving renal failure live with other chronic diseases. Between 2010 and 2013, Medicare patients with chronic conditions accounted for $8 billion of the total $9 billion in Medicare spending growth. Seventy percent of Medicare spending for CKD patients over age 65 had diabetes, congestive heart failure, or both.

Health insurance has funded medical advancements, yet these have come with a significant advance in costs.

Early History of Health Insurance

If health care costs are now routine, expected and predictable, then a financing model designed for a rare event is not a model for successfully financing healthcare nor for improving the health status of Americans. How did we land in our current circumstances?

Is there an evil cabal pulling the strings? Or, is there a series of unfortunate decisions and non-decisions, coupled with ideology?

The USA is the only "industrialized" or "first world" country without a national health care plan — some model of nationalized coverage. How we historically got into this situation is the lack of national leadership, coupled with competing ideas of individual responsibility versus collective responsibility.

In early America, individual health was an individual and family responsibility. There were few medical interventions, and these were not costly. Birth was at home, often attended by older women from the community. "Preventive care" meant "an apple a day keeps the doctor away." No immunizations. No cancer screening. If you got sick, you recovered or died without costly interventions.

As cities grew, people living in close quarters raised concerns of communicable diseases. In port cities, efforts were made to stop sailors or immigrants from carrying diseases. Early hospitals cared for those without families and quarantined those with identifiably communicable illnesses. Medical care, if available, cost little.

Before widespread immunization, for example, tuberculosis (TB) ravaged the urban poor in the late 19th and early 20th centuries. The response was to build TB sanitariums in rural areas.

Payments by all members of a 'benevolent' association funded the payments to any member who became ill or injured.

Immigrants from the "old country" formed associations to help each other in the new one. Early "benevolent" associations, such as the fraternal order of Elks and Foresters, early credit unions, and burial societies, often served ethnic or religious communities. Regular payments by all members funded payments to any member who became ill or injured.

Commercial insurance started before the Civil War to provide coverage for injuries related to travel by railroad or steamboat. Massachusetts Health Insurance in Boston offered an early group insurance policy in 1847.

As America industrialized, employers began to pay for the health care of employees and the families of employees. Their motivation: You can't run a factory if your employees are out sick. "Company towns" offered company physicians and clinics. Otto von Bismarck in 1884 mandated health coverage for all Germans from the same motive: A strong military requires a healthy population.

Health insurance got its real start during the Great Depression. With fewer patients able to pay, and those with jobs facing hardship if they became ill, hospitals began to offer insurance for the costs of hospital care. A network of local insurance companies united as the Blue Cross, based on a 1920s offer by Baylor University Hospital to

Dallas public school teachers. Baylor provided hospital services to teachers for 50 cents a month. Physician charges were not included, so physicians formed the national Blue Shield in 1939. The separate federations, Blue Cross and Blue Shield, merged in 1982.

The Great Depression sparked commercial health insurance, and World War II spawned employer-sponsored health insurance.

Military conscription created labor shortages, yet factories had to increase their labor force to meet wartime production. Government wage controls limited the ability to offer higher wages, so factories turned to fringe benefits for attracting workers. Health benefits, the more generous the better, became a major recruitment tool.

Employer-sponsored health insurance got a boost in 1943 when the Internal Revenue Service ruled that the cost of health insurance, if provided through an employer, was tax-free to the employee and tax-deductible for the employer. This tax advantage for employer-sponsored health insurance was reconfirmed in 1954.

Nine percent of the population was covered by voluntary private health insurance in 1940, growing to 63 percent by 1953 and then 70 percent in the 1960s, according to an NPR "Planet Money" report. Private health insurance seemed to be working for America.

Advent of Medicare and Medicaid

Two dark clouds hovered over private health insurance from both not-for-profit insurers like Blue Cross and Blue Shield and the commercial for-profit companies like Aetna. The poor people not in the workforce, and those who aged out of the workforce, the elderly over age 65, were not being covered by health insurance.

Medical care had extended people's lives beyond their working years, yet older people were being impoverished by health care costs. The poor and unemployed, relegated to charity services, were being squeezed by the costs of medical advances.

Americans don't like the idea of people dying on the street, or seeing their parents, who spent a lifetime working, retire into abject poverty brought on by health care costs. Something had to be done. The government responded in 1960 with the Kerr-Mills Act to match state funds to cover patients' bills, but that was not enough.

After extensive wrangling, as part of President Lyndon Johnson's Great Society, Congress in 1965 enacted Medicare for people over age 65 and Medicaid for the poor.

Medicare's fiscal model is based on insurance, funded during a person's worklife by payroll deductions and employer contributions. Medicaid is funded by federal taxes, allocated based on state poverty levels, plus state and local taxes. The state controls Medicaid benefit levels. Local counties control individual enrollments.

Health insurance companies did not oppose Medicaid, for poor people were not potential customers. For the medical community, especially for hospitals, Medicaid meant more reliable money than was possible from charity.

Physicians were different. Many physicians had willingly provided care to their poor patients without compensation, so now they could be paid. However, a bureaucracy now intervened in what physicians saw as their moral duty. Changing the physicians' moral duty into a commercial transaction shifted the focus from healing to business. Some physicians refused Medicaid participation and yet still provided unpaid health care to the poor.

> Changing physicians' moral duty to a commercial transaction shifted the focus from healing to business.

Medicare, in contrast, was initially opposed by the commercial insurance industry, then logic prevailed. People work until age 65 and retire in relative health. When their big medical bills roll in, they are no longer on private insurance, so no loss of profits!

The medical community itself was harder to convince. Medicare could be a boon to physicians' incomes since patients needing their services now had a reliable funding source. Initially, services were virtually unconstrained, and payment reflected a high percentage of customary medical fees. The medical community's enthusiasm then was dampened by the potential of government, a third party, taking a greater role, influencing or commanding care activities, impacting the physician-patient relationship.

Here was the vision: Employer-sponsored health insurance for the workers, Medicare for the elderly. Medicaid for the poor. Gaps in coverage from unemployment were handled by the Consolidated Omnibus Budget Reconciliation Act (COBRA), enabling individuals to extend employer-sponsored health insurance up to 18 months, paying the premiums themselves until they found another job.

Virtually everyone was covered. What could go wrong?

What Went Wrong

In theory, all was right with the world. What went wrong was cost emulating the New York State motto, *excelsior*, ever upward.

Health care costs grew from a nominal expenditure by employers and taxpayers into expenditures sucking up more and more dollars. The Centers for Disease Control reported health care costs in 1960 were $26 billion, 5.2 percent of the Gross Domestic Product (GDP). Costs by 1990 reached $725 billion at 12.4 percent of GDP, and they are projected to reach $5 trillion by 2020 at 20 percent of GDP.

Meanwhile, worker's compensation insurance reduces take-home pay, and so do increased Medicare payroll deductions. Medicaid keeps pushing up federal, state and local taxes. The health insurance model worked until the costs of providing care drove premiums and tax support to the point of pain.

The new gold mine of health insurance financed physicians, hospitals, pharmaceutical firms, medical device manufacturers, and care providers of all types. As new and improved services rushed to meet ever-growing patient needs, costs continued to grow.

> # The insurance model worked until the costs of care drove premiums and taxes to the point of pain.

Hospitals had to purchase the very latest diagnostic equipment. Radiology offered a CT scanner and then an MRI. By 2016, the USA had nearly 37 MRI machines for each million people, according to Statista. Canada had nine MRIs for each million people. All of this hiked hospital costs.

The payment model for health care services was both simple and inflationary. Policyholders accepted whatever services the medical community offered, each effective and medically necessary, and the insurance would cover the costs up to the policy limits. Those limits were generous, a high percentage of "usual and customary" charges. U&C charges skyrocketed. As long as physicians agreed to accept insurance payments in full, patients willingly played along.

Health insurance paid for it all, virtually without any question. Multiple visits for the same condition, even hospitalization for the convenience of a family, such as admitting Mom so children could go on vacation. Effectiveness was not tracked, nor was quality. If some medical error required hospital re-admission, health insurance paid the bill without question. Happy days in healthcare.

As the cost of healthcare rose, so did health insurance premiums, so did Medicare premiums, and so did taxes to support Medicaid. The easy focus was — and to a large degree remains — on the cost of health insurance, Medicare, and what taxpayers pay for Medicaid. The real culprit is the cost of medical services. As costs grew, so did the schemes and plans to constrain them.

States stepped in to limit the "unit costs" of services provided to Medicaid recipients. Medicare created a schedule of allowable fees. Commercial insurance passed on cost increases to the employers, who often passed them to employees as increased payroll deductions. Hospitals in many states came under laws that tried to control the rates they charged. Medicare moved from payments based on length of hospital stay to payments based on diagnosis.

Commercial plans reduced premiums by reducing benefits, such as not covering physician visits unless the patient had an illness (so much for preventive care) increasing co-pays at the time of service, and by tightening underwriting on who they would insure.

Managed Care

The most impactful scheme to "bend the cost curve," to restrain the rate of cost growth, was a model that Henry Kaiser developed during construction of the Hoover Dam, later used in the shipyard where Liberty ships were mass-produced during World War II.

The "managed care" model of health maintenance organizations, HMOs, approached costs, quality and bureaucracy differently.

The original Kaiser model became the Kaiser Permanente Health Plan. It called for the insurer to control the medical delivery system, to manage individuals' care throughout the system, eliminate waste and duplication, monitor quality, and implement treatment plans that prove to be the most effective for the least cost. As a result, the cost to the patient and to the employer could be constrained.

The goal of managed care was to serve the long-term interests of patients' health. Offer them easy access to a primary care physician, so patients saw physicians early in an illness. Early interventions lowered costs. Benefits were enhanced. Lifetime caps were removed. By owning a system of hospitals, outpatient services and physicians, HMOs were motivated to provide care in the least costly setting.

The one fly in the medicinal ointment? Patients were required to use only the HMO's system, its hospitals and physicians. Channeling or corralling Americans into such a system met with resistance.

President Richard Nixon in 1973 signed the Health Maintenance Organization Act, known as the Federal HMO Act. Sen. Edward M. Kennedy was the principal sponsor.

HMOs took off. What started as a movement expected to enroll 20 percent of the population has become the universal model for delivering coverage, not only for employer-sponsored health plans, but also for Medicare and Medicaid. HMOs were able, initially, to put the brakes on costs, chiefly unit costs, as they contracted with medical providers and hospitals at discounted rates.

As HMOs moved past controlling costs to managing care, sparks began to fly.

Just as physicians had feared with the advent of Medicare, adding a third party to the patient-physician relationship affected that relationship. As HMOs moved past controlling unit costs to actually managing care, sparks began to fly.

Patients did not want to stay restricted to the HMO's network, and they did not want to go get permission to go see a specialist. Medical providers did not want to be told to whom they could refer patients, nor to be pressured to use alternatives to traditional treatment plans, such as outpatient care. Horror stories told of patients limited to "in network" coverage and deficient access to quality care by in-network providers.

Although much went wrong with HMOs, much went right, too. For a period of time, cost increases stabilized. However, the initial HMO strategy could not hold down costs long term.

Market resentment toward "managed care" (by both patients and physicians) doomed the underlying model. Over time, inflationary fee-for-service models returned as the norm.

The Affordable Care Act

Health insurance premiums kept increasing by double digits, two to three times the rate of inflation. Employers balanced the costs by passing along rate increases through higher payroll deductions and fewer wage increases. States grappled with Medicaid costs by cutting fees paid for Medicaid services. Medicare restrained costs by cutting hospital rates and limiting increases in physician fees.

As premiums rose, insurance companies dug back into their bag of tricks to slow rate increases. Individual and small group policies became either unavailable or unaffordable. Small businesses gave up and dropped coverage completely.

The Great Recession of 2008 became the great disrupter in health insurance. The ensuing reform, the Affordable Care Act, proudly or derisively called Obamacare, changed health insurance dramatically while changing the structure of care delivery.

The concept is simple. Get 100 percent of the U.S. population insured. With everyone insured, every citizen would have coverage, forever removing economics as a barrier to healthcare services. All would be protected from financial devastation for necessary care. Wisely, the cost of delivering care would be spread over the entire population by mandate, in effect nationalizing the cost of medical care but not the delivery of care. No exclusions for pre-existing conditions. No lifetime caps. No longer would affordable health care insurance be available only through an employer.

Under the ACA, hospitals, doctors and other caregivers would no longer carry the load of providing services without payment, uncompensated care, passing on the costs to others.

Don't force people into one plan. Let them choose from among comparable plans. Let them pick a plan based on price, reputation and the plan's included providers, hospitals and physicians. Keep confusion out of plan selection by mandating four benefit packages, labeled as Bronze, Silver, Gold, and Platinum.

For those of low income, expand Medicaid coverage by bringing Medicaid insurance to those with incomes up to 132 percent of the Federal Poverty Level. For those of modest means, subsidize the purchase of "approved" insurance plans, available to those between 133 and 400 percent of the Federal Poverty Level.

The ACA's promises were more political than practical.

The ACA's promises were more political than practical.

President Obama's promise — "If you like your doctor, you can keep your doctor." — should have included a qualifying asterisk. The ability to keep your doctor depended on whether or not your physician chose (or was chosen) to participate in a plan "approved" under the ACA. Turned out that expanding Medicaid eligibility did not expand the number of participating physicians.

For approved plans with standard benefits under metallic labels, differences rested on price and network — the medical community contracted to provide care under the insurance policy.

Narrow Care Networks

The products offered through a Health Insurance Exchange do not cover out-of-network care except in an emergency, which often means no coverage. These "narrow" networks are claustrophobic.

Each insurance carrier uses propriety data, propriety algorithms, to decide which providers can be in its narrow network. This lacks transparency and disregards existing patient-physician relationships. Is cost the only criteria? What about quality or efficiency?

For example, Empire BlueCross BlueShield created the narrow "Pathways" network for its 2014 offering by excluding all academic medical centers in New York City, such as Sloan Kettering, plus all the physicians associated with those institutions. For 2015, Empire broadened that network, but it could shrink in the future. The only insurer offering products on New Hampshire's exchange, Anthem (BlueCross BlueShield) excluded ten of the state's 26 hospitals. Hospitals are included or excluded based on unit price.

These narrow networks often are state-specific. You can't cross state lines for covered care, even if your insurance company sells the product in every state. This may not be known until care is needed, or after it's obtained, increasing the patient's economic risk.

Who fits in these "chosen" networks is a source of confusion and mystery to patients and physicians alike. Health plans do not make it easy. Network and product names constantly change, and so do the rules for participating physicians.

UnitedHealthcare has products called Core, Metro and Charter. Physicians participating in the networks called Freedom and Liberty do not participate in these products unless a patient is in a hospital, and if the physician is participating. How is a physician or a patient to keep this nuance clear? Patients get caught in the confusion.

Verifying if your physician is in a narrow network is a challenge in itself. Reviews of the online directories by the health plans have revealed high degrees of inaccuracy, such as the lack of availability of the listed physicians, who are not accepting new patients. The Los Angeles Times in 2014 reported that 12.8 percent of the physicians in Anthem's online directory for California were not accepting new patients, and 25 percent of the office locations were inaccurate.

'You Can Keep Your Current Plan'

"If you like your current health insurance plan, you can keep it." This politic statement also needs an asterisk. Yes, you can keep your plan, but only if it meets federal requirements.

The ACA set up essential benefits that all health insurance plans must cover. If your current health insurance plan did not include all these essential benefits, it was not approved under the ACA.

Non-conforming policies get labeled as "junk policies" because of large gaps in the health benefits. Junk policies do satisfy the needs and desires of some younger and healthier purchasers, who care about affordability more than benefits. A single male does not need maternity benefits, for instance, so 66 percent of male purchasers chose that cost savings, according to Healthcare.org.

However, limitations in junk policies often are discovered only when the excluded care is most needed, creating economic burdens for patients causing medical debt for their caregivers.

In fairness to the ACA, it makes sense to set minimum standards on what must be covered under a health insurance policy.

The Trump administration policy allows states to approve non-conforming policies, those with less coverage and lower premiums. Excluding coverage for mental health, substance abuse treatment or maternity care does reduce premiums. Why pay a higher premium for services you do not expect to use? However, short-term savings on premiums may be regretted long-term when superior coverage is needed. One needs to balance costs and risks.

Metallic Plans and Medical Debt

More than half of the personal bankruptcies in this nation relate to medical bills and the economic stress on families and individuals by the cost of care. The ACA was designed to address this tragedy, but does it really solve the problem?

Bronze, Silver, Gold, and Platinum insurance plans. Not all that glitters is good. Each of these metallic labels carries a different level of patient financial responsibility. None of these coverage categories offer full protection from medical debt and financial ruin.

Healthpocket.com explains the situation. Bronze plans with the most affordable premiums cover only 60 percent of the care costs, leaving 40 percent of the responsibly on patients and families. Bronze plans have a $3,000 deductible for individuals and $6,000 for families. The out-of-pocket cap is $6,350 for individuals and $12,700 for families. Gold plans, in contrast, cover 70 percent of the costs with a $2,000 deductible for individuals and $4,000 for families, plus a $5,500 out-of-pocket maximum for individuals and $11,000 for families. Clearly, those of modest means risk personal or family economic devastation.

> Bronze, Silver, Gold, and Platinum insurance plans. Not all that glitters is good.

Patient's financial responsibility is not eliminated by ACA. The public may be lulled into a false sense of security. Those deductibles are hefty, adding to cost-sharing by the healthcare providers like physicians and hospitals. As the patient's financial responsibility for a claim goes up, so does the provider's risk and likelihood of non-payment. Medical debt remains a big problem for all.

Patient's eligibility is not guaranteed. Even if a provider verifies coverage at the time of care, individuals who purchase coverage on an exchange are given a grace period to pay their monthly insurance premium. Care providers will receive a confirmation the patient is covered even if a premium remains unpaid up to 90 days after it was due. About 20 percent of those buying individual policies on health exchanges default before the end of their grace period.

The ACA removed barriers to buying health insurance, removed bans on pre-existing conditions, provided coverage for children up to age 26 under a family plan, made coverage available to individuals without employer-provided plans, and expanded the availability of Medicaid. All of this, along with premium subsidies, increased affordability for a large segment of the middle class.

The result has been a clear decrease in the number of uninsured. According to Kaiser Family Foundation research, the number of uninsured non-elderly Americans decreased from 44 million in 2013 (the year before ACA coverage provisions took effect) to fewer than 28 million uninsured at the end of 2016.

The same Kaiser report warns that the affordability of insurance policies remains an issue. High costs are the principal reason most often cited by those who remain uninsured.

The ACA Is Really Insurance Reform

One of the key provisions of the ACA converted health insurance companies into public utilities, and so regulated their profitability. Insurance products must pay out 85 percent (80 percent for a small group policy) for medical services, leaving 15 to 20 percent for both administration and profitability. Spending more on medical clams, insurance companies adsorb the loss, spend less, and must refund the difference to the policyholders. Profitability is not what it once was for insurance companies.

The cost of health insurance is still tied to the cost of care — unit cost and the volume of services. There's been little impact here.

From 2008 to 2016, health plan costs rose by 50 percent, reflected in the higher insurance premiums paid by employers and the higher payroll deductions of employees.

Employers offset the increases by applying the deductible models

ACA did little to change the fundamental structure for the delivery of health care.

of the ACA marketplace plans. If anything, the ACA legitimized and reintroduced the deductible as a major tool for shifting the cost of care to the patient. By 2016, Money magazine reports, deductibles above $1,000 were standard, and 51 percent of insured employees were exposed to high out-of-pocket costs.

The ACA did little to change the fundamental structure for the delivery of health care. It did not move hospitals to communities where most needed, increase the supply of primary care physicians, increase ambulatory care options, nor end medical debt.

The necessary re-engineering of care delivery has been left to the healthcare industry, which has proven itself to be more dedicated to protecting the status quo and their bottom line than in adopting reforms that meet evolving community medical needs.

I believe that insurance is the wrong way to finance healthcare. We cannot end medical debt without addressing the core structures driving high health care costs. We need to rethink our approach.

I attribute my success to this:
I never gave or took any excuse.

— Florence Nightingale

CHAPTER 8

No Thank You
For Your Service

Jerry Ashton

Writing this chapter was difficult for me. It was difficult to write without getting angry. I'll tell you why.

On November 11, 2017, for the first time in more than 50 years, I put back on my old Navy uniform to march in the New York City Veterans Day Parade. I was joined by Mikel Burroughs, retired Army colonel, and Hutch Dubosque, a Vietnam-era Army sergeant. We're there for RIP at America's largest annual Veterans Day parade.

As I marched in uniform that day (amazed it still fits), someone called out, "Thank you for your service!" I appreciated and accepted acknowledgement of the years I served many decades ago as a Navy journalist. Even so, I heard those words with mixed emotions.

I felt compelled to write a blog about the experience, suggesting that we replace the words, "Thank you for your service," with action. This was my polite way to request that the person shaking my hand express a more useful form of gratitude. I provided a way this might be done — forgive veterans' medical debt! I touched a nerve.

Back in 2014, after Craig Antico and I co-founded RIP as a tax-deductible way for any American to help us locate, buy and forgive medical debt, we realized helping hard-pressed people in the general population was not enough. As donations came in and we purchased debt, we noticed a surprising percentage of the medical bills forgiven were from veterans and active-duty military. That's off.

We realized that RIP must be anchored in two different worlds, both debt buying and military charities. A referral led me to Mikel Burroughs. Perfect fit. Mikel (say like "Michael") served as an Army brigade commander in Kuwait and Iraq. Retired as a bird colonel, Mikel is a veteran C-suite collections industry executive who's bought and sold billions in medical debt. He rides a Harley and likes to drum. He's active on RallyPoint for vets.

Mikel felt as ardently about forgiving veterans' medical debt as do Craig and I. We began a campaign, #NoVetMedDebt, that's been crucial in reaching our 2018 goal of forgiving $50 million in veterans' medical debt. Our efforts barely scratch the surface.

Vets Do Have Medical Debt

You may be asking, how can any men and women in the service, (active-duty or veterans), have medical debt? What about Veterans Affairs (VA) and the Veterans Benefits Administration?

Like most Americans (including myself as a veteran), I believed our country fully covers the medical needs of men and women who serve our country. Many return from deployments suffering severe disabilities, visible or not. Our nation would and should care for our warriors as a patriotic way of showing our thanks, right?

When entering the military, men and women sign a blank check, saying, "I'm yours to use as needed, America, up to and including my death." Year after year, America cashes that check. So, of course, we take care of all our troops in return. Certainly, we do!

I've learned it's not quite that way, not in every case. Consider the regs and hoops a vet must jump through to get medical care at the VA. Consider VA refusals to cover vets for off-site care by non-military physicians, clinics and hospitals, or for emergency transport. "Uncle Sugar" does not

Billions in medical debt are landing on the backs of our veterans.

cover everything. Millions, no, billions of dollars in medical bills are landing on the backs of our veterans.

Consider our veterans' vital statistics: About 20 veterans a day commit suicide. More than 50,000 homeless vets seek shelter nightly. More than 50 percent of returning vets suffer from PTSD. Many vets discover their long-term health care needs outlast their Veterans Affairs benefits. In 2010, roughly 1.3 million uninsured veterans had out-of-pocket medical costs beyond their disposable income.

As evidence of the scale, Paige Kutilek at GoFundMe says the site hosts campaigns by tens of thousands of military veterans plagued with unpaid medical debt. Bill collectors hound them.

Medical debt is no way to thank those who risked their lives.

Hard reality is why RIP decided early to forgive veterans' debt as our special focus. This was a development I did not expect, not even as a Navy sailor. I still thought, isn't our government supposed to be responsible for all who serve, who have served, all who sacrifice for our country? We surely do right by them, yes? Not quite, not nearly well enough, I've learned, and sometimes not at all.

From buying and forgiving veterans' debt, I have identified ways the VA (which is you and me) evades or avoids its responsibilities to veterans. I'll offer three varied examples of the situation.

The Case of 'Veteran Alpha'

We were contacted for debt relief by a 73-year-old Army veteran ("Veteran Alpha") unable to pay his high medical bills. On Veterans Day 2016, Veteran Alpha visited his ailing wife at the local hospital. While there, he suffered a cardiac arrest and underwent emergency heart bypass surgery. Before the surgery, the hospital duly advised the area's largest VA medical center about his precarious condition. They wanted to send an ambulance from 75 miles away to transport him back to the VA for any further care.

The hospital staff put Alpha on the phone with the VA center. He groggily told the VA person that he already was being prepped for surgery, and he wasn't going to wait for them. His life was at risk. He ended the call and went into surgery. He survived.

After his surgery, Alpha was swamped with medical bills the VA declined to pay because he had "refused emergency transport."

The hospital surgery bill was $180,000. Medicare paid about 80 percent. The hospital pursued the $35,000 balance. Alpha emptied a $7,000 savings account and borrowed $7,000 from the Navy Federal Credit Union. This left the married couple with $15,000 still due to the hospital. Alpha depended upon regular federal payments for his service-related 100 percent disability. Adding monthly loan payments atop household costs, plus pittances to the hospital, had put Alpha and his wife in jeopardy of losing their home.

Liver Fluke Cancer and the VA

Hutch DuBosque has been waging a fight to secure VA coverage for a rare bile duct cancer and liver disease caused by the parasite, *Platyhelminthes.* Several of Hutch's Vietnam-era vet friends came down with a "weird disease" from an obscure parasite called a "liver fluke." Before two of them passed, Hutch and his crew promised their dying friends to research this disease and save others' lives.

The river fluke, according to the American Cancer Society, is a freshwater-borne flatworm found in military men and women who served in eastern and southeastern Asia. It produces a protein called "granulum," which is highly carcinogenic, basically a death sentence. If caught in its dormancy, the parasite is treatable. If not discovered, it inevitably presents Stage 4 cancer in the pancreas or liver.

Hutch insists the VA resists covering treatment for the parasite, denying claims by arguing, "It's not been proven."

The VA denied claims, arguing, 'It's not been proven.'

Hutch and four of his friends (John Ball, Gerry Wiggins, Larry Noon, and Ralph Goodwin) volunteered for a 50-person pilot study by the VA Medical Center at Northport, NY. Veterans who reported eating undercooked freshwater fish while in Vietnam donated blood samples for serological exam at Seoul National University College of Medicine in South Korea. The blood went there since no U.S. facility can reliably identify the antigen marker of the Asian parasite.

The January 2018 issue of Infectious Diseases in Clinical Practice published Norfolk's study report, "Screening U.S. Vietnam Veterans for Liver Fluke Exposure 5 Decades After the End of the War."

Hutch and his friends were interviewed by their area newspaper, Newsday, for a story about the Long Island study. The VA found almost one in four of the 50 Vietnam veterans harbored the parasite, which can live dormant in a body for decades, Newsday reported. One in four of the study group tested positive for bile duct cancer. Since 2013, Newsday said, the VA had received 240 claims for bile duct cancers attributed to the liver fluke, and the VA had "rejected more than 76 percent of those claims."

Hutch says, "This disease is three times as big as Agent Orange, but its victims are systematically being denied disability claims by the VA." Three million GIs served in Vietnam. More serve today in the parasite's range, including South Korea. Neither the VA nor the Department of Defense routinely screens for the parasite.

The five Long Island veterans next reached out to Sen. Chuck Schumer (D-NY) and Rep. Tom Suozzi (D-NY), who then released statements calling for a broader study.

The Department of Veterans Affairs initiated a mortality study of Vietnam-era vets going back 60 years to determine any connection between parasite exposure and liver bile cancer. However, Newsday said, the announcement has done little to calm nerves.

Hutch's buddy, Gerald Wiggins, tested positive for bile cancer. In 2018 he had cancerous cysts removed from his liver at Memorial Sloan Kettering Cancer Center. He'll return every year for a new CT scan, but he's unsure how to pay for any further care.

"Friends are dying," Wiggins complained, "but no one at the VA can give us any direct answers on what's going on with disease coverage, if they are going to treat us, so we can live. The VA dances around this whole thing while vets get more medical bills."

For me, his story conveys, "No thank you for your service."

Burn Pit Veterans

This one was new to me, discovered only when RIP received this one veteran's request for help at our website.

"I realize that you buy bundles of old debt, so debt forgiveness is random, and you can't help individuals. But us burn pit veterans get short shrift. We don't get real help from the VA. I have not found a fund that helps burn pit veterans afford medications or inhalers or oxygen to benefit their daily living."

Burn pits? What in blazes are they? I began doing research.

The VA dances around while vets get more medical bills.

The Department of Veterans Affairs defines a "burn pit" as the common way the military got rid of its waste at military sites in the Middle East war zones. They burned chemicals, paint, medical and human waste, munitions, and unexploded ordinance — just about everything combustible went into a burn pit, fouling the air.

In response to growing concerns from mounting evidence that military personnel and contractors who worked at or near "burn pits" were suffering from excessive lung diseases, in June 2014, the VA launched the "Airborne Hazards and Open Burn Pit Registry." Had the registry made a difference for burn pit veterans?

A referral led me to the D.C. offices of U.S. Rep. Raul Ruiz (D-CA), himself a physician. "Burn pits absolutely are a major concern," he declared, "and I'm doing something about it."

Dr. Ruiz in 2018 launched the bipartisan Congressional Burn Pits Caucus with Brad Wenstrup, GOP chair of the House Veterans' Affairs subcommittee with 21 bipartisan members. The "Helping Veterans Exposed to Burn Pits Act" became law in September 2018. The bill directs the Department of Veterans Affairs to establish a center of excellence in the prevention, diagnosis, mitigation, treatment, and rehabilitation of health conditions relating to exposure to burn pits or other environmental exposures in Afghanistan or Iraq.

Now that's real help! Thank you for your service.

After Veterans Day, What?

The 20 million men and women alive today who have served a grateful nation deserve attention. After Veterans Day, after the flags are furled, after the marching bands return home, then what?

If you are akin to many Americans, you take time each Veterans Day to honor those who have fought and still fight for our country. Perhaps you stand to watch or join a parade in the smallest towns to the largest cities across the country.

More probably, you only watch a parade snippet on the evening news, perhaps after visiting the shopping mall to take advantage of "Veterans Day Bargains!" Sadder still, maybe the day passed without you ever noticing or giving vets any thought.

The attention paid to veterans tends to fade after Veterans Day. Vets starve for attention the other 364 days of the year. The parades are over. The cemetery salutes are done. The vets we thank for their service are still here, and too often they are underserved.

Veterans' Medical Debt

Among the segments of American society most indebted by our healthcare system, the military and veterans stand out.

Herb Weisbaum at NBC News covered the Consumer Financial Protection Bureau (renamed by Acting Director Mick Mulvaney as the Bureau of Consumer Financial Protection). Half the complaints received from service members in 2015, Weisbaum reported, dealt with debt collectors. Veterans also file twice the level of complaints as does the general public.

> ## Veterans with medical debt are stones squeezing out blood.

NBC News said that military members and veterans "report being hounded to pay medical bills that should have been covered by insurance" (e.g., the VA, Medicare, Medicaid, and private).

Military members are easily pressured by bill collectors to pay a bill (even if not owed or not correct) for fear a collection agency may (illegally) contact their commanding officer, hurting a military career, or (legally) place a bad mark on a credit report, hurting their financial recovery. They may dread the stress, perhaps knowing it may harm their health.

To our shame as a nation, in my eyes, a large part of our veterans' burden comes in the form of medical debt. No matter what they do or say to each collection agency, they are stones squeezing out blood. The calls and letters never stop. This is why RIP makes a special effort to forgive veterans' medical debt, such as abolishing more than $50 million in vet debt in 2018 alone. We thank the allies joining forces with us in a priority emergency mission to complete with honor.

Veterans' Unemployment

Sen. Bob Casey (D-CA), a ranking Finance Committee member, reported that, on average, 30 percent of all returning vets aged 18-24 are unprepared for the road ahead, not ready for the struggles with personal finances, low-paying jobs, and unemployment. Regardless of their willingness to protect their families, they lack the experience and resources to handle serious financial adversity.

Almost 50 percent of the 20 million U.S. veterans participate in the labor force. So, more than 10 million veterans are not working or not actively looking for work. Some veterans give up on ever finding a job. Some veterans are retired or on disability. Some may be in school. There are many reasons for not being in the labor force.

We have 9.9 million employed veterans, reported the U.S. Bureau of Labor Statistics in 2017.

Nearly one third of all working vets are deemed underemployed, according to ZipRecruiter as well as the Call of Duty Endowment, which helps veterans find jobs.

Millions of vets hold jobs they are overqualified to do. They risk their lives for our country, and we do not value their skills.

Homeless Veterans

Due to poverty and inadequate support networks, 1.4 million veterans risk homelessness, reported the VFW Magazine. An Iraq war member helping homeless veterans in Missouri told the magazine, "I was leaving as many vets on the streets as I was helping. They took the oath just like me. Why am I treated better?"

Few homeless vets qualify for VA help. Too many such vets are being told "no." They haven't served long enough, for instance, or they don't qualify for VA benefits after getting in legal trouble, like a DUI, in which case all VA benefits may be taken away.

Military Times in 2017 reported the number of homeless vets has risen for the first time in seven years. Some 50,000 sleep in shelters nightly across America. The story cited VA Secretary David Shulkin admitting that "zero homeless veterans" is not a realistic target.

Veterans' Suicides

The U.S. Department of Veterans Affairs (VA) released findings from its most recent analysis of veteran suicide data for all 50 states and the District of Columbia.

This report yields several important insights:

• Suicide rates increased for both veterans and non-veterans, underscoring that suicide is a national public health concern.

• The average number of veterans who died by suicide each day remained unchanged at 20.

• The suicide rate increased faster among the veterans who had little used the Veterans Health Administration care plan, compared to those who had sought coverage.

(For the full analysis, see the "VA National Suicide Data Report 2005-2015." Based on 55 million civilian and veteran death records, the report grounds the VA's Suicide Prevention Program.)

Any part medical debt plays in veterans' suicides is too much.

Charity for Veterans

GrantSpace estimates 1.5 million nonprofit organizations in the USA. GuideStar estimates 45,000 nonprofits devoted to veterans and their families. Did you know only 18 percent of these are 501(c)(3) charities that can accept tax-deductible contributions?

These organizations come in every stripe and color, according to a CNBC report on the "Top 10 Charities That Support Veterans." Some were formed by military wives or focus on specific branches of service. One charity, Puppies Behind Bars, trains prison inmates to raise service dogs for wounded war veterans.

The organizations most Americans might recognize include the Veterans of Foreign Wars (VFW) and Disabled American Veterans (DAV). A relative newcomer is Wounded Warriors, begun 2003 in Roanoke by a group of Virginia veterans and their friends who chose to take action to help injured service men and women.

We can tell you from experience that Americans are incredibly giving once they're aware of a need deserving attention. RIP met our 2018 goal to abolish $50 million in veteran debt in a #NoVetMedDebt campaign. Next year, we're shooting for $100 million.

RIP is able to help any organization — military or civilian — raise funds to abolish unpaid and unpayable medical bills for military and veterans. As a way to say, "Thank you for your service," let's commit to leaving no man or woman behind.

A billion here, a billion there,
sooner or later it adds up to real money.

— EVERETT DIRKSEN

CHAPTER 9

Health Is a Goal, Not an Industry

Robert Goff

We Americans have an odd concept of healthcare. We will not tolerate people being deprived of it, yet we just don't want to pay for someone else's care. Services essential to a whole community must be paid for by each individual. This results in medical debt for individuals without the resources of insurance or cash.

We debate who should pick up the tab, missing the reality that we all pay for healthcare for everyone. Each of us picks up the tab for the health insurance plan premiums, payroll deductions for premiums, deductions for Medicare, taxes for Medicaid, and taxes to subsidize the deficits of hospitals and clinics that aren't making it financially. Each of us are paying for the losses and consequences of sickness in public disability payments, public support of medically impoverished families, and economic losses from lost job productivity.

The $3 trillion healthcare spending tab in the USA is about sick care, about accident care, health restoration. It is about the business of providing care, which is not the true business of health.

Shouldn't the discussion or debate be far wider?

Shouldn't we be as concerned, or more concerned, about health itself? How can the health status of Americans be lifted? If we'd focus on health not costs, I propose, the costs of care would be positively impacted, stabilized or reduced. Acting to prevent or mitigate illness or injury is not widely seen as the mission of health care. Meanwhile, our health costs keep going up. This defies reason.

Acting to prevent or mitigate illness or injury is not widely seen as the mission of health care.

In my ideal, a health system concerned with patient health would better influence the trajectory of needed care. Utilization of medical services would be decided using a *failure analysis model* to determine the causes of health issues and implement corrective actions. When a patient requires a higher-cost, more intensive service, that would be taken as a "failure to intervene" earlier with lower-cost, less intensive services. Pay a little now to avoid paying more later.

Too little effort is made to avoid care costs by addressing causes. We know the causes of most illness, but efforts are limited for the interventions that reduce the incidence of illness, reduce costs and improve health outcomes. We know the causes of most injuries, but efforts are limited for the interventions that reduce the incidence of injuries, reduce costs and improve outcomes.

Preventive care helps avoid medical spending. Each intervention forestalls or avoids a later, costlier intervention. A healthcare industry that's paid for delivering care services has no such interest.

The medical care of Americans today is the business of the U.S. healthcare industry. The mission and business of the health industry is treating illnesses and accidents after they occur, not before. The care industry is compensated for the production and delivery of care services, by service units, a silo of sickness and accident care in the health restoration and repair business.

Medical spending should go where it can best improve health. In the trillions spent annually on medical care, consider the scale of all the missed opportunities. A Kaiser Family Foundation study, for instance, identified factors increasing risks of premature death. Ten percent of premature deaths were due to the care provided. Another 20 percent were due to social or environmental factors, 30 percent to genetics, and 40 percent for personal behaviors.

Health research and treatment has advanced. Illnesses that in the past meant a premature death today are livable as chronic conditions, which lead to higher medical costs. Becker's Hospital CFO Report says unhealthy behaviors are largely responsible for chronic illnesses like heart disease, cancer and diabetes, which cause about 70 percent of all deaths in the USA and are the most expensive to treat. No one wants to pay for the unhealthy habits of "the other guy."

Personal Responsibility

Personal responsibility is an ethical or a moral tenet in America. Freedom entails responsibility to better oneself, such as responsibility for one's health. The ideal of *self-reliance* explains pushback against all national healthcare proposals that reduce personal responsibility. People should face the consequences of their choices. If the economic risk from not taking care of oneself is borne by others, says this view, then nothing motivates us to engage in healthy behaviors.

Personal responsibility for health is left to individuals. Illness is widely perceived as a consequence of poor personal behavior, so even premature death is a fitting consequence. I see this as a throwback to the times when poor health was a sign of a failure in individual piety. The righteous are granted health; the sinful are made to suffer.

By this view, if your behavior increases your risk of illness, if you suffer economic harm as a result, so be it. Equating illness with risky behavior falls apart when that illness is the result of factors outside the control of the individual., such as genetic predispositions, birth defects, environmental factors, or social conditions.

> In the name of personal responsibility, we shifted the economic cost of health care to patients, making it harder for people to be responsible for themselves.

Self-preservation really should motivate wise choices, but we may do self-destructive behaviors (such as smoking, drinking, drugs) from societal factors (such as poverty). Many causes of illness can't be addressed by lone individuals (such as water and air pollution). We also can't yet alter our genetics after the fact of our birth.

In the sacred name of personal responsibility, we have shifted the economic cost of health care to patients (such as with deductibles and coverage limits). This yields economic hardship for individuals and families, actually making it harder for people to be responsible for themselves.

Self-Destructive Behaviors

Let's look at unhealthy personal behaviors that drive up the costs of healthcare yet begin outside the healthcare system itself.

Smoking: Smoking-related illness costs society more than $300 billion yearly, says the Centers for Disease Control (CDC), including $170 billion for direct medical care with $5.6 billion for secondhand smoke exposure. Taxes on cigarettes to help reduce consumption are offset by manufacturers' discounts to retailers that lower prices for consumers, with $5.8 billion spent in 2016 to subsidize smoking.

Alcohol: Alcohol abuse costs U.S. society more than $249 billion a year, according to the CDC. Healthcare costs account for only 11 percent of that. The primary cost is lost job productivity.

Drug Abuse: The aggregate cost from drug abuse in the USA is $1 trillion, including costs for medical care and criminal justice. Janet Yellen, former chair of the Federal Reserve, attributes drug abuse to a lack of job opportunities among prime-age workers. Other factors include escape from pain, as with opioid addiction.

Gun Violence: Gun violence costs an average of $700 per year, per person, with an annual hit to the economy of $229 billion, reports Mother Jones. Direct expenses for emergency and medical care from gun violence are $8.6 billion. "It does not matter whether we believe that guns kill people or that people kill people with guns," wrote a team of doctors in the April 2017 Annals of Internal Medicine. "The result is the same: A public health crisis."

The Obesity Crisis

America, the "land of plenty," has ample portion sizes feeding our waistlines. The National Heart, Lung, and Blood Institute calculated that in the past 20 years, a simple bagel grew three inches in diameter to six inches. A cheeseburger grew from 3.5 to 8 ounces. A "normal" serving of sugar-laden soda grew from 6.5 to 20 ounces.

The CDC reports almost 40 percent of all U.S. adults are obese as are nearly 20 percent of all adolescents. NBC News in 2017 said the "obesity crisis" appears more unstoppable than ever.

Obesity is the underlying cause, a contributor or a complicator of heart disease, stroke, high blood pressure, diabetes, gout, gallbladder disease and gallstones, osteoarthritis, and breathing issues like sleep apnea and asthma. Being overweight or obese further is associated with increased risk for 13 types of cancer, accounting for 40 percent of all the cancers diagnosed in the United States.

Other countries use taxes to fight obesity. Mexico's sugar tax cut soda consumption by 5.5 percent the first year and 9.7 percent the next. Similar taxes are working in Canada, United Kingdom, Ireland, Portugal, France, Saudi Arabia, South Africa, Australia, and Thailand. Portugal added a salt tax on fattening snacks.

Seven countries have started food fights with junk food. Mexico, Chile, Norway France, India, Japan, and Australia seek to motivate behavioral change in the population. These efforts range from taxing the fat content in prepared foods to banning advertising to children that use toys as incentives to buy sugary foods. Each approaches the obesity problem differently, yet each aims to shift unhealthy behavior by raising the costs at decision time for unhealthy behaviors.

All these countries have national health coverage, so they can use governmental taxing authority to impact behaviors that increase the cost to health care programs. America could learn from them.

In the USA, where two-thirds of all Americans are obese, no such national efforts exist. We have local initiatives. Philadelphia introduced a tax on sugary drinks that cut soda consumption 38 percent in 30 days and 40 percent in 60 days, reported Philadelphia Magazine, and energy drink consumption fell 64 percent. Consumption of bottled water rose 58 percent.

The New York Board of Health tried to tax sugary drinks, but an

Countries with national health coverage use governmental authority to impact health behaviors.

appeals court found the city exceeded its authority, Beverage Daily reported. I believe that win for sugary drinks was a loss for health.

Embracing the digital life (TV, games, internet) contributes to a sedentary lifestyle, which contributes to obesity. The State of Obesity estimates 45 percent of all U.S. adults are not active enough to get daily health benefits. Diseases related to inactivity cause $117 billion in direct healthcare costs. Our vaunted healthcare system does little to address this source for high healthcare demand and rising costs. At best, health insurance reimburses a gym membership.

Employers are showing leadership by matching economics with behavior. Some levy higher payroll health insurance deductions for employees that smokes or have a high BMI (Body Mass Index, a ratio of body fat to height and weight). Some offer employee benefits for gym memberships (and usage). Others design their offices for more walking around with more stairs to climb. It's a good start.

Genetics and Health

Genetics are powerful when it comes to our health and longevity. Genetics impact 30 percent of our premature deaths. We benefit by knowing in advance our genetic predispositions to diabetes or kidney disease or obesity. We might act to avert illnesses. Early interventions like a change of diet or monitoring can make a huge difference in not only our own lives but in reducing overall medical care costs.

Genetic testing plays a role in identifying fetuses likely to be born with life-ending or threatening birth defects. Sampling amniotic fluid during pregnancy, amniocentesis, a screening for fetal abnormalities, is nearly routine. Such testing can detect the likelihood of sickle cell disease, Down syndrome, cystic fibrosis, muscular dystrophy, Tay-Sachs disease, or any diseases where the brain and spinal column do not develop properly, such as spina bifida and anencephaly.

How do we act on that information?

In Iceland, fetal testing and abortions have virtually eliminated babies being born with Down syndrome, "CBSN: On Assignment" reported. In developed nations, termination of pregnancies for birth defects is becoming widespread, even in nations with strong anti-abortion cultures and laws.

The Genetic Literacy Project reports genetic testing is becoming part of matchmaking for arranged marriages among Hasidic Jews, who do not sanction abortion. Hasidic high school students get their blood drawn for genetic testing. Later, when a match is proposed, the matchmaker or families use the tests to spot a risk of genetic diseases or birth defects, then they bless or discourage the marriage.

Environmental Factors

Twenty percent of us are at risk of premature death from social factors and environmental factors.

A link exists between lower health status and higher health costs among lower-income groups. Lack of education limits employment, limiting income, which limits access to healthy working and living conditions, limits access to quality food, limits access to quality child care, limits access to health care services, increasing health care costs, which increases medical debt, which is a pox upon society.

Nothing in the scope of health insurance can or will address the ecological and social issues contributing to higher health care costs. The healthcare system is not demanding upstream solutions.

Today's anti-regulation wave erodes environmental protections, yet the impact on healthcare costs should be considered.

More than 1,000 people a day are admitted to hospitals because of chronic lung diseases like asthma, costing the nation $56 billion annually in both direct costs (such as hospitalization) and indirect costs (such as missed work and decreased productivity), according to the National Environmental Education Foundation.

Air pollution contributes to 16,000 premature births each year, adding $760 million in direct healthcare costs plus $3.57 billion in lost productivity costs from physical and mental disabilities, reports Business Insider. The Rand Corporation found that between 2005 and 2007 in California, air pollution added $193 million in hospital costs — Medicare paid $104 million, Medicaid paid $28 million, and private insurances paid the balance of $56 million.

Theory and Reality

Cigna CEO David Cordani told Business Insider magazine, "We spend the majority of our money and resources addressing people once they're sick. We need to spend more of our resources keeping people healthy in the first case, and identifying people who are at risk of health events, and lowering those health risks."

> The health care industry inadvertently has been allowed to become a big monster that threatens to devour every dollar of America's GDP.

No amount of tinkering with insurance models will change the fact our health care costs reflect the demand for care and the costs to deliver care. Both the demand side of the equation and the structure of care delivery add to the costs of delivering health care services. The health care industry inadvertently has been allowed to become a big monster that threatens to devour every dollar of America's GDP.

Hospitals have emerged as the concentrated economic powers in our healthcare system. They have evolved from the local community institutions into networks of care providers composed of urgent care centers (once denigrated as a "doc-in-the-box"), ambulatory surgery centers (ACS), and hospital-owned practices employing 42 percent of all practicing physicians, says Becker's Hospital Review.

In theory, such a system could provide great benefits for patients. In-system treatment should assure coordination among caregivers, who share patient medical records, avoid costly duplicative testing and avoid conflicting drug interactions. In theory, all this lowers the cost of health care by squeezing out unnecessary services within the delivery of care. Such a health care structure should lower costs and improve quality. What could be better?

Reality is different. These systems have become additive to health care costs rather than reductive. Hospital-dominated systems put the economic needs of the system before the fiscal impact on patients. Revenue is produced by the system and for the system (a pay-into system). Efficiencies and economies benefit the system. Patients pay more in the process, as do their health insurance companies.

Market Watch tells a tale that is far too common. Jackie Thennes switched to an in-network doctor at a health system facility near her. Her bill suddenly included charges for each doctor visit along with something extra — an added $235 "facility fee."

Concern for maximizing mission has been replaced by concern for maximizing margins.

National Healthcare Policy

All this brings us back to the central problem of medical debt, the proposals and solutions and schemes for who pays and how.

Regardless of your support for national health insurance, or your opposition, the reality is that the crisis in health insurance coverage and affordability is a crisis in the cost of delivering healthcare.

Hiding those costs in the current insurance model or in a nationalized tax scheme does not change the structure of care nor all the factors driving a demand for care. If a national health insurance program were created, the issue of costs would continue to be a problem.

The current system or a single-payer system will both be expensive.

Opposition to national health insurance, in part, is from a belief the costs will be too great. At the current trajectory of spending, this objection is valid, to a point. The Centers for Medicare and Medicaid Services (CMS) has projected that health care spending by 2026 will surpass $5.7 trillion dollars. Investor's Business Daily, estimates that a "Medicare for All" plan would add $32 trillion to federal spending over 10 years. The current system or a single-payer system will both be expensive.

Health insurance is only a scheme to finance health care services. Whether premiums are funded by individual purchase, by employers paying for care benefits or by taxes, it's just a mechanism for funding the healthcare system to provide care services.

Focusing only on health insurance misses the real issues — the demand for services and the costly way that services are delivered. Both must be addressed.

For instance, a nation concerned about the quality of its citizens' lives can use taxes to motivate healthier behaviors that reduce the need for care services. Tax deductions for charity donations support the generosity of the American. Home mortgage deductions support home ownership for family and community stability. By increasing taxes on our unhealthy behaviors, the cost of such behaviors shifts to the point of decision. It's wrong to make cost a barrier to seeking help for treating the consequences of unhealthy behaviors, as costs delay care, resulting in higher costs and poorer outcomes. This is especially true if an illness stems from factors outside a person's control, like genetic ailments or respiratory disease caused by secondhand smoke.

The healthcare industry cannot be expected to reform itself, to become efficient and effective, to find ways of delivering care faster, better and cheaper. It is not structured to do so. Hospitals' focus on profits do not reduce their costs to the communities they serve. From noble charities, they've evolved into economic carnivores.

We need a holistic approach to healthcare costs.

Separate silos for health services of public health or social services just is not working. Underfunding public health and social services results in a greater demand for public healthcare services. Likewise, underregulating environmental quality issues results in a greater demand for healthcare services. Our health care silos raise our costs. We need a holistic approach to healthcare costs.

The totality of costs being spent on medical care, public health and social services needs to be considered along with what we know reduces the need for care. Let's allocate services accordingly. A national healthcare policy needs to be established as a guide.

What matters most is caring for the ill and injured. Returning to this focus will produce a healthier population, which will reduce the cost of care, and so reduce medical debt.

A national healthcare policy needs to support a country that is healthy and an economy that is strong. From such a policy, decisions can be made to support the goal of health, not just care delivery.

Tax policy influencing self-care decisions need not result in some "nanny state" that erodes personal responsibility. The actual costs of pollution, in terms of health and productivity, for instance, need to be moved from the healthcare system to the polluters. For me, that would be taking real responsibility for our economic freedoms.

From a national healthcare policy aimed at improving the health of Americans can flow sensible health benefit plans that promote and support preventative and routine care as well as early interventions for illness along with health maintenance for chronic care.

The structure for delivering care needs to be reconstituted for the betterment of the population. A sustainable, affordable funding model then becomes a possibility, be it insurance, Medicare for All, or some other national health plan.

The present system is rigged against citizen health. This is being done not by design, not by a cabal of evil doers, but by the historical evolution of our healthcare delivery structure. We need an evolution to higher thinking for the health of everyone in America.

To paraphrase the famous old Pogo comic strip, "We have met the problem, and it is us."

My doctor gave me six months to live,
but when I couldn't pay the bill
he gave me six months more.

— WALTER MATTHAU

CHAPTER 10

Personal and General Medical Debt Solutions

Craig Antico

Every day I see our healthcare system causing financial ruin to millions of Americans, their friends and families. Many of them would be financially ruined no matter what they or we can do. That's unacceptable. I want to help ensure this does not happen to them or you. I later will speak to systemic things we can do as a country to avoid those outcomes.

Until then, let's get personal.

Illnesses or accidents often cause unexpected shocks, and material hardship often ensues. There are useful steps you can take — or your friends and family can take — that are in your personal control, so you can mitigate the risk of the medical debt hardship.

Nothing is sadder to me than seeing people make poor decisions about their own health care and wellness because of ignorance or an unwillingness to act. Nothing makes me angrier than the number of people in positions of authority who are unwilling to educate and support people in need, so they can actually help themselves.

There is no other nation in the world like the United States that tries as hard to make up for the system disparities, inequalities and government inefficiencies, or that donates more time and money for the good of others. When we Americans are made aware of others' unmet needs, such as after a wildfire or hurricane, we do our best as givers, and as recipients of giving. This gives me hope.

Personal Responsibility Solutions

Many of us are just one illness or accident away from financial ruin or material hardship from medical debt. Hardship can occur for you and others when you or another person...

1. Doesn't take or have the time to stay current on their bills.

2. Waits until they're in a crisis to act.

3. Doesn't read through the medical bills they get.

4. Asks you or another to pay any bill for them.

5. Ignores health care billing notices.

6. Puts bills on a credit card (worse if you co-signed).

7. Doesn't feel the need to have any health insurance.

8. Doesn't understand that if you secured insurance for them, then you are doomed to pay for their medical debt hardship.

When it comes to material hardship, I've seen it all in my work. As one whose family has experienced material hardship, I wish to help you avoid or mitigate such deep scars by teaching you how to take much better personal responsibility for your own health care costs.

If you have everything under full control, and you're properly insured, you can ignore the tips below. These

Take better personal responsibility for your own health care costs.

are tips I've garnered in the 30 years that I've been in this business of cleaning up the debt mess created by our healthcare system. I've also learned what to do from my own hardship. These can help.

Below is a self-help guide with basic how-to information.

Learn About Health Insurance

Research how health insurance works and doesn't work (reread this book). Understand the concepts of co-insurance, co-payments, deductibles, and those out-of-network benefits and pitfalls.

If you are insured, approximately 25-30 percent of your cost for healthcare comes out of your pocket in the form of deductibles, co-pays and co-insurance. Know exactly what your own plan covers. Read the fine print. According to The Commonwealth Fund, being uninsured or underinsured affects 68 million people in America.

Determine What Services Are Covered In-Network

If you live in a region with only one hospital, you are especially vulnerable to not having any in-network doctors. However, this can happen in any hospital if they participate in few insurance plans.

Before you need care, find out if which local care providers are covered by your in-network insurance plan, such as radiologists, anesthesiologists and laboratories. The hospital may be in-network, but every caregiver in the hospital might not be.

Above all, find out in advance of a medical crisis whether or not your local ambulance company and hospital emergency room staff is in-network. They may not be. If not, you could get a bill five to ten times the cost of in-network charges for the same services.

Know Consumer Rights Around 'Balance Billing'

A New England Journal of Medicine study in 2016 found that 22 percent of emergency room visits nationally involve care by an out-of-network doctor, putting the patient at risk of a surprise medical bill, known as "balance billing," or billing for the unpaid balance. Balance billing is prohibited for people on Medicaid or Medicare.

Zack Cooper, assistant professor of health policy and economics at Yale University, stated in an interview with Kellie Schmitt of the USC Annenberg Center for Health Journalism, "These sorts of surprise bills can tally up into the hundreds or thousands of dollars and really wreak financial havoc on people's lives."

Lynda Washburn at NorthJersey.com covered the governor of New Jersey, Phil Murphy, in April 2018 signing a new law against balance billing, calling it "one of the strongest consumer protection laws in the country." Murphy said at the bill signing, "An estimated 168,000 patients receive out-of-network bills that total $420 million annually," noting this adds $1 billion annually to health costs.

Other states have similar bills proposed or enacted. No such national law exists. Always ask if a care provider is in-network.

Examine Bills Carefully

Adria Goldman Gross from MedWise Insurance Advocacy in Monroe, New York, warns that "about eighty percent of all medical bills have errors." You need to know what to look for. Gross says to search the internet to find the "reasonable and customary charges" for the medical procedure codes on your bill (and what they mean). Compare what you find to your own charges.

Mistakes on bills often are due to miscoding, but wait 30-45 days before calling because it often takes three months for insurance billing to go through. If you are on Medicare, carefully review your quarterly Medicare Summary Notice.

Get everything pinned down in advance, she says, stressing the importance of written estimates: "Whatever agreed fee amount you have with your medical provider, make sure you have it in writing."

Beware of Facility Fees

Hospital-owned physician practices charge "facilities fees" above the usual service charge. In Washington state, for instance, a patient paid $125 out-of-pocket to visit an employed doctor, but visit costs skyrocketed to more than $500 to reflect a new facility fee charge.

The Physician Advocacy Institute asserts facility fees are being charged much more than before because hospitals now own about 30 percent of physician practices and employ over 42 percent of all physicians (a 100 percent increase since 2012).

These practices have the legal right to charge facilities fees, even if a physician practice is off-campus from the hospital. The problem is that patient don't expect to get charged more when they are going to the same place they always went for care services. Facility fees can occur even if the doctor is just "affiliated" with a hospital.

> Alway ask in advance of the visit if you will be charged a facility fee

Ask in advance of a visit if you will be charged a facility fee. If so, find out whether your procedure can be done at another location that doesn't charge a fee. Always ask *before* the service is rendered because fighting the fee afterwards is close to impossible.

Always File Out-of-Network Claims

An insurance company can process and pay an out-of-network bill as much as seven years after an "OON" bill has been generated. This can happen even after a bill was paid by you, by friends or by family ($55 billion each year is given by friends and family for medical expenses and debt repayment). So, always submit your out-of-network charges to your insurance company.

If you are not filing a claim for your own benefit, do it to repay the friends and family who gave to you until it hurt.

Do not ask your doctor for hospital file the OON claim for you, It's not in their interest to make sure you get reimbursed. Either do it yourself or go to GetBetter.co to have them process your claim.

With more than $115 billion a year being billed OON, and an accumulated $450-500 billion left unpaid over the last seven years, there's a potential of recovering about $45-60 million dollars from insurance companies. Get OON it!

Determine if Underinsured. If Uninsured, Get Insurance

The cheapest health insurance likely is no bargain. If you make less than two times the Federal Poverty Level (FPL), your deductible should not exceed five percent of your gross income. If you earn more, your deductible should not exceed 10 percent of your gross income. If you earn $30,000, your deductible should be not more than $1,500 a year. If you earn $60,000, is $6,000 a year.

If you do not yet have insurance, or your deductible is higher than the above guidelines, your family is underinsured. If you have one major illness or accident, you and your family are vulnerable to material hardship that could last from three to five years.

Determine Eligibility for Charity Care Before You Need It.

Search the internet for your local hospital name and the phrase, "financial assistance." Find the hospital "financial assistance policy," perhaps called a "charity care policy." Independent doctors do not offer charity care, as a rule, for they cannot afford to do so.

Most hospitals offer free charity care for low income patients. To qualify, you usually need to make below two times (200 percent) the FPL. If you are over that, there will usually be a sliding scale from 10 percent to 80 percent of the bill you will end up paying, if approved — but you must ask. (While online, find a Federal Poverty Level guidelines calculator to assess your situation.)

FYI: We as a nation every year on average give to charity about two percent of our gross domestic product (GDP). What's stunning is that the 33 percent of the population that earns less than two times the FPL — about $40,000-$50,000 — are the most generous givers to charity as well as to needy friends and family (F&F). As a percentage of adjusted gross income, this segment gives away more than those in much higher income brackets. Lower-income people give more, even if it brings them hardship, because they know first-hand what a big difference generosity makes in people's lives.

Apply for Medicaid in Case of Low Income

Although low income lasts a lifetime for some, poverty is often a temporary situation. I'm talking from experience. Medicaid is the health insurance for all low-income citizens who cannot afford their medical care expenses. Income qualification criteria vary by state, so contact your state Medicaid office to see if you qualify. Your child may be eligible for Medicaid even if you are not.

If you qualify, Medicaid may fully pay for the medical expenses already incurred, but only within a certain timeframe, about 90-180 days. Apply as soon as possible after receiving a medical bill.

If you are up to age 26 and on your parent's insurance, consider applying for Medicaid. We don't know anybody on Medicaid with medical debt problems, including recent graduates looking for a job. Consider yourself fortunate if you

> **Medicaid may fully pay for medical expenses already incurred.**

have parental plan coverage, yet they'll consider themselves fortunate if you have a major illness or accident and your Medicaid spares them from financial ruin.

Communicate with Providers and Collectors if in Hardship

Do not be one of the 30 percent of all the people with hospital accounts at collection agencies who earlier had qualified for charity care but did not accept it, or did not know to ask for it.

If you did not apply for charity care, and if paying the bill you received will cause you and your family real hardship, contact your hospital or their collector, or answer their call.

Only Visit the ER in a Genuine Emergency

Call your doctor if an issue is not life-threatening. Go to the ER if your doctor says to go. My spouse did make that call, but she was in excruciating pain and later couldn't remember who said to go to the ER. We had to pay a $700 ER bill that could have been a $150 co-pay. So, get the name of whom talks to you at the doctor's office, note the time you spoke, and have them make a notation in your records that they felt your condition warranted an emergency visit.

Pay only Three to Six Percent of Your Gross Income on Out-of-Pocket Expenses or Past Medical Debt

Financial hardship can occur when medical expenses reach as little as two percent of gross income. Only you know how much you can afford to pay for out-of-pocket (OOP) medical expenses and past debt. Your savings, a second job, or family and friends can all mitigate hardship, foster resiliency and reduce stress.

Although research shows that most people experience hardship when their OOP expenses rise above 2.5 percent of gross income, you may have more or less resiliency than others.

Stay within three to six percent of your gross income. Make a yearly projection of up to six percent of your gross income. Only pay out what you can afford. Even if you are getting collection calls, be resolute that you will not stop taking your medications, going to the doctor, paying rent or utilities, or putting tires on your car. No one can force you to pay for a bill instead of life necessities. You always control who and how much you pay.

> No debt collector can force you to pay for a bill instead of necessities.

Don't Pay with Credit Cards or Interest-Bearing Loans

The main way medical debt from a hospital or doctor becomes an interest-bearing "debt" is when you ignore it, get sued, ignore that or lose the case, and find a judgment entered against you.

Trouble can ensue if you pay the bill with a credit card or loan. If you have debt at a high-interest rate debt, such as a credit card or a payday loan, get to know the "Rule of 76." (Low rate loans like home equity lines use the "Rule of 72.") Researching both rules will help you understand the likely cost of using financial instruments to pay off medical expenses or medical debt.

The Rule of 76 calculates how soon the amount you owe will double. To do it, divide your interest rate (say 24 percent) into 76 (76 ÷ 24 = 3.17). This is the number of years it will take to double how much you owe. The Rule of 76 tells you that the $3,000 you put on a credit card turns into $6,000 in about three years! Ouch.

If possible, make an interest-free installment payment agreement with the medical provider. No credit is needed for that, and it won't show on your credit report. Never miss that payment!

Start or Max-Out Your Health Savings Account

A 2017 Kaiser Family Foundation survey found 46 percent of enrollees in high-deductible health plans (HDHP) report difficulty affording deductibles. About 60 percent of those with employer-sponsored health insurance have high deductible of at least $1,300 for an individual and $2,750 for a family. A Health Savings Account (HSA) can foster resiliency and avert medically-induced hardship. Try to fund the maximum annual contribution in your HSA.

An HSA has a significant tax benefit. You don't pay taxes on the money put into the plan, nor do you pay taxes on the amount you use on medical expenses or premiums. Once you are on Medicare, you can't contribute to an HSA, so start now. Stop funding an HSA six months before you join Medicare to avoid HSA issues.

IRS rules for 2018 let you contribute up to $3,450 per year as an individual ,or $6,900 if you have family coverage. The IRS allows a catch-up contribution up to $1,000 a year for those age 55 or over.

Sign up for Medicare on Time to Avoid Penalties

The Forbes Finance Council warns about significant penalties for late enrollment into Medicare. These penalties accumulate the longer you wait to enroll and can be very costly. You can avoid any penalties by signing up for Medicare when you are first eligible.

> If you can afford a good Medicare supplemental plan, be sure to buy one.

You have a seven-month initial enrollment period starting three months before and after you turn 65. Enroll in Medicare Parts A, B and D during this period if you don't have better health insurance coverage.

Medicare only covers 80 percent of an authorized charge. If you can afford a good Medicare supplemental plan, be sure to buy one. That 20 percent difference can mean the difference between solvency and hardship in case you have a major illness or injury.

Prepare for Healthcare Expenses in Retirement

A 65-year-old couple that retires today would need an estimated $280,000 to cover their expected health care costs in retirement, according to a Fidelity analysis. Acquiring supplemental coverage is one of the most important things you can do to limit or completely avoid medical debt during retirement.

Get The Caregiving Tax Credit

With more than 25 million seniors living below 250 percent of the FPL, more caregivers are needed, and families just can't cope. If you are one of the 35 million adult children caring for a parent, or one of the 15 million caring for a spouse, or one of the 35 million parents taking care of adult children with disabilities, you are keenly aware of the costs involved. The average paid for OOP expenses per year is more than $,7000, but figure in lost wages, less Social Security benefits later in life, added stress, and other hidden costs.

Those providing care for a family member can get a tax credit under the Credit for Caring Act. According to AARP, the IRS gives eligible family caregivers the opportunity to receive a tax credit for 30 percent of qualified expenses above $2,000 paid to help a loved one. The maximum credit amount is $3,000.

Get Compensated as a Caregiver

There also are programs and mechanisms that enable you, as the caregiver for a family member, that can ease the added expense and lost income — paying you for your service. These payers could be a long-term care insurance plan, Medicaid or worker's compensation claim. The VA may honor a claim if the care receiver is a veteran.

The National Academy of Elder Law Attorneys is the leading attorney network working with consumers on the legal problems of aging Americans as well as people of all ages with disabilities. They can help you draft a formal "eldercare contract," normally between family members, which outlines care responsibilities and provides a way for a caregiver to be paid. Such an agreement potentially clears up any confusion among family members.

A care agreement lets the family pool resources to pay for a caregiver, if the care recipient lacks means. If the care recipient has ample resources, an agreement can mitigates feuds between family members on who inherits money or gifts. It further can ensure the caregiver is treated with respect, especially if a caregiver must stop working to help a loved one.

If your loved one is a veteran, contact Veteran Directed Home and Community-Based Services (VDHCBS), which pays vet family members to act as caregivers.

> A care agreement lets a family pool resources to pay for a caregiver.

Use a Medicaid-Paid Caregiving Program

Medicaid in your state may offer a way to get paid for taking care of a family member, friend or neighbor. New York State offers the Consumer Directed Personal Assistance Program (CD-PAP), a Medicaid-funded program that allows care recipients to hire almost any caregiver they choose, including the family member currently providing care. Freedom Care NY provides services statewide.

Most state Medicaid programs offer some form of self-directed care, which is used by more than 800,000 patients nationwide, according to an Open Minds report authored by Athena Mandros, a market intelligence editor focusing on Medicaid trends.

The above tips are by no means comprehensive, but if you apply them, you may spare yourself from hardship due to medical debt.

General Solutions

The cost of health care is expected to double in the next seven to ten years with income at a slower growth rate. It doesn't matter who pays each medical bill — government already pays 70 percent of the costs — it will be impossible to pay for all care without a revolution in cost reduction or an increase in effectiveness and wellness.

While we search for a way to increase wellness, which will reduce the health care costs trajectory, we can make a significant impact through the following strategies:

• Shifts in data sharing, trusts, ownership, control, monitoring.

• More transparent, responsive, impactful financial assistance policy education, plan design and real-time delivery.

• More finance industry social responsibility.

• Use of shared burden platforms for elimination of medically-induced financial hardship.

Make Charity Care and Medicaid Opt-Out

A simple solution for part of our medical debt epidemic, at least on the nonprofit hospital side (where more than a third of medical debt is created), would be to make charity care and Medicaid opt-out. Those who quality under the financial assistance policy (FAP) of the hospital would automatically get vital care for free. Patients could decline or opt-out of free care, but few would, I expect.

Hospitals, until now, required patients to provide extensive verification of income, assets or hardship to qualify for charity care. The onus has been on the patients so too few even apply.

RIP can now provide hospitals (using their current technology), with our data and analytics to connect their clinical data with federal Health and Human Services networks for patient verifications. This innovative linkage between a Health Information Exchange (HIE) and Community Information Exchange (CIE) shows great promise for identifying qualified and verified charity care patients along with providing medical debt abolishment on the spot.

As a proof-of concept, RIP is engaged in a first-of-its-kind pilot with 2-1-1 San Diego, a social service resource and information hub. Using their CIE, we are connecting two participating hospitals and 6,000 health and human services providers in San Diego to identify charity care cases and to abolish medical debt for qualified patients. (Jerry gave a detailed description of the project earlier as an example of the John Oliver Effect.) The project shows the possibilities.

Build Data Trusts Where Consumers Control Their Own Data

Wellness and health care services, like all ventures, expend a lot of money finding people who need their services while constantly improving their services to make them more attractive.

Personal data on our wellness (mental, physical, and emotional health), finances, and consumer behavior is, and should be, private. Lack of privacy breeds distrust between consumers and providers.

With a system of trustworthy data-sharing controlled by people themselves, products and services could be designed and marketed more ethically. Health care services could be provided to people in real time, based on reliable anonymized data about people, families, and communities — driven by evidence and data-informed impacts. This could lower health care costs across the board in all sectors.

To accomplish this worthy goal, I support using the data flow science created and pioneered over two decades by OBASHI in Scotland, which is accredited and deployed internationally.

> **'Data trusts' would let us own, control and monitor our private personal data.**

I envision "data trusts" where people (patients and consumers) could own, control and monitor their private personal data, which would belong to them, not to corporations. Europe is way ahead of the USA in adopting this principle of personal data ownership.

Have Specialty Finance Companies Abolish Medical Debt

Hospitals and doctors have started getting out of the business of letting you owe them — incur medical debt — in lieu of immediate cash payment. They elect not to participate in any insurance plan at all, government or private, and take only cash, or have you provide a credit card. Some bring in a bank specialty finance company, such as CareCredit. You may owe the bank directly without ever realizing you don't owe the hospital or doctor.

In my mind, this trend could be harmful to patients financially, as I discussed in an earlier chapter. To offset the risks of medical debt owed to banks rather than to care providers, I propose that these specialty finance companies establish a fund to abolish (forgive) the medical debt of those in hardship. Such a fund could be created by each company or the special finance industry acting in unison.

Build a Charity Fund to Pay Caregivers for Caregiving

With caregiving becoming more and more of a hardship on our dwindling caregiver base, there needs to be a safety net for them. We need more education of the programs out there for caregivers, and their caregiving needs to be better funded. I propose that we unite to establish state and national charitable funds for this purpose.

About $400 billion in caregiving services are rendered each year, and much of that is lost income. Remember, this is the same amount as the $400 billion that citizens, corporations and foundations give to charities every year. Caregivers rarely get trained in the financial matters affecting them. Few even know that some states and entities actual pay F&F caregivers. We can do more to support them.

Abolish the Debt-of-Necessity Causing Material Hardship

RIP, with a $500,000 donation from a caring couple, abolished $50 million in veterans' medical debt in late 2018 as part of a larger donation that wiped out more than $250 million in medical debt for the poor and those in hardship because the incurred medical debt-of-necessity from unexpected illnesses or injures. Some good news, certainly, but what else can be done? A lot more debt is out there.

Shift Who Pays for Severely Past Due, Unpayable Debt

I've run collection companies all my adult life, and more than 50 percent of the collection work done by my industry is for medical debt. Before co-founding RIP with Jerry Ashton, himself a debt collections veteran, we worked in a broad industry that made $19 billion a year in revenue — $8 billion from medical debt collections, $6 billion in debt settlement and debt consolidation, and $5 billion in repairing people's credit. The industry earned an additional $50 billion for debts from settlements, collected for creditor clients.

I estimate that 20-25 percent of those debtors were in hardship at the time they paid those debts. If we educated those in hardship to safely and privately self-identify their hardship, our communities could pay off their debts for them through debt purchases and abolishment. We would share the debt burden and reduce material hardship to practically nothing.

A shift in our wealth can make a large dent in U.S. medical debt.

With a shift of just $2 billion of our national wealth to abolish medical debt, we could eradicate all medical debt hardship in this country by abolishing $200 billion in medical debt. This wide debt forgiveness could be made possible by donations from those without debt and by those with debt who can donate without hardship.

Given $1 trillion in unpayable healthcare bills in America, such a shift in our wealth can make a large dent in U.S. medical debt. We can find more permanent answers for finally ending medical debt by increasing wellness, reducing costs, and changing how we finance health care in our nation.

*A hospital bed is a parked taxi
with the meter running.*

— GROUCHO MARX

CHAPTER 11

National Health Care:
To Be or Not To Be?

Jerry Ashton

W e're in a particularly difficult period of time in society today (or what passes for society). When it comes to healthcare, forget about "reasoned discourse." You are damned if you pick a side, such as for or against single-payer, damned for the side you pick, or condemned by all sides for not picking any side.

As we three authors have made clear in our own ways, blaming others avoids responsibility. A clearly destructive path is being taken, but we have consented to it. Fixed positions on healthcare are now required for every social group, economic class, religion, or political persuasion. A justification for any position will and must be found. Minds are closed. Why argue? Move on. Nothing to see here.

Meanwhile, our broken healthcare system screams for change. We are experiencing a "global warming" in healthcare economics. Every tiny degree that costs go up for insurance, drugs, hospitals and other care, in turn, creates a hotter, costlier future. Deniers refuse to admit that our structure ensures costs and medical debt will rise.

Our society is as fractured as our healthcare system. Each given healthcare "solution" is well defended, and too often by those same interests that are creating the problem. Some of us feel locked into the current system by a career or paycheck. Others of us are devoted to a bedrock ideology of right and wrong. Our refusal to compromise is moral, and all doubts are treason.

What stance are we willing to give up to make healthcare work? What are we willing to do to make America healthier, equitable and sustainable? No matter what solution we pick, implementation will not be easy, and that solution may never be perfect.

Is medical debt forgiveness the solution? Well, yes and no.

The "no" is because medical debt forgiveness treats the symptom but does not cure the disease. The many sources of medical debt reside "upstream." Righting a wrong by forgiving debt, however sincere and well-intended, is not a real solution for ridding America of medical debt. Given $1 trillion of medical debt in America, and rising, even if RIP can grow to abolish two or three billion

> # Medical debt forgiveness treats the symptom but does not cure the disease.

dollars in medical debt every year, that will not change the existing healthcare system. Debt forgiveness, by itself, will never make a real dent in all the debt that has been created, is being created and is yet to be created. We need a structural change in the system.

The "yes" is because RIP is becoming a voice that calls attention to the problem of medical debt and the process of finding solutions that work. As a 501(c)(3) tax-exempt charitable organization under U.S law, we cannot directly engage in politics. However, we can ally ourselves with people and organizations active in the monumental efforts to inform America and change public opinion. We can help to repair our nation's conscience as well as its wallet.

Our charity will keep fulfilling our mandate of debt forgiveness, making a persistent person-by-person, family-by-family dent in the financial anguish and pain of the medical debt burdening millions of people. We are grateful to be their champions.

We further will call public attention to the problem of medical debt and the healthcare system creating it. We will raise awareness, touch hearts, educate with integrity, and call for action. By our sheer numbers, the collective voice and actions of those concerned about the issue will finally end medical debt.

Within RIP, we would love to see our charity put out of business. No medical debt would mean no need to forgive it. This is likely a ways off, but it can happen once Americans agree we need essential changes in the financial model of healthcare delivery.

The tide is turning. I see Americans removing their blinders and challenging the status quo, honestly looking at alternatives. We are seeing that not only are we our brother's keeper, we are our brother. This final chapter looks at ways to create such positive changes.

A Modern Barn Raising

Back in the 19th and 20th century, if a rural family's livelihood was ruined by a major financial loss, like a barn destroyed by a fire or tornado, the community would show up and pitch in, unpaid, to build a replacement barn. Some contributed labor, some lumber or nails, others money, but they all contributed from their hearts.

There was enlightened self-interest in those community actions. People recognized, "It could be me someday," so they all pitched in vigorously, even joyfully (as with Habitat for Humanity). People knew that should a disaster happen in their own lives, their friends, neighbors, and relatives would return the social investment.

Today, for the donors and fans of RIP Medical Debt, perhaps at an unconscious level, we serve a similar role for social investment. Many of our donors know, at some level, that medical debt on their credit report, bankruptcy, job loss, failure to finance a car or rent an apartment, or other issues, could well be in their future. We accept that our own "barn" could need raising someday.

> # If nothing changes in healthcare financing, none of us are safe from catastrophic medical bills.

If nothing changes in healthcare financing, none of us are safe from catastrophic medical bills. Your own family will not save you. Social rank will not save you. Wealth will not save you. Education will not save you.

The failure of the current system is epitomized in an October 3, 2018, obituary for the Nobel Prize-winning physicist, Leon Lederman, age 96. His wife told the Associated Press that in 2015 he'd sold his Nobel Prize at auction for $765,000 "to help pay for medical bills and care."

Therefore, in the spirit of civic education and open discourse, let's take a look at the four most common solutions proposed for improving healthcare and lowering medical costs:

1. Repeal and Replace Obamacare.
2. Regulate insurance and drug prices.
3. Add a Medicare option to the ACA.
4. Offer Medicare for All or single-payer healthcare

A caveat: None of what follows is comprehensive. You will not find here all you need to know. Our goal is raising public awareness. What you do with that awareness — such as seeking more education or becoming more actively involved — is up to you.

Repeal and Replace Obamacare

The battle cry of "Repeal and Replace" went silent in response to voter outrage in the 2018 mid-term elections, rejecting politicians who favored stopping coverage for pre-existing conditions. Still, the case is instructive should this idea ever be resurrected.

Writer and gadfly John Hecht wrote a great 2017 Bustle article, "Repeal and Replace is Dead: A Definitive Timeline of Republicans' Zombie Obamacare Bill That No One Can Kill." Hecht tracked the Republican efforts and gave reasons for its failure.

The chief reason was that "Republican lawmakers couldn't quite stomach it." Defunding the ACA would drive up health insurance premiums to stratospheric levels. Repealing the ACA subsidy would cause 32 million voters to lose their insurance. Also chilling House GOP enthusiasm was the pummeling at town hall meetings by angry constituents, who in 2018 voted many of them out of office.

A number of cobbled-together iterations failed to get the votes. A bold thumbs down by Sen. John McCain hammered the stake through the heart of his party's one possibly viable offering.

When a GOP "skinny bill" failed to pass, Sen. Lindsey Graham summed up the GOP's seven years attempting to replace the ACA. (Replace with what?) He said, "I thought everybody else knew what the hell they were talking about, but apparently not."

Regulate Insurance and Drug Prices

Insurance and pharmaceutical price reform is a Sisyphean task. The healthcare industry, including the hospital conglomerates and physicians, resists changes. Money keeps things as they are.

Big Insurance, Big Pharma and Big Hospitals benefit from the system as it stands. I believe they are mostly concerned about how "the other" is charging too much, thereby making it harder for them to charge more for their own piece of the healthcare pie.

Robert Goff gave his views on hospitals and their profit system. Let me look at two other so-called "bad boys" in healthcare costs — insurance companies and pharmaceutical companies.

Health insurance company profits are booming. Bob Herman at Axios found the five largest U.S. insurance companies reported $4.5 billion in net earnings for the first quarter 2017. The insurers employ 2.5 million people. A robust industry with healthy margins.

In an NPR interview, Herman said that since Obamacare began, the cumulative salaries of insurance and pharma CEOs has tallied $9.8 billion. The top earner was John Martin, former CEO of Gilead Science, who took home in excess of $900 million.

You might think all this quality brainpower would make great allies for reformers trying to bring about financial reforms to relieve the burdens carried by you and me. Not so. No motivation. Herman said executives are not paid to slow spending. Much of their pay is in stock or stock options. "Their incentive is to do whatever it takes to make that stock go up." The stock market drives drug prices.

Raising prices to lift stock values is the opposite of what we need to heal a broken system. Why not try to lower prices, eliminate unnecessary care and drugs, and coordinate care better? My opinion is that none of the Republican and Democratic proposals really address the core causes of rising costs in our healthcare system.

This leads me to the drug industry and their profit structure. Among all the "out-of-control" healthcare sectors, the one most unanimously attacked by the general public is the drug industry. Why all the outrage?

'Free market' economies shun limits on profits, so pricing regulations are unlikely.

Eric Reguly, European Bureau Chief for The Globe and Mail, wrote a scathing article, "Rx for Excess: The truth behind big pharma spending," He asked why prices of name-brand drugs keep soaring? His simple answer: "Because they can."

Reguly alleges that both governments and consumers have been "brainwashed" into thinking all the double-digit price increases are necessary to fund world-class research and development programs. investing in inventing products to make us healthier.

This rationale, apparently, let Gilead Sciences charge $84,000 for a 12-week treatment course (at about $1,000 a pill) for Sovaldi, an antiviral treatment for hepatitis C. Médecins Sans Frontières called the price "shocking," noting it would cost $227 billion to treat the 2.7 million Americans with hep C, "let alone the rest of the world."

Reguly labels the argument of "sumptuous prices for sumptuous R&D" a blatant fraud. What's really driving up drug prices are share buybacks and dividends, he said, naming Valeant Pharmaceuticals' CEO, Michael Pearson, who in 2018 saw the valuations of his stock holdings and options swell to almost $3 billion.

Can we reduce U.S. healthcare costs by regulating the profits of insurance and pharmaceutical companies? "Free market" economies shun limits on profits, so pricing regulations are unlikely.

Add Medicare Option to the ACA

People are making a strong argument for adding a "Medicare Option" to the ACA. This would offer a voluntary "Opt-In" from age 50 or 55 to age 65 (Medicare today starts at age 65). Supplemental insurance would cover the 20 percent that Medicare does not cover (same as Medicare now). This would modestly expand Medicare.

The main Medicare Option bills now in congress are led by Sen. Debbie Stabenow (D-Mich.), who sees it starting at age 55, and Rep. Brian Higgins (D-NY), who wants it to start at age 50. The Stabenow and Higgins bills both rely on marketplace subsidies and employer participation. Both offer assurance that any Medicare buy-in would not compete with commercial marketplace plans.

No matter what form any Medicare Option takes, detractors will deride it as "creeping socialism." Never give a dog a bone, even with scant meat on it, and try to take it back. Look at Medicare itself, and Social Security; such socialism rots moral character, undermines personal responsibility.

Here's a point of reference. Imagine America 50 years ago when only 48 percent of all "senior citizens" had health insurance. About 35 percent of all seniors were living in poverty. The life expectancy for men was 66 years and 73 years for women. All that changed on July 30, 1965, with the passage of Medicare. Today, only two percent of us over age 65 lack healthcare coverage. Better yet, poverty among those of us age 65 and older has been reduced by two-thirds.

Now picture mature people from age 50 to 65 enjoying a similar improvement in their life and health. If you think it was painful to try to "repeal and (never) replace" the ACA, imagine the howls from people younger and more ready to march on Washington!

Picture a future United States of American in which all people at age 50 enjoy all the benefits of Medicare, with little or no medical debt. Might the younger population be a tad envious?

A bipartisan Medicare Option could now pass in the House, and it could pass in Senate if enough Republicans are willing. Is this the best solution for us? Do you prefer a more sweeping change?

Medicare for All or Universal Healthcare

A 2018 Reuters survey determined that 70 percent of Americans support "Medicare for All," the current popular title for single payer healthcare. Reuters quoted Larry Levitt, senior vice president for health reform at the Kaiser Family Foundation, "The advantage of

Medicare for All, which is much closer to how the rest of the world provides health care to their residents, is that you can achieve universal health care at a lower cost."

Joel Segal, co-author of the legislation, HR 676, "Expanded and Improved Medicare For All," lays out the three main advantages of such a proposed single payer solution:

- No out-of-pocket costs.
- No hospital or physician bills to pay.
- No more medical debt.

Patients, physicians and hospitals would make decisions based on needs to foster health, not the needs of insurance companies and medical providers in business to generate profits.

Under HR 676, Joel said to me, the healthcare system would be publicly financed, but privately operated, same as with Medicare. "This is different from the 'socialized' medicine in England, or what we have here in America with the VA, where the government itself owns and operates the healthcare system."

Under HR 676, he added, as with Medicare now, "you would show your card, receive care services and go home, no worries about bills to pay, or bill collectors if you can't pay."

Both proposed laws, sponsored by Rep. Keith Ellison (D-MN) and Sen. Bernie Sanders (D-VT), would cut the current 12 percent rate of uninsured people to zero. Everyone would enroll in one plan without deductibles or co-payments. No one could opt out.

People could still buy supplemental private health insurance, similar to the Medicare supplemental plans today.

Healthcare would be publicly financed, but privately operated, same as Medicare.

Unlike Medicare, there would be no age limits. All Americans would be fully covered from birth to grave. All other form of private health coverage would vanish. Most of the existing public programs, including Medicare as it exists today, Medicaid, and CHIP, would be replaced. Healthcare financing would shift away from households and employers to the federal government.

Naturally, the proposal has enemies. Beyond the ideological or morality issues (in a number of quarters), critics raise the spectre of cost. The Mercatus Center in Virginia (Koch-funded) projected a $32.6 trillion increase in federal spending over ten years.

Sanders' answer: "If every major country on earth can guarantee health care to all and achieve better health outcomes while spending substantially less per capita than we do, it is absurd for anyone to suggest that the United States cannot do the same."

Could universal health care cost less and save money? That depends on who you ask. Physicians for a National

Americans need to take a moral stand that health is a human right.

Health Plan say a national health insurance program would save at least $150 billion annually on just paperwork alone. Under private insurance, more than 25 percent of every health care dollar earned by insurance companies goes for marketing, billing, utilization review, and duplication, what some call "waste."

The Peterson-Kaiser Health System Tracker reported that other wealthy countries, on average, spend half as much per person on healthcare as the USA. This means that $10,000 in care charges here are $5,000 "over there." Anybody with a capitalist bent might love a solution that costs less and saves money, but I guess that depends on the capitalist — and the circumstances.

Universal healthcare would offer a valuable social side-benefit: Equity in health care delivery. If universal healthcare or single-payer is constructed in such a fashion that my doctor is certifiably as good as your doctor, if our treatments are equal and my medicines are the same quality as yours, then we both have better health outcomes and a better quality of life ahead of us. We need not compete for care. The healthcare system can focus on health not finance.

In Canada's single-payer system, assessed Newsweek, "Medicine is not a commodity to be sold to the highest bidder, but a right that must be distributed equitably to one and all, and (like the Canadian character) ferociously egalitarian, but thrifty at the same time."

Why do we Americans resist such a sensible, moral social value? Seems to me this is where Americans reveal a form of Stockholm Syndrome. We've been lifelong captives of "the system," and we love our captors. We believe down is up and white is black.

To call single payer a moral issue, to claim every citizen deserves equal access to quality healthcare, somehow turns advocates into something unamerican — socialists! Really? Forget the labels.

We Americans need to take a moral stand that health is a human right. Let's be vocal and active until our country finally join the ranks of other enlightened nations.

I favor America no longer being a healthcare have-not nation.

The American Medical Debt Commission

I'm learning to think outside my box in response to Joel Segal, referred to me by a colleague in November 2018. In a long freeflow phone conversation, I learned he'd been senior legislative assistant to retired Rep. John Conyers, Chair of the Congressional Universal Health Care Task Force. Joel helped to write the ACA. He shared with me his own struggles with medical debt. As we explored our thoughts on healthcare in America, I had an "aha!" moment.

It's one thing to begin a charity that forgives medical debt, yet it's something else to grasp the tools for changing the law governing medical debt. Joel has been drafting laws for years. He has shaped public policy in practical ways that effect our daily lives. His efforts made me realize that RIP has been playing too small.

Showing what's possible, within days after we met, Joel drafted the "The American Medical Debt Commission Act of 2019." He said he would get it introduced in Congress, and it could pass!

Congress would establish an independent bipartisan "Medical Debt Commission that provides factual information on an annual basis to Congress and the general public on the medical debt crisis in America." A 25-member commission, chosen by the House Energy and Commerce Committee, would represent physicians, academics, hospital administrators, civil society organizations, local and state elected officials, foundations, think tanks, universities, medical debt experts, and patients impacted by medical debt.

The Commission would convene four times a year. Their tasks would include publishing at the CMS website an annual report on America's medical debt crisis, available for download. The report would offer Commission recommendations on how to address the medical debt crisis with the broadest possible spectrum of solutions, based on best practices, to end the medical debt crisis.

Twice a year, Commission members would appear before the House Energy and Commerce Committee to testify about the status of the U.S. medical debt crisis, reporting facts and results from the various attempted solutions addressing U.S. medical debt.

Joel could rapidly draft such a law because he knows how to do it. He has an enviable record of crafting bills that actually get passed. Joel's mastery of the legislative process sparked in me a vision of the bold and audacious world in which I want to be living!

Now is the time to get involved. Your voice truly does matter.

Not in Conclusion, in Anticipation

By the time this book was published in December 2018, RIP had forgiven a half-billion dollars in medical debt for about 250,000 individuals and families. Double that amount is now in our pipeline. Laudable, but we do not delude ourselves. We are only "sweeping up after the parade." As we clean up behind this ugly parade, I grow increasingly convinced our deeper purpose is awakening America to the problem of medical debt and galvanizing us into action.

Most Americans know our current healthcare system is broken. Despite the propaganda bash-label of "socialism" and the tired bleat of "we can't afford it," we Americans want healthcare coverage for ourselves and our families with no more medical debt.

We Americans somehow cough up enough in taxes to support the protections provided by our military, by our police and our fire departments. The same willingness to be taxed needs to happen for universal healthcare. We accept it for Medicare and Social Security. Can enough of us educate ourselves out of hopelessness, investigate our healthcare alternatives and choose new solutions?

To realize America's founding promise of "Life, liberty, and the pursuit of happiness," let's notice the order these words appear. Life, which depends on health, comes first. Without health, liberty has little value, and the pursuit of happiness is meaningless. Whenever our vote is cast, America's health needs to come first.

"If you have your health, you have everything," goes the saying. Let's stop depriving ourselves of that everything.

End medical debt.

*Hope lies in dreams, in imagination,
and in the courage of those who dare
to make dreams into reality.*

— JONAS SALK, M.D

About the Authors

Jerry Ashton — Jerry has more than 40 years' experience in the credit and collections industry. In 1995, dissatisfied with the way he saw debtors treated, he formed CFO Advisors in New York City. His debtor-centric teams in several states annually serviced a half billion in  receivables. Inspired by Occupy Wall Street's "Rolling Jubilee" debt forgiveness campaign, he joined with Craig Antico, his CFO partner, to co-found RIP Medical Debt. Jerry is the Executive VP.

Robert Goff — Retired from 40 years in the healthcare industry, Robert E. Goff is a consultant in care delivery, organization and financing. His senior leadership roles include hospital administrator, regulator, managed care executive, association executive, educator, and  entrepreneur. He developed one of the first for-profit HMOs in New York State. He was head of the University Physicians Network. Robert is RIP's founding board member.

Craig Antico — A financial industry leader in collections, debt buying, outsourcing, and consulting, Craig's 30-year career features work with IBM, Johnson & Johnson, collection agencies, and medical distributors. An expert in data analytics, he co-founded a distressed debt  exchange, eDebt. He joined Jerry at CFO Advisors. Craig is the co-founder, chair and CEO of RIP Medical Debt.

"Before you heal someone, ask him [her] if he's willing to give up the things that made him sick."

— HIPPOCRATES

About RIP Medical Debt

RIP Medical Debt is a 501(c)(3) not-for-profit national charity based in New York, incorporated in 2014, which locates, buys and forgives unpayable medical debt for those burdened by financial hardship.

RIP to date has abolished $500 million in medical debt for about 250,000 Americans. They support communities across the country in conducting local medical debt forgiveness campaigns. They have a special interest in forgiving the medical debt of veterans.

RIP buys large batches of medical billing accounts in "portfolios" for about a penny on the dollar, so donations to RIP deliver "a lot of bang for the buck." A $100 donation can forgive $10,000 in debt.

RIP cannot yet forgive medical debt for individuals on request, but people in need can apply for future debt relief at the RIP website by joining the Debt Forgiveness Registry.

Surprised people who receive in the mail a yellow RIP envelope enjoy no tax consequences from the charitable gift. Debt forgiveness from RIP is a freely given "random act of kindness."

For more information, visit RIPmedicaldebt.org

Made in the USA
Middletown, DE
17 December 2019